Conversion to Modernities:
The Globalization of Christianity

SERIES:

ZONES OF RELIGION

Edited by
Peter van der Veer

Conversion to Modernities:
The Globalization of Christianity

Edited by

Peter van der Veer

ROUTLEDGE

NEW YORK & LONDON

Published in 1996 by
Routledge
29 West 35th Street
New York, NY 10001

Published in Great Britain by
Routledge
11 New Fetter Lane
London EC4P 4EE

Printed in the United States of America on acid-free paper.

Library of Congress Cataloging-in-Publication Data

Conversion to modernities : the globalization of Christianity
  / edited by Peter van der Veer.
     p. cm.
    Papers presented at a conference held at the Research Centre
Religion and Society of the University of Amsterdam, June 1994.
    Includes bibliographical references and index.
    ISBN 0–415–91273–3. — ISBN 0–415–91274–1 (alk. paper)
    1. Conversion—History—Congresses. 2. Church history—Modern
period, 1500—Congresses. 3. Indigenous peoples—Religious life—
Congresses. I. Veer, Peter van der.
BV4916.C68 1995
306.6'4824—dc20   95–11009
                                              CIP

CONTENTS

PREFACE

*T*HIS VOLUME IS THE RESULT of a conference on conversion, held at the Research Centre of Religion and Society of the University of Amsterdam in June 1994. The conference was organized by Ton Otto, José van Santen, and Peter van der Veer. It received financial support from the Universities of Amsterdam, Leiden, and Nijmegen as well as from the Royal Dutch Academy of Sciences and the International Institute for Asian Studies, for which I am very grateful. A great number of papers (25), ranging from conversion to Islam to conversion in Japanese religions, were presented over three days. The initial idea had been to look comparatively at conversion in a number of religions; however, an overwhelming number of contributions focused on conversion to Christianity, so it has become the subject of the present volume.

The conference on conversion was the first of a series of conferences to be held at the Research Centre of Religion and Society. The next conference will be in November 1995, on Religion and Nationalism in Europe and Asia. A third conference will be in December 1995, on Border Fetishisms. It is the mission of the Research Centre to give a new impetus to the anthropological, historical, and political understanding of religion in the contemporary world. Its approach is interdisciplinary and comparative.

I would like to thank Ton Otto and José van Santen for their organizational and intellectual contribution to the shaping of the conference on conversion. I also thank Ingrid van den Broek for her detailed attention to the needs of the conference and to the preparation of the manuscript. Finally, at Routledge I owe special thanks to Marlie Wasserman for her strong support of this project.

Peter van der Veer
Amsterdam, March 1995

INTRODUCTION

Peter van der Veer

*I*N THE BEGINNING OF THE EIGHTEENTH CENTURY, a man with the unusual name of George Psalmanazar presented himself to British society
as a Formosan pagan converted to Christianity. In 1704 he published *A
Historical and Geographical Description of Formosa, an Island Subject to the Emperor of Japan*. Psalmanazar's account was highly successful, but after a number of years he was discovered to be a forger and impostor who had never
been to Formosa. Most of what we know about his "true" identity is derived from his own posthumously published memoirs, but of course there
is a paradox in looking for the "true" identity of a self-professed impostor
in his own work.

In a brilliant analysis of both Psalmanazar's description of Formosa and
his memoirs, Susan Stewart argues that they contain an interplay between
description/testimony and confession/conversion: "These two gestures—
one reaching out to the world within a stance of distance and objectivity,
the other reaching inward in a claim of transformation that in itself asserts
or posits the very subjectivity that is its 'motivating' cause—run in an obvious course from the halted narrative and ensuing lyricism of Augustine's
'confessions' to the paired volumes of ethnographic description and personal memoirs produced by anthropologists even today." (Stewart 1994, 56,
57). The description of the "old" religion that one has left is often a part
of the conversion narrative, but Psalmanazar's description is even more interesting than usual, since it describes his "old" religion as that of a cultural
Other, totally unknown to his British audience.[1] Religion is the real sign
of difference between Formosa and Britain, and the "description" of Formosa begins with "an account of the religion, customs, manners, etcetera,

of the inhabitants." This account shows the strangeness of Formosan religion in all kinds of detail, but especially in the annual ritual of child sacrifice. Some kind of human sacrifice is a standard element in the description of the barbarity of non-Christian religion in this period, and highly marketable in a rapidly expanding print market for exotic stories. The description of Formosa is followed by the story of Psalmanazar's conversion from his Formosan religion to Anglican Christianity. An important element in this part of the story is his rejection of the Jesuits (by the way, the only ones who could challenge his "knowledge" of Formosa thanks to their missionary presence on it), skillfully comparing Formosan and Catholic priests and playing on Protestant anti-Popery attitudes. The "old" religion of both author and audience is represented as awful.

What can the conversion narrative of a man who writes a forged description of his "old" religion tell us about the authenticity of his conversion? In his memoirs Psalmanazar is primarily concerned with demonstrating that at the end of his life he is "truly" converted and that he has broken with the world. It is in the truth of his confession that his Christian self is authenticated. As such it is a very modern truth since it is a personal, autobiographical account of a "private" experience that is not authorized by a social institution such as the Church. The authenticity and sincerity of the double gesture of description and conversion become central problems in modernity. Their delicacy is enhanced by globalization. Print capitalism, to use Benedict Anderson's term, transforms notions of self and community. The widening universe of communication allows for modern forms of private and public that, at the same time, unsettle the grounds of authentication. Often, it is not enough recognized to what extent these transformations in the West are connected to the expansion of European power to Asia, Africa, and the Americas. This connection is captured by the dual rhetorics of description of the Other and the conversion of the Self in Psalmanazar's forgery.

Obviously, it is not only forgery but also the writing of "history" in terms of progress and novelty that enables the British to reflect on their modernity (Pocock 1961). A century after Psalmanazar, the Utilitarian thinker James Mill published a *History of British India* in which a long chapter on "the Religion of the Hindus" can be found. While Psalmanazar's Formosa was remote and unknown to the British, India was in the process of being colonized by the British East India Company, James Mill's employer. Despite these considerable differences in the relation between knowledge and power, there are interesting parallels in Psalmanazar's and Mill's "descriptions." Like Psalmanazar, Mill was against the rule of priests who had greater authority in India than in any other part of the world, in his view. Mill's description of the authoritarian irrationality of India's religion resembles Psalmanazar's Formosan fantasy closely: "Everything in Hindustan was transacted by the Deity. The laws were promulgated, the people were classified, the government established, by the Divine Being. The astonishing exploits of the Divinity were endless in that sacred land. For every stage of life from the cradle to the grave; for every hour of the day; for every function of nature; for every social transaction, God prescribed a number of religious observances."

These endless priestly rituals were, as such, abhorrent to a Utilitarian, but what really captured the immorality of Hinduism was the practice of widow burning (sati), which became a trope in the descriptions of Hindu horrors equal to Psalmanazar's description of child sacrifice in Formosa. In this period the British could not, however, revel any longer in the representations of other far-away realities, since they were in command and their rule was expanding. In 1829 the British showed that Hindu horrors could not be tolerated under modern rule, and abolished the practice of widow burning in Calcutta. The authenticity of the Hindu ritual, shown by an act of free choice for self-immolation by the widow, is the main issue in the colonial debate. Freedom is also definitely the great subject of debate in the metropole, and it is in the opposition of freedom and unfreedom that the Christian West distinguishes itself from its Others. Again, however, as in Psalmanazar's case, we can come to know only very little about the Hindu practice, since its representation is framed in this particular colonial narrative of liberation.

Historical description, such as that of Mill, functions less as an entertainment for an emerging, reading public than as as a legitimation of colonial rule under the rubric of progress and rationality. As in Montesquieu's *Lettres Persanes*, the exotic serves also as a foil for thinking about "liberty" and about social and political conditions "at home." Under colonial conditions, however, there is not only room for thought but also experimentation. The nineteenth-century colony was an ideal arena for heated debates among the British about the location of religion in modernity, and about experiments in secular education that could not yet take place in Britain. Conquest and conversion's relationship to each other stood precariously in India, Britain's largest colony. There was a fear in the East India Company that direct interference with Indian religion could upset its expanding political dominance. At the same time, a clear need was felt to rule India through a class consisting of "brown gentlemen," to use an expression of Thomas Macaulay. Indian religions were seen as backward obstacles to progress. As it is put in Macaulay's famous Minute on Indian Education of 1835: "These are the systems under the influence of which the people of India have become what they are. They have been weighed in the balance, and have been found wanting. To perpetuate them, is to perpetuate the degradation and misery of the people. our duty is not to teach, but to un-teach them—not to rivet the shackles which have for ages bound down the minds of our subjects, but to allow them to drop off by the lapse of time and the progress of events."

In her book on English education in nineteenth-century India, Gauri Viswanathan has argued that English literature, as the mirror of the true self, was the medium through which this transformation of Indian back-wardness had to take place. At the same time, literature was the site of con-testation between missionaries and Utilitarian administrators. Viswanathan showed that while literature was a source of the regeneration of an innately depraved self in nineteenth-century Protestant Evangelicalism, it was a means of exercising reason and free will in Utilitarianism (Viswanathan 1989, 19). This debate was a real one, and we would be wrong to think that the missionaries were backward-looking conservatives while the secular-ists were progressive forces in the liberation of mankind. In fact, in this very period missionary societies were extremely active in the struggle for the abolition of slavery, while utilitarians were equivocal on this subject. Nev-ertheless, beyond the complexities of this conflict we may see a fundamen-tal agreement of both parties to the effect that the colonized had to be converted to modernity.

This conversion to modernity in the interplay between Europe and the colonized world is what the present volume seeks to address. It is a subject that has to be understood both historically and anthropologically. The modern problem of the authenticity of conversion and of the description of those who have to be converted, which is taken up by Psalmanazar and Mill under very different conditions at the beginning and at the end of the eighteenth century, originates in seventeenth-century debates about the lo-cation of "religion" in society. With the rise of Protestantism, the univer-sality of the Truth of the Church and of Christendom as the sacred community of believers gave way to a plurality of religious truths and com-munities. This plurality caused large-scale civil strife based on religious dif-ference, especially in Germany, England, and France. These new political conditions had important implications for the understanding of conver-sion, as shown in this volume by Luria and Pollmann. These two papers deal with an early modern situation in which conversion is still a major issue in the European polity itself and has not yet been transported outside of Europe. As I have argued elsewhere, a solution to the European situation of religious civil warfare was a call for religious tolerance and syncretism, but also an interiorization of belief and a privatization of conversion (van der Veer 1994a).

Another, related solution was the emergence of Natural Religion as a belief in and worship of a supreme power. The Deist perspective in the early eighteenth century was that the great truths of religion were all universal and that true religion was ultimately natural religion, open to reason and not bound to particular historical events of revelation that divided one religious community from another (Taylor 1989, 273–74). These theories made a modern, universalist concept of religion possible. In an analysis of Clifford Geertz's (1973) celebrated essay, "Religion as a Cultural System," Talal Asad (1993) argues that the modern understanding of religion, of which Geertz's essay is an example, is very different from what medieval Christians would have regarded as religion. Asad's strategy illuminates the specific historicity of Western "universal" concepts by showing that a definition of religion drawing from modern Christianity cannot be applied to pre-modern Christianity. Briefly, Asad's position is that the boundary between secular and religious has been constantly redrawn in Christianity, but that a major shift occurred when, in the seventeenth century, the Roman church lost its authority to make these distinctions. What comes to be called "religion" is now both universal in the widest sense, as in the ideas about Natural Religion, which exist in every society, and individual in the deepest sense; that is, really part of the inner beliefs of individuals. As a consequence, conversion becomes more and more a depoliticized, private matter of the individual conscience in Europe after the seventeenth century, while missionization campaigns are directed at the colonized areas. In his contribution to the present volume, Asad points out that the problem of the sincerity of coerced conversion raised in seventeenth-century political theory is related to the grand themes of global progress on one hand and religious toleration on the other.

The modern understanding of religion and conversion is not only developed as an answer to political problems in Europe, it is the result of the expansion of the European world-system and the encounter with different religions and cultures that were gradually subjected to colonization. Clearly, this globalization was not only economic in nature, but also cultural and religious. In his *Orientalism*, Edward Said argues forcefully that Western knowledge about the Orient was a "systematic discourse by which Europe was able to manage—and even produce—the Orient politically, sociologically, militarily, ideologically, scientifically, and even imaginatively." According to Said, Western views created a reality in which the "Oriental" had to live. Said's construction of colonial discourse itself is too monolithic, since it is precisely through the debate between different factions in the colonial project that conversion to modernity takes place, as we have seen above.

Another criticism of Said's argument in *Orientalism* is that it seems to deny the agency of the colonized by showing the force of colonial discourse (cf. Breckenridge and van der Veer 1993). To counter the notion that the colonized are the passive objects of a history of world capitalism, Marshall Sahlins relates the story of the killing of the missionary John Williams in Vanuatu on November 20, 1839:

> Already famous as "the Apostle of Polynesia," Williams was abruptly translated to martyrdom by certain Melanesians, purportedly in blind revenge for outrages earlier inflicted on them by White sandalwood traders. Or so runs the pious description of the event which, like calling it "murder" or them "savages," characteristically inscribes the actions of islanders in the notions of Westerners. The historiographic tradition of such incidents has since improved, but not to the extent of ridding itself of the Christian virtue of understanding the Melanesians on the grounds that it was not them who cast the first stone. As if they could have no reasons of violence of their own devising. Never mind that the indigenous meaning of Williams' death—in its ceremonial details strangely reminiscent of the fall of Captain Cook at Hawaii—never mind that the local meaning seems to have been nothing less than deicide." (Sahlins 1994, 412).

Sahlins is definitely right in his view that local meanings tend to disappear in the master narrative of global capitalism, as they do in the story of Christian conversion, but he seems to overestimate the possibilities of retrieving local meanings that are, as it were, untainted by the "outside." Again, description and conversion are double gestures, and it is very hard to escape from the play of memory and forgetfulness in the colonial and missionary archive. The project of modernity that is crucial to the spread of colonial power over the world provides new forms of language in which subjects understand themselves and their actions. In a sense, Western history has indeed shaped world history, including what is understood as "history" (cf. Asad 1993). Actions that cannot be seen as significant within the modern conceptualization of history are thus not part of "history." And one could add that it is almost impossible to escape from categories of Western history, such as "public," "private," or "religion" when writing the history of other societies (Chakrabarty 1992). As Asad reminds us in his contribution to this volume, this is also true for the category of "agency," which is a crucial element in Western modernity. Nevertheless, one has to agree with Sahlins that the globalization of modernity is played out in very different ways in different locales, and that the colonized attach their own meanings to this process. This is in this volume, the subject of Margaret Jolly's contribution, which deals precisely with conversion on Vanuatu, from which Sahlins's example derived. What is indeed so interesting is the interplay between the global and the local through which these very spatial points of reference are constituted.

The present volume seeks to develop an understanding of the interaction between the developments in the colonizing and the colonized worlds. This should lead us away from the commonsensical simplicities of theories of modernization and secularization in which modern Europe unilaterally modernizes its Others, whose role is limited to reaction, both in the sense of weak response and retrograde action. The immense creativity in colonial encounters, both on the part of the colonizers and the colonized, is often done little justice in accounts that rather stress failure than innovative practice. The colonial era makes new imaginations of community possible, and it is especially in the religious domain that these new imaginations take shape. In that sense, conversion to another faith is part of a set of much larger transformations affecting both converts, nonconverts, and the missionaries themselves. Conversion is an innovative practice that partakes in the transformation of the social without being a mechanical result of it. And again, this is true for both the colonizer and the colonized, the missionary and the convert. As I have argued above, conversion of others is gradually marginalized in modern Europe and transported to the non-Christian, colonized world. At the same time, the rise of missionary societies, accompanied by intensive fundraising and missionary propaganda, deeply affects Christianity "at home." The Christian missionary project becomes a crucial part of the related, world-historical phenomena of colonialism and nationalism in the nineteenth and twentieth centuries. No doubt the colonizing state both supports and limits the activities of missionary societies, just as it does with trading companies, and surely there is nothing monolithic in colonialism. The point is rather that the missionary societies are active in the heart of both colonialism and nationalism, the transformation of the religious domain.

An obvious research strategy is to look at Christian missionary societies. There is a rich literature from which one can draw. By far, most of that work focuses on what happens in the target areas in Asia, Africa, and Latin America. Only recently, however, has some work been published that looks simultaneously at the activities of the mission societies at home and in the target areas. I am thinking here, for instance, of the sophisticated work done by John and Jean Comaroff on the Christianization of South Africa. They argue forcefully that "the missionary encounter must be regarded as a *two*-sided historical process: as a dialectic that takes into account the social and cultural endowments of, and the consequences for, *all* the actors—missionaries no less than Africans. Second, as this suggests, a comprehensivé study of that encounter, and of its place in the past and present of Third World peoples, ought to begin in Europe." (Comaroffs 1991, 54). They examine at length the social conditions in Britain from which the London Missionary Society, founded in 1795, and the Wesleyan Methodist Missionary Society, established in 1813, both active in the South African field, emerged. In their analysis, the great eighteenth-century evangelical movements out of which the missionaries came were both causes and consequences of the rise of European modernity, a process that turned upon newly salient differences between civilization and savagery. The heathen "other" of the dark continent provided a language for talking about the rising working classes, the "dark satanic" populations at home (Comaroffs 1991, 43). This suggests that one should look at the rhetoric of the uplifting of the working class and the urban poor as a parallel to the civilizing mission in the colonized areas.

In this volume, Peter van Rooden examines the social mobilization of the Dutch Missionary Society, founded in 1797, as part of a profound shift in the place of religion in Western society. He argues that the Protestant missionary project in the nineteenth century promoted a thoroughly modern distinction between a public and a private sphere by organizing religion outside of the state. The Protestants had hardly been interested in missionization overseas, and the only activities Protestant ministers developed had been firmly under the umbrella of the state and the trading companies. This changed quite dramatically at the end of the eighteenth century, when a distinction between the public and the private allowed voluntary Protestant organizations to develop a whole number of innovative social and religious practices involving Bible translations, poor relief, antislavery activities, and missionary projects. One can hardly overestimate the enormous range of these new practices, which played a crucial part in refiguring the relation between private conscience and public morality. It is important to note here that the transformation of Western society probably was the most important effect of the missionary societies (contrary to what is commonly thought), but that at the same time these very societies tried to create the same dis-

tinctions and relations in the target areas of colonization and missionization (see also Birgit Meyer in this volume).

The connection between bourgeois respectability in Holland and the
missionary project in Indonesia is brilliantly explored in one of the finest
novels in nineteenth-century Dutch literature, *Max Havelaar* by Multatuli
(1860). The coffee trader Droogstoppel summarizes a sermon by his fa-
vorite preacher, the Reverend Wawelaar, about the conversion of the Javanese and Malays in the Netherlands Indies. The gist of the sermon is that
the Netherlands are elected by God to save the heathens, the sons of Ham
who are misled by a false prophet and are punished for that with deep
poverty. The ships of the Netherlands sail the oceans to bring civilization
and Christianity to the misguided Javanese. The pastor has at least two practical suggestions to enhance conversion: (1) to bring the Javanese to God by
labor and (2) to give a free bible with every sale of opium (Multatuli 1860,
138–40). A direct link between missionary activities at home and in the target areas lies, of course, in the fact that these societies had to recruit missionaries among the home population and that they had to raise money at
home for their activities in the field. At the end of his sermon, the reverend
Wawelaar urges his church community to give lavishly to the missionary
society and to the bible society. The Dutch can only fulfill their great task
when they are themselves (and this is the crucial passage): hard-working,
respectable bourgeois who may then justifiably profit from the coffee trade.
Again, the connection between Europe and its Others is historically salient.
Modern Protestants were engaged in transforming civil society in Europe
under conditions of urbanization and rapid industrialization, while at the
same time reorganizing relations of production and disciplining the workers in the target areas of missionization.

The issue here, as Max Weber (1958) realized, is the modern conception
of the individual person, essential to both capitalism and Protestantism.
Surely this modern conception had a much longer Christian ancestry, as
Louis Dumont, among others, has argued, but it is under capitalism that
the entrepreneurial bourgeois self with his urge for self-improvement becomes the bearer of modernity. It is to this new personhood that Europe's
Others have to be converted. I would argue that both Catholic and Protestant missions carry this new conception of the self, of bourgeois domes-
ticity, of citizenship to the rest of the world. This volume tries to relate the
European development of modern notions of personhood to the missionary project of conversion. The complexities of this relation can be captured
in the following three themes, which are explored in the various contributions: identity politics, translation, and transformation.

Identity Politics

Weber's (1978) account of the relation between modernity, disenchantment, and Protestant individual conscience does not sufficiently take political conditions into account. The state is almost completely absent from his analysis, which focuses on "belief" and "rationality." Consequently, this absence is also marked in a Weberian research agenda for the study of conversion to Christianity (e.g., Heffner 1993). In this volume, contributions by Luria, Viswanathan, Spyer, and Dirks, which range from the absolutist state to the colonial state and the nation-state, show the immense importance of the demands of the state, of questions of citizenship and subjecthood for the understanding of conversion both in Europe and in the colonies.

Keith Luria demonstrates that there was a direct connection between conversion and political loyalty in seventeenth-century France. The Counter-Reformation harped on the theme of "cujus regio, ejus religio" (the religion of the ruler is the religion of his territory) to argue that Protestants were disloyal to their Catholic king by the very fact of their Protestantism. In missionary campaigns, a theocratic conception of the monarchy was emphasized so that loyalty to the king could be presented as a religious motive to convert to Catholicism. Although Protestants had theological difficulties in accepting the sacredness of kingship, they went out of their way to protest their political loyalty. What French Protestants asked for was a distinction between religious choice and political subjecthood, a truly modern demand that was accepted by Henri IV in his Edict of Nantes (1598) but rejected by his grandson Louis XIV, who revoked the edict a century later.

Despite the Catholic emphasis on the religious nature of monarchy and subjecthood, their narrativization of conversion is deeply troubled by the problem of insincerity, of "ulterior motives." Luria shows in rich detail the extent to which Catholic conversion stories are overdetermined by a theme that they seek to suppress: conversion as a matter of the individual conscience. There is a nagging doubt in these stories about conversion for political reasons. This doubt of conversion's authenticity is a constant theme in modern Christianity, as documented here also in papers by Spyer on Indonesia and Dirks on India. In a fascinating discussion of Locke's theory of toleration, Talal Asad shows the extent to which the relationship between sincerity of professions of belief and political coercion became the focus of debate in Enlightenment philosophy. He argues that with Descartes and Locke, a new psychology emerges that identifies "religious belief" as a phenomenon of "consciousness," together with other internal phenomena.

In the French case, there is an interesting contradiction in the fact that the conversion stories that have to show "sincerity" are written for polemical, political reasons. This is also true to some extent for a number of the stories of conversion to Protestantism in the sixteenth century, explored by Judith Pollmann, which were often written in answer to political attacks. In seventeenth century France it was the Protestants who, by the very logic of their growing marginality, had the better of this religious truth-game: The less one gains materially and politically from one's religious affiliation, the more sincere it is. Luria does not explore this, but his assessment of conversion by force in his conclusion leads one to hypothesize that after the revocation of the Edict of Nantes, it became the act of political resistance—open or silent—in which one could show one's true conversion. Indeed, the truth of conversion can only be found discursively in the tensions between Protestantism and Catholicism, between individual conscience and political authority.

A century after Louis XIV's decision, the French Revolution put an end to royal absolutism—it is striking how anticlerical that revolution was. Indeed, the legacy of that revolution still inspires the French Government to be extremely secularist in its views on the separation of state and religion, especially in the field of education. Ivan Strenski recently argued that the Protestant-Catholic dichotomy, though grown far beyond the original communities, still characterized French society until the twentieth century: "In this sense, it was common in late-nineteenth- and early-twentieth-century France, to associate republican, rationalist, individualist, moralist tendencies with the so-called Protestant or Free Thinker spirit, while monarchism, authoritarianism, corporatism, and ritualism were attributed to Catholics." (Strenski 1992, 214) Although it is always somewhat dangerous to make these grand dichotomous generalizations over a long period of time, one might safely argue that one of the unintended consequences of the emphasis of the Catholic nature of the monarchy was that it was nearly impossible to disentangle the Church from Absolutism.

That it is the structural relation between Protestants and Catholics rather than their doctrinal differences that determines their position toward state authority per se is shown by the case of nineteenth-century England in which Catholics were the religious, disenfranchised community. While the Catholics were the state Church in France, the Protestant Anglicans were the same in England. After the seventeenth-century religious conflicts in England, Catholics continued to be distrusted as agents of foreign powers. It was only in the nineteenth century that Parliament passed bills for the legal emancipation and enfranchisement of the Catholics. In England, therefore, Catholics as well as dissenting Protestants were the bearers of a tradition of resistance against state power. As Gauri Viswanathan shows in her contribution, the most famous convert of the nineteenth century, John Henry Newman, wanted to draw precisely on that tradition of dissent to claim a space for religious identity that was not simply subsumed within the secular nationalism of the nation-state. In a fascinating move, Newman invented a pre-Reformation popular Catholicism in his struggle against both the secularism and class elitism of the modern nation-state. Newman tried to combine a Catholicism of the popular masses that was truly national with a Catholicism that was truly transnational, and thus capable of criticism of the nation-state. His conversion to Catholicism as an act of both religious and political resistance was thus riddled with contradictions.

Newman's case introduces the complicated relation between conversion, class, and the modern nation-state. In many modernization theories, modernity implies secularism; that is, the privatization and political marginalization of religious belief. The great number of modern nation-states that are not (or only partly) secularized is a problem for these theories. Moreover, as van Rooden shows in his contribution, religious organizations play a significant role in the transformation of modern Western society. In many modern nation-states, one may therefore find forms of religious nationalism in which discourse on the nation and discourse on the religious community are combined. Newman tried to develop a religious nationalism as a form of resistance to the secularization, implied in the nationalism of his time. He saw that the emancipation of Catholics (and Jews, for that matter) would turn them into secular Englishmen, whose class position, not their religious beliefs, would determine their participation in the nation-state.

The problems raised but not solved by Newman are not specific to Britain. Viswanathan takes the admirable step of putting them in a comparative framework by examining another convert for political reasons: Bhimrao Ramji Ambedkar. A crucial difference in the political situation of Newman and Ambedkar is that in nineteenth-century England, religious identity became the point of entry to the more encompassing national identity, with full rights of citizenship, while in twentieth-century India, religious identity had become the site of resistance to a secularizing colonial power that did not grant citizenship but merely subjecthood. In the era of political mobilization, Hindu and Muslim identities were no longer relegated to the private sphere but began to dominate the public sphere in the form of separate, religious nationalisms (van der Veer 1994b).

An enduring theme of Hindu nationalism has been that Hindus, as India's majority, could only be strong if they were united. "Foreign" religions, such as Islam and Christianity, threatened to convert Hindus and thereby diminish Hindu numerical strength. Even very recently, in the 1980s and 1990s, some limited cases of conversion to Islam in South India have caused a major panic and an upsurge of Hindu nationalism. One of the reasons for this numerical anxiety is that the incorporation of untouchable castes in the Hindu fold is only partial. Conversion of all untouchables in India to another religion would immediately cause the collapse of Hindu political dominance. It is this anxiety that the famous untouchable leader (and writer of India's constitution) B. R. Ambedkar has tried to use for the benefit of the untouchables. In 1935 he announced that he would leave Hinduism and convert to another faith, but only twenty years later, just before his death, he actually took the step of converting to Buddhism.

Like Newman, Ambedkar tried to make use of religious difference to express his dissent from a secular national identity in which social disabilities continued to exist. Again, like Newman, he invented an ancient religion of the popular masses that had been suppressed by the ruling elites of the country, namely Buddhism. Conversion to Catholicism in Newman's case, and to Buddhism in that of Ambedkar, had a utopian, radically dissenting character: against the grain. Nevertheless, both were unable to resist the discourse of nationalism. Newman made Catholicism into something truly English, and Ambedkar chose Buddhism, a religion of Indian soil, as it were, rather than a "foreign" (much more threatening) import like Islam or Christianity.

Ambedkar's choice of Buddhism rather than of Christianity is interesting. Although conversion to Christianity in India has been relatively minor compared to Africa, the mission was especially successful among untouchable castes. As Nicholas Dirks shows in his discussion of South India, conversion was intimately tied up with a Christian critique of caste that had great implications for South Indian politics. Missionaries attacked the Brahman caste and Brahmanism fiercely because they saw them not only as the cause of the "immorality"of Hindu society, but also as the reason for their lack of success in converting Indians. One of the strategies was to show that untouchables or tribals were not Hindus originally, but subjected by Brahman priests at some point in history and "made" untouchable by them. Such a missionary theory provided the terms of the anti-Brahmanical discourse of the Dravidian movement, still the most important political movement in the Southern state of Tamil Nadu today. In the case of the Dravidian movement, language and history could form the basis for a regional identity that could soon forget its Christian missionary genealogy. Ambedkar's discursive strategy was similar to that of the Christian missionaries in constructing an "original" non-Brahmanical religion of the untouchables.

Striking in the seventeenth-century French case, as well as in the nine-teenth-century British and the twentieth-century Indian cases, is the impor-tance of the relationship between majority and minority for the issue of conversion. The Indian obsession with numbers definitely is one of the results of the peculiar importance of the colonial census in restructuring Indian so-ciety (Cohn 1978), but, more generally, numbering is an intrinsic part of the modern nation-state and the crucial feature of its most important ritual: elec-tions. In modernity the role of numbers becomes gradually more important, especially in the form of statistics, until it reaches the very margins of the na-tion-state. In Patricia Spyer's discussion of recent conversion to Catholicism in Aru, a remote island in Eastern Indonesia, the simultaneous arrival of con-version and "numericality" is almost uncanny. The Indonesian state has linked full citizenship, including the right to vote, to adherence to one of five world religions (*agamas*): Islam, Hinduism, Buddhism, Protestant Christianity, Catholicism. After the mass killings of 1965 that accompanied the establish-ment of the current New Order regime of President Suharto, it is simply seen as subversive not to adhere to any of these religions. To follow local religious customs (*adat*) is to be against development, antirational. In an ironic twist, the Indonesian government appears to implement Weber's model of rational-ization from magic to religion in its attempt to replace *adat* with *agama*. This shows not only the connections between knowledge and power, but also, again, the importance of state power for the understanding of conversion.

Spyer describes a mass conversion that is simultaneously a missionary's dream and nightmare. Although the question of sincerity does not fail to come up in a situation in which thousands are converted in a short period, this is not Spyer's concern. Marshall Sahlins's theme of local agency and in-terpretation in processes of globalization (see above) appears to be explored here by paying close attention to the ways in which the government and the missionaries' obsession with numbers has penetrated into the very dis-course of the specialist of customary religion (appropriately called "*adat* of-ficial"). Customary religion, in her analysis, does not so much become a site at which to resist the outside imposition of the nation-state, but of a local inflection of conversion to modernity.

Translation

The narrativization of Christian conversion often follows the model of Paul's sudden conversion to Christianity, as told in the New Testament, or that of Augustine, as told in his Confessions. These narratives speak of an individual insight, a deliberate change. Although some of them mention the occurrence of an external event, such as a miracle, there is in general an extraordinary emphasis on the inner experience. It is this interior struggle for change that receives a new boost in Protestant Pietism and is taken to be the core of conversion by William James in his Gifford lectures on conversion, delivered in 1901–1902. Rodney Needham (1972) has rightly argued that belief, language, and experience are connected in a specific way in European thought. If belief is an "interior state," as assumed in the English language, one has to trace that interior state in converts via "belief-statements" in other languages. Needham points out, however, that most languages do not have an equivalent for the English "belief," although there are often concepts that have family resemblances to the English concept. Given the cognitive element in the Western usage, the problem is often best approached by relating the concept of belief to that of knowledge (cf. Kopytoff 1981). However, this does not solve the problem for missionaries who locate the sincerity of conversion in "inner" experience. As missionaries have always realized, it is precisely the problem of translation that is at the heart of conversion. Translations of the Bible and of religious doctrine are among missionaries' first tasks, only preceded by the description in grammar and lexicon of the language of those who are to be converted.

In a fascinating book on translation and conversion in Tagalog society in the Philippines from the late sixteenth to the early eighteenth century, Vicente Rafael (1993) points out that conversion (changing one thing into something else) is synonymous with translation (changing one language into another). He asks the simple but profound question of what conversion means to a colonized people whose language radically differs from that of the colonizers. One of his answers is that the translation of Christian doctrine from Latin and Spanish into Tagalog transformed not only that language but also the Christian doctrine. There is an obvious communicative necessity to master the language of those who are to be converted (and colonized), but it is less obvious that in most missionary projects the vernacular first had to be "tamed" in grammars, based on the sacred language of Latin and lexicons. To an important extent, the vernacular had to be converted into a translatable language within a global hierarchy of languages that could carry the holy Christian message. Rafael, however, shows, in rich detail that the language of the colonized can never be totally "mastered." Moreover, from the missionary point of view, the Tagalog did not quite seem to understand to what religion they converted to. This clearly opens up again the entire problem of the indeterminacy of interpretation and the authenticity of representation. In the Spanish case, this problem, however, has a specific political history that is unfortunately not explored by Rafael. After the reconquest of Spain, leading to the expulsion of Jews and Muslims at the turn of the fifteenth century, the Spanish state made a sharp distinction between original Christians (those with only Christian ancestors) and *conversos* (those who had converted from Judaism or Islam). In the period that the Philippines were conquered and the Tagalog converted, blood statutes and the Inquisition's attention to genealogy in Spain itself made conversion and its insecure determination a problem of immense political implications (Shell 1993, 24–32). Rafael's description of the "totalitarian" nature of the Spanish demand that nothing be held back in confession may well have had something to do with this particular history of Spain (Rafael 1993, 102). The anxieties about the sincerity of conversion and the authenticity of speech in general seem to be embedded in a certain history of power.

In her discussion of the Marist mission in Vanuatu (Western Pacific) in the late nineteenth and early twentieth century, Margaret Jolly follows Rafael in looking not only at the translation of concepts but of practices that embody contesting ideas of sacred potency. Like Webb Keane in his contribution on Sumba, she examines the larger discursive context in which not only speaking is significant but also silence and the refusal of conversation, a subject too often neglected in the ethnography of speaking. Such a refusal to speak is obviously deadly for missionaries who try to learn a language that is not yet "mastered" in grammars and dictionaries. They totally depend on native assistance, and Jolly shows convincingly that that assistance was often refused. In the end the natives did convert, but Jolly warns rightly against the teleology of the conversion narrative that glosses over the sometimes long period of resistance. In a detailed analysis of the translations by the French priest Elie Tattevin, Jolly shows the extent to which the notions of God, spirit, sanctity, or sacred power were contested terrain. Translation actually meant an outright struggle against the sacrality of ancestor religion and the men's house.

A few decades before Tattevin started to work in the western Pacific, the Anglican missionary Robert Caldwell, discussed by Dirks, finished his work in India. One of his major contributions to knowledge was an ethnography of the people among whom he worked, the untouchable Shanars of South India. In his book he argued that these people were Dravidians, the original inhabitants of the land, and had therefore nothing to do with Brahmanical ideas and practices. By demonstrating that the words for local gods (demons or devils) worshiped by the Shanars were all Tamil, and the words for higher gods were all Sanskrit, he wanted to show not only that the Shanars had a separate language and religion but also that they had nothing to do with Brahmanism, so that Brahman priests could be circumvented in their conversion to Christianity. Through the publication of an immensely influential grammar of the Dravidian languages, Caldwell extended his argument to the entire South Indian region, making it as a whole into a mission area. Modern science—that is, linguistics and ethnology—was put to missionary use by Caldwell, but, ironically, his project led to a new non-Christian cult around Tamil Tay (the mother goddess of Tamil) rather than to conversion to Christianity. It had immense political implications in the development of the Dravidian movement, to which we have referred above. Dirks argues convincingly that it is this appropriation in regional politics of a missionary ideology, originating in the peculiar project of conversion, that carried the day. It is clearly not helpful to understand the intricate politics of conversion and translation in terms of a simple resistance or acceptance of the Christian message.

One of the most useful approaches to the conceptual problems involved in conversion is the analysis of its discourse in different historical and ethnographic contexts. A good example of such an analysis is Susan Harding's recent discussion of fundamental Baptist conversion. She argues that American fundamental Baptists do not only talk about conversion, but convert by talking: "Witnessing, and conversion talk more general (testifying, evangelizing, gospel preaching, spreading the Word), is rhetorical in the sense that it is an *argument* about the transformation of self that lost souls must undergo, and a *method* of bringing about that change in those who listen to it. Fundamental Baptist witnessing is not just a monologue that constitutes its speaker as a culturally specific person; it is also a dialogue that reconstitutes its listeners" (Harding 1987, 167). Harding shows that conversion comes through listening and speaking, through discourse: "Among fundamentalist Baptists, the Holy Spirit brings you under conviction by speaking to your heart. Once you are saved, the Holy Spirit assumes your voice, speaks through you, and begins to reword your life. Listening to the gospel enables you to experience belief, as it were, vicariously. But generative belief, belief that indisputably transfigures you and your reality, belief that becomes you, comes only through speech. Among fundamentalist Baptists, speaking is believing." (Harding 1987, 179). Indeed, it is only through the learning of a Christian discourse, a particular set of rules that determines what can be said and what not, what can be done and what not, that one gets converted.

Discourse itself is therefore the subject of the politics of conversion. As Webb Keane shows in his paper on conversion to Protestantism in Sumba,

Indonesia, there is a clash between different perceptions of discourse, of authentic speech. An example is the difference between addressing God directly in prayer and shutting one's eyes while praying, as the Protestants do, or having priests do a formulaic prayer with eyes open, as the "traditional" Sumbanese do. It is not only the authenticity of speech that is a bone of contention but also the valuation of things in the ritual use of objects, as well as the very relation between words and things. It is especially sacrifice, and the distribution of sacrificial meat with its implied commensality, that leads to great debate among missionaries, since it forces them to confront the role of missionary discourse in the transformation of Sumbanese society. Some missionaries realize that conversion to Protestantism entails a separation of subject and object, as well as words and things that will destroy the social fabric of Sumbanese society, in order to replace it with both a modern subjecthood and modern, economic rationality. Like Marcel Mauss in his famous study of gift exchange, these missionaries express a feeling of loss in the modern transformation. Keane's story, however, is not about the triumph of modernity but precisely about the challenge to modern conceptions entailed in the missionary encounter with converts and nonconverts who value "things" differently. His contribution brilliantly shows how important the analysis of the discourse of conversion is for a critical understanding of modernity.

Transformation

Conversion and modernity have something in common—they both view change positively. Raymond Williams reminds us in *Keywords* that change was generally regarded as negative in premodern Europe, and that the positive value of the term "modern" and the spread of its use is in itself an important sign of modernity. The authentication of the present is often in terms of a continuity with the past, but in both modernity and conversion there is a deep ambivalence about the past. There is a tension in modernity well expressed by Baudelaire in his essay "The Painter and Modern Life": "Modernity is the transient, the fleeting, the contingent; it is the one half of art, the other being the eternal and immutable" (quoted in Harvey 1990, 10). This tension is perhaps even stronger in conversion, since religious truth has the tendency to make itself unassailable by ignoring or denying historical change. It is therefore not surprising that the sixteenth-century converts to Protestantism, described by Judith Pollmann, did not enthusiastically proclaim that they were doing something entirely new. It is only in the seventeenth century, when modernity was more fully accepted, that conversion narratives abounded. As Pollmann argues, "The condition for the writing—or even thinking—of such a narrative is a willingness to contrast past and present and to assert that the old was wrong and the new was right." Only few in the sixteenth century were willing to be so radical.

An important element in the need for continuity is a respect for the religion of the ancestors, and, by that token, for the integrity of the larger family. By abandoning the religion of the ancestors, one does not want to cut loose one's family ties. From Luria's account it is clear that converts and nonconverts continued to marry each other and be buried in the same grounds, but that the Capuchin mission did everything to sever these social ties so that conversion to Protestantism really came to mean a total break with the past. A similar problem is addressed by Birgit Meyer, who describes the efforts of a nineteenth-century German Pietist mission among the Ewe in Ghana. However, her analysis gives an interesting twist to the problem, since she argues effectively that the conceptualization of the new constantly needs the imagining of the old. The Pietist missionaries were truly modern in emphasizing a radical break with a past that was governed by the Devil. By claiming that the Ewe cult of the ancestors was, in fact, the worship of the Devil, they endowed the past of their converts with a new, evil potency. A similar problem was faced by the missionaries in Vanuatu, discussed by Jolly. Especially in the field of disease and death, missionary and indigenous understandings of power and evil were deeply entangled. Instead of eradicating past beliefs, the missionary invention gave missionaries a new place in the religious ideas of the converts. Meyer demonstrates that this is not merely a cognitive issue but a social one, since the missionaries tried (as in the case of the Sumbanese, described by Keane) to transform society by dismantling the larger lineage networks. This project of creating the modern individual was, as usual, as partial as the incorporation in a modern, global economy was. Despite the development of a cocoa industry by the missionaries, the land remained in the hands of the lineage heads. And, also, despite the greater efficacy of Western medicines, people continued to be dependent on their larger families in times of illness.

The manicheistic dichotomy between good and evil, between past and present, made by the Pietist missionaries illustrates aptly the discontents of modernity. The topic of conversion allows us to penetrate deeper than usual into the peculiar ambiguities of modern power. Christian conversion is a "technology of the self," to use Foucault's notion, which, under modern conditions, produces a new subjecthood that is deeply enmeshed in economic globalization and the emergence of a system of nation-states.

Not only does conversion to Modern Christianity (both Protestant and Catholic) seek to transform the Self by changing its relation to Others, it enables a new organization of society. As Foucault (1982) argues, this process produces "two meanings of the word 'subject': subject to someone else by control and dependence; and tied to his own identity by a conscience or self-knowledge." The contributions to this volume show different aspects of this production of the modern subject in a variety of historical settings.

Note

1. Formosa was better known to the Dutch because the Dutch East-India Company had occupied it between 1627 and 1661 (see Blusse 1984). Since Psalmanazar had been a soldier in the Netherlands, his choice of Formosa may have derived from there, a possibility not considered by Stewart.

References

Asad, Talal. 1993. *Genealogies of Religion. Discipline and Reasons of Power in Christianity and Islam.* Baltimore: Johns Hopkins University Press.

Blusse, Leonard. 1994. "Dutch Protestant missionaries as protagonists of the territorial expansion of the VOC on Formosa." In Dick Kooiman, Otto van den Muijzenberg, and Peter van der Veer (eds.) *Conversion, Competition and Conflict. Essays on the Role of Religion in Asia.* Amsterdam: Free University Press, 155–85.

Breckenridge, Carol A. and Peter van der Veer (eds.). 1993. *Orientalism and the Postcolonial Predicament. Perspectives on South Asia.* Philadelphia: University of Pennsylvania Press.

Chakrabarty, Dipesh. 1992. "Postcoloniality and the artifice of history: Who speaks for 'Indian' pasts." *Representations* 37: 1–30.

Cohn, B. S. 1987. *An Anthropologist among Historians.* New Delhi: Oxford University Press.

Comaroff, Jean and John. 1991. *Of Revelation and Revolution. Christianity, Colonialism, and Consciousness in South Africa.* Chicago: University of Chicago Press.

Foucault, Michel. 1982. "The subject and power." Leslie Sawyer, trans. *Critical Inquiry* 8, no. 4: 777–78.

Geertz, Clifford. 1973. *The Interpretation of Cultures.* New York: Basic Books.

Harding, Susan. 1987. "Convicted by the holy spirit: The rhetoric of fundamental Baptist conversion." *American Ethnologist*, 14, no. 1: 167–82.

Harvey, David. 1990. *The Condition of Postmodernity.* Oxford: Basil Blackwell.

Heffner, Robert. 1993. Introduction in Robert Heffner (ed.), *Conversion to Christianity; Historical and Anthropological Perspectives on a Great Transformation*. Berkeley: University of California Press, 3–47.

James, William. 1985. *[1901–1902] The Varieties of Religious Experience*. London: Collins.

Kopytoff, Igor. 1981. "Knowledge and Belief in Suku Thought." *Africa* 51, no. 3: 709–723.

Macaulay, Thomas Babington. 1935. *Speeches, with the Indian minute on education*. G. M. Young (ed.). London: Oxford University Press.

Multatuli (Eduard Douwes Dekker). 1860. *Max Havelaar*.

Needham, Rodney. 1972. *Belief, Language, and Experience*. Oxford: Basil Blackwell.

Pocock, J. G. A. 1961–62. " The origins of the study of the past: A comparative approach." *Comparative Studies in Society and History* IV, 209–246.

Rafael, Vicente. 1993. *Contracting Colonialism. Translation and Christian Conversion in Tagalog Society under Early Spanish Rule*. Durham: Duke University Press.

Sahlins, Marshall. 1994. "Cosmologies of capitalism: The trans-pacific sector of 'The world-system.' " In Nicholas Dirks, Geoff Eley and Sherry Ortner (eds.) *Culture/Power/History. A Reader in Contemporary Social Theory*. Princeton: Princeton University Press, 412–57.

Shell, Marc. 1993. *Children of the Earth. Literature, Politics and Nationhood*. New York: Oxford University Press.

Stewart, Susan. 1994. *Crimes of Writing. Problems in the Containment of Representation*. Durham: Duke University Press.

Strenski, Ivan. 1993. *Religion in Relation. Method, Application and Moral Location*. London: MacMillan.

Taylor, Charles. 1989. *Sources of the Self*. Cambridge: Harvard University Press.

van der Veer, Peter. 1994a. "Syncretism, multiculturalism and the discourse of tolerance." In Charles Stewart and Rosalind Shaw (eds.) *Syncretism/Anti-Syncrteism. The Politics of Religious Synthesis*. London: Routledge, 196–212.

———. 1994b. *Religious Nationalism. Hindus and Muslims in India*. Berkeley: University of California Press.

Viswanathan, Gauri. 1989. *Masks of Conquest. Literary Study and British Rule in India*. New York: Columbia University Press.

Weber, Max. 1958. *The Protestant Ethic and the Spirit of Capitalism*. New York: Scribner.

———. 1978. *Economy and Society: An Outline of Interpretive Sociology*. Guenther Roth and Claus Wittich, eds. Berkeley: University of California Press.

1

THE POLITICS OF PROTESTANT CONVERSION TO CATHOLICISM IN SEVENTEENTH-CENTURY FRANCE

Keith P. Luria

There are those who have believed it good, useful or necessary to abandon the religion of their ancestors and embrace another for timely reasons—to make a so-called "mixed" marriage, to be integrated into society, or because of political circumstances that do not tolerate those of certain origins. These are conversions of opportunity, and the expression is not meant in any way to be perjorative. *Honni soit qui mal y pense.* We will not be speaking of them here. . . . Of whom then do we speak? Of other converts, *of true converts.* Of believers who have changed religion as part of a voyage (en cours de route). For some there was a rupture, clear, radical, sometimes brutal, following upon an equally sudden Revelation. For others, this deviation from a well-traced spiritual itinerary was made more gently, after a slow and long maturation, after a series of encounters, or through the detour of a book. (Assouline 1992, 15–16, my translation and emphasis)

CLAIMING NO PERJORATIVE INTENTION, Pierre Assouline speaks here of those who convert for reasons of circumstance or opportunity. Yet barely has he signalled his impartiality, by invoking the old malediction against those who think evil, when he suggests that such convenient conversions are not "true" ones. Real conversions have nothing to do with worldly desires, social obligations, and political pressures—the realm of historical contingencies. Real conversions are sparked by something less mundane—a book, a long spiritual searching, a revelation—and they emerge from an inward spiritual movement, a "radical rupture" at once deep and irrevocable. The conversions Assouline dislikes mix worldliness with sanctity and demean the gravity of a spiritual change.

This distinction between true and false conversions is hardly new. Within Christianity, for example, it is as old as the paradigmatic conversions of Saint Paul and Saint Augustine, which stand as the prototypes of a momentous interior change, a "turning to God" in the etymological sense of the word convert (latin *convertire*). God works this turn, and it is manifested in the convert by an inner change of belief and an outward change of life. Ever since Paul and Augustine, the inward transformation has been central to the Christian understanding of conversion. For scholars, such as William James, it has sometimes constituted the sole meaning of the conversion experience (James 1985).[1]

But examinations of conversion's meaning at specific historical moments reveal considerable variation. Sociologists working on our contemporary notions of conversion have demonstrated how it responds to the larger cultural framework within which converts live, and particularly to the ideas propagated by the religious groups they join.[2] The same was true in the past. Paula Fredriksen has shown how Paul understood his experience in the terms offered by his religious tradition, as a "call" to an Old-Testament-style prophet. Augustine reinterpreted Paul's change, and thereby explained his own conversion, in the light of a different tradition. His neo-platonism and his theological concerns at the time he wrote the *Confessions* led him to think of Paul's experience as a "drama of human will and divine grace." For Augustine, "Paul becomes the sinner inexplicably redeemed from his former life by the unmerited gift of God's grace" (Fredriksen 1986).

Augustine's interpretation of Paul's momentous, interior transformation has had an enduring importance for Christians, but later eras found other ways to understand both Paul's experience and the general concept of conversion. Karl Morrison contrasts a view (such as is current today) that focuses on Paul's sudden experience on the road to Damascus with that of the Middle Ages, which saw all conversion, including Paul's, as a long "process of adoption, or transformation . . . In fact, all of life, rightly lived, was conversion" (Morrison 1992, xii. See also Harran 1983, 31–41, 52). Monastic life was thus the truest form of conversion. In the seventeenth century, this conception of conversion was far less evident than those that stressed either a change in religious creed or a turning of one's life—in the world not the monastery—away from sin and toward virtue (Dumonceaux 1983, 7-17). Thus, the understanding of conversion responds to certain dominant cultural codes and symbols; those who encourage it or undergo it describe conversion by means of certain conceptions of self and religion whose meanings can be studied as historically specific (Hefner 1993, 4).

The Seventeenth-Century Model of Conversion

The meaning of conversion was very much at stake in seventeenth-century France because of the side-by-side existence of competing faiths—Catholic and Protestant—each of which encouraged converts from the other. The confessions constructed models of conversion that reiterated the depiction of it as a profound inner transformation worked by God. However, in the context of religious rivalry, conversion was not just a turning to God—it was also a submission to an institution that represented, indeed that defined, truth. Each model stressed the sincerity of converts to its faith and the worldly, self-interested reasons that goaded its deserters. No true conversion resulted from "human considerations." But the rival polemicists faced the rather evident problem that worldly means—social and political pressures or enticements, such as government posts and pensions—were often the motives behind conversions. And the issue was complicated for the competing clergies because of what they saw as the converts' easy back and forth movement between the two faiths. Relapses particularly smelled of worldly interests. As the Protestant minister of Charenton, Charles Drelincourt, remarked: "The comings and goings of certain people who play at changes of religion are very lucrative" (Drelincourt 1654, 7). To stop what they considered false changeovers, the Catholic and Protestant clergies wanted conversion understood as irrevocable, serious, and impervious to social and political imperatives.

Worldly motives, however, could be very compelling because religious affiliations criss-crossed other social groupings such as kinship ties, family alliances, communal institutions, patron-client networks, and class. Perhaps nothing speaks more strongly to the permeability of religious boundaries than intermarriage. In many mixed-confessional areas, family interests and strategic planning dictated frequent unions of Catholic and Protestant spouses (Labrousse 1985, 83-84; Sauzet 1979, 165–68; Dompnier 1985, 154–57; Bertheau 1970, 522). More common than even the truly mixed weddings were matches in which one spouse converted to the other's religion and then, quickly or at a later moment, returned to his or her original faith. These conversions for the sake of marriage were common not just in aristocratic or bourgeois families, for whom such alliances were an important means of social ascension, but also in poorer families, who needed to make cross-confessional matches for economic partnership and survival. An advantageous marriage was an advantageous marriage, despite its interconfessional inconvenience, the complaints of the clergy, and even royal legislation (Labrousse 1985, 83; Diefendorf 1989, 85; Dompnier 1985, 157; Benoist 1983, 328; Bertheau 1970, 522–23; Debon 1983, 141).

Robert Sauzet has disparaged these confessional changes as a "comédie des abjurations pro matrimonio," which suggests a particularly modern suspicion of non-religious motives in conversion (Sauzet 1979, 268). But rival early-modern clergymen would have agreed: they also complained of religious indifference in cross-confessional marriages (Labrousse 1985, 83; Diefendorf 1989, 85).[3] The practice of intermarriage, however, corresponded to very real social imperatives. It may not have indicated a lack of religious belief, as clerics liked to believe, but a kind of religious belief different from what they propagated, a faith that incorporated the social and political concerns of its believers.[4] And clerical insistence on religious endogamy did hide a certain ambivalence. Regardless of the injunctions of Catholic priests and Protestant consistories against such matches, those who took partners of the other faith were not punished harshly (Dompnier 1985, 155; Labrousse 1985, 83). Each side could hope that a conversion for the sake of marriage might eventually become sincere and lasting, and each expected spouses to help insure that their converted mates would stick to their new faith (Dompnier 1985, 156; Diefendorf 1989, 85).

The conversion of clergymen produced especially sharp polemics and accusations of insincerity. Propagandists on either side made much of clerical conversions, which seemed, even more than the winning of lay converts, to indicate the truth of their faith. Indeed, the converted ministers and priests themselves often became champion polemicists for their new religions (Desgraves 1983, 89–110). In many cases, however, converted clergymen were no more steadfast than their lay counterparts. The former Cordelier, Olivier Enguerrand, became minister of the Reformed Church of Chef-Boutonne (Poitou), but a decade later returned to his original faith. He published accounts of both changes (Desgraves 1983, 94, 103). Likewise, the Dominican Gabriel Boule, from Carpentras, converted to Protestantism sometime between 1610 and 1612 and eventually became a pastor, first at Orange and then at Vinsobres. Boule published a polemical work on behalf of his new faith. Joseph-Marie de Suarez, Bishop of Vaison (the diocese within which Vinsobres lay) lured Boule back, perhaps by ameliorating the minister's difficult economic situation. By the late 1630s, Boule was serving Suarez as an agent, providing the prelate with lists of Protestant books along with information about synods and Huguenot ministers. In 1642 he abjured his Calvinism and returned to the Church. He then turned his polemical talents against his former Huguenot coreligionists (Feuillas 1983).

The Jesuit Pierre Jarrigue undertook a similar trajectory. In 1647 he asked the La Rochelle consistory to receive him as a Protestant. For the elders, the conversion was a true movement of conscience in which "God's grace had opened [Jarrigue's] eyes and made him recognize, on the one hand, the errors and superstitions in the Roman Church and particularly in the Jesuit order and, on the other hand, the true and pure beliefs of the reformed churches. . . . He was now determined to give glory to God by the free confession of the truth" (Archives départmentales de la Charente-Maritime 1628-1662).[5] Catholic apologists suggested that the ambitious Jarrigue had converted because he felt ill-used by his Jesuit superiors, and further, they claimed he had committed gross sacrilege by dissimulating his change and continuing to celebrate the Mass until he felt able to go public (Filleau 1668, 715–16). Three years after his initial conversion, he returned to Catholicism and even rejoined the Jesuits (Hanlon 1993, 206). He, too, published polemical accounts of his conversions at each stage of his itinerary.

Catholics experienced the same sorts of disappointments and embarrassments, such as in the conversion of the Poitiers minister, Samuel Cottiby. Antoine Denesde, a merchant of Poitiers and a fervent Catholic, recorded Cottiby's religious trajectory in his journal. In an entry for March 8, 1637, he reports:

> Monseigneur of Poitiers led by the hand to the sermon at St. Pierre's church, the one named Cotiby, of around 19 years of age, oldest son of Sieur Cotiby, minister of the religion of Calvin at Poitiers. . . . The son received absolution of the heresy in public the next day. . . . He had studied his humanities at Saumur and was on the point of preparing for the ministry with a pension from the Huguenots, but he frustrated their expectations. God give him the grace to persevere and die a true child of the Roman Church.

The Catholics seemingly had triumphed. An aspiring minister, the son of a minister and the object of great local Protestant expectations, had abjured. But Cottiby's new coreligionists were to be disappointed. Denesde concludes the entry with a laconic, "Three weeks later, Cottiby reverted to his errors" (Denesde 1885, 78). Eventually, however, Catholicism did claim a victory. Twenty-three years later, Denesde's wife, Marie Barré, who continued the journal after her husband's death, reported Cottiby's final change of religion. A "multitude" of people attended the abjuration ceremony, "giving as much joy and satisfaction to Catholics as confusion to the Huguenots because [the convert] was a person of consequence, thanks to his great knowledge and eloquence. May God, by His holy mercy, grant him the grace to persevere in that which he has so gloriously begun" (Denesde 1885, 184, 187). He, too, would enter into the polemical arena to defend his ultimate change (Cottiby 1660).

The apostasies of clergymen made for ardent polemics but brought few tangible results in the form of further converts. Their motives, especially if they received financial assistance or the patronage of powerful new coreligionists, were easily belittled. Catholics claimed that the ex-pastor Jacques Métayer (of Lusignan in the Poitou) had been "fortified by the inspiration of God" in giving up his ministry. Protestants just argued that Métayer was a troubled person and had been lured to Catholicism by a pension (Métayer 1617, Mestayer 1620).[6] Catholics might rejoice at capturing a redoubtable opponent like the minister Jérémie Ferrier, but Protestants were quick to dismiss him and his importance. Elie Benoist's denunciation of Ferrier's 1613 desertion, though admittedly written much later, no doubt reflected the aspersions his predecessors had cast: Ferrier "had labelled fidelity to the King that which the *reformez* saw as a betrayal of their secrets; what he argued was compensation for his good services they decried as payment for treason; what he thought of as his free and sincere preaching, in which he spoke only the true sentiments of his conscience on their affairs, they viewed as seditious" (Benoist 1693, 2, 125).

Relapses were an embarrassment to all concerned. The loss of a Cottiby was a disappointment to Protestants, but his switching back and forth did little to encourage other conversions. Gabriel Boule's name became abhorrent to his former Protestant congregation. Even if Catholicism would most often claim the converts' ultimate loyalty, changeability served no one's cause very well. As one Catholic observer of Boule's career remarked: "The conversion of a nobleman is more efficacious than that of a minister. The minister just makes himself odious, and he is quickly replaced" (Feuillas 1983, 188).

To counteract the seeming self-interestedness of conversions and the embarrassing turnabouts, each faith presented to potential neophytes a model of conversion that stressed the importance of conscience and deep interior motivation, as well as true doctrine and the role of intellect and emotion in adhering to it. (Luria 1993, 65–81). Here I will concentrate largely on the Catholic model, because the evidence for it is more plentiful and the flow of conversions over the century favored it. But the Catholic model also deserves attention because it contains a distinctive element that seventeenth-century French Protestants could not readily include within their representation of religious change; namely, political obedience to the monarchy. Conversion to Catholicism was described as a turning not only to God but to the king and his religion. The emphasis on a political motive in conversion would seem incongruous in a model that otherwise under-scored the role of conscience, but Catholic converts and polemicists de-scribed the return to political loyalty as prompted by the sincere recognition of a religious as well as a political error. Loyalty to a monarch was not, there-fore, another worldly concern or obligation imposed by custom, law, or so-cial interest. Just as true religious feelings of the conscience were to be above such matters, so too was political fidelity. It came from the heart.

The linkage of obedience and conversion stemmed directly from the Catholics' theocratic conception of the monarchy, in which political loy-alty, religious uniformity, and Catholicism were inextricable. By a process stretching over centuries, the French monarchy had accumulated a sacred mystique and had become the object of a cult, which overlapped with Catholic beliefs. The cult adapted Catholic rituals in particular in the con-secration of new kings at the Reims cathedral, in the practice of the royal touch by which kings miraculously cured scrofula, and in royal funeral cer-emonies during which an effigy of the monarch continued to represent the mystical body politic of the realm while the king's mortal remains were en-tombed (Bloch 1972; Giesey 1960; Kantorowicz 1957). Propagandists of this royal religion equated the king's relation to the kingdom with that of Christ to the Church. The early-modern theorists of divine-right monar-chy further elaborated the royal cult by arguing that God granted the king his position, and, as a result, the king was answerable only to God. It was the monarch's duty to advance his subjects' quest for salvation by insuring peace and justice in the realm and good order in the Church (Labrousse 1985, 107).

Calvinists could not easily share the belief that an earthly being par-took of God's divinity. And their denunciation of miracle working, sacred images, and relics put them at odds with the royal religion's Catholic trappings. Thus, Catholics saw Protestants as inherently disloyal, and the minority faced frequent accusations of lèse-majesté (Garrisson 1985; 81–90, Dompnier 1985, 82–87; Labrousse 1985, 110–112). Despite the Huguenots' frequent and fervent protestations of political obedience, Catholic propagandists could effectively paint them as rebels, or at least as potential rebels. The accusation of disloyalty was only one among a vari-ety of means by which anti-Protestant campaigners were successful in segregating Protestants from the social and political life of the kingdom, constructing them as a danger to the state that could only be alleviated by their conversion to the state religion.

Catholics deployed this image through polemics, notably accounts of Protestants converting to Catholicism. These published works of contro-

versy were especially numerous in the decades after Henry IV's promulga-
tion of the Edict of Nantes (1598). The edict allowed members of the
French Reformed Church to worship in France within strictly defined legal
and geographic limits. Although they could practice their religion legally,
the edict did not effectively create a situation in which Protestants were
truly tolerated in the Catholic state. Early-modern Europeans—Protestants,
too, in countries in which they were the majority—found the notion of religious pluralism unacceptable. The belief that confessional uniformity was
essential for national unity was still widespread (Labrousse 1985, 106–108).[7]
In France, the Catholic clergy argued that the Edict of Nantes was an out-
rage to the true faith and a sign of royal weakness; kings swore in their coro-
nation oaths to eradicate heresy. In a situation of legal coexistence, however,
the Catholic clergy had to pursue its goals through political pressure, missions, and polemics. French Protestants could apply political pressure only
locally, and they could not actively proselytize through missions, but they
did respond to Catholic polemical attacks with their own publications.

The public disputes grew especially heated when they were provoked by
Catholic missionary campaigns organized to promote mass Protestant conversion. One of the earliest such missions in France started in the western
province of the Poitou in 1617. Its founder, the Capuchin Père Joseph of
Paris (Joseph du Tremblay, future *éminence grise* of Richelieu), was well-ac-
quainted with religious conditions in a province that presented an attractive
target for his missionaries.[8] The Poitou had a large, socially complex, and
politically powerful Protestant population. At the beginning of the seventeenth century, approximately 100,000 Protestants lived there in congregations spread throughout the province (Pérouas 1964; Favreau 1988,
132–34, 144–45). Huguenots comprised as much as forty percent of the
population of some towns. In certain regions, they made up seventy-five to
ninety percent of rural parishes. They were well represented among the
local elite of nobles, officers, professionals, and merchants. And at the top
of Poitevin society sat the great aristocratic Huguenot clans of La Trémoille,
Rohan, and Vérac.

Reports to the crown complained of the Huguenot domination of
provincial society and politics (Archives nationales 1618, 232–35). But in
the Poitou, relations between the religious groups were not always tense; in
many ways local Catholics and Protestants achieved a coexistence in the
decades immediately succeeding the Edict of Nantes. Poitevins crossed the
confessional boundary in a variety of ways, of which I can only cite some
very brief examples. Concern with familial interests led to frequent intermarriage within both higher and lower social groups (Bertheau 1970, 525).

Family political ambitions also dictated the filling of local offices by means of patron-client rather than religious ties. The powerful La Trémoilles, a Huguenot clan in the early decades of the century, had both Protestants and Catholics among their clients. Townspeople of different religions often shared civic duties, such as service on councils or in militias, though generally by means of a strict ordering designed to insure positions for each side (Dez 1936, 253; Bibliothèque municipale de Poitiers 1621, 68, 357–61). Perhaps more surprising than cross-confessional social alliances and cooperation in civic duties was the sharing of sacred space, especially cemeteries. Poitevins wanted to be buried with their kin, even if they were of the rival faith. Agreements between the religious groups sometimes established common cemeteries and spoke of communal consent to share and even of the "amitié ancienne" that had governed joint cemetery use (Archives départmentales de Vienne 1634; Benoist 1983, 343–44). In other words, despite the sometimes considerable tensions between the two religions, substantial evidence suggests a mutual recognition of the right of each group to exist within Poitevin communities as well as a willingness to live together. The missionaries' conversion campaign would quickly undermine the process of building such social coexistence.

The mission promoted a rupture between Catholics and Protestants in provincial society by emphasizing the religious boundary over and above the other social and political divisions that separated Poitevins from each other (Dompnier 1983, 270). Missionaries, along with their local and national supporters, did not create tensions where none had previously existed, but they accentuated certain local differences and imbued them with doctrinal and political orthodoxy. Their campaign estranged the two confessional groups, and, with the help of royal legislation and the judicial system, excluded Huguenots from full participation in the daily life and governance of the province's communities. Once separated from their accustomed social bonds, Protestants could only be fully reintegrated into local and national, Catholic and monarchical society through religious conversion.

The Capuchin mission in the Poitou began in Lusignan on Christmas of 1617 with a spectacular ceremony—a prayer vigil of Forty Hours (Luria 1993). Capuchins made this ceremony the hallmark of their missions in France. It proclaimed belief in the real presence in the Host, a crucial point of doctrinal difference between Catholicism and Calvinism. Central to the Forty Hours ritual was a watch before the Blessed Sacrament, exposed on an altar for three days. The missionaries focused attention on the Host by decorating altars to resemble small stages with the Host in the center, surrounded by veils or drapes and bathed with hidden lights (Luria 1989,

115–16; Dompnier 1981, 1983, 262–70; Weissman 1982, 229–33). In the Poitou, the friars enhanced the ceremony by adding public preaching and processions. Capuchins frequently employed the Forty Hours devotion to attack Protestantism directly by performing it at the same time and place as Huguenot synods. But they also opened their missions among Catholics with the ritual, and found it especially useful as a means of drawing the faithful away from carnival celebrations or other such "popular" festivities (Sceaux 1958; Dompnier 1983, 262–63). The overriding purposes of the event—to hear Capuchin preaching and to proclaim the real presence—rallied the Catholic faithful. The vigils for the Eucharist, the sacred songs and litanies for the Virgin, the processions that paraded the Blessed Sacrament from church to church combined to produce an impressive spectacle of Catholic piety, one quite foreign to Calvinist beliefs and modes of worship. As the accounts of the Poitou mission show, it was precisely by directing the ceremony toward Catholics, to revive their faith and their orthodox religious behavior, that the Capuchins reinforced the boundaries between them and their Protestant neighbors.

The chronicle of the Poitou mission claimed that as many as 50,000 people from throughout the province attended the Forty Hours and the preaching at Lusignan (Bibliothèque municipale d'Orléans 1673, 51–70; Pérouas 1964). Similar ceremonies conducted elsewhere also attracted large crowds. The figures might well be exaggerated, but it is clear that the devotions had a large impact. Despite the baroque, Catholic style of the ritual, Protestants also came, and the Capuchin staging of it provided them with a role. Those who converted during the Forty Hours were illustrative examples of how former heretics could be reintegrated through the ritual back into the majority community (Luria 1993, 71–72).

The Forty Hours devotions, as well as sermons, processions, pilgrimages, and public debates with Protestant ministers, all became part of both the practices of the conversion campaign and the Capuchin discourse about conversion. The model the friars constructed linked the intellectual appeal to proper doctrine, as elucidated in sermons and debates with ministers, to the emotional appeal of baroque ceremonies. This discourse, in a sense, masked the possibility that quite different considerations prompted Protestant conversions to Catholicism. Pensions paid to ministers, the desire to avoid social ostracism, the need to obtain or retain official positions, the attraction of attaching oneself to the Catholic elite or to a particular patron, the importance of demonstrating loyalty to the crown—for all these reasons and others it made good sense for Protestants to change religions. The power of such reasons only increased across the century.

But Capuchin discourse on conversion (and that of Catholics more generally) could not easily admit such rationales. They smacked of insincerity, of "human considerations," rather than the moralistic or spiritual meaning of true conversion. Thus, the abjuration of someone like Métayer could only have followed upon "violent movements of his conscience" and "violent interior reproaches that stung him to the bottom of his heart" (Métayer 1617, 7; Mestayer 1620, 21–22). This conversion was no mere sellout but a heartfelt movement of conscience in which one could see, as was said of another conversion during the Poitou mission, "a work of God's hand, so pure and so clean that nothing human or of any particular interest entered into it" (Anonymous 1628b, 4). In his private correspondence, Père Joseph wrote that the fervor of the mission's neophytes was proof that the conversions came from God and not from "considérations humaines." The converts were moved by God, who "had put His hand in their hearts, and not by human considerations, which, on the contrary, would have prevented them [from converting]" (Mauzaize 1978, 1035). Neither Capuchins nor other converters refrained from using worldly incentives to encourage abjurations, but in the polemics that surrounded the missionary campaign, conversions motivated by such inducements were open to easy Protestant attack.

Conversion and Political Loyalty

It is ironic, therefore, that to deflect attention from the self-interested political motives lurking behind many actual individual religious changes, Capuchin conversion discourse and missionary practice emphasized a supremely political rationale, obedience to the king. The political motive was glorified as a religious one.[9] Or it might be better to say that loyalty was construed not just as a political concern but as a religious one. Père Joseph, for instance, politicized the originally penitential Forty Hours ritual by ordering his missionaries to add public prayers for the prosperity of their majesties. Those who marched in processions to the site of each ceremony were to chant litanies for the blessed Virgin with a "Vive le Roi" added to each refrain (Dedouvres 1894, 2, 161). Louis XIII made his interest in the mission known in various ways, such as, in 1620, requesting from Rome extended authorizations for the missionaries and, in 1621, permitting the friars to preach in public marketplaces—an activity usually prohibited because of its potentially inflammatory consequences (Formon 1955, 221–22). Conscience would answer not only to God but also to the king.

The polemical works the mission produced were framed by reference to the monarch and political loyalty. Protestant rebellion was brewing in 1617, when one of the friars' first converts, the Lusignan pastor Jacques Métayer, wrote his conversion account. In it, he demonstrated his loyalty by deriding his former colleagues for attempting to provoke a war against the king. He wanted no part of a ministry of anger, of condemnation, and of death. The Protestant Church was no longer "reformed" but "deformed by seditious troubles and movements that would lead only to confusion and anarchy." "I detest," he wrote, "the rebellions against the King and his state by ministers who have the direction of their churches' public affairs" (Métayer 1617, 3, 7–9, 18). When Samuel Cottiby converted in 1660 (not as a result of the mission), he, too, raised suspicions about Protestants, who, "for a religious motive have interests separate from those of their natural prince and their dear country" (Cottiby 1660, 5). Louis XIV faced no Huguenot rebellion in 1660, but the interregnum in England provided French Catholics with plenty of ammunition to use against French Protestants. Huguenot apologists went to great lengths to proclaim their fidelity and criticize English Calvinists, but it was easy for Catholic propagandists to associate the two groups of coreligionists (Labrousse 1985, 111). With religion and politics so closely intertwined, a conversion to Catholicism was inevitably an integration into the monarchical order as well.[10]

The point was made clear in conversion accounts both by demonstrating the way in which the convert was officially accepted back into the community of loyal French subjects and by exclamations of the neophytes' newfound political orthodoxy. When in 1620 the Capuchin missionaries converted a Parthenay inhabitant, the Sieur de la Verdure, the town's Catholic elite, consisting of ecclesiastics, nobles, and judicial officers, came to welcome him into the faith. The canons of the chapter of Sainte Croix chanted a *Te Deum* in a church filled with a great crowd that had assembled in Parthenay for a market day. When in the same year the Dame de la Poste of Sanxay converted, a Capuchin missionary led to her house a procession that included local Catholic noblemen (Mestayer 1620, 27–32, 52–54).

The attendance at Cottiby's first conversion in 1637 was similar. Denesde reports in his journal: "Present were Messieurs the lieutenants civil and criminal, several counsellors, all the *gens du roy*, Monsieur the Mayor, several echevins, and a great number of other people." Their presence lent the conversion a social and political as well as religious significance; it welcomed the convert into the city's social and political elite and into a position of political orthodoxy. Four months after Cottiby's second and final conversion to Catholicism, the king arrived in Poitiers to lay the foundation stone of a Carmelite convent. Denesde's widow pointedly notes that the recent convert attended the ceremony and was presented to the "King, Queens, and Mr. le Cardinal [Mazarin], all of whom paid him much honor . . . and congratulated him on his fortunate conversion." Here again, a Catholic witness made the link between religious and political orthodoxy. Each would insure the other (Denesde 1885, 79, 184, 187).

In 1628, the Protestant grandee Henry, Duke de La Trémoille converted to Catholicism in the presence of Louis XIII, Richelieu, and the royal army besieging La Rochelle. The renewed religious wars of the 1620s sparked the defection of many Protestant magnates, who felt pressured by royal propaganda decrying their disloyalty, were troubled by angry divisions among their coreligionists, and were lured by royal positions and favors (Imbert 1867, 9; Parker 1980, 122). But La Trémoille, the most important nobleman in the Poitou and a guardian of the Reformed Church, was a special catch. Catholic polemicists described the conversion so as to make the duke's change an example others would follow (Anonymous 1628a, 1628b). They were quick to extol the duke and to acclaim his political loyalty as a sign of his "true" conversion. They also rushed to praise the king and, even more so, Richelieu for bringing about the change. The writers stressed the duke's moderate character, evident even in the ardor of his youth. He had exhibited "none of the pride and insolence common to those of his creed." Such moderation made him open to instruction in the true faith, which he received over a period of months from Capuchin friars and then from Richelieu. But the teaching had only allowed his true self to emerge; he found it easy to "follow the instincts that the hand of God had touched." His Protestant faith was only "borrowed." "God had permitted him to be born and to live for some time in error so that, by his example, the pride and insolence [of the heretics] could better be repressed" (Anonymous 1628a, 2, 8; La Trémoille 1895, 4, 86–87). Henry's return to the true faith reversed his father Claude's desertion of it, and restored the duke to his rightful place within the illustrious La Trémoille lineage, which had formerly served Church and king so well (Anonymous 1628a, 8; 1628b, 3).

Those present at Henry's public renunciation of error remarked on the "profound humility" with which he received Richelieu's encouragement. His tears of regret for his sins proved his inner change; one could see "on the face of this penitent the true movements of his soul."[11] These movements, however, brought him back not just to God. For as the duke presented himself to the king, he "offered [the monarch] as proof of his fidelity a new conscience with a desire to serve him without exception" (Anonymous 1628a, 6–7). Henceforth, his conscience belonged not just to God but also to his sovereign. The king received him with joy, and "promised to take communion with him at the next festival." And "to show how interested he was in the salvation of his subjects," Louis honored the duke by making him "mestre de camp" of the light cavalry (La Trémoille 1895, 87). Protestant writers would seize on the king's favor as a payoff for the duke's change of religion.

Privately, ministers bemoaned the loss in letters to the duke's Huguenot mother, the Duchess Charlotte de Nassau. But they did not give up hope. The prominent pastor, André Rivet, a professor in Leiden and formerly the La Trémoille chaplain, assured the duchess that he would continue his prayers for her son's rectification: "For God is powerful enough to touch his heart and make him regret the bad deal he has made with the world, so far removed from that of Moses . . . who chose to be afflicted along with the people of God rather than enjoy for a short time the delights of sin. . . . God knows those who are His, and He knows how to bring them back into the sheepfold when they stray" (Archives nationales 1628, 207).

The letter has two implications. The loss of the duke to Catholicism may not be permanent. From the immediate vantage point of 1628, the duke's conversion might not have seemed any more likely to last than so many other religious changes. Or, at least, one could pray that it would not. In public, clerics might denounce conversions that did not endure but, in private, relapses might seem perfectly desirable. The other suggestion is that the desertion was prompted by some sort of worldly desire; it was not sincere. God would find a way to make the convert realize his mistake. But, in fact, God did not: La Trémoille never left Catholicism. From a later vantage point, therefore, it became necessary to denigrate the duke's motives in converting as well his role in religious rivalry after 1628. Elie Benoist did so with disdain and dispatch in his history of French Protestantism, published in the 1690s:

> [La Trémoille] abjured the Reformed religion between the hands of the Cardinal [Richelieu] before the taking of La Rochelle. He received in recompense the command of the light cavalry, in which he served . . . during the Italian wars. . . . Some years after, he grew disgusted with life at court and retired to his home in Thouars. He became a bigot and a controversialist, and he died finally having reached a very old age. He never lived up to the reputation of his father (Benoist 1693, 2, 481).[12]

Henry's son, Henry-Charles de La Trémoille, Prince de Tarente, returned to the bosom of the Church in 1671. Better said, his last religious change occurred that year. His first conversion to Catholicism followed soon upon his father's. But his mother, the Huguenot Marie de la Tour d'Auvergne, spirited him off to Holland, where under the tutelage of his great uncle, the Protestant Prince of Orange, he returned to Calvinism in 1640. This change might have seemed to Catholics no less self-interested than his father's 1628 abjuration appeared to Protestants; the prince was about to take up a command in the army of the Dutch Estates. But Protestants, of course, celebrated it. Rivet wrote of how "all the *gens de bien* rejoiced." And the contrast is marked between his praise of the prince and his derision four years later of Tarente's younger brother, the Comte de Laval, who took up a Catholic religious life: Laval "has thrown himself into the college of the Fathers of the Oratory, angering his parents a good deal. He has been lured by great hopes for ecclesiastical dignities."[13]

After Tarente's return to Calvinism, his father wrote to him that, although the change had brought him "a very real sorrow, it had not destroyed the paternal affection he had for his son." He hoped God would pardon him and "inspire him with the means and counsel" that would bring him to serve the Church "with me and after me." "I hope," he added, "that [God] will give you the grace to conserve your fortune and your honor, providing that you have for your principal goal His glory and your salvation. To which end I exhort you never to deviate from the obedience and fidelity you owe the King, nor from the respect and services to which the favors of their Highnesses oblige you" (Archives nationales 1640, 397).

As Tarente relates in the memoir of his final conversion to Catholicism, he fulfilled his father's wishes three decades later (Archives nationales 1671). Here he describes how in Holland, and also England, he had enjoyed the liberty of depending only on himself, but it led him into a totally disordered existence. He returned to France and participated in the Fronde, a revolt (1648–1652) against the government during Louis XIV's minority. His rebelliousness was not surprising, he wrote, "for I was living in such a great forgetfulness of God and myself that I threw myself into revolt against the king, when I thought my interests were opposed to his service and my duty" (Archives nationales 1671, 5). The prince's personal independence had resulted in confusion and rebellion, just as the independence of new sects causes disorder in souls. "Submission to the Church," on the contrary, "is a great consolation to a Christian" (Archives nationales 1671, 12–13). So, too, was submission to the monarch. His conversion, thus, was a return to God and to the king.

The association of religious change and political fidelity in France remained a constant theme of Catholics across the century. While presiding over the abjuration of two ministers in 1683, the Bishop of Angers, Henri Arnauld, turned his speech into a panegyric of Louis XIV and the royal role in protecting religious truth. He reminded the two converts that the king's "zeal for the ruin of heresy should excite yours for the conservation of his *personne sacrée*. In the future, you should consider this most redoubtable enemy of the error, which you renounce today, as the protector of the truth you embrace, so that in accomplishing all the duties of our holy religion, you may merit the recompense that God promises to those who live and die in the communion of the saints" (Blanc 1983, 51).[14]

As André Blanc points out, such rhetoric mixed "the juridical principle of *cujus regio, ejus religio* (see note 7) with a loyalist mystique to which the Protestants, too, always proclaimed themselves desperately faithful" (Blanc 1983, 52). But those who converted to Protestantism could not portray their change as a political submission. Catholic propagandists played on this difference, emphasizing the separateness of Protestants, isolating them from Catholics whose religion was intertwined with communal, social, and political existence. Huguenots tried to counter with protestations of their absolute obedience. The Charenton minister Charles Drelincourt, writing during the politically troubled 1650s, disputed the charge that his coreligionists were inevitable opponents of the monarchy by arguing that "we let pass no occasion to preach the inviolable fidelity and sincere obedience that we owe to superior powers and to teach that we are subjected to them [not only outwardly] but also by our consciences" (Drelincourt 1654, 39). Declarations of Protestant political loyalty stretched the limits of religious belief. Synods— for example, that of Loudun in 1659 or of Châtellerault in 1663—offered public prayers for the "personne sacrée" of the king, a concept that fit well within the royal religion of the French state but was a dubious proposition, at best, in Calvinist theology.[15] Huguenot resisters of royal persecution in the 1680s criticized those who issued such proclamations as being "idolators of royal authority" (Labrousse 1986, 16). But for many Huguenots before the Revocation of the Edict of Nantes in 1685, any act of collective resistance to royal policy, outside of prayer and fasting, remained unimaginable.

Concluding Remarks

Studies of conversion often focus on the adherence of individuals to new religious movements, those that challenge a society's religious norms. In such situations a conversion may be seen as a form of resistance or rebellion, or even of social deviance (Pollock 1993, 171). One benefit of examining the conversion of Protestants to Catholicism in seventeenth-century France is that it reminds us conversion can be to a norm; it can reinforce the status quo. As Judith Pollmann points out, early-modern converts to Protestantism also stressed the continuity of their beliefs with accepted tradition, so as to diminish the possibility that they would be accused of socially disruptive innovation (Pollmann, this volume).

Catholic (and Protestant) rhetoric about conversion in the seventeenth century emphasized the importance of the interior movements within a convert's conscience. Thus, it forms another link in the chain of "interiorist" understandings of true religious change that runs from Augustine to William James to our own day (although not necessarily meaning exactly the same thing at each moment). But this element was only part of the Catholic conception of conversion in the religiously divided France of the seventeenth century. For the majority religion in the monarchical order of the Bourbon state—where the Church and regime were mutually reinforcing—conversion to Catholicism and political loyalty were inseparable. Missionaries and others involved in the campaign to convert Protestants propagated the notion through rituals, sermons, debates, polemical literature, and conversion accounts. And we can see its reflection in, for example, the private journal of Antoine Denesde or in the correspondence of the La Trémoille family.

Conversions made for political reasons may seem purely opportunistic; certainly seventeenth-century French Protestant writers insisted on as much. But before we are too quick to agree with them, we should remember the power the discourse had not only to construct a model of conversion but also to shape the way converts reported and, indeed, understood their experience. Religious conversion may have entailed an internal movement of conscience, but to be acceptable the change had to bring the conscience in line with external authority—the Church, and, in the French Catholic case, the monarchy. Although Huguenots thoroughly believed in the monarch's political authority and expressed their loyalty at every opportunity, they could not claim that their consciences were aligned with their Catholic sovereign. Indeed, they insisted that, with the liberty of conscience granted them by the king in the Edict of Nantes, their consciences were not subject to their monarch's control. Catholic discourse posed a challenge to Protestant proclamations of loyalty that would be difficult for the religious minority to combat. It was thereby able to construct a political difference where Protestants and the laws that governed their existence in France had tried to eliminate one. Huguenots appealed to the law and to a concept of the state as based on, and as the administrator of, laws. Catholics appealed to a theocratic conception of the monarchy that associated political loyalty, religious uniformity, and Catholicism, and bound them together with the cult and rituals of the royal religion. The theocratic concept was eminently powerful in seventeenth-century France, and Protestants could never be full members of the mystical body of the kingdom without converting to the majority religion.

Thus, Catholic campaigners had a powerful advantage in formulating their model of true conversion—or at least they might have had but for the *dragonnades* and the Revocation of the Edict of Nantes in the 1680s. Early in this decade, zealous royal officials started sending troops into Protestant areas to force conversions. In 1685, Louis XIV revoked the right his grandfather had granted Protestants in 1598 to practice their religion legally. The campaign of persecution and forced conversions quickly intensified. A demand that Protestants convert because "le roi le veut" might seem the logical outcome of associating political fidelity and religious faith. But matters were more problematic. Protestants, drawing on a long tradition within Christian thought as well as reacting to their immediate circumstances, denounced the idea that forced conversions could ever be sincere. The Catholic clergy mostly applauded the long-sought change in government policy, and they could defend coerced conversions by referring to an equally long tradition that justified the constraint of heretics with the scriptural phrase "Compel them to come in" (Luke 14, 23; Labrousse 1973, 115). Those compelled to convert and participate in Catholic observances might, in time, become true members of the faith. And even if they did not, their children would be raised as Catholics. But despite the royalism of Catholics and their willingness to resort to force, the Revocation also posed problems for their understanding of conversion. Its rhetorical construction of religious change contained an element of voluntarism. The Duke de la Trémoille "offered" his conscience to the king; the Prince de Tarente chose to give up his personal independence to submit to the monarch. True conversion, in any case, was not the result of human endeavor, not even the king's: it was God's work. Some of the Catholic clergy quietly expressed doubts about the sorts of conversions the "booted missionaries" would achieve. Their doubts were soon enough confirmed. The optimistic reports of thousands of abjurations flooding into Versailles in the period immediately before and after the Revocation gave way, a few years later, to more realistic assessments. Protestants might come to the Mass when they had no choice, but given the slightest opportunity they avoided priests and their religion. For the king turned tyrant, there would be very few true conversions.

Notes

I would like to thank for their suggestions on this essay: Mary D. Sheriff, David Gilmartin, Peter van der Veer, and the conference participants.

1. James, of course, does not explain conversion as God's work, though he recognizes the psychological importance of such an explanation in the conversion accounts upon which he draws. Nonetheless, for him conversion is still an individualized and inner experience that he characterizes as a psychological "process of unification," bringing relief to a "discordant," heterogeneous personality or to a "divided will." The subject feels "something welling up inside." It might occur gradually or abruptly, but if sudden it is actually the result of longer-term subliminal processes. The "self hitherto divided, and consciously wrong, inferior and unhappy, becomes unified and consciously right, superior and happy, in consequence of its firmer hold upon religious realities" (James 1985, 140, 143–44, 146, 156, 157). Robert W. Hefner has recently criticized the Jamesian psychological account of conversion by pointing out that it "project[s] an interiorist bias onto a phenomenon that comes in a wide array of psychocultural forms" (Hefner 1993, 17).

2. See, for example, James A. Beckford's study of conversion to the Jehovah's Witnesses in the 1970s (Beckford 1978).

3. The clergies of both churches denounced the practice of intermarriage. Catholics threatened excommunication, and the Catholic Church's frequent complaints to the government were finally rewarded in 1663 by an ordinance outlawing relapses. Conversions of convenience for marriage would no longer be allowed (Dompnier 1985, 157; Benoist 1983, 328, n. 21). Protestant authorities were just as exacting. National synods, such as that of Saint-Maixent in 1609, insisted on an exact observance of the Discipline: pastors were to perform a marriage involving a former Catholic only after she or he had received instruction in the faith and properly abjured papism. The synod of Charenton in 1623 confirmed that anyone deserting the faith for marriage, or their parents, who had permitted the wedding (more likely, since the consistory had no control over a convert unless she or he asked its forgiveness), would be publicly suspended from communion (Bertheau 1970, 522–23; Debon 1983, 141).

4. Élisabeth Labrousse has suggested in a series of articles that, in regions of confessional coexistence, neighbors of different faiths recognized that they were all Christians who shared many concerns about salvation and moral issues. Their local religion may have been an irenic amalgam of the two confessions (Labrousse 1978, 1980, 159–76; 1983, 161–74). Conversion, then, was far less momentous for these people than it was for their clergies. A change of religion did not entail an acceptance of an entirely different core of beliefs but an acceptance of a less crucial set of rites. Much evidence exists to support Labrousse's contention (see Pollmann, this volume). If she is correct, then the clergies' interest in imbuing the notion of conversion with a more serious intent becomes that much clearer.

5. An account of Jarrigue's conversion to Protestantism has been inserted into a register that otherwise contains records of conversions to Catholicism.

6. Joseph de Morlaix, a Capuchin, later wrote of the advantages Métayer had given up in abandoning his ministry, without any likelihood of finding similar ones in the Catholic Church. He had therefore changed religion only for the "interest of his conscience" (Morlaix 1641, 6).

7. This belief found its most succinct expression in the principle *cujus regio, ejus religio*: the religion of the prince is the religion of his territory. The Peace of Augsburg (1555) and the Peace of Westphalia (1648) applied the principle to Germany. Each German territorial ruler determined whether his principality would be Catholic or Lutheran (and later Calvinist), and could impose religious uniformity. Subjects of the disallowed religion were given the option of emigrating to a territory in which their faith was established. Some have seen the Edict of Nantes as an application of the same principle because it consisted of a state-sponsored political solution to the problem of religious division in France (Garrisson 1985, 17–18). It seems more appropriate, however, to apply the term to the edict's revocation in 1685, which once again made Catholicism the only legally recognized religion in the kingdom.

8. He had been involved in the establishment of the Calvarians at Poitiers; he had participated in negotiations at Loudun (1616) between rebellious nobles and the royal government; he had preached on various occasions in the province; and he was developing a close relationship with one of the local bishops—Richelieu (Mauzaize 1977; Sceaux 1965; Piat 1988; Huxley 1969; Fagniez 1894; Dedouvres 1894, 1918).

9. It is entirely possible, as Mary D. Sheriff has suggested to me, that the discourse's stress on political loyalty might also have been a means for Catholics to lobby the king for an eventual revocation of the Edict of Nantes.

10. Conversion to Catholicism was thus described as a return to political tradition, just as conversions more generally were construed not as a change to something innovative but as a return to religious traditions. According to Judith Pollman, Protestants also saw conversion in this light, as a continuity rather than a break with tradition (Pollmann, this volume).

11. Tears were taken as an expression of true repentence and conversion (Bayne 1981, 1983).

12. The duke's father was Claude de La Trémoille, Huguenot military leader during the Wars of Religion, whom Elie Benoist celebrates as having been instrumental in protecting Protestant interests in the negotiations over the Edict of Nantes.

13. Letters of June 25, 1640 and February 18, 1644, from André Rivet to Claude Saumaise (Le Roy and Bots 1987, 211, 338).

14. For the Jansenist Arnauld, the occasion also presented a useful opportunity to insist on his own political loyalty.

15. For Loudun, "Extraict des actes du synode national des églises reformées de France . . . Loudun, le 10ème novembre 1659," (Cottiby 1660, part 1); for the provincial synod of Châtellerault, (Bibliothèque d'histoire du protestantisme français 1663). The phrase also appeared in Protestant political writings (e.g. Bouillon 1622).

References

Anonymous. 1628a. *La conversion de Monsieur de la Trimoüille duc et pair de France faitte en l'armée du roy devant La Rochelle le 18 iour de juillet mil six cens vingt-huit.* Paris: Toussainct du Bray.

———. 1628b. *Dicours [sic] theologique sur la conversion de Monsieur le Duc de la Trimoüille, à la Religion Catholique, Apostolique & Romaine, contenant une sommaire narration des raisons & motifs qui l'ont porté à ce changement.* Paris: Jean Bessin.

Archives départmentales de la Charente-Maritime. 1628–1662. Registre contenant les noms de tous ceux qui ont abjuré la RPR dans les diverses églises et couvents de La Rochelle entre la réduction de La Rochelle et la révocation de l'Édit de Nantes. Series C. 134.

Archives départmentales de Vienne. 1634. Sommaire des raisons que ceux qui font profession de la religion refformée ont de se plaindre de l'arrest du seiziesme septembre 1634. Series C. 49.

Archives nationales (Paris). 1618. Estat de la religion en Poictou. Series TT. 262 (8).

———. 1628. Letter of October 21, 1628 from André Rivet to the Duchess de la Trémoille. Series 1AP. 353.

———. 1640. Letter of October 20, 1640. Copie de la lettre de Monseigneur à Monseigneur le prince de Talmond. Series 1AP. 397.

———. 1671. Motifs de la conversion de feu Monsigneur le prince de Tarente écrits par luy-mesme vers l'année 1671. Series 1AP. ★441.

Assouline, Pierre. 1992 [2nd edition]. Les nouveaux convertis: Enquête sur des chrétiens, des juifs et des musulmans pas comme des autres. Paris: Gallimard.

Bayne, Sheila Page. 1981. Tears and Weeping: An Aspect of Emotional Climate Reflected in Seventeenth-Century French Literature. Tübingen: G. Naar.

———. 1983. "Le rôle des larmes dans le discours sur la conversion." In La conversion au XVIIe siècle, Actes du XIIe Colloque de Marseille (janvier 1982). Roger Duchene, ed. Marseille: Centre Méridional de Rencontres sur le XVIIe siècle.

Beckford, James. 1978. "Accounting for conversion." British Journal of Sociology 29: 249–62.

Benoist, André. 1983. "Catholiques et protestants en "moyen-Poitou" jusqu'à la révocation de l'Édit de Nantes, 1534–1685." Bulletin de la société historique et scientifique des Deux-Sèvres (2nd series) 16, 235–439.

Benoist, Elie. 1693. Histoire de l'Édit de Nantes contenant les choses les plus remarquables qui se sont passées en France avant & après sa publication. 5 vols. Delft: Adrien Beman.

Bertheau, Solange. 1970. "Le consistoire dans les églises réformées du moyen-Poitou au XVIIe siècle." Bulletin de la société de l'histoire du protestantisme français 116: 333–59, 512–49.

Bibliothèque d'histoire du protestantisme français. 1663. Collection Auzière: Synodes et colloques du Poitou. Ms. 579 (1).

Bibliothèque municipale de Poitiers. 1621. Establissement des gardes de la ville de Niort au service du roi. Fonds Fonteneau 68: 357–61.

Bibliothèque municipale d'Orléans. 1673. Recueil pour l'histoire generalle en abbregé de touttes les missions des capucins depuis le commencement de la reforme jusques l'an 1673. Ms. 916.

Blanc, André. 1983. "Le Mercure Galant et la propagande catholique: L'écho sonore." In La conversion au XVIIe siècle, Actes du XIIe Colloque de Marseille (janvier 1982). Roger Duchene, ed. Marseille: Centre Méridional de Rencontres sur le XVIIe siècle.

Bloch, Marc. 1973. *The Sacred Touch: Sacred Monarchy and Scrofula in England and France.* J. E. Anderson, trans. London: Routledge & Kegan Paul.

Bouillon, [Henri, duc de]. 1622. *Le manifeste de Monsieur de Bouillon envoyé a messieurs de la religion.* n.p.

Cottiby, Samuel. 1660. *La lettre de M. Cottiby, envoyée le 25 mars au pasteurs et anciens de l'eglise réformée de Poictiers.* [published with Daillé, Jean. 1660. *Lettre escrite a Monsieur Le Coq Sieur de la Talonniere sur le changement de religion de M. Cottiby.*] Charenton: Louis Vendosme.

Debon, René. 1983. "Religion et vie quotidienne à Gap." In *Le protestantisme en Dauphiné au XVIIe siècle: Religion et vie quotidienne à Mens-en-Trièves, Die, et Gap.* Pierre Bolle, ed. Poët-Laval: Curandera.

Dedouvres, L. 1894. *Politique et apôtre: Le Père Joseph de Paris, capucin: L'éminence grise.* 2 vols. Paris: Beauchesne.

———. 1918. *Le Père Joseph de Paris. Sa vie. Ses écrits.* Angers: Siradeau.

Denesde, Antoine. 1885. "Journal d'Antoine Denesde et de Marie Barré, sa femme (1628–1687)." In *Archives historiques du Poitou.* E. Bricauld, ed. Poitiers: Oudin.

Desgraves, Louis. 1983. "Un aspect des controverses entre catholiques et protestants, les récits de conversion (1598–1628)." In *La conversion au XVIIe siècle,* Actes du XIIe colloque de Marseille (janvier 1982). Roger Duchene, ed. Marseille: Centre Méridional de Rencontres sur le XVIIe siècle.

Dez, Pierre. 1936. *Histoire des protestants et des églises réformées du Poitou.* La Rochelle: Imprimerie de l'Ouest.

Diefendorf, Barbara. 1989. "Houses divided: Religious schism in sixteenth-century Parisian families." In *Urban Life in the Renaissance.* Susan Zimmerman and Ronald F. E. Weissman, eds. Newark: University of Delaware Press.

Dompnier, Bernard. 1981. "Un aspect de la dévotion eucharistique dans la France du XVIIe siècle: Les prières des Quarante-Heures." *Revue d'histoire de l'église de France* 67: 5–31.

———. 1983. "Pastorale de la peur et pastorale de la séduction: La méthode des missionaires capucins." In *La conversion au XVIIe siècle,* Actes du XIIe colloque de Marseille (janvier 1982). Roger Duchene, ed. Marseille: Centre Méridional de Rencontres sur le XVIIe siècle.

———. 1985. *Le venin de l'hérésie: Image du protestantisme et combat catholique au XVIIe siècle.* Paris: Éditions du Centurion.

Drelincourt, Charles. 1654. *Avertissement sur les disputes et le procédé des missionaires.* Charenton: Louis Vendosme.

Dumonceaux, Pierre. 1983. "Conversion, convertir, étude comparative d'après les lexicographes du XVIIe siècle." In *La conversion au XVIIe siècle,* Actes du XIIe colloque de Marseille (janvier 1982). Roger Duchene, ed. Marseille: Centre Méridional de Rencontres sur le XVIIe siècle.

Fagniez, G. 1894. *Le Père Joseph et Richelieu.* 2 vols. Paris: Hachette.

Favreau, Robert, ed. 1988. *Le diocèse de Poitiers.* Paris: Beauchesne.

Feuillas, Michel. 1983. "Gabriel Boule (v. 1580–1652): Frère prêcheur, ministre calviniste et apologiste catholique." In *La conversion au XVIIe siècle,* Actes du

XIIe colloque de Marseille. Roger Duchene, ed. Marseille: Centre Méridional de Rencontres sur le XVIIe siècle.

Filleau, Jean. 1668. *Décisions catholiques ou recueil general des arrests dans toutes les cours . . . concernant l'exercice de la religion pretendue reformée.* Poitiers: Jean Fleuriau.

Formon, Marcelle. 1955. "Henri-Louis Chasteigner de la Rocheposay, évêque de Poitiers (1612–1651)." *Bulletin de la société des antiquaires de l'ouest et des musées de Poitiers* (4th series). 3: 165–232.

Fredriksen, Paula. 1986. "Paul and Augustine: Conversion narratives, orthodox traditions, and the retrospective self." *Journal of Theological Studies* (NS) 37, 3–34.

Garrisson, Janine. 1985. *L'Édit de Nantes et sa révocation: Histoire d'une intolérance.* Paris: Éditions du Seuil.

Giesey, Ralph E. 1960. *The Royal Funeral Ceremony in Renaissance France.* Geneva: E. Droz.

Hanlon, Gregory. 1993. *Confession and Community in Seventeenth-Century France: Catholic and Protestant Coexistence in Aquitaine.* Philadelphia: University of Pennsylvania Press.

Harran, Marilyn J. 1983. *Luther on Conversion: The Early Years.* Ithaca: Cornell University Press.

Hefner, Robert W. 1993. "Introduction: World building and the rationality of con-
version." In *Conversion to Christianity: Historical and Anthropological Perspectives on a Great Transformation.* Robert W. Hefner, ed. Berkeley: University of California Press.

Huxley, Aldous. 1969. *Grey Eminence.* (new edition). New York: Carroll & Graf.

Imbert, Hugues, ed. 1867. *Registre de correspondance et biographie du duc Henri de la Trémoille, 1649–1667.* Poitiers: A. Dupré.

James, William. 1985. "The varieties of religious experience." In *The Works of William James.* Cambridge: Harvard University Press.

Kantorowicz, Ernst H. 1957. *The King's Two Bodies: A Study in Medieval Political Theology.* Princeton: Princeton University Press.

Labrousse, Élisabeth, ed. 1986. *Avertissement aux protestan[t]s des provinces (1684).* Paris: Presses Universitaires de France.

———. 1973. "Religious toleration." In *Dictionary of the History of Ideas: Studies of Selected Pivotal Ideas.* 4. Philip P. Wiener, ed. New York: Scribner.

———. 1978. "La conversion d'un huguenot au catholicisme en 1665." *Revue d'histoire de l'église de France* 64: 55–68, 251–52.

———. 1980. "Les mariages bigarrés: unions mixtes en France au XVIIIe siècle." In *Le couple interdit, entretiens sur le racisme: la dialectique de l'alterité socio-culturelle et la sexualité,* Actes du colloque tenu en mai 1977 au centre culturel international de Cerisy-la-Salle. Léon Poliakov, ed. Paris: Mouton.

———. 1983. "Conversion dans les deux sens." In *La conversion au XVIIe siècle,* Actes du XIIe colloque de Marseille (janvier 1982). Roger Duchene, ed. Marseille: Centre Méridional de Rencontres sur le XVIIe siècle.

———. 1985. *Une foi, une loi, un roi? La révocation de l'Édit de Nantes.* Paris: Payot.

La Trémoille, Charles-Louis. 1895. *Les La Trémoïlle pendant cinq siècles.* 4 vols. Nantes: E. Grimaud.

Le Roy, Pierre and Hans Bots, eds. 1987. *Claude Saumaise & André Rivet: Correspondance échangée entre 1632 et 1648.* Amsterdam: APA-Holland University Press.

Luria, Keith P. 1989. "The Counter-reformation and popular spirituality." In *Christian Spirituality: Post-Reformation and Modern.* Louis Dupré and Don E. Saliers, eds. New York: Crossroad.

———. 1993. "Rituals of conversion: Catholics and Protestants in seventeenth-century Poitou." In *Culture and Identity in Early Modern Europe: Essays in Honor of Natalie Zemon Davis.* Barbara B. Diefendorf and Carla Hesse, eds. Ann Arbor: University of Michigan Press.

Mauzaize, Jean [Raoul de Sceaux]. 1977. Le rôle et l'action des capucins de la province de Paris dans la France religieuse du XVIIème siècle. 3 vols. Thesis, Université de Paris.

Mestayer [Métayer], Jacques. 1620. *Recit de plusieurs conversions signalées depuis peu de jours par l'entremise des peres capucins de la mission de Poictou.* Poitiers: J. Thoreau.

Métayer, Jacques. 1617. *La conversion du sieur Mestayer cy-devant ministre du Lusignan, faicte en la ville de Poictiers le 23 mars 1617.* Poitiers: A. Mesnier and J. Thoreau.

Morlaix, Joseph de. 1641. *Lettre du Sieur Crescentian de Mont-Ouvert adressée par forme de relation au Sieur Mettayer, jadis ministre de Lusignan & maintenant professeur de la foy catholique en eglise romaine.* Reims: François Bernard.

Morrison, Karl F. 1992. *Understanding Conversion.* Charlottesville, Va.: University Press of Virginia.

Parker, David. 1980. *La Rochelle and the French Monarchy: Conflict and Order in Seventeenth-Century France.* London: Royal Historical Society.

Pérouas, Louis. 1964. "La 'Mission de Poitou' des capucins pendant le premier quart du XVIIe siècle." *Bulletin et mémoires de la société des antiquaires de l'ouest et des musées de Poitiers* (4th series). 7: 349–62.

Piat, Colette. 1988. *Le Père Joseph, le maître de Richelieu.* Paris: Bernard Grasset.

Pollmann, Judith. (this volume). "A different road to God: The Protestant experience of conversion in the sixteenth century."

Pollock, Donald K. 1993. "Conversion and 'Community' in Amazonia." In *Conversion to Christianity: Historical and Anthropological Perspectives on a Great Transformation.* Robert W. Hefner, ed. Berkeley: University of California Press.

Sauzet, Robert. 1979. *Contre-réforme et réforme catholique en bas-Languedoc: Le diocèse de Nîmes au XVIIe siècle.* Paris: Publications de la Sorbonne.

Sceaux, Raoul de. 1958. "Le Père Honoré de Cannes, capucin missionaire." *XVIIe siècle* 41: 349–74.

———. 1965. *Histoire des frères mineurs capucins de la province de Paris (1601–1660).* Blois: Éditions Notre-Dame de la Trinité.

Weissman, Ronald F. E. 1982. *Ritual Brotherhood in Renaissance Florence.* New York: Academic Press.

2

A DIFFERENT ROAD TO GOD: THE PROTESTANT EXPERIENCE OF CONVERSION IN THE SIXTEENTH CENTURY

Judith Pollmann

C ONVERSION NARRATIVES AS A WAY OF EXPLAINING personal change are deeply embedded in Western culture. Tales of "a deliberate turning ... which implies that a great change was involved, that the old was wrong and the new was right," as the classical definition of conversion has it, are omnipresent in religious discourse, and even tales of secular change are often modeled on this tradition (Fredriksen 1986, 5).

The Christian tradition of the conversion narrative goes back to the times of the early church. The New Testament tells how divine intervention made Saul, the persecutor of Christians, into Paul, the zealous defender of Christ and his message. Even more important as a model for the experience of conversion were Saint Augustine's *Confessions*, in which he told of his long struggle for faith.

Paul and Augustine provided an archetype of conversion for the tales of later converts and perhaps even for their experiences themselves. Medieval hagiography tells us of sudden insights or even visions that turned worldly youngsters into candidates for sainthood, as in the case of Saint Francis. And although few tales became as famous as Ignatius Loyola's *Pilgrim's Testament* and John Bunyan's *Pilgrim's Progress*, there are—particularly from the seventeenth century onward—hundreds of conversion accounts from people of all walks of life.

Nevertheless, there is a peculiar gap in the long tradition of the conversion narrative. The tens of thousands of Europeans who in the course of the sixteenth century turned to Protestantism left very few accounts of their experiences of conversion.

Biographers of sixteenth-century converts have devoted much attention to the experiences of individuals, but in the absence of direct evidence, only a few scholars have attempted to deal with the experience of conversion in the sixteenth century in general (Kingdon 1966, 105–106; Cameron 1991, 168–85). Donald Kelley devoted a chapter to the subject in *The Beginning of Ideology* (1981, 53–87) and gave a fascinating analysis of the material he had found, but he did not devote much attention to the apparent reluctance on the part of converts to explain why and how they had converted.

Right as Kelley was in making the most of the available material, I think that the lack of conversion narratives cannot be dismissed as an accident but should be approached as a phenomenon that requires explanation in itself. Conversion was, after all, a subject of prime importance in Reformation thought and one for the description of which literary models were readily available.

Sixteenth-century learned culture loved modeling its own experiences on those of the Bible and classical antiquity. One can hardly accuse the Reformers of a lack of interest in Paul, and the godfather of Renaissance culture, Francesco Petrarca, had shown in the fourteenth century how Augustine's *Confessions* could serve as a model for one's own experiences. Of course, Paul and Augustine were gentiles when they converted to Christianity, not Christians who converted to a different type of Christianity. However, the few sixteenth-century examples that exist, and the widespread use of the Pauline and Augustinian models of conversion in the seventeenth century, indicate that this objection was not structural. Protestantism, furthermore, was not at all averse to the creation of contemporary "exempla," as we can see from the flood of Protestant martyrologies with their long and detailed accounts of the interrogation, torture, and death believers had to undergo for their faith.

Because conversion narratives in the tradition of Paul and Augustine are so common in European Christian culture, they have come to determine our expectations of what a convert ought to experience. When biographers of sixteenth-century converts tell us that they cannot pinpoint the "moment" of conversion, they implicitly do so because the tradition of the conversion narrative tells them that such a "moment" ought to exist (e.g. Kelley 1973, 42; Braekman 1960, 37; Van Schelven 1939, 8).

Attempts to reconstruct the experiences of sixteenth-century converts have often led to disproportionate attention to and overinterpretation of any source that appears to fit the traditional model. Traces of Ulrich Zwingli's experience of conversion have, for instance, been detected in a rather conventional poem written in consequence of his recovery from the plague. It can perhaps be taken as proof of a deepening faith as a result of his illness, but it does not explain why he became an evangelical Christian (Potter 1976, 62; 69–70). The reconstruction of the conversion of Guy de Bres is based on a pious letter in which he states his readiness to die as a martyr for his faith but —to my mind—no more than that (Braekman 1960, 37–41).

The idea that conversion experiences of the Pauline/Augustinian type were common in the sixteenth century has undoubtedly been stimulated by the extreme significance attributed to the so-called "Tower Experience" of Martin Luther (Cargill Thompson 1978). Indeed, Luther's "Tower Experience" can be interpreted as a conversion experience, but when reading through the many brief accounts of it—the earliest of which dates from at least fifteen years after the event—it seems that Luther's claim that his understanding of the phrase "the righteousness of God" from Romans 1:17 had come "as a thunderbolt in my conscience" was essentially intended to explain how he arrived at his theology. Only in his most extensive statement on the subject in the preface to the edition of his collected works thirty years later, did he say he had felt "reborn" and had sensed that he had found the gate to paradise (Luther 1928, 179–87). Although we can take it for granted that Luther indeed had a significant experience, he himself was very slow in giving it a central role in his development (Cargill Thompson 1978, 211).[1]

As far as I know, only two other prominent Protestant Reformers published conversion narratives of the traditional type: Theodore Beza and Hugues Sureau. A third was written by Guillaume Farel but not published until the nineteenth century (Meylan 1973).[2] Attempts have been made to attribute a conversion experience to Calvin. He did, indeed, write a brief account of how God's providence had "by an unexpected conversion tamed to teachableness a mind too stubborn for its years," but, as William Bouwsma has recently summed it up, further evidence for a "conversion" following the Pauline model is "negligible" (Bouwsma 1988, 10–11).

The remarkable thing about the accounts of Beza and Sureau is that they were produced from motives other than the wish to testify to the conversions themselves. In 1560, Calvin's successor, Theodore Beza, told the tale of his conversion experience in a letter to a friend, which served as a preface to his *Confessio Christianae Fidei*. There he recalled how in 1548

> Behold, [the Lord] inflicted a very serious illness on me, so that I almost despaired of my life. What should I do in this wretched state, when nothing stood before my eyes beyond the horrific judgment of a just God?

After endless torments of mind and body, God, taking pity on his fugitive slave, so consoled me that I no longer doubted that I had been granted forgiveness. Thus in tears I cursed myself, I sought forgiveness and I renewed my vow to openly embrace His true worship and finally I dedicated myself wholly to Him. And so it came about that the image of death placed before me in earnest aroused in me the slumbering and buried desire for the true life, and that this disease for me was the beginning of true health . . . And as soon as I could leave my bed, having severed all my ties and gathered my possessions, I once and for all abandoned my country, parents and friends to follow Christ, and together with my wife I retired into voluntary exile in Geneva.[3]

Kelley gave this account a central role in his analysis of the experience of conversion, but did not relate it to the circumstances that led to its being written. As Beza's star was rising in Geneva, Catholic adversaries continued to harp on the theme that the young Beza had not been as righteous a man as he now professed himself to be. His *Poemata*, which were published just before his conversion in 1548, contained rather frivolous poems, while his relationship with the woman who was to become his wife had also attracted criticism. To explain the contrast between his past failings and his present status, Beza resorted to the traditional model of the conversion narrative. In the introduction to the second—and revised—edition of his *Poemata* of 1569, he specifically states that he had written it as a defense.[4]

With Sureau's conversion narrative the apologetic character is even more obvious (Kingdon 1985, 105–112). In 1572 the French Calvinist minister Hugues Sureau abjured his Calvinism and reverted to the Catholic Church. Under pressure from officials of the royal court and the church establishment, he produced a "confession" regarding his abjuration. According to his tale, he had had grave doubts about the legitimacy of the claims of himself and his fellow pastors to spiritual leadership. The actual conversion had been the result of the onslaught upon his brethren in the massacre of Saint Bartholomew in the summer of 1572, which had made him doubt the favour of Providence.

A year later, however, out of deep unhappiness over the Catholic theology of the Mass, Sureau decided to revert to Calvinism. Again he wrote an account, this time

of his lapse into Papacy and the horrible scandals committed by him, serving as an example for all the world of the fragility and perversity of a man abandoned by himself and of the infinite mercy and firm truth of God towards his elect.[5]

It is very doubtful whether Sureau would have written and published this second account had it not been for his first publication. It was, one might say, the least he could do.

These conversion narratives were thus written in a context in which the authors had more to justify than their conversions alone. Beza had to dissociate himself from his past because it contained more dangerous elements than just his former Catholicism. Sureau was trying to make up for the highly demoralizing effect of converts who had renounced their Reformed ideals. Their conversion narratives were not intended as shining examples for future converts, but were written to defend themselves or their ideals against criticism from others.

The traditional conversion narrative was a genre to which Protestant converts resorted rather than one in which they indulged. As a rule, converts about whom we possess a wealth of material, and who have left us a great deal of information about their lives in general, are collectively silent about their decision to convert. Peter Martyr did indeed explain why he decided to flee Lucca for the existence of a Protestant exile, but he never described how and when he converted to the new ideas in the first place (McNair 1967, 143ff., 263–68). The early Reformer Wolfgang Capito never reflected on the change in his opinion of Luther (Kittelson 1975, 206–214). François Hotman, a prolific writer and the son of a member of the Chambre Ardente, the court that was trying French heretics, apparently did not produce an account of his decision to become a heretic himself (Kelley 1973, 43, 47). And Joseph Scaliger, who even produced an autobiography, does not tell us why he converted to Calvinism (Grafton 93, I,104; Scaliger 1594). Philips van Marnix, Lord of Saint Aldegonde, an indefatigable propagandist for both the Dutch Revolt and Calvinist Protestantism, did not leave a single hint as to the time and place of his conversion, and his biographer had to place the moment of Marnix's conversion "sometime" between 1553 and 1559, when he went to study at Geneva (Van Schelven 1939, 5–10).[6] Ubbo Emmius lost his position as rector of the Latin school in Norden because of a conflict with his Lutheran opponents, so we can hardly assume that he thought the differences between Lutherans and Calvinists were negligible. Nevertheless, he felt no need to reflect on or explain his decision to leave his father's faith (Bergsma 1994, 107–109). John Donne, born into a family of Catholic martyrs, developed into a highly serious Anglican clergyman without revealing how this change had come about (Carey 1990, 16).

To understand why sixteenth-century converts did not write conversion narratives, it is of course necessary to understand the reasons for which people do write them. In her important article on the conversion narratives of Paul and Augustine, Paula Fredriksen concluded that the content of conversions:

> does not lie in the clear moment of radical change that the classic literature presents to us . . . The conversion account, never disinterested, is a condensed, or disguised, description of the convert's present, which he legitimates through his retrospective creation of the past and a self (Fredriksen 1986, 33).

Fredriksen thus stresses that conversion narratives cannot tell the historian what conversion experiences are like; they are retrospective accounts of what the convert thinks or wants others to think he has experienced. An essential function of the conversion narrative is to explain and justify change, and therefore to legitimize the conversion. The contrast between the wicked culture of his past and the blessed culture of the present constitutes one of the essential features of this legitimization, and the suddenness of the conversion increases both the effect of this contrast and the dramatic impact of the story.

Nevertheless, the creation of a conversion narrative in the tradition of Paul and Augustine is not something in which every convert may wish to engage. The condition for the writing—or even thinking—of such a narrative is a willingness to contrast past and present and to assert "that the old was wrong and the new was right." There are, however, other ways of dealing with the experience of change. Rather than as a revolutionary process, a convert may well want to think of it as evolutionary and try to underplay the radical nature of his decision. He may not, for instance, want to think of his past life and the culture in which he lived as totally bad, or he may want to claim that he really has always been what he is now and minimize the contrast between his former and his present self.

In both the political and the religious discourse of the sixteenth century, the juxtaposition of new (and therefore evil) developments with old (and therefore good) traditions is overwhelmingly present. It is one of the peculiar paradoxes of sixteenth-century culture that despite the enormous changes it wrought, it was simultaneously characterized by a universal dislike for innovation; to say that something was "new" in itself amounted almost to a negative judgment. Political debate in the French Wars of Religion and the Dutch Revolt centered around mutual accusations of a desire for novelty. Similarly, the term "new" religion for Protestant worship was intended and received as an insult.[7]

The Reformers were extremely sensitive to critics who branded their ideas as "novelties," and they constructed their own interpretation of church history to withstand this challenge. In the Protestant interpretation of history, it was the Church of Rome that had changed and corrupted original Christianity and that was defending a "new" religion (e.g. Bouwsma 1988, 82–85; Van Haemstede 1598, 150r.). The Reformers were not promoting change but combating it, and they were doing so in a long tradition of critics of Rome. Yet this argument, however compelling it may have been to theologians, remained problematic for many believers. They witnessed the Reformers introducing forms of religious worship that seemed very "new" indeed, and for that very reason to be stirring up a great deal of social unrest.

In 1522 the author of a widely circulated Reformation pamphlet described how:

> The shining of the fiery Sword had pierced the eyes of the hearts of many, so that great dissension has sprung up, the son [stands up] against his father, the daughter against her mother, so that there is disagreement within families, monasteries are factional, scholars muted and the simple lay people utter highly wondrous things, the one from this, the other from that. For which reason a common phrase has developed: 'I abide by my old God, with my old beliefs, with the old teachings.'[8]

It was a reaction that was to be heard for decades to come. At least in the Netherlands people remained Catholic because they did not like 'new' things and wanted to stick with tradition. Thus the Dutch gentleman Johan Stephenszoon de Wit wrote to a friend as late as 1614

> I am not changing from Peter's ship, outside of which, I have learned, there remains no salvation. Herein my dearest parents placed me; herein my faithful guardians have kept me; herein I shall readily live and die.[9]

Religion for him was not a matter of theology, but of family tradition.

Even Protestants themselves were sometimes worried about the 'novelty' of their religious doctrines. The Utrecht lawyer Arnoldus Buchelius, who had developed into a moderate Protestant in the 1590s, resigned to religious change rather than welcomed it. Around 1595 he wrote about his native town

> This is the eagerness for novelty of the mortals; a simpler form of religious worship has been introduced, but the common people is drawn to

piety by the packaging; spectacles of empty piety often influence even evil minds.[10]

The merchant Andries van der Muelen, who in 1606 discovered that a suitor for his daughter was refusing to become a member of the Reformed church, wrote to his cousin

> I find that he is not a libertine but religious, but that his heart is most attached to the Papist religion because it has the oldest possession and through the Pope and all its orders has the greatest authority, and that the other religion is but novelty.[11]

Interestingly enough, the suitor was not a Catholic, but a regular attendant of the Reformed church. Formal membership was a step he did not want to take since the 'novelty' of his church still bothered him.

The cultural unacceptability of novelty posed a grave dilemma for the Reformation as a movement; although it was absolutely necessary to stress how different Reformed religion was, first of all from the teachings of Rome, but increasingly from the competing Protestant churches, too, its social success was largely dependent on its ability to underplay the innovative elements in its teaching. The tension existed in the Reformers themselves. Calvin voiced annoyance at the blind call to tradition and condemned people who stuck with the faults of their fathers, but at the same time he instinctively disapproved of "new" things himself (Bouwsma 1988, 144–49, 178–79).

In the face of this widespread ambiguity toward the desirability of change and the efforts to disguise new ideas as old ones, the Pauline/Augustinian model of conversion was perhaps not the obvious ideal to present to prospective converts. This might explain why conversion narratives were not used by the Reformation movement as "exempla" of how conversion could and should be experienced, despite the fact that Catholic opponents published many accounts of the conversions of Calvinists who had returned to the old faith (Wolfe 1993, 15). Instead of contrasting the old and the new man, the Reformers provided believers with an alternative strategy of merging the two into one.

The Reformation movement presented its program to believers as one of learning old truths and of unlearning bad habits, not as one of changing personality.[12] Despite its stress on the innate sinfulness of man, it adressed prospective converts not as wicked unbelievers but as simple and misguided children.[13] When conversions were accounted for, they were, as Kelley noticed, more often than not described as the result of learning (Kelley 1981, 64–66). In his autobiography the Reformer Heinrich Bullinger described his religious development exclusively in terms of reading, learning, and understanding (Bouvier 1940, 10–12, 445–46). The martyrologies of Adriaen van Haemstede and Jean Crespin usually deal with conversions in brief phrases like "after he had gained knowledge of the Gospels" or "after they had gained the knowledge of the truth from the books of Luther" (Van Haemstede 1598 and Crespin 1560).

It was in similar terms that parents transmitted the tales of their conversions to their children. In the early seventeenth century, Wilhelmus Baudartius in his autobiography said of his parents:

> This I do know, that my father and mother, when the light of the Holy Gospel began to break through in the Netherlands, received this grace from the Lord God, that by reading Holy Scripture and other good books, as principally through the instruction of men who were divinely blessed and experienced in God's word, they have seen and understood the gross errors and misunderstandings of popery and have taken on the true Reformed Religion.[14]

Divine inspiration had to guide converts in their learning, as would the ordeals of the martyrs. Constantin l'Empereur claimed that his grandparents had been so impressed by the steadfastness with which the first Calvinist martyr of the Netherlands had undergone his execution that they started to read the Bible for themselves (Van Rooden 1985, 22). In the rare instances in which the martyrologies mention sudden conversions, these usually follow the witnessing of the plight of a martyr (e.g. Van Haemstede 1598, 142v.).

Learning and martyrdom were essential features of sixteenth-century Reformed ideology; it is therefore quite understandable that converts should have described their development in terms of these two notions. It was both a logical and an attractive solution. For all practical purposes, belief started with the acquisition of knowledge, and just as a child can learn without blaming itself for the fact that it ever was a child, the believer could learn about the truth without feeling that he had been totally wicked before.

"Certainly I was still a rough and grating boy . . . but pardon my impetuosity of that time, which had not yet come to know the new birth through God" the Reformer Heinrich Bullinger wrote to a fellow believer.[15] He, indeed, used the words "new birth," but to pardon his former self, not to condemn it. Bullinger had nothing to be ashamed of, as he stated more than twenty years after his conversion: "Thank God, you will find nothing over which I should blush, other than that I am a sinner before God, my Lord."[16]

Rather than presenting their conversion as a total break with the past, their culture and their personalities, many converts seemed set on underplaying the difference between past and present. An example of this attitude can be found in one of the rare seventeenth-century tales of a Dutch conversion. In 1654 the minister Coccejus held a funeral oration over his colleague Jacobus Trigland. He claimed to base his account on a letter that Trigland had written to his children about his conversion to Calvinism, which had taken place more than fifty years earlier.

Trigland came from a staunchly Catholic family that was supporting the missionary activity in the Dutch Republic and that had destined him for the priesthood. According to Coccejus, Trigland had already been dissatisfied with Catholicism while he was studying at Louvain. He came to doubt the Catholic doctrine on good works, and eventually reached the conclusion that justification could not be earned and that salvation was dependent on Christ's sacrifice alone. It was only then that he began to read Reformed theology. Irrespective of whether this account of Trigland's development was genuine or was concocted by Coccejus, it is remarkable that it stressed the continuity in Trigland's piety rather than the changes it had undergone. Or, as Coccejus put it: Trigland "had already been reformed, before he knew the doctrine of the Reformers."[17]

When Arnoldus Buchelius in 1595 reflected on the variety of religious opinions that had developed in the past decades, he too tried to minimize the importance of the differences between past and present.

> When we are all gazing at the same stars, and all aim for the same goal of eternity, what does it matter by which knowledge someone seeks the truth, by which road he shall reach the end of his course ? . . . It is not possible to arrive at such a great mystery by one route alone; however, one goal is set for all, and one door is open to all those hurrying there; we seek Christ and him we follow, albeit along different routes; and he who sets himself this goal cannot be lost. The road of our ancestors to this true end was different from that of those who live now.[18]

Buchelius and his forebears shared the same goal, they just chose to approach it by different routes.

As John Bossy has pointed out, medieval religion had conceived of sin as a social act. Sin was a state of mind that primarily expressed itself through sinful acts that harmed other people, just as piety and virtue were fundamentally social attitudes (Bossy 1985, 35–56). People who broke with their families because of religion were thereby committing an act that could easily be perceived as irreligious. Luther and his followers were severely criticized for causing a breakdown of the social order, which was expressing itself as much in dissension within families as in social unrest, phenomena that were the exact opposite of what people expected of religion. Kelley has noted that while the desire to break away from tradition and parental authority may have steered many in the direction of the Reformed teaching, many converts immediately looked for new father figures to take the place of the old (Kelley 1981, 78–87). However, although Reformers claimed that following the word of God took precedence over family loyalty, and indeed thousands of people were prepared to break with parental authority and tradition, many tried to keep the rifts as small as possible. There are indications that converts actively tried to minimize the social damage of conversion, for instance by postponing conversion until after their fathers had died. Ubbo Emmius is a case in point, as is Joseph Scaliger. François Hotman did break away from his father, but tried to hide his Protestant publications from his family (Kelley 1973, 47).

Converts were not keen to condemn their relatives as sinners destined for eternal damnation, nor to shun all contact with those who did not share their religious convictions. By describing their ancestors as ignorant, the earliest converts could safeguard the idea that those of their forebears who had died in the old faith could still be in heaven, as the martyr Johan van Oostende pointed out to his interrogators in 1551.

> Then the monks asked: Are all our parents doomed then? Johan replied: that I will leave to God's judgment. God will take the ignorance of the age into account and will have mercy upon them. But now that the light of the Gospel, which has been concealed for a long time, is shining, everybody should look out, so that he will perceive it.[19]

Those whose relatives refused to see the light of the Gospel faced a potentially difficult dilemma. However, believers in the Dutch Republic worked out a strategy for avoiding emotional conflict. While they could wholeheartedly believe in the importance of religious orthodoxy and denounce the activities of other churches, they would go on judging their fellow human beings through a theologically rather unspecific notion of piety. If somebody was a good man, he had to be pious and was therefore eligible for salvation (Pollmann 1996).

In the Dutch republic it was almost impossible to avoid meeting people who held other confessional allegiances. But elsewhere, too, a de facto tolerance appears to have been practiced. Even in France, where religious struggles had been exceedingly bitter, Catholics and Protestants not only worked together and maintained friendships but actually went on to intermarry after the persecutions were over (Luria, in this volume.) German Protestant autobiographers were remarkably tolerant about the Catholics they knew personally (Greyerz 1984, 227).

Many lay believers took their religious ideals very seriously and were willing to die for them, but their first concern was not to dissociate themselves from the past to justify their present. As it was, a change of confessional allegiance was probably often not the result of a sudden conversion but of a gradual development.[20] The desire to find one dramatic point in time and place that would explain this development was apparently not felt. Rather, converts wanted to preserve their present as the natural outcome of the past, as the result of reasoning and learning rather than as a second birth.

Of course, the conversion narrative became immensely popular with Protestants of later generations—so popular indeed that it has hindered scholars from noticing how exceptional it was in the sixteenth century. In Pietist and Puritan circles, people started to tell stories of long processes of doubt and despair, of signs of Grace, of the sudden realization that the conversion was not complete, and hence of renewed agony until final release came (Ebner 1971; Watkins 1972; Caldwell 1983; Seaver 1985; Van Lieburg 1991).[21] However, these conversion accounts are not descriptions of changes in confessional allegiance. The typical Protestant conversion narrative was written by someone who had been raised in the Protestant tradition himself or herself, and who described a spiritual development within that tradition; these converts were indeed rejecting their past selves, but not the faith of their fathers.

Sixteenth-century conversions took place in a cultural and emotional setting that radically differed from that of the Protestant soul-searchers of the seventeenth century; sixteenth-century converts probably had good reasons for experiencing a conversion without turning it into a conversion experience of the Pauline and Augustinian type. Paul and Augustine provided models for the experience of conversion that keep recurring in the Christian tradition, but we should also allow for the fact that people sometimes could and did convert without them.

Notes

The research for this paper was undertaken as part of the work on a Ph.D. thesis on religion in the world view of Arnoldus Buchelius (1565–1641), funded by the Stichting voor Historische Wetenschappen in The Hague. I would like to thank Gabrielle Dorren, Alastair Hamilton, Paul Knevel, Malcolm de Mowbray, and Henk van Nierop for their stimulating comments, and Wiebe Bergsma and Luuc Kooijmans for sharing some of their unpublished results with me.

1. It seems that this last account is usually read outside the general context of the preface, which tried to explain that Luther's earlier works reflected an initial attitude toward the Roman Church and the papacy that had been far more conciliatory than his later stance (Luther 1928, 179–80). That he dated the "Turmerlebnis" as late as 1519 in the preface might well have to do with the rhetorical function the story fulfilled in the preface as a whole.

2. Rather more complex is the case of Pier Paolo Vergerio. Vergerio, who had been preaching evangelical ideas in Italy for a considerable time, decided to break with the Roman church and flee to Switzerland after witnessing the total despair of Francesco Spiera when Spiera renounced his evangelical sympathies under pressure from the Inquisition. Vergerio wrote an account of the miseries of Spiera that was later published with a few other texts to prove that the "example" of Spiera was something one could learn from—with Vergerio as the first proof of this. It is not quite clear to me whether Vergerio had written his original account to explain why he gave up trying to accommodate himself and fled to the north rather than become a martyr for the faith, or was really presenting it as the moment of his "conversion" (Jacobson Schutte, 238–65).

3. *"Ecce enim gravissimum morbum mihi infligit, adeo ut pene de vita desperarem. Hic ego miser quid facerem, quum nihil mihi praeter horrendum justi dei judicium ob oculos observaretur ? . . . Post infinitos et corporis et animi cruciatus, Dominus fugitivi sui mancipii misertus ita me consolatus est ut de venia mihi concessa nihil dubitarem. Meipsum igitur cum lacrymis detestor, veniam peto, votum renovo de vero ipsius cultu aperte amplectendo denique totum illi meipsum consecro. Ita factum est mortis imago mihi serio proposita, verae vitae desiderium in me sopitum ac sepultum excitaret, et morbus iste verae sanitatis mihi principium esset . . . Simulatque igitur licuit lectum reliquere, abruptis omnibus vinculis, sarcinulis compositis, patriam, parentes, amicos semel desero ut Christum sequar, meque una cum mea conjuge Genevam in exilium voluntarium recipio."* Beza to Melchior Volmar, 12 March 1560 repr. in Beza 1963: 43–52, there 47.

4. *"Iam tum enim coniiciebam fore quod postea evenit, ut ii ipsi qui nostros antea versiculos in deliciis habebant (quandiu nimirum in ipsorum lustris versabar) mihi postea, Evangelii odio, illorum editionem exprobarent: nempe quod aliud nihil quod mihi obiicerent, nisi manifeste confictum invenirent. Quod autem sposponderam an reipsa praestiterim, testabitur praefatio duplex, una quidem Gallica, Tragoediae cui titulus est Abrahamus sacrificans, praefixa et ante annos octodecim a Conrado Badio excusa; altera vero Latinae meae Confessioni addita et iampridem quoque in publicum emissa."* (Beza 1569: 8)

5. From the title of the *Confession et recognoissance de Hugues Sureau dit du Rosier touchant sa cheute en la Papauté, & les horribles scandales par lui commis, servant d'exemple a tout le monde, de la fragilité, & perversité de l'homme abandonné a soi & de l'infinie misericorde de dieu envers ses esleuz* (Heidelberg 1573), cited in Kingdon 1985: 106.

6. It is only on the basis of a story in an admittedly unreliable seventeenth-century biography that he pins it down to 1558, when Marnix's brother Jan had allegedly challenged him for clinging to the "fleshpots of Egypt" (Van Schelven 1939: 5–10)

7. A good example of the anxiety the accusation of "novelty" caused is to be found in the "Praefatio" of Flacius Illyricus 1556: a[1]- a[4].

8. *"Mer dat schijnsel des vurigen sweerts heeft die ooghen veelre herten doordrongen, also datter een grote tweedracht op gestaen is, dat kint tegen sinen vader, de dochter teghen haer moeder, dat huysgesin onder malkanderen in tweedracht, de cloosteren partijch, de hoochgeleerden verstommet, ende die slechte leecken spreken hooghe wonderlike dinghen, die een hier uut de ander daer uut. Van welcke een ghemeyn bijsprake opghestaen is, Ick blijven bij mijn olden God, bij mijn olden gheloove, bij die olde leer."Vanden olden en nieuwen God geloove ende leere.* Anonymous Dutch edition of 1524 edited by S. Cramer, F. Pijper (1903: 45–46). I do not agree with Pijper's attribution to Thomas Münzer or his followers.

9. Johannes Stephansz de Wit to Lambert van der Burch, 13 August 1614 *"Interim ego Petri cymbam non commuto, extra quam didici nullam superesse salutem. In hac me charissimi imposuere parentes, tenuere fidi rectores, in hac vivam lubens, in hac moriar lubens"* University Library Utrecht Ms. 836 f. 5v.

10. *"Mortalium haec novitatis curiositas, simplicior introducta religionis species, at involucris ad pietatem trahitur vulgus; afficiunt etiam maleferiatos animos pietatis saepe vanae spectacula"* (Buchelius 1906: 259)

11. Andries van der Muelen to Nicolaes de Malapert, 27 May 1606. Rijkarchief Utrecht, family archive Van der Muelen, Inv. no. 35. *"Ick vinde dat hij niet libertins, maer religieus is, dan dat sijn herte meest hangt aen de paepse religie, midts d'outste possessie hebben ende door den paus ende alle haere orderen de grootste autoriteyt, ende dat de andere religien maer nieuwicheijt en is."* I am greatly indebted to Dr. Luuc Kooijmans for bringing this correspondence to my attention.

12. Only representatives of the radical Reformation like the Anabaptists, "who defined themselves against Protestantism rather than against Catholicism" (Hamilton 1994: 3), systematically presented conversion as a radical break with the past. In the *Offer des Heeren*, a collection of writings of Dutch anabaptist martyrs, the authors frequently contrast the 'new clean life' entered into after adult baptism with the wicked 'world of the flesh' that converts left behind (Anonymous 1904: 83, 105–106, 121, 128, 138–40, 178). However, even they rarely discussed how they themselves had come to accept this life. The best known conversion narrative from these circles to do so, that of the Dutch minister Menno Simons, was written as an apology. To counter the Calvinist charge that Simons had belonged to the militant Anabaptists who had forcibly tried to build a new Jerusalem in Münster, he described a conversion process in which he had been guided by divine inspiration. His primary aim in this was to disclaim the influence of these militant Anabaptists on his religious development (Voolstra: 1986).

13. It should be noted, of course, that Reformation thought did not idealize the innocence of children. They had a share in original sin and required taming (Strauss 1978: 85–107).

14. *"Dit weet ick wel dat mijnen vaeder ende moeder, doe het licht des H. Evangelii in Nederlant begost door te breken, van Godt den Heere die genaede hebben ontfangen, dat sij door het leesen der H. Schriftuijre ende andere goede boeken, als oock principalijck door de onderrichtinge van Godt salighe ende in Godes woort ervaerene mannen, gesien ende verstaen hebben de grove*

dwalingen ende misverstanden des pausdoms ende sij [hebben] de waere Gereformeerde Religie aengenomen." (Baudartius 1947: 204)

15. *"Bien sûr, j'étais encore un gaillard rude et tranchant, à la Suisse, mais pardonne mon impetuosité d'alors, qui n'avait pas connu la nouvelle naissance selon Dieu"* Quoted in French translation in Bouvier 1940: 12.

16. *"Déjà comme adolescent j'arrivai à la vraie foi; déjà à cette époque, je me plongeai dans la lecture d'Ecriture sainte et des Pères. Je n'ai jamais été lié par les voeux à qui que ce soit, évêque, abbé ou prieur: jamais non plus n'ai-je prononcé des voeux monastiques. Je vivais comme laïque et homme privé, consacré à la science, et zélé dans l'étude des belles lettres et du saint savoir. Enquiers-toi seulement; Dieu merci, tu ne trouveras rien dont j'aie à rougir, sauf que je suis un homme pécheur devant Dieu, mon Seigneur."* Quoted in French translation by Bouvier 1940: 11.

17. *"Ita noster jam Reformatus erat, antequam sciret quae esset Reformatorum doctrina."* Coccejus 1673: 50.

18. *"Eadem tamen cum omnes astra spectemus, et ad eundem aeternitatis finem tendamus; quid interest, qua quisque prudentia verum requirat, qua quisque via curriculi metam attigerit? Vere ille, uno itinere non posse perveniri ad tam grande secretum; unus vero omnibus finis propositus, et una properantibus janua aperta: Christum petimus, eumque sequimur, diversa licet via; nec potest errare, qui sibi statuit hunc scopum. Alia majorum via ad verum illum terminum; alia horum qui iam vivunt."* Arnoldus Buchelius, "Traiecti Batavorum Descriptio," S. Muller Fz. *Bijdragen en Mededelingen van het Historisch Genootschap* 27 (1906), 258–59.

19. *"Doe seyden de Monnicken. Zijn dan alle onse ouders verdoemt? Johan antwoorde: dat wil ick den oordeele Gods bevelen. Godt sal den tijt der onwentenheyt aensien ende haer genadich sijn. Maer nu het licht des Evangeliums schijnt, dwelck een seer lange tijt verborghen is geweest, soe sie een yegelick voor hem, dat hij het waerneemt."* (Van Haemstede 1598: 107)

20. It was described as such by Guillaume Farel (Meylan 1973). Calvin, too, stressed that conversion took a long time (Bouwsma 1988: 11), as did Vergerio (Jacobson Schutte 1977: 250).

21. Although Puritans and Pietists were particularly active, the writing of conversion narratives was not limited to these groups only. One of the earliest autobiographical accounts of a Protestant conversion was that of the French Reformed minister François du Jon, who, significantly enough, had been raised in a Protestant milieu. His conversion narrative was not about changing religions, but about his spiritual development. (Junius 1595).

References

Printed Primary Sources

Baudartius, Wilhelmus. 1947. "Autobiografie" (1628) in O. C. Broek Roelofs, *Wilhelmus Baudartius* Kampen: Kok 201–223

Beza, Theodore. 1569. *Theodori Bezae Vezelii Poematum Editio secundum, ab eo recognita . . .* [Geneva]: Henricus Stephanus.

———, 1963. *Correspondance de Théodore de Bèze* Hippolyte Aubert, Henri Meylan, Alain Dufour, eds. Vol. III (1559–1561) Travaux d'Humanisme et Renaissance 61. Geneva: Droz.

Buchelius, Arnoldus. 1906. "Traiecti Batavorum Descriptio" S. Muller Fz., ed. *Bijdragen en Mededelingen van het Historisch Genootschap* 27: 131–268.

Coccejus, Johannes.1673. "Oratio in funere . . . d. Jacobi Triglandii P.M. 17 Apr. MDCLIV' in: idem, *Opera Omnia Theologica* 6. Amsterdam: Joh. à Someren *Orationes*, 49ff.

Crespin, Jean. 1560. *Actiones et Monimenta Martyrum* [Geneva]: Joannes Crispinus

Flacius Illyricus, Mathias. 1556. *Catalogus Testium Veritatis qui ante nostram aetatem reclamarunt Papae* Basel: Joh.Oporinus

Haemstede, Adriaen van. 1598. *De historien der vromer martelaren, die om het ghetuygenisse des H. Evangeliums haer bloedt vergoten hebben.* Delft: Bruyn Harmanssz. Schinckel for Amsterdam: Laurens Jacobsz.

Het Offer des Heeren, naar de uitgaaf van 1570. 1904. In S. Cramer and F. Pijer (eds.) *Bibliotheca reformatoria Neerlandica. Geschriften uit den tijd der hervorming in de Nederlanden.* The Hague: Martinus Nijhoff, Vol. II, 1–486.

Junius, Franciscus. 1595. *Vita nobili et eruditi viri Francisci Junii (. . .) ab ipso conscripta.* Paulus Merula, ed. Leiden: Raphelengius

Luther, Martin. 1928. Preface to the *Opera Omnia* (Wittenberg 1545) repr. in: idem, *Werke.* K. Drescher, ed. kritische Gesamtausgabe (Weimarer Ausgabe) Weimar: Hermann Böhlaus Nachfolger 54: 179–87.

Scaliger, Josephus Justus. 1594. *Epistola de vetustate et splendore gentis Scaligerae, et Jul. Caes. Scaligeri Vitae.* Leiden: Raphelengius

Simons, Menno. 1600–1601. Facsimile of *Sommarie ofte by een vergaderinge van sommige schriftelijcke bekentenissen des gheloofs* . . . Hoorn: Jan Jansz. In: "Uyt Babel gevloden, in Jeruzalem ghetogen. Menno Simons' verlichting, bekering en beroeping" W. Bergsma and S. Voolstra, eds. *Doperse Stemmen* 6 (1986).

Van den olden en nieuwen God geloove ende leere (1522). 1903. In S. Cramer and F. Pijper, eds. *Bibliotheca reformatoria Neerlandica. Geschriften uit den tijd der hervorming in de Nederlanden.* The Hague: Martinus Nijhoff, Vol. I, 201–223.

Secondary Sources

Bergsma, W. 1994. "Het godsdienstig wereldbeeld van Ubbo Emmius" in: *Ubbo Emmius. Een Oostfries geleerde in Groningen/Ubbo Emmius. Ein Ostfriesischer Gelehrter in Groningen.* W. J. Kuppers, ed. Groningen: REGIO PRojekt 106–129.

Bossy, John. 1985. *Christianity in the West, 1400–1700.* Oxford and New York: Oxford University Press

Bouvier, André. 1940. *Henri Bullinger, réformateur et conseiller oecuménique, le successeur de Zwingli.* Neuchatel: Delachaux & Niestlé and Paris: Droz.

Bouwsma, William J. 1988. *John Calvin. A Sixteenth-Century Portrait.* New York, etc.: Oxford University Press

Caldwell, Patricia. 1983. *The Puritan Conversion Narrative. The Beginnings of American Expression.* Cambridge etc.: Cambridge University Press

Cameron, Euan. 1991. *The European Reformation*. Oxford: Clarendon Press

Carey, John. 1981. *John Donne. Life, Mind and Art*. London: Faber and Faber, 1st ed. 1981

Cargill Thompson, W. D. J. 1978. "The Problems of Luther's 'Tower Experience' and its Place in His Intellectual Development" in: *Religious Motivation. Biographical and Sociological Problems for the Church Historian* Derek Baker, ed. Studies in Church History 14. Oxford: Blackwell for the Ecclesiastical History Society 187–211.

Ebner, Dean. 1971. *Autobiography in Seventeenth Century England. Theology and the Self.* The Hague and Paris: Mouton

Fredriksen, Paula. 1986. "Paul and Augustine: Conversion Narratives, Orthodox Traditions and the Retrospective Self." *Journal of Theological Studies* new series 37: 3–34.

Grafton, Anthony. 1983. *Joseph Scaliger. A Study in the History of Classical Scholarship I*. Oxford: Clarendon Press

Greyerz, Kaspar von. 1984. "Religion in the Life of German and Swiss Autobiographers (Sixteenth and Early Seventeenth Centuries)." In *Religion and Society in Early Modern Europe, 1500–1800* idem (ed.) London: German Historical Institute, 223–39.

Hamilton, Alastair. 1994. "The Development of Dutch Anabaptism in the light of the European Magisterial and Radical Reformation" in: Alastair Hamilton *et al.* (eds.). *From Martyr to Muppy (Mennonite Urban Professionals). A Historical Introduction to Cultural Assimilation Processes of a Religious Minority in the Netherlands: the Mennonites* Amsterdam: Amsterdam University Press.

Jacobson Schutte, Anne. 1977. *Pier Paolo Vergerio: The Making of an Italian Reformer*. Geneva: Droz

Kelley, Donald R. 1973. *François Hotman. A Revolutionary's Ordeal*. Princeton N.J.: Princeton University Press

———, 1981. *The Beginning of Ideology. Consciousness and Society in the French Reformation*. Cambridge etc.: Cambridge University Press

Kingdon, Robert M. 1985. "Problems of Religious Choice for Sixteenth-Century Frenchmen." In idem, *Church and Society in Reformation Europe*. London: Variorum Reprints, 105–112. Reprinted from *Journal of Religious History* 4 (1966).

Kittelson, James M. 1975. *Wolfgang Capito. From Humanist to Reformer*. Studies in Medieval and Reformation Thought XVII. Leiden: Brill

Lieburg, F. A. van. 1991. *Levens van Vromen. Gereformeerd piëtisme in de achttiende eeuw*. Kampen: De Groot Goudriaan

McNair, Philip. 1967. *Peter Martyr in Italy. An Anatomy of Apostasy*. Oxford: Clarendon Press

Meylan, Henri. 1973. "Les Étapes de la Conversion de Farel." In: *L'Humanisme Français au Début de la Renaissance* colloque international de Tours (XVIe Stage) Paris: J. Vrin: 253–59.

Pollmann, Judith. 1996 "Public Enemies, Private Friends. Arnoldus Buchelius' Experience of Religious Diversity in the Early Dutch Republic" in: *The Public and the Private in Dutch Culture of the Golden Age* Arthur Wheelock ed. to appear with the University of Delaware Press.

Potter, G. R. 1976. *Zwingli* Cambridge etc.: Cambridge University Press

Rooden, Peter van. 1985. *Constantijn l'Empereur (1591–1648). Professor Hebreeuws en Theologie te Leiden: theologie, bijbelwetenschap en rabbijnse studiën in de zeventiende eeuw* thesis VU Amsterdam.

Schelven, A. A. van. 1939. *Marnix van Sint Aldegonde* Utrecht: Oosthoek

Seaver, Paul S. 1985. *Wallington's World. A Puritan Artisan in Seventeenth-Century London* London: Methuen

Strauss, Gerald 1978. *Luther's House of Learning* Baltimore and London: Johns Hopkins University Press

Voolstra, S. 1986. "Menno Simons' verlichting, bekering en beroeping" *Doperse Stemmen* 6: 17–35.

Watkins, Owen C. 1972. *The Puritan Experience* London: Routledge

Wolfe, Michael 1993. *The Conversion of Henri IV. Politics, Power and Religious belief in Early Modern France* Cambridge Mass. and London: Harvard University Press

3

NINETEENTH-CENTURY REPRESENTATIONS OF MISSIONARY CONVERSION AND THE TRANSFORMATION OF WESTERN CHRISTIANITY

Peter van Rooden

*I*N THIS PAPER I WANT TO REFLECT upon a well-known but analytically neglected historical phenomenon. Protestant missions as an ongoing and regular activity only emerged at the very end of the eighteenth century. Although this is generally recognized, histories of missions tend to obscure the originality of this emergence (Latourette 1937–45; Neill 1964). Missionary histories usually focus on the results of missions in the field. When paying attention to the mobilization for missions, they associate the missionary impulse with revival, a periodic recurrence of pious enthusiasm for the essentials of Christian belief (van Rooden 1990). On theological grounds, missionary endeavor is considered part of the transhistorical essence of Christianity. The historian's task is reduced to describing how these intrinsic justifications of the missionary project were grasped or forgotten by Christians, were acted upon or neglected (van den Berg 1956). Implicitly, or, more seldom, explicitly, such conceptions justify the biographical and theological approach characterizing most historical writing on Christian missions. This individualized approach makes it possible to construct a series of missionary heroes and pious endeavors, of which the organizing for missions around 1800 was an integral part, remarkable only for its extent and widespread support.

In a curious twist, anthropological work on missions tends to obscure the originality of modern missionary endeavors in a similar way. Like historians of missions, anthropologists focus on the effects of missions in the field, describing the various ways in which local populations appropriate or reject Christianity. They too consider Christianity in possession of inherent missionary impulse, basing their thoughts on Weberian speculations about its character as a world religion (Hefner 1993). The growth of missions around 1800, if observed at all, is thought to find a sufficient explanation in the expansion of the West.

In this essay I contend that to neglect the historicity of the emergence of modern missions is to miss an important point. The mobilization for missions at the end of the eighteenth century was part of a profound shift in the social and discursive place of religion in European and North-American societies. Missionary endeavors are a modern phenomenon, not only in the sense that they presupposed and propagated the modern distinction between a public and a private sphere, but also because they acted to transform Western Christianity itself.

I shall pursue my argument in four steps. First, I offer an analysis of the representation of conversion in the journal of the Dutch missionary society—the first of its kind on the continent—during its first half-century. In this journal, Christianity is depicted as a moral force that transforms the public, societal world by operating in the private sphere. The following section contrasts this missionary conception of the social place of religion with the nature of early-modern religious establishments. Classical Protestantism lacked the discursive framework to conceive of the spread of Christianity as distinct from political expansion, and in any case did not possess the resources to engage in such an endeavor. A third section makes the same point, by stressing how the new missionary endeavors at the end of the eighteenth century were undertaken by groups that emerged where traditional ecclesiastical and political establishments were weakened. The final section illustrates this process with a description of the transformation of the place of religion in Dutch society, and in doing so contextualizes the propositions of the first section.

The main Dutch Protestant missionary society, the *Nederlands Zendelings-Genootschap*, was founded in 1797 and was thus one of the oldest missionary societies in the world (Craandijk 1869; Kruijf 1894; Gedenkboek 1897; Boneschansker 1987). In the second half of the nineteenth century, the society would be torn by conflicts between liberal and orthodox Protestants. Several new missionary societies were founded, as the growing organizational pluralization of Dutch Protestantism affected the missionary endeavor. As in other countries, Dutch missionary efforts increased markedly during the last quarter of the nineteenth century, reaching their greatest extent in the twentieth century. During this period, the number of missionary journals grew rapidly as well (Jongeneel 1990).

During its first half-century, the *Nederlands Zendelings-Genootschap* sent out only a small number of missionaries. To focus on its relative lack of success, however, would be to repeat the error of most of the missionary literature, which is only interested in the efficacy of the missions "out there," in the missionary field. I want instead to ask what the mobilization for missions was supposed to mean in the Netherlands. One of the original aspects of the Dutch missionary society was its journal, *Berichten en Brieven* (Reports and Letters), since 1828 called *Maandberigten* (Monthly Reports). This was one of the first truly religious journals in the Netherlands. During the eighteenth century several theological journals were published, devoted to the review of religious and theological books. These did not, however, like the *Berichten en Brieven*, attempt to further the piety of their readers directly, strengthening their personal commitment to Christianity. *Berichten en Brieven* was supposed to be read in local prayer meetings of members and sympathizers of the missionary society. Such meetings were organized on every first Monday of the month, not only by the Dutch but by all missionary societies. The meetings were meant to further the members' commitment to the world-wide missionary endeavor; consequently, the missionary journal offered information not only about the activities of the Dutch Missionary Society but about other European and American missionary societies as well. If one reads through its first fifty years, it becomes clear that the Dutch missionary journal offers a consistent image of the spread of Christianity.

In the first place, missions are depicted as a worldwide enterprise. The missionary journal orders its information according to a geographical principle, by continents and by countries. Every issue is devoted to one or more areas. The journal thus emphasizes an image of the world as a single whole, including, for instance, numerical estimates of the populations of its various parts (1816, 134). However, the most important geographical distinction is the opposition between Europe and the rest of the world. Europe was Christian, and therefore the most civilized and the most powerful area of the world. This distinction was used to articulate the necessity of the missionary endeavor. God does not want to be only a God of Europe or of the whites. Black-skinned or poor people can be more sincere in their piety than the whites or the rich (1816, 151). Obviously, such a dialectic between outward social position and inward conviction is one of the most recurrent of Christian discursive strategies. Yet in the missionary review, the dialectic takes on a new, geographical form. The annual lecture for the Dutch Missionary Society in 1821, for instance, elaborated upon the intentions of

> "the God of the Bible, the God of the Christians, the God we worship . . . We do not have a God, who takes pity only on the European, and reserves salvation to the whites only, or, on the other hand, elects only the poor and despised while repudiating the powerful and rich. . . ."

In such ways, the actual particularity as well as the potential universality of the Christian faith are transformed into a geographical opposition between nations. The missionary endeavor is depicted as a geographical obligation falling upon European societies. In 1820, a native Christian of Celebes in the Dutch East Indies, now called Sulawesi, is introduced as saying that the Christians of Europe are unfeeling and devoid of interest in the happiness of their fellow human beings because they do not understand the necessity of spreading the gospel (1820, 43). In the same way the spread of Christianity, which is the result of missions, is represented as the transformation of whole societies outside Europe. In 1826, the missionary journal contained a humdrum observation of Madagascar, which I will quote in full because it concisely illustrates this societal conception of conversion.

> "Madagascar, in former days unknown, in recent days forgotten, is worth our attention as well, because the number of inhabitants of this island is estimated to be four million. The London Missionary Society has been working here for some years with marked results. The missionaries are progressing in learning the national language, and the most important inhabitants let themselves be taught, not only in the English language, but in various arts and sciences as well. The artisans that have been sent there have been well-received, to the advancement of civilization. Here, too, the use of schools is to be noted, as they have already produced assistants to the missionaries who help them in their labours." (1826, 8–9)

This short paragraph contains at least five elements that illustrate the image of conversion to Christianity projected by the missionary journal. Madagascar is situated as an element in a series of similar areas, a part of a knowable geographical world of which the center is Europe. In the second place, it is depicted as a nation with a definite number of inhabitants, a national language, and its own social and political hierarchy. Third, the work of the mission is depicted as civilizing, a societal transformation. Fourth, the work done there by another missionary organization, the *LMS*, can be taken up in this Dutch review as a matter of course. The advancement of Christianity is represented as the work of different national societies, all of them of the same purpose and character, engaging in the transformation of other nations. In the fifth place, this transformation is depicted as taking place apart from politics and power, in the sphere of education and personal persuasion.

This last element also plays an important role in recurring discussions of the relationship between European colonialism and missionary endeavor. In general, such discussions defend the mission against the accusation that it endangers colonial authority. Christianity is represented as a moral force that influences individuals quite apart from objective power structures. Christian belief does not shape the public sphere directly, but inhabits and informs private worlds, creating only indirectly a public world of enlightened laws and legitimate authority. Because the influence of Christianity is essentially moral, it cannot become a political challenge to established colonial rule, and all distrust by colonial authorities of the missionaries is unfounded. By introducing the distinction between private and public sphere, Christianity actually takes the sting out of the political ambitions of colonial subjects (1820, 23; 1826, 91–93; 1827, 26). Conversely, societies thought to possess the beginnings of a distinction between the public and private sphere were thought of as offering auspicious conditions for the introduction of Christianity. High hopes were expressed about the mission in Celebes, for instance, because of its thrifty and clever population and the relative lack of despotism in its government, which recognized private property and personal freedoms (1840, 152).

The depiction of Christianity as a moral force operating in the private sphere immediately poses the problem of the sincerity of belief. Quite often, *Berichten en Brieven* illustrated the official policy of the Dutch missionary society of accepting converts only after establishing the true and personal character of their conversion (1820, 247–48; 1821, 175; 1828, 59). Anecdotes and little stories stress that doctrinal knowledge and a virtuous life alone are not sufficient to count as a Christian and to be allowed to join the new Christian communities. The journal occasionally reverts to rather childish rhetorical strategies to establish belief as truly authentic and personal, not part of a social transaction. In 1832, for instance, it published a letter from a missionary on Ambon describing how he went around his village at night eavesdropping on the natives, reporting on the heartfelt prayers he overheard (1832, 101ff). More usual are stories about long, drawn-out processes of conversion, in which detailed descriptions of the length of the process and the conflicts of the convert with his family, neighbors, and friends are used to establish his sincerity for the reader.

Such stories, attempting to establish the truth of what is depicted as the ultimate inner and individual experience, always rhetorically link individual conversion to the societal transformation in which the Christian mission is supposed to result. The description of the conversion of a Buddhist priest on Ceylon, relating the slow growth of his inner conviction of the truth of Christianity, culminates in his public confession of his new belief on the solemn anniversary of the start of the missionary work on the island (1828, 32–36). A highly detailed report on a Persian youth describes his conversion, following a polemical argument stemming from the seventeenth century (van Rooden & Wesselius 1987), as originating in an intellectual recognition of the truth of Christianity caused by discussions about the relative reliability of Islamic and Christian traditions concerning revelation. The main thread of the story, however, is formed by descriptions of his daily meditations and thoughts about Christ and his conflicts with his Muslim father. The story ends with the biblical image of the yeast and the dough, applied to this first convert who is expected to help transform the condition of his people (1824, 87–101).

As these rhetorical linkings of individual conversion and societal transformation suggest, the journal does not recognize a difference between the two aspects of the missionary enterprise. It locates Christianity within individual conscience. Therefore, the distinction between private and public sphere, the hallmark of civilization, is the most important social aspect of Christianity, too, because it is the precondition of sincere conversion. As Europe is made up of various nations, each with only a minority of committed Christians supporting the missions, so the Sandwich Island mission on the Hawaiian islands, the great nineteenth-century example of a successful societal conversion, is depicted as having created a civilized society that offers the possibility of personal belief. This is an offer only a minority of committed believers within a multitude of formal Christians embrace (1820, 233–34).

This dialectic between objective knowledge and personal conviction, between civilization and piety, the result of the way in which the missionary journal represented Christian belief, made it possible also to come to terms with the lack of success in obtaining a large number of sincere, personal conversions. The truly successful aspect of the missions, the establishment of schools and hospitals, could be interpreted as the introduction of the distinction between public and private sphere, and therefore as a precondition of Christianity (1836, 95–96).

The importance of the distinction between private and public sphere for Christianity, as depicted by the missionary journal, is highlighted by the way in which the journal hierarchizes cultures. It uses two criteria, not distinguishing between their civil and Christian aspects. The first criterion concerns the location of the sacred. Idolatry and especially fetishism, dislocations of the sacred in objects instead of in individual consciousness, are clear indications of barbarism. (1820, 90). The second criterion concerns gender. When women are used for crude physical labor, are sold to be married, or are mistreated in other ways, both civilization and Christianity are lacking. (1832, 60; 1836, 185) Adherence to the proper relationship between the sexes, with the woman presiding over the private sphere, is the standard by which the various cultures that the missionaries encounter are graded. This second criterion is extremely important and one of the most recurrent motives in the missionary journal. For example, in the single year 1824, *Berichten en Brieven* uses it to describe the lack of civilization of Caucasian tribes, Egyptian Jews, natives on Menado in the East Indies, inhabitants of the South Sea Islands, and widow burners in India. (1824, 14, 115, 123–24, 177–78, 238).

The importance of gender to this concept of religion suggests an explanation for one of the more puzzling features of the missionary tales in the *Berichten en Brieven*. Representations of Christian missions have always shown them to be fascinated by death. But whereas tales about early modern Roman Catholic missions focus on the public heroic martyrdom of the missionary, in the Dutch missionary journal the fascination with death expresses itself in stories about the private deaths of wives and children of missionaries. These stories do not represent death as a public testimony of the presence of Christianity, but as a shattering experience in the private sphere that individual faith can overcome.

To support this interpretation of the representations of conversion to Christianity as the introduction of the modern difference between a private and a public sphere, I want to stress their affinity, in the Weberian sense of a *Wahlverwandschaft*, with the social form of the missionary society. Societies with a religious purpose were a new and original form of Christian sociability emerging at the very end of the eighteenth century. They were a late fruit of the drive toward voluntary associations of the Enlightenment. Strangely, both the recent and the older scholarly literature on the emergence of a new public sphere in the era of the Enlightenment has neglected these societies with a religious purpose. (Nipperdey 1976; Im Hof 1982; Dülmen 1986; Mijnhardt 1988; LaVopa 1992; Goodman 1992). Literature about these societies, which typically sent out missionaries to foreign parts, organized home missions, tried to convert Jews, and published, translated, and distributed Bibles and all kinds of religious tracts, mostly consists of works published on the centennial or demicentennial anniversaries of the societies themselves. Predictably, such jubilee volumes focus on the societies' accomplishments, on their success or failure in reaching their stated goals. Recent research on the secular sociability of the eighteenth century, on the other hand, is inspired by the sociology of knowledge. It examines the internal functioning of the societies, the consequences of participating for the values and behavior of their members, and the contribution of the new sociability to the emergence of a public sphere and civic culture. The study of the attainment of explicit goals is replaced by the evaluation of the indirect consequences of the societal movement. A similar appraisal of the workings of the societies with a religious purpose illuminates the representation of conversion in the missionary review sketched above.

The Dutch missionary society, like societies with a religious purpose elsewhere, was not an ecclesiastical organization. Membership was voluntary and individual. It was not subject to formal requirements concerning ecclesiastical adherence or religious belief, requiring nothing more than endorsement of the stated purpose of the society. The society was organized as a nationwide association of full members. Local branches, including poor sympathizers who were not full members, met on the same day every month to hear the journal produced by the society read aloud. Such monthly meetings facilitated the imagining of a community of committed Christians active throughout the nation. The nature of the missionary society itself was in perfect accord with the view of the social place of religion offered in the missionary review. This affinity between the representation of conversion and the societal movement suggests that to locate the conceptual roots of this peculiar mixture of experimental religion and civilizing project in Pietism and the Enlightenment would be to miss an important point (Gäbler 1989). The concept of religion implied in the missionary representation of conversion was not simply the result of a new theory but an articulation of new social practices. What is needed is not only a history of Christian or missionary thought but a genealogy of this concept: a search for the societal and discursive changes that led to this new construction of religion in the world (Asad 1993, 27–79).

Such a search has been singularly lacking in the historiography of Protestant missions. Missionary histories consider the missionary enterprise such an essential part of Christianity that they are embarrassed by its virtual absence, both in theory and practice, in early modern Protestantism. Strategies developed to deal with this embarrassment include the search for precursors, focusing on those few-and-far-between attempts at spreading Protestantism outside Europe and European colonies, and the provision of excuses stressing the adverse objective circumstances in which the Protestant churches found themselves. Both strategies attempt to construct a continuity in religious endeavor and agreement on the place of religion between the early modern Protestant establishments and the Protestant churches of the nineteenth and twentieth centuries. No one tries to use the late emergence of missions as a means to define the originality of modern Western Christianity.

❧ ❧ ❧

In opposition to the Catholic view of the church as a corporate, visible, and hierarchized clerical body, the Protestant magisterial reformers of the sixteenth century developed the concept of the church as the communion of true believers. As true believers are only known to God, by necessity this church could not take on a visible, social form. As for the question of where it might be found, Luther answered that true believers could be supposed present wherever God's word was preached purely and his sacraments administered in the right way. He called on political authorities to ensure that this would happen in their territories. All magisterial reformers followed Luther on these points, expecting reform to come from civil authority.

As true believers cannot become known to each other, this conception ensured that in Protestant areas, religion in its visible form would be part of the structure of the body politic. All Lutherans and most Reformed subscribed to Erastianism, the doctrine that the visible church, the ecclesiastical establishment as opposed to the invisible church of true believers, is legitimately subject to political authority. Only some Reformed, Calvin amongst them, wished ecclesiastical establishments to possess a certain autonomy from civil authority, exercising a jurisdiction of their own. But even then, ecclesiastical establishments were considered part of the structure of authority that made up the body politic. In the 1550s, French Calvinists more or less by accident—in any case, without direction from Geneva—stumbled upon the possibility of setting up an ecclesiastical organization completely apart from political authority. This would prove, in France as well as in the Netherlands, an excellent means to organize resistance against persecuting central governments (Augustijn 1993). Still, such churches considered their opposition to civil authority to be provisory. They aimed to replace the Catholic hierarchy and hoped to be allowed to determine the public order of religion. In France their bid for power failed. In the Netherlands, a revolt against the central government of the staunchly Catholic Habsburgs resulted in the emergence of a new state, the Dutch Republic, which introduced the Reformation. The formerly persecuted Reformed became its new public church.

The religious settlement of the Dutch Republic deviated in two important ways from the common early modern pattern. In the first place, after a series of bitter internal disputes and conflicts with public authority, the new public church, although it was in fact very much subject to the secular governments, theoretically upheld the principle of the independent nature of ecclesiastical authority (Conring 1965). In the second place, in the core areas of the Dutch Republic not all subjects were considered to automatically belong to the public church. Public authority allowed the emergence and organization of various dissident religious groups: Catholics, Mennonites, Arminians, Lutherans, Jews. Moreover, the public church itself reserved formal membership for those willing to subject themselves to its discipline and pass an examination of their knowledge of its doctrine. Yet even in the Dutch Republic, the public church conceived of itself as an aspect of the order of society. In annual jeremiads, which were the only public ritual of this markedly decentralized state, ministers of the public church characteristically first reviewed the duties of the various holders of authority—magistrates, bearers of ecclesiastical office, heads of households—and ended with appeals to the converted and the unconverted, leaving it to their hearers to determine to which category they belonged. In this way, the ministers of the public church of the Dutch Republic reproduced the Protestant location of religion in the visible order of society on one hand, and the invisible hearts of individual believers on the other (van Rooden 1995a).

Within the conceptual world of magisterial Protestantism, it is very difficult to conceive of the necessity to engage in missionary endeavors, in the sense of spreading Christianity beyond the given geographical extension of political authority. Even Dutch theologians who, more than any other Protestants, upheld the distinction between the church and public authority, and who were confronted with the problem of the Christian religion outside the Republic because of the trading posts of the Dutch East India Company, did not think of missions in any kind of modern sense. This becomes very clear in the extensive writings of Gisbertus Voetius. Voetius, professor of theology at Utrecht from 1634 to his death in 1676, was the most influential Dutch theologian of the seventeenth century. He combined, in a curious way, a neoscholastic theological method with a Puritan-inspired program of societal and individual disciplinary reform. He was a staunch defender of the autonomy of ecclesiastical authority claimed by the Dutch public church. In thousands of pages of academic disputations he discussed all aspects of Reformed theology and church order. Scattered throughout his works one finds disputations devoted to the refutation of Islam and Judaism, to the founding of new churches in the past and present, to the

Roman Catholic missions and their claim to continue the work of the Apostles, to the situation of Christianity in the areas subject to the Dutch East India company. Yet these various themes do not make up a separate conceptual whole in his thought. Voetius does have a concept of "missions," but this includes all manners in which the church acts toward that which is alien to it (Voetius 1663–1676, no. 4, 332–34). He focuses on the legitimacy of such acts, that is, on the manner in which legitimate ecclesiastical authority is constituted. Here he rejects both the Roman Catholic view, which bases the legitimacy of ecclesiastical agency on the continuity between bishops and apostles, and Erastian arguments, which derive ecclesiastical legitimacy from civil authority. Attempts to isolate his utterances on subjects resembling missions in the modern sense from his general remarks on ecclesiastical agency spectacularly miss the point (van Andel 1912; Jongeneel 1989). Voetius assimilates reports about Roman Catholic missions and the spread of Protestantism in the East Indies into his interest in the nature and legitimacy of ecclesiastical authority, denying the legitimacy of the Roman Catholic church as a missionary body and pleading for the independence of the ecclesiastical establishment in the East Indies from the Dutch East India Company. Voetius treats the expansion of Christianity only because he treats theology in an encyclopedic way. Tales of heroic missionary endeavor or the spread of Christianity are not in themselves important to what is clearly his main interest, the establishment of a Christian commonwealth informed by public authority, both in its political and ecclesiastical aspects. Voetius, like all theologians of early modern Protestant ecclesiastical establishments, had no ideological need for missions.

Moreover, Protestant churches did not possess or control independent means. The public church of the Dutch Republic was ideologically and organizationally the most independent Protestant ecclesiastical establishment of the continent. Yet its synods functioned almost exclusively as courts of appeal. They were not boards of organizations that possessed their own resources or formulated their own policies. At no level of ecclesiastical organization did the church as a body command independent financial means. If a local church or provincial synod thought a new ecclesiastical office was necessary, it had to petition the competent political authorities—a city council or provincial estate—to provide the necessary funding. The same was true for the churches in the areas administered by the Dutch East India Company. Usually, secular authority had no interest in ecclesiastical endeavors outside its own territories.

The importance of ideological need and independent resources is strikingly brought out by the two main examples of Christian missionary endeavors in early modern times: the work of the Roman Catholic orders in Japan, China, and India and the efforts of the Moravians in Greenland, Labrador, the West Indies, and South Africa. Medieval Latin Christendom had expanded territorially, but this expansion had been the result of an aggressive process of conquest and settlement, which spread a highly particular form of culture and society (Bartlett 1993). Although the introduction of Christianity in the newly conquered Spanish and Portuguese areas of Latin America followed this medieval pattern, the sixteenth- and seventeenth-century missionary endeavors in Japan, China, and India were forms of Christian expansion not immediately tied to conquest. They belong to the most strikingly original aspects of the Counter-Reformation. Late medieval Christianity had been a rather loose association of national and territorial churches, with the papacy not much more than a symbol of unity. The Erastianism of the Protestant churches, resulting in national or territorial churches subordinated to political power, radicalized these late medieval tendencies. An important element of the Counter-Reformation's program followed similar lines. The strengthening of the Catholic church as a working institution always involved a much closer collaboration with the Catholic states. Yet in a movement contrary to these parallel developments of Catholic and Protestant national and territorial churches, the papacy became far more politically active on a European scale, presenting itself once more as an institution of universal authority. This ideological reorientation was coupled with a reliance on new religious orders, the most famous being the Jesuits, that exemplified and made possible this new universal ethos (Evennett 1968). Missionary endeavors on a worldwide scale, independent of any particular Christian political power, were a fitting symbol of these new universalist aspirations.

In the long run, the two aspects of the Counter-Reformation would run afoul of each other. The strengthening of the ties between political authorities and territorial churches involved the absolutist Catholic rulers in conflict with the papacy, conflicts that they easily won (Chadwick 1981; Wright 1982). At the end of the eighteenth century, the Catholic states forced the papacy to dissolve the Jesuit order. With the weakening of the the factual basis for the universal aspirations of the papacy, Catholic missionary endeavors faltered (Chadwick 1981). Catholic missions in early modern times were organized apart from national and territorial ecclesiastical establishments out of an important ideological need for symbols, and they were funded by independent resources.

The same goes for the only important example of Protestant missionary endeavors in these years. In the second half of the seventeenth century and the first half of the eighteenth century, Eastern European Protestants, not protected by the Peace of Westphalia of 1648, lived under the continuous threat of Catholic political authorities. In areas like Silesia and Carinthia, they were deprived of a regular ministry and forced to improvise means to sustain their religious identity. In the course of the eighteenth century, the methods developed by these Protestants, such as an unlearned ministry, a strong focus on lay piety, and a simple structure of belief, were spread throughout the Protestant world by the Moravians (Ward 1992). The Moravians, uprooted and exiled Eastern European Protestants recruited by Count Zinzendorf, were a small but extremely influential group. They did not consider themselves a sect or a new church; instead, they were dedicated to bringing true believers of all confessions and nations in contact with each other, without changing their formal confessional identity. Their commitment to missionary endeavors was an integral part of this attempt to create new spaces for belief. A world open to missionary endeavors was the ultimate symbolic expression of an imagined worldwide community of believers, apart from the daily social world of existing political, social, and ecclesiastical structures of authority.

In both these cases, missionary endeavors in early modern times were undertaken by groups apart from national or territorial political establishments, possessing their own resources (Zinzendorf displayed an uncanny talent for raising money), and using the image of these missionary endeavors to symbolize their main purpose. The sudden explosion of missionary endeavors all over the Protestant world at the end of the eighteenth century and beginning of the nineteenth century illustrates these same mechanisms. It was intimately related to a fundamental transformation of the political and social place of Protestantism. To make this point, it is useful briefly to sketch the developments in Britain and the United States.

❧ ❧ ❧

The new Protestant missions emerged in England in the early 1790s, were almost immediately emulated in the Dutch Republic, and were followed some years later by other continental Protestants as well as in the United States. The missionary endeavor was part of a great upsurge of voluntary religion, the extent of which was in directly inverse proportion to the strength of the ecclesiastical establishments in the different countries (Ward 1972b). The ecclesiastical establishments of the United States collapsed as a result of political revolution. That of England was severely shaken by the demographic and social effects of the industrial revolution. The continental Protestant establishments managed to contain what was the most visible aspect of the new, voluntary religion in the United States and England: the extraordinarily rapid numerical growth of a new kind of dissent.

In both countries, classical Protestant ecclesiastical establishments had held a near-monopoly on the exercise of religion until the end of the eighteenth century. And in both countries, this monopoly was destroyed by the emergence of evangelical Protestant groups. Around the middle of the nineteenth century, Methodists, various kinds of Baptists, Disciples of Christ, and other evangelical groups would make up a majority of American Protestants (Mead 1963). Dissenters in England had reached parity with the Anglican Church at that time (Ward 1972a; Gilbert 1976). These evangelical groups, in part completely new, like the Methodists or the Disciples of Christ, in part transformations of older forms of Protestant Dissent, like the English Congregationalists and some American and English Baptists, located religion in a private space, apart from politics. Ruthlessly subordinating questions of theology and church order to the overriding concern of missionary growth, they recruited new adherents at an astonishing rate. Although these groups did not invest many resources in foreign missions, the symbolic function of the missionary endeavor was important to them. They considered their churches to be missionary bodies, existing in a free social sphere, apart from the structures of public and national authority. Missionary societies were an organizational refinement, not a radical renovation involving a conceptual change in the way these new churches thought about themselves. From the beginning, they kept apart from interdenominational societies for foreign missions and organized their own missions.

The second great organizational renewal in these crucial years, the interdenominational societies with a religious purpose, emerged in England (Foster 1960; Brown 1961; Martin 1983). The *London Missionary Society* was founded in 1795, the *Religious Tract Society* in 1799, the *British and Foreign Bible Society* in 1804. In the United States and on the European continent, similar societies sprang into being. Those in Britain and the United States became the first examples of modern mass organizations, run by a professional staff, using and developing modern techniques of advertising and fundraising. As early as 1814, for instance, the *British and Foreign Bible Society* possessed auxiliary societies in each English county. By 1824 it had 859 of them, organizing more than two thousand Bible associations and some five hundred groups for women. In America, various regional societies with the same religious purpose merged into national bodies after 1810, especially in the 1820s. The various national organizations collaborated closely, developing joint fundraising campaigns. The close collaboration, organizational sophistication, and sheer size of this societal world justify its characterization as an "Evangelical Machine." By the 1830s, the American societies with a religious purpose had raised and spent an amount of money that almost equaled the total of the annual budgets for internal improvements of the federal government since the Revolution (Oliphant 1938).

Whereas the new American and British evangelical churches recruited their members from among the lower classes, both in the countryside and the fast-growing cities, the societies with a religious purpose mainly rested upon the urban bourgeoisie. Most of their members belonged to traditional Protestant groups. The American societies were dominated by members of the Congregationalist churches of New England and the Reformed churches of the Middle Colonies. The former were still a state church, the latter were organizationally and ideologically modeled on the Scottish state church. In England, the societies with a religious purpose mainly recruited among members of the Anglican Church and Old Dissent, those Protestant groups that had tried to supplant the Anglican Church as state church during the Civil War. Yet all societies with a religious purpose were free from clerical control, were organized apart from ecclesiastical establishments, and were the result of the voluntary joining of individuals. In all of these aspects, they fundamentally differed from the Anglican *Society for Promoting Christian Knowledge* and the *Society for the Propagation of the Gospel in Foreign Parts*, both founded around 1700 and modeled on Catholic examples. These were ecclesiastical bodies, meant to further the interests of the Church of England both in England and its colonies (Duffy 1979, 1981).

The new voluntary societies with a religious purpose, on the other hand, did not mean to serve ecclesiastical interests. Even in England, where evangelical members of the Church of England founded the *Church Missionary Society* (1797) instead of joining the interdenominational *London Missionary Society*, they did not do so with a desire to expand their church (in its first years, the *CMS* mainly supported Lutheran missionaries). They did it for tactical reasons, to avoid a bitter struggle with their high-church opponents over the principle of collaborating with dissenters (Best 1959). The overwhelming concern of these societies was the spread of a nondenominational Christianity. They shared the conception of the new evangelical churches of Christianity as something apart from the public world of objective power structures, firmly located in a private sphere. Yet whereas the new evangelical groups used their missionary endeavors to build communities located apart from yet not in opposition to the public world, the societies with a religious purpose attempted to provide the means for individuals to convert, expecting that such individual conversions would transform society indirectly.

Missionary societies were therefore only an element of a larger societal world, which included societies dedicated to the publication and propagation of religious tracts, the spreading of Bibles, or, in the United States, the training of ministers for the newly settled territories on the frontier. The societal movement was aimed not only, or even in the first place, at the transformation of foreign societies. Societies publishing and spreading religious tracts and Bibles mainly worked for the conversion of individual citizens of the nation in which they were organized. Small wonder, given that even the new evangelical churches have been interpreted, in the case of English Methodism, as a religion of despair, offering solace to those members of the working class whose political and social ambitions were thwarted (Thompson 1968, Hempton 1984), that this aspect of the religious societal movement has been depicted as an attempt to keep the lower classes in their place. Apart from the literature celebrating anniversaries of the various societies with a religious purpose, most studies about both the British (Quinlan 1941; Howse 1952; Foster 1960; Brown 1961) and the American (Bodo 1954; Cole 1954; Foster 1960; Griffin 1969) societal movements focus on their conservative political intentions, interpreting their work as an attempt to contain the dangerous example of the French revolution.

This is a shallow treatment of the religious societal movement. In the first place, it is rather doubtful that the message of the societies with a religious purpose was received and appropriated in the intended way. The English laboring classes, for instance, used the Sunday schools, set up to teach them to be content with their lot, for their own purposes and to reproduce their own values (Laqueur 1976). Second, the ideology of the religious societal movement was much more sophisticated than a crude representation of its counterrevolutionary intentions makes it out to be. The American societies with a religious purpose, for instance, developed an ethos that has been characterized as Christian Republicanism, stressing the importance of a virtuous and pious citizenry as the basis of the new Republic (Handy 1984; Banner 1973). This ethos not only informed all kinds of reforming movements, the most prominent being Abolition, but also decisively contributed to the definition of the emerging American nationalism (Tuveson 1968; Moorhead 1984). In Britain, too, the religious societal movement opened up spaces for moral crusades and reforming movements by propagating a view of religion as located within individual citizens contributing to the welfare of the nation. Here too, Abolition became an important issue that mobilized people against governmental policies.

Third, quite apart from the ideology propagated, the working of the societal world itself contributed to the transformation of the relation between religion and politics and the emergence of a public sphere. Ford K. Brown's quip about the *British and Foreign Bible Society* can be applied to the whole religious societal movement: "If everyone of the 4,252,000 Bibles issued by 1825 had been printed in the language of the Esquimaux and piled up on the frozen tundra, the Bible society would still have been, next to Abolition, the most powerful agency of Evangelical Reform" (Brown 1961, 261). Just as the new evangelical churches contributed to the emerging modern conception locating religion in a private sphere by actually organizing their communities apart from the world of politics and power, so the societal movement is to be considered important mainly for its actual introduction of a distinction between a private and a public sphere, locating religion firmly in the former and making possible the emergence of the moral citizen involved in politics. Both in the United States and in England, societies with a religious purpose played an important role in the transformation of traditional ecclesiastical bodies. In England, for instance, the *London Missionary Society* over time became the core around which the Congregationalists became a modern denominational organization. In the United States, various kinds of Presbyterians and the Congregationalists became modern denominations in similar ways, in the wake of ruptures of interdenominational societies (Smith 1962; Pearson 1969; Hood 1980).

The contrast between Britain and the United States makes it possible to further contextualize the emergence of Dutch missionary efforts. Like the ecclesiastical establishments of other continental countries, the Dutch Reformed public church was strong enough to contain outbreaks of revival (van den Berg 1968). On the other hand, the Dutch missionary society, founded in 1797, was the first continental imitator of the *London Missionary Society*. In the Netherlands, even more than in Britain, the management of the missionary society was securely in the hands of a social and cultural elite. Full members were only allowed after passing a ballot, and members of the former public church, many ministers among them, predominated. In general, the Dutch missionary society was allied far more closely with the Dutch churches than, for instance, the German missionary societies were integrated with ecclesiastical establishments. This strong and early presence of the missionary society, coupled with the virtual absence of evangelical Protestantism, marks a peculiar characteristic of the emergence of Dutch missionary endeavors.

In contrast to England, where the industrial revolution opened up social spaces for the growth of evangelical Protestantism, the Dutch economy contracted during the second half of the eighteenth century. While in the United States traditional ecclesiastical establishments, weak to begin with and weakened further by the separation of church and state, were unable to contain the numerically and geographically expanding population, the Dutch Republic of the eighteenth century had seen the growth of a religiopolitical order that incorporated various dissenting religious groups, rendering them recognized parts of a hierarchized social landscape of which the public church was only the most eminent element (van Rooden 1995b). Both of these conditions militated against the growth of new religious movements comparable to Anglo-Saxon evangelical Protestantism, as they effectively precluded the emergence of free social spaces. On the other hand, they furthered a moral interpretation of national and religious life, and facilitated the rise of a societal movement.

The Dutch Republic's loss of great power status, caused by its economic difficulties, was interpreted in moral terms as a loss of ancestral virtue. This led to proposals for educational and moral reform, meant to restore a virtuous citizenry. The eighteenth-century religious order tended to have a similar effect. Yearly jeremiads, organized by civil authority and observed by all religious groups, upheld what is best called a civil religion. This civil religion found the reason for the welfare of the Republic not in the presence of particular religious groups or confessions but in its tolerant religious order, which made possible the exercise of individual virtue and piety (van Rooden 1992).

These moral interpretations of public life were suddenly politicized in the 1780s, in the aftermath of a disastrous naval war with Great Britain (van Sas 1987, 1988). The reforming program of the so-called patriot party aimed at a national moral regeneration and culminated in the first European revolution in the age of democratic revolutions (Palmer 1959–1964). The revolution was put down by Prussian troops in 1787, and tens of thousands of revolutionaries fled to France. In 1795, invading French troops put the revolutionaries of the 1780s back into power. One of the first important acts of the new government of 1795 was to separate church and state. This act was almost unanimously supported in the national assembly, but it led to passionate debates about the new place of religion in the state. These debates have been adduced as evidence of the Christian character of the Dutch Enlightenment, and the distinctness of the Dutch experience in the age of democratic revolutions has been found in the Christian, even pious interests of the revolutionaries (Schama 1977). I would argue that the importance of religion in the revolutionary debates in the Netherlands reflects the specific nature of the social order of the Dutch *ancien régime*, which to a great extent was based on religion. The separation of church and state in the Netherlands was thus not about the destruction of the power of an ecclesiastical establishment—the former public church had been neither powerful nor rich—but about a reshaping of society. It brought a formal end to social and political discrimination based on religious difference. In this sense, it was much closer to the American than to the French model of the separation of church and state. The new unitary Dutch nation-state would know only citizens, not various religious groups. The role of religion and the churches was to be limited to the moral education of individuals. Religion was not to become an element constitutive of societal difference. On the other hand, its importance was generally recognized. A viable state could only be established on the basis of a virtuous citizenry, its morality shaped by religion.

This view of the relation between religion and the body politic was staunchly defended by the Dutch missionary society, founded only two years after the separation of church and state. Its vision of the public relevance of Christianity, propagated in its missionary journal, fitted the new circumstances perfectly. A fundamental discursive shift had taken place. The late-eighteenth-century concept of a hierarchized social order of various religious groups had been changed into the conception of a homogeneous nation of moral citizens, in which the task of churches was to further the moral education of individual citizens. In organizing for missions and representing the spread of Christianity as a moral transformation of societies, the Dutch missionary society imagined the new place of religion in the Netherlands themselves. The former public church supported the missionary endeavor because it helped it to come to terms with its new situation after the separation of church and state. Dissenters joined the missionary society because it offered them a possibility to be involved with a common, national religious endeavor, expressing a view of the place of religion in society with which they agreed.

∾ ∾ ∾

The more or less general acceptance of societal mobilization for foreign missions was particularly Dutch. Yet over time, the same would happen in all Western societies. By the late nineteenth century, implicit or explicit opposition to missionary endeavor had ceased among all Western Christians. Roman Catholics as well as liberal, orthodox, evangelical, and high-church Protestants considered missions extremely important and invested considerable resources in missionary endeavors. For all of them, representations of the spread of Christianity became an important means for imagining the position of Christianity in their own societies. Views of the relationship between civilization and piety, between societal transformation and individual conversion, similar to the conception expressed in the Dutch missionary journal, were shared by all. Consequently, the modern spread of Christianity would always be accompanied by fundamental ambiguities about the relationship between civilizing and converting aspects of the mission (Hutchison 1987), and about the relationship between the missionary endeavor and colonial authority (Comaroff and Comaroff 1986). These ambiguities were the result of the discursive dependence of the nineteenth- and twentieth-century missionary endeavor on the modern distinction between a private and a public sphere. Locating Christianity within a private sphere, expecting it to effect societal change indirectly, the missionary effort was both indication and cause of a fundamental discursive shift in the relation between religion and politics in the West.

References

Andel, H. A. van. 1912. *De zendingsleer van Gisbertus Voetius*. Kampen: J. H. Kok.

Asad, T. 1993. *Genealogies of Religion: Discipline and Reasons of Power in Christianity and Islam*. Baltimore: Johns Hopkins University Press.

Augustijn, C. 1993. "De opmars van de calvinistische beweging in de Nederlanden." *Theoretische Geschiedenis* 20: 424–38.

Banner, L. W. 1973. "Religious benevolence as social control: A critique of an interpretation." *Journal of American History* 60: 23–41.

Bartlett, R. 1993. *The Making of Europe: Conquest, Colonization and Cultural Change 950–1350*. London: Allen Lane/Penguin Press.

Berg, J. van den. 1956. *Constrained by Jesus' Love. An inquiry into the motives of the missionary awakening in Great Britain in the period between 1698 and 1815*. Kampen: Kok.

———. 1968. "Een opwekking te Nijkerk in 1821." *Nederlands Archief voor Kerkgeschiedenis* N.S. 48: 293–312.

Berichten en Brieven, voorgelezen op de maandelijksche bedestonden van het Nederlandsch Zendeling Genootschap. 1799–1827.

Best, G. F. A. 1959. "The Evangelicals and the established church in the early nineteenth century." *Journal of Theological Studies* N.S. 10: 63–78.

Bodo, J. R. 1954. *The Protestant Clergy and Public Issues, 1812–1848*. Princeton: Princeton University Press.

Boneschansker, J. 1987. *Het Nederlands Zendingsgenootschap in zijn eerste periode: Een studie over opwekking in de Bataafse en Franse tijd*. Leeuwarden: Gerben Dykstra.

Brown, F. K. 1961. *Fathers of the Victorians: The Age of Wilberforce*. Cambridge: Cambridge University Press.

Chadwick, O. 1981. *The Popes and European Revolution.* Oxford: Clarendon Press.

Comaroff, J. and Comaroff, J. 1986. "Christianity and Colonialism in South Africa." *American Ethnologist* 13: 1–22.

Cole, C.C. 1954. *The Social Ideas of the Northern Evangelists.* New York: Columbia University Press.

Conring, E. 1965. *Kirche und Staat nach der Lehre der niederländischen Calvinisten in der ersten Hälfte des 17. Jahrhunderts.* Neukirchen–Vluyn: Neukirchener Verlag.

Craandijk, J. 1869. *Het Nederlands Zendelingsgenootschap in zijn willen en zijn werken geschetst.* Rotterdam: M. Wyt & Zonen.

Dülmen, R. van. 1986. *Die Gesellschaft der Aufklärer. Zur bürgerlichen Emanzipation und aufklärerischen Kultur in Deutschland.* Frankfurt am Main: Fischer.

Duffy, E. 1979. "Correspondence Fraternelle: The SPCK, the SPG and the Churches of Switzerland in the War of the Spanish Succession." In D. Baker (ed.), *Reform and Reformation in England and the Continent, c. 1500–c. 1750.* Oxford: Blackwell.

———. 1981. "The Society for Promoting Christian Knowledge and Europe: The background to the founding of the Christentumsgesellschaft." *Pietismus und Neuzeit* 7: 28–42.

Enklaar, I. H. 1978. "Motive und Zielsetzungen der neueren niederländischen Mission in ihrer Anfangsperiode." In J. van den Berg and J. P. van Dooren (eds.), *Pietismus und Reveil.* Leiden: Brill.

Evennett, H. O. 1968. *The Spirit of the Counter-Reformation.* Cambridge: Cambridge University Press.

Foster, C. I. 1960. *An Errand of Mercy. The Evangelical United Front 1790–1837.* Chapel Hill: University of North Carolina Press.

Gäbler, U. 1989. "Erweckung im europäischen und amerikanischen Protestantismus." *Pietismus und Neuzeit* 15: 24–39.

Gedenkboek. 1897. *Gedenkboek uitgegeven ter gelegenheid van het Honderdjarig Bestaan van het Nederlandsch Zendelinggenootschap.* Rotterdam: M. Wyt & zonen.

Gilbert, A. D. 1976. *Religion and Society in Industrial England: Church, Chapel and Social Change, 1740–1914.* London: Longman.

Goodman, D. 1992. "Public Sphere and Private Life: Towards a Synthesis of Current Historiographical Approaches to the Old Regime." *History and Theory* 31: 1–20.

Griffin, C. S. 1969. *The Ferment of Reform, 1830–1860.* London: Routledge.

Handy, R. T. 1984. *A Christian America. Protestant Hopes and Historical Realities.* Second edition, New York: Oxford University Press.

Hefner, R. W., ed. 1993. *Conversion to Christianity. Historical and Anthropological Perspectives on a Great Transformation.* Berkeley: University of California Press.

Hempton, D. 1984. *Methodism and Politics in British Society 1740–1850.* London: Hutchison.

Hood, F. J. 1980. *Reformed America: The Middle and the Southern States, 1787–1837.* Alabama: University of Alabama Press.

Howse, E. M. 1952. *Saints in Politics: The "Clapham Sect" and the Growth of Freedom.* Toronto: University of Toronto Press.

Hutchison, W. R. 1987. *Errand to the World: American Protestant Thought and Foreign Missions.* Chicago: University of Chicago Press.

Im Hof, U. 1982. *Das gesellige Jahrhundert. Gesellschaft und Gesellschaften im Zeitalter der Aufklärung.* München: Beck.

Jongeneel, J. A. B. 1989. "Voetius' zendingstheologie, de eerste comprehensieve protestantse zendingstheologie." In C. Graafland e.a., eds., *De onbekende Voetius.* Kampen: Kok.

————. 1990. *Protestantse zendingsperiodieken uit de negentiende en twintigste eeuw in Nederland, Nederlans Indië, Suriname en de Nederlandse Antillen.* Utrecht: IIMO.

Kruijf, E. F. 1894. *Geschiedenis van het Nederlandsche Zendeling-Genootschap en zijne zendingsposten.* Groningen: Wolters.

Laqueur, T. W. 1976. *Religion and Respectability: Sunday Schools and Working Class Culture 1780–1850.* New Haven: Yale University Press.

Latourette, K. S. 1937–1945. *A History of the Expansion of Christianity.* Seven vols. New York: Harper.

Maandberigten (. . .) van het Nederlandsch Zendeling Genootschap, betrekkelijk de uitbreiding van het Christendom, bijzonder onder de heidenen. 1828–1917.

Martin, R. H. 1983. *Evangelicals United: Ecumenical Stirrings in Pre-Victorian Britain 1795–1830.* London: Scarecrow Press.

Mead, S. E. 1963. *The Lively Experiment: The Shaping of Christianity in America.* New York: Harper.

Moorhead, J. H. 1984. "Between Progress and Apocalypse: A Reassessment of Millenialism in American Religious Thought, 1800–1880." *Journal of American History* 71: 524–42.

Mijnhardt, W. W. 1988. *Tot Heil van't Menschdom. Culturele genootschappen in Nederland, 1750–1815.* Amsterdam: Rodopi.

Neill, S. 1964. *A History of Christian Missions.* Harmondsworth: Penguin.

Nipperdey, T. 1976. "Verein als soziale Struktur in Deutschland im späten 18. Jahrhundert. Eine Fallstudie zur Modernisierung." In T. Nipperdey, *Gesellschaft, Kultur, Theorie. Gesammelte Aufsätze zur neueren Geschichte.* Göttingen: Vandenhoeck und Ruprecht.

Oliphant, J. O. 1938. "The American Missionary Spirit, 1828–1835." *Church History* 7: 125–37.

Palmer, R. R. 1959–1964. *The Age of the Democratic Revolution: A Political History of Europe and America, 1760–1800.* Princeton: Princeton University Press.

Pearson, S. C. 1969. "From Church to Denomination: American Congregationalism in the Nineteenth Century." *Church History* 38: 67–85.

Quinlan, M. J. 1941. *Victorian Prelude.* New York: Columbia University Press.

Rooden, P. van. 1990. "The Concept of an International Revival Movement around 1800." *Pietismus und Neuzeit* 16:155–72.

———. 1992. "Dissenters en bededagen. 'Civil Religion' ten tijde van de Republiek." *Bijdragen en Mededelingen betreffende de Geschiedenis der Nederlanden* 107: 703–712.

———. 1995a. "Het begrip 'vaderland' in bededagspreken." In N. C. F. van Sas, ed., *Vaderland. Een begripsgeschiedenis* (forthcoming).

———. 1995b. "Secularization, Dechristianization and Rechristianization in the Netherlands." In H. Lehmann, ed., *Secularization, Dechristianization and Rechristianization* (forthcoming).

Rooden, P. van, and Wesselius, J. W. 1987. "The Early Enlightenment and Judaism: the 'Civil Dispute' between Philippus van Limborch and Isaac Orobio de Castro. 1687." *Studia Rosenthaliana* 21: 140–53.

Sas, N. van. 1987. "Opiniepers en politieke cultuur." In F. Grijzenhout and N C. F. van Sas, eds., *Voor Vaderland en Vrijheid. Revolutie in Nederland 1780–1787.* Utrecht: Centraal Museum.

———. 1988. "Drukpers, politisering en openbaarheid van bestuur in de patriottentijd. Enkele kanttekeningen." In Th. S. M. van der Zee et al. eds., *1787: De Nederlandse revolutie?* Amsterdam: De Bataafsche Leeuw.

Schama, S. 1977. *Patriots and Liberators: Revolution in the Netherlands, 1780–1813.* New York: Knopf.

Shiels, R. D. 1980. "The Second Great Awakening in Connecticut: Critique of the Traditional Interpretation." *Church History* 49: 401–415.

Smith, E. A. 1962. "The Forming of a Modern American Denomination." *Church History* 311: 74–99.

Thompson, E. P. 1968. *The Making of the English Working Class.* London: Penguin.

Tuveson, E. L. 1968. *Redeemer Nation: The Idea of America's Millennial Role.* Chicago: University of Chicago Press.

Voetius, G. 1663–1676. *Politica Ecclesiastica.* Four volumes. Amsterdam: apud Johannem Janssonium.

La Vopa, A. J. 1992. "Conceiving a Public: Ideas and Society in Eighteenth-Century Europe." *Journal of Modern History* 64: 79–116

Ward, W. R. 1972a. *Religion and Society in England 1790–1850.* London: Schocken.

———. 1972b. "The Religion of the People and the Problem of Control." In G. J. Cuming and Derek Baker, eds., *Popular Belief and Practice.* Cambridge: Cambridge University Press.

———. 1992. *The Protestant Evangelical Awakening.* Cambridge: Cambridge University Press.

Wright, A. D. 1982. *The Counter-Reformation: Catholic Europe and the non-Christian World.* London: Weidenfeld and Nicolson.

4

RELIGIOUS CONVERSION AND THE POLITICS OF DISSENT

Gauri Viswanathan

Religious Minorities and Citizenship

In the great secularization movements of the nineteenth and twentieth centuries from which emerged the concept of the tolerant modern state, it is possible to discern, if not the origins of modern religious and ethnic strife, at least prototypical enactments of the drama of citizenship—a drama that unendingly complicated itself by questioning and rethinking the possibilities of dual allegiances brought on by such things as—in England, for instance—legislation to enfranchise religious minorities in the wake of national union and disestablishment: Could an Englishman be both English *and* Catholic, Jewish, Nonconformist? These challenges suggest that the very concept of nationality, hitherto relying on an unquestioned equation of Englishness with mainstream Anglicanism, had to be revised because of altered relations between church and state, now no longer bound by formal oaths of allegiance to doctrine and creed but by the incorporative logic of law, administrative rationality, and constitutional principles of liberty.

If nationalism can be defined as the total set of representational practices that establish the grounds of nationality,[1] then terms like "cultural nationalism" or "religious nationalism" already assume a seamless unity of aspirations, goals, and agendas, a selection and filtering that irons out the contradictions embedded in the construction of national identity from the fragments of religious, racial, cultural, and other forms of self-identification. Peter van der Veer cautions us against this totalizing approach and urges that "we should take religious discourse and practice as constitutive of changing social identities, rather than treating them as ideological smoke screens that hide the real clash of material interests and social classes."[2] However forcefully allegories of the nation, constituting the history of modern secularism, might draw attention to the teleology of its own formation, the narratives produced in the crucial space of negotiation between national and religious identity shed the most visible light on the strains and stresses in community self-identification, especially when community or individual self-perceptions conflict with the definitions accorded them by the nation-state.

This is as true of European state formation as it is of the colonies that Europe, particularly England, subjugated to its own rule. Juxtaposition of the narratives representing both metropolitan and colonial locations reveals that in the period between 1790 (the time of the infamous Gordon riots in England over Catholic emancipation) and 1850 (when the Gorhams judgment was passed by the Privy Council, which declared the determination of religious belief outside the purview of the courts and thus effectively disempowered ecclesiastical authority), English colonial influence in India simultaneously grew to the point that England, in assuming responsibility for the education of its subjects in Western sciences, languages, and culture, was able to incorporate colonial subjects into the civil structures of governance while denying them the full political rights attendant on such assimilation. The delicate balance sought by English educational policy in India was essentially a secular project to transform Indians into deracinated replicas of Englishmen while they remained affiliated with their own religious culture—a project, however, that did not necessarily imply giving English-educated Indians a place in the English political system. The strategic objective of turning Hindus into "non-Hindu Hindus," or Muslims into "non-Muslim Muslims,"[3] has been memorialized in Macaulay's infamous pronouncement on the goal of an English education—to produce Indians who would be "Indian in blood and colour but English in taste, in opinions, in morals, and in intellect."[4] Less remarked upon is that by 1850, there occurred a parallel process in English social and political life that aimed to turn Jews into non-Jewish Jews, Catholics into non-Catholic Catholics, Dissenters into non-Dissenters, Nonconformists into non-Nonconformists, and so forth.

At first glance, these two secular developments—the lifting of religious discrimination against non-Anglicans in England and the Anglicization of Indians—would appear to have little or no relation to each other. Indeed, they almost have the semblance of contrary developments. To be sure, the mid-nineteenth-century relaxation of penalties imposed on religious minority groups in England for pursuing their own religious creeds is more in tune with the policy of involvement with India in the early years of East India Company (coincident with the Orientalist phase of scholarship), when indigenous systems of learning, culture, and religion were allowed to flourish without any interference from the company officials. But I would argue that Macaulay's program of Anglicization in India has strong parallels to the bills in England to enfranchise Jews, Dissenters, Nonconformists, and Catholics. In much the same way that religious tolerance and emancipation were inevitable secular trends that grudgingly won acceptance even by the most diehard Tories and Anglicans, with the expectation that if it was not possible to have a nation of good Anglicans, at least it was worthwhile to aim for a nation of good Englishmen, it was deemed profitable to make good Englishmen of colonial subjects—even if it was unlikely or even undesirable for them to be good Christians, as long as they were no longer practicing Hindus or Muslims. The Macaulayan educational project in India coalesced imperceptibly into the emancipatory legislation admitting hitherto excluded religious minorities into the English nation. It is no accident that the British figure most responsible for the Anglicization of Indians also happened to be one of the most strident voices in the English parliament for the lifting of restrictions against Jews. As Israel Finestein points out, Macaulay's "robust advocacy" of the cause of Jewish civil emancipation blended indistinguishably with the radical agenda of the Whigs to enfranchise the Jews as a necessary step in the teleological progress of English liberalism.[5] A program that had a colonial provenance facilitated the construction of the secular English state, in which the central issue of national identity dispersed the demands of particularized religious differences. The debate on citizenship is clearly less focused on cultural adaptation than on progressively secularizing religious identity into an autonomously conceived national identity.

The overlapping of a secular educational agenda for colonial subjects with the decline of ecclesiastical authority in England, along with emancipatory legislation to enfranchise excluded religious minorities in England, has several implications: First, it introduces a politics of identity into both English and colonial political life, where the grounds for Englishness are increasingly determined by the individual's ability to detach from the *concept* of local or regional affiliations while maintaining their form; second, the strengthening of the English state is predicted not by a single unified framework of ecclesiastical or missionizing doctrine but by the absorption of racial and religious "others" into a secular, pluralistic fabric; and third, a centralized administrative machinery is set in place whose legislative capacity displaces the authority of religious bodies in determining the criteria for membership in the community.

But the overlay also contains a number of problematic dimensions that suggest the uneven development of colonizing and colonized societies, even while both may be driven by a similar trajectory. The "othering" of religion takes different forms in the metropolitan English and colonial Indian contexts, despite the fact that both result in legislated religious identities that marginalize the content of belief systems. The difference crucially hinges on the issue of civil enfranchisement, the possibilities of which, in the English situation, permit religion to be more "naturally" identified as a necessary prior state in the progression toward nationhood—the point at which religious differences, while present as established social categories, are neutralized as they are subsumed under a national identity. The split occurs along the axes of citizenship and subjecthood: Religious tolerance in England is definitionally the process that emancipates religious minorities from all existing civil disabilities and enables hitherto marginalized groups to participate in the nation-state. Of course, the fact that religious enfranchisement effectively displaces the extension of the franchise across social classes creates tensions of another kind that have persisted in English social history, as exemplified most vividly in Charles Dickens's *Barnaby Rudge*.

But while the English secular state is constructed on the premise that formerly excluded religious groups are duly given the rights of citizenship, such a premise can be no more than conditional in colonial societies, and religion continues to be an unassimilatable and resistant marker of political difference. Secularization in the colonies remains a flawed project, even more than in England, because of the absence of an emancipatory logic that steers a once-monolithic religious culture into the gradual absorption of pluralized groups into the nation-state. Secularization in India has always been a fraught process driven by unresolvable tensions, due partly to the fact that parliamentary reform, which enabled religious minorities in England to be absorbed as citizens, failed to perform a comparable function in India. There, state formation is basically incorporation of subjects into a *colonial* state and, following national independence, into a hegemonic state in which the social relations sanctioned by colonialism continue virtually uninterrupted. Furthermore, England's policy of religious neutrality had always officially resisted endorsing missionary proselytization, and substituted "Englishness" for "Christianity" as the defining principle of subjecthood. The administration of colonial law clearly indicates that even when Hindus were converting to Christianity, the decisions made by the civil courts denied the fact of such conscious change and treated the Christian convert as essentially *not* having converted. The particular situations that brought the British resistance to religious change out into the open also challenged them, paradoxically, to defend the rights of converts against the punitive actions of Hindu or Muslim personal law. But while seeming to protect the rights of converts, the administration of English law dissociated Christian converts from the larger communion of Christians to which native converts may have believed they were admitted, and recast their religious identity in the form of the religion they had renounced.[6]

Despite the British inclination to treat the sectarian differences between religious faiths in India as a purely internal affair, in much the same way that judicial decisions in England tended to treat questions involving religion as entirely a matter for the ecclesiastical establishment, the clamor for self-rule by Indians turned these religious differences into a political matter. An obvious case in point is the great controversy over the communal awards sanctioned by the British in India, which gave Muslims separate electorates in the legislatures and established the grounds for the pursuit of political power on sectarian lines. On the same principle, Bhimrao Ramji Ambedkar, leader of the untouchable (or "dalit") community in India, demanded separate electorates for the untouchables, insisting that if Muslims were given this privilege as a significant religious minority, untouchables as an oppressed minority equally deserved a similar guarantee of self-representation in order to protect their own interests against the encroachments of Hindu majority rule. Ambedkar rejected the identification of untouchables with Hindus—a classification that both caste Hindus and British administrators were eager to retain—and argued that no other religious constituency had the right to make political representations on behalf of the untouchables: Only untouchables can speak for untouchables, he announced categorically. Over the objections of members of the Indian National Congress, who clamored for a united India to throw off the British yoke, Ambedkar refused to yield and only reluctantly agreed to a compromise solution when Gandhi threatened to go on a hunger strike to protest Ramsay MacDonald's communal award, which acceded to the untouchables' demand for separate electorates. This compromise, known as the Poona Pact, made provisions for the reservation of seats for untouchables in exchange for Ambedkar's conceding to joint rather than separate electorates. Many critics are of the opinion that Ambedkar's famous declaration of his intention in 1935 to leave the Hindu fold and convert to another faith can be traced to his intense frustration and anger over failing to secure a separate electorate for untouchables. However, his twenty-year decision to convert to Buddhism developed in much more complex ways than conveyed by this description, indicating that his conversion cannot be attributed solely to political disappointment.

As a dissenter bent on dismantling the Hindu caste system, Ambedkar fulfilled the historical role of dissent not only to question hateful religious dogma but also to unbuckle the consolidating ambitions of the secular state under which former religious orthodoxies are subsumed. The deliberateness with which he planned his conversion, all the time negotiating with Hindu leaders for legal measures against untouchability and courting Muslim, Sikh, and Christian organizations, while also developing formidable scholarship in Buddhist studies and writing his own version of the *Dhammapada*, indicates that his conversion was far from being a knee-jerk reaction to failed political solutions, as mass conversions tend to be read. Ambedkar's vast body of work on Buddhism, conversion, and caste ideology attempted to steer a steady course between a separatist, sectarian stance and an unconditional citizenship function in which the identity of untouchables would be subsumed under Hinduism. The final section of this essay will consider what was entailed by Ambedkar's conversion, and examine its implications for the possibilities of nationhood for a social class denied access to political power through self-representation, yet seeking a course of action that *preserves* rather than eradicates difference. As more than one scholar of modern Indian history has noted, consciousness of difference was once the preserve of the upper castes, but recent history has shown that the victims of religious difference invoke religion to stake their own claims to identity: "Precisely those who should seek obliteration of the divisions and disparities that characterize the deeply hierarchical nature of the caste systems are found to use it the most, hoping to undermine it . . . and do precisely what the larger secular order has failed to provide: a society free of exploitation and oppression and indignities."[7]

Church–State Relations and Catholic Conversions in England

If Ambedkar is arguably the most important convert of the twentieth century, John Henry Newman can justly be described as the most celebrated convert of the nineteenth century. Both are towering figures whose conversions were as public as their participation in the political life of their respective nations, India and England. And while for both conversion was a clear political statement of dissent against the identities constructed by the state (through legislation, for example), they were not merely reacting to centralized authority in the name of asserting difference but exploring the possibilities offered by conversion (especially to "minority" religions) in developing an alternative epistemological and ethical foundation for a national community. In this transitional section, I focus briefly on John Henry Newman in nineteenth-century England, and, in the remainder of the essay, will move on to a discussion of B. R. Ambedkar in twentieth-century India. The point of comparison lies in the fact that both Newman's conversion to Catholicism and Ambedkar's to Buddhism sought to reclaim cultural identities located at an originary point (pre-Reformation Catholicism for Newman, the triumph over caste-ridden Brahmanism by Buddhism for Ambedkar), defined as the historical model for enlightened nationhood.

Just as much as Ambedkar, Newman was acutely aware of the critical nature of dissent to succumb to the fatal alternatives of citizenship or separatism. His major philosophical treatise, *A Grammar of Assent* (1870), works through a number of carefully considered critical moves that retrace the stages of his own conversion, ultimately to posit Catholicism as a transreligious, transnational force—which, far from being separatist or sectarian, appears to Newman to perfect the idea of the English nation.[8] *A Grammar of Assent* could easily be retitled "A Grammar of Dissent" because of its detachment of Catholic belief from established structures and institutional practices. Its clear aim is to turn Newman's own conversion into praxis— the action of belief on the world, or what Newman calls a real assent—to distinguish it from notional assent to abstract propositions that attach themselves to systems, including the superstition and ritualism with which Catholicism itself was identified. *A Grammar of Assent* attempts to resolve the ambiguity of a cultural identity split between religion and nation by forging a middle ground that might be termed "the worldliness of belief."[9] But in the long run, what promises to be a work that attempts to guide cultural criticism toward belief as an expression of dissent turns into a mere protocol of possible critical strategies, a description of mental phenomena that outlines a dynamic critical practice aimed at disempowering notional assent to foundational premises, yet never is fully engaged in the materiality of historical change.

Ironically, Newman, who was suspicious of tolerance as a real aim of parliamentary reform, initially opposed the Catholic emancipation bills proposed by parliament because he thought they were part of a progressive strategy to erode the authority of the Church of England. But he later did an abrupt *volte-face* and began to subscribe to the course of national developments in limiting the reach of the Anglican church. In 1845, he converted to Roman Catholicism partly out of a recognition that the narrow sectarian interests of preserving Anglicanism were no longer politically tenable. Thereafter, Newman proposed the "stark alternative" of Roman

Catholicism as the only bulwark against the infidelity toward which all other forms of Christianity tended. If Newman's conversion was deeply motivated by a fundamental urge to restore unity of religious opinion, it was substantially assisted by his gradual acceptance of disestablishment, in order, he claimed, to "fight the enemy on better ground and to more advantage."[10] Personally, he believed that "the most natural and becoming state of things" was for the "aristocratical power" to be the upholder of the Church; yet he could not deny "the plain fact" that "in most ages the latter has been based on a popular power."[11]

Newman's work simultaneously embraces contrary positions within a wide spectrum of possible positions, ranging from an identification with aristocratic privilege to an espousal of popular radicalism. This is largely because his unbuckling of the ideology of tolerance shifts alternatively between a class-based critique, in which he freely draws upon libertarian notions, and an orthodox religious position, which seeks to unmask the anti-ecclesiastical impulses of the modern secular state. While he defended reactionary establishment principles, his populist turn also enabled him to argue that the reforming party's aim of removing civil disabilities against religious minorities obscured its resistance to what should have been an equally pressing parliamentary cause, the extension of the franchise to all social classes. His conversion of the parliamentary discourse of religious enfranchisement into the language of heresy enabled him to restrict the idea of inclusiveness to principles of social equality, and so preclude religious or cultural relativism as admissible in the tolerant state's incorporative philosophy. Newman's religious discourse included the problem of articulating the political aspirations of what he called the uneducated masses, for whom religious identification is increasingly represented as a means of contesting the selective logic of legislative reform. Repositioned thus in the politics of disestablishment and prospective national union, Newman's conversion is less a private event of sudden spiritual illumination than an interpretive index to the main currents of contemporary social legislation and the direction of national consolidation upon which he imagined it to be premised.

Newman's own dissent from the established church, while influenced by his increasing interest in "look[ing] to the people,"[12] was based on an *a priori* reasoning that distinguished between centralization and democratization. In identifying himself with the people to restore the power of Christian belief to English society, Newman consciously separated the "nation" from the "state." He associated the "state" with pernicious bureaucratic, hierarchical, and classificatory tendencies, and the "nation" with community-centered local experience. But though Newman did acknowledge that centralization, while destroying local influences, also proceeded simultaneously with the Reform Bill of 1832, the democratization that the Reform Bill ideally embodied appeared to him to represent the autonomous power of the popular will, which aimed "to supersede the necessity of a government, and to make the House of Commons, and so the people, their own rulers."[13] Indeed, Newman's enthusiasm for a recentering of English politics in the people led him to see a disestablished and popular Roman Catholicism as the only credible means of recovering the unified religious culture of the primitive church, lost since the time of the early church fathers.

Newman's call for reinstituting structures of authority that are not derived from the nation-state (i.e., from Catholicism) was nothing short of a desire to dissolve the state altogether. The Catholicism that Newman affirms, which is much closer to the faith of pre-Reformation England, is a more diluted version of the ultramontanism (a movement advocating papal supremacy) that was then fashionable in Roman Catholicism but with which Newman was by and large uncomfortable. Embedded in this universalist affirmation is a return to origins that prescribes a specific agenda for the English nation, which is resituated globally not as the renegade nation that broke away from Rome but as the imperial center of the only true world religion. Newman's vision for English Catholicism readily incorporated England's colonial ventures as a logical and inevitable part of its own self-definition as global in reach.

Newman's ultimate purpose is to show that an English Catholic, far from being "a member of a most un-English communion,"[14] is in fact more English than is an Anglican, because he is more in touch with his national and religious origins. Catholicism's sharing of features with both Hindu priestly ritualism and pan-Islamic extraterritorial bonding doomed it to a debased, "oriental" status in English culture, as Indianists like James Mill, who were hostile to superstitious religious traditions, repeatedly depicted it—an attribution that spurred Newman to prove his own patriotic credentials amidst the general prejudice against Catholics as "foreigners" whose loyalties were presumed to lie toward Rome rather than England.[15] On another front, he had also to ward off charges of effeminacy and celibacy, with which Catholicism was notoriously identified, and assert his heterosexual English manliness by proclaiming his allegiance to those most English of virtues—scientific objectivity, rationality, and evolutionary progress.[16] Newman's struggle to demonstrate his Englishness against the hostile skepticism of his contemporaries ironically reflects the extent to which belief itself was marginalized in nineteenth-century England, even as his more accommodating Catholic position led him to be regarded as "the most dangerous man in England" by both Anglicans and Catholics.[17]

Newman's inability to realize the radicalism of his initial move to assert religious difference is a measure of his own difficulties in negotiating a viable relationship between religion and nation. His universalism seeks to go *beyond* the nation, but it ends up working regressively, not only by reintroducing religious identity as both contained in and transcending national identity, but also by locating in the authority of Catholicism the foundational structure of true Englishness. Newman's transnational solution cannot effectively disentangle belief from structures of authority, despite the privileging of popular imagination and intuition over rationality and elite modes of intellectual apprehension. Caught between the demands of secular national identity and local religious differences, Newman turns his back on conversion as a dynamic principle of change to embrace one of self-confirmation and discovery of what is already latently present as religious teleology. The radical revisionist possibility of conversion is reversed, as achieving a point of compatibility between Catholicism and Englishness replaces the earlier challenge to the desirability of nationhood posed by his conversion. The sustained tension between Catholicism and Englishness inevitably diluted the efficacy of Newman's dissent from Anglicanism and rendered it homogeneous with assent to prevailing secular norms—in short, to the construction of English nationhood, in the service of which his own conversion is then sacrificed.

Ambedkar and Dalit Conversions

"Mahatmaji, I have no country." These words of exasperation and barely disguised fury were uttered by B. R. Ambedkar as he left his first meeting with Gandhi in 1931, a meeting marked by a confrontational intransigence on Gandhi's part to the claims of untouchables on the sharing of political power with the Indian National Congress.[18] Ambedkar's frustrations in throwing his lot with the movement for national independence, while simultaneously fighting for the autonomy of untouchables against the incorporative tendencies of a brahmin-dominated Indian National Congress, appeared to take the form of split loyalties, which his opponents were swift to exploit as evidence of a factional streak in him.[19] Ambedkar's inflammatory speeches were construed as antinationalist, particularly when he asserted that it was the caste system that crippled India, not the British. His public burning of the Hindu code of ethics, the *Manusmriti*, was intended to show that the main enemy of untouchables was Hinduism, not British colonialism.

Among Ambedkar's critics, perhaps the most scathing was C. Rajagopalachari, who blatantly called Ambedkar's demand for separate electorates for the untouchables as an antinational tactic that undermined the unified efforts of the Indian National Congress to gain independence from Britain.[20] In an openly hostile and partisan attack, Rajagopalachari maintained that Ambedkar was never interested in the political incorporation of dalits into the Indian nation-state and opposed constitutional provisions for including dalits in the new schedules (from which derives the official appellation of untouchables as "scheduled castes"), because he wanted to keep them isolated. Even more inflammatory was Rajagopalachari's charge that Ambedkar chose passive gestures like conversion, which had the effect of derailing the dalit platform from real political emancipation, in order to protect his own hold over those whose debased condition was the *raison d'etre* of his leadership function. Rajagopalachari saw Ambedkar's resistance to the social reform measures of the Indian National Congress as no different from the reticence of "Christian and Muslim proselytizers" toward reform in Hinduism, since such reform would eradicate the exclusionary tendencies from which other religious groups had long benefited in their pursuit of new members.

The main thrust of Rajagopalachari's polemic, however, was directed at what he called Ambedkar's manipulation of the dalit agenda in order to undermine the manifesto of political freedom upon which the Indian nationalist movement was based. Without directly alluding to Ambedkar's impending conversion, Rajagopalachari insinuated that his separatist demands were divisive because they undermined the Indian National Congress's struggle against British colonialism, and indeed capitulated to colonialist manipulation of dissident voices in the Indian subcontinent.

Ambedkar's declaration to leave Hinduism, made soon after that disastrous meeting with Gandhi, was similarly interpreted as a piqued reaction against the forced compromise to give up separate electorates in return for reserved seats in the legislature. A number of pamphlets appeared, purportedly by untouchables but sounding suspiciously like Indian National Congress propaganda, which rejected Ambedkar's "pseudo-theories" of dalit liberation and denounced him as a stooge of the British, while praising Gandhi's nonpartisanship.[21]

For twenty years, Ambedkar kept people guessing to which religion he, along with his dalit supporters, was going to convert. In 1956, just a few weeks before he died, Ambedkar led one of the largest mass conversions witnessed in modern history and, by converting to Buddhism, fulfilled his promise that though he had no choice in being born a Hindu, he was resolved not to die as one. Born in 1891 into a Maharshtrian Mahar untouchable family and overcoming insuperable obstacles of caste prejudice, Ambedkar rose to become one of the most highly educated Indians of his time, with a Ph.D. from Columbia University in political science and further advanced work in law and economics at the London School of Economics. His academic achievements, however, did not exempt him from the disdain of caste Hindus. Returning to India to work in a law office, Ambedkar suffered the humiliation of clerks throwing files at him so as not to be defiled by his touch. Inflamed by these experiences, he threw himself into the uplifting of the untouchables; not, however, by working for reform within Hinduism but by asserting the rights of untouchables to full equality before the law—what he called the only positive legacy of British colonialism.[22] Ambedkar's uncompromising appeal to principles of political liberty overrode what might have easily been a more modest project of eliminating the civil disabilities under which untouchables suffered daily harassment.

Ambedkar's momentous conversion on October 16, 1956, was preceded by two decades of frantic maneuvers by Hindu leaders to persuade him not to leave Hinduism and to work for change within the Hindu structural fold. Ambedkar's unshakable resolve to convert was blatantly read as a crude and vindictive attempt to split Hinduism, as well as disable the consolidating strength of the dalit movement. This is because by converting to Buddhism, Ambedkar and his followers sought the identity of a distinct religious minority group that had no special, favored status under the law, though under the earlier personal law officially recognized by the British, Buddhism was categorized as an offshoot of Hinduism, as were Sikhism and Jainism.[23] But in his speech at Nagpur on October 15, 1956, on the eve of what has come to be known as the "Great Conversion," Ambedkar defended himself against charges that by leading his followers away from their now constitutionally recognized status as untouchables, he was gravely disadvantaging them at a time when compensatory legislation was being considered for the officially named "scheduled castes." None of his opponents had the courage to deny that conversion to Buddhism offered Ambedkar a way out of the hateful hold of caste prejudice, but they nevertheless tried to press upon him that his renunciation of Hinduism was invariably at the cost of also renouncing whatever new incorporative measures were being made for the dalit classes under the schedules laid down by the Indian Constitution, in the writing of which Ambedkar himself was a key figure.

Why then, in this secular climate of emancipatory legislation, did Ambedkar choose conversion as his favored mode of leading the dalits to political equality, while many of his own followers preferred a combination of organizational strength and constitutionalist methods to promote upward social mobility? And why Buddhism in particular rather than the more obvious alternatives, Islam or Christianity? Most important of all, why did Ambedkar reject the Marxist model of fighting social inequities and take what must surely appear on the surface to be a regressive step in turning to religion for liberation purposes? After all, the Marxist route was the chosen alternative of many groups similarly oppressed by caste discrimination, particularly in south India; the iconoclast Periyar E. V. R. Naicker launched his anticaste "Self-Respect" movement in Madras presidency under the banner of atheism, and denounced all religions as essentially discriminatory.

Recent critical approaches to Ambedkar's conversion are as disparate as his contemporaries' interpretations of his motives. By and large, the split is straight down the line, dividing the private from the public, the spiritual from the political. Critics like Gail Omvedt see Ambedkar's religious conversion as purely reactive, a mode of mass mobilization of dalits to retrieve them from the hostility of caste Hindus on the one hand and, on the other, the refusal of political groups like the communist party to regard caste and religious oppression as distinctly separate from class factors.[24] In this reading, Ambedkar's conversion is a political stunt, albeit a highly successful one that altered forever the demographic equation between religious groups: The population of Buddhists in India increased dramatically with the mass conversions of dalits, from the figure of 141,426 given in the 1951 Census to 3,206,142 in the 1961 Census.[25] Most mass conversions continue to be attributed to political motivation and social mobility, including the 1981 large-scale conversions of scheduled caste groups to Islam in the southern town of Meenakshipuram.

At the other extreme are interpretations of Ambedkar's conversion as an entirely spiritual event connected to the discovery of moral truths with the power to liberate oppressed dalits. Critics who take this view are prone to emphasizing Ambedkar's early-childhood influences, particularly pious parents who enveloped his life with the music and poetry of Hindu saints in the belief that Marathi saint-poets like Moropant, Mukteshwar, and Tukaram were saviors of the poor and the lowly. Of particular appeal was the Bhakti school of Kabir, which sought to abolish the inflexibility of the caste system and initiate an unmediated relation between devotee and deity. The cultural mythology of dalit households often borrowed from archetypal images of the past in which religious dissenters were central figures. One such powerful image for a dalit liberation theology is provided by the "dalit martyr" of twelfth-century South India, Nandanar, who inaugurated an activist tradition of protest from below against the Hindu denial of entry into temples by untouchables and claimed the right to worship as an equal. Another historical model for the definitive possibilities of realizing a compassionate, egalitarian religion is the central one of Ashoka, whose conversion to Buddhism is seen as marking the beginnings of an era of tolerance, justice, and service to humanity. Ambedkar is often referred to in this literature as the "Ashoka of modern India," whose rejection of militant solutions to caste oppression and embrace of a nonviolent religious ethic are "a triumph of the spiritual side of this noble and sensitive soul."[26] This line of scholarly inquiry seeks to reclaim Ambedkar from the main role assigned him by history as chief architect of the Indian Constitution and political leader of the untouchables, placing him instead as one of the most significant interpreters and practitioners of Buddhism in recent times. The relevance of Ambedkar's conversion to the construction of the national community he strove for, most apparently in his writing of the Indian Constitution,[27] remains marginalized, however, as is all too clear in the divorce between Ambedkar the politician and Ambedkar the commentator of Buddhist texts—a split that modern scholars of Indian history have continued to observe in their own work.

Linking his two roles, one of the most compelling interpretations of Ambedkar's conversion is offered by Christopher Queen, who reads both Ambedkar's life and his conversion as a move from premodernity to modernity. From being a lowly untouchable whose "destiny" it was to endure the strictures of Hindu caste society, Ambedkar *chose* to leave Hinduism and embrace Buddhism, and in that act, Queen suggests, he fulfilled one of the conditions of modernity: the exercise of individual choice based on reason, careful deliberation, and historical consciousness. As meticulously as his predecessor John Henry Newman, who considered in minute detail the attractions of Roman Catholicism in an increasingly secular and pluralistic England in which predetermined, legislated identities usurped self-definitions, Ambedkar, after systematically studying available alternatives for creating an ethical nation that would guarantee fundamental rights to his fellow dalits, finally adopted Buddhism as the faith that met his complex requirements of reason, morality, and justice. But having announced his choice of Buddhism, Ambedkar, as Queen points out, "went on to become the paradigm of postmodern man, who is driven not only to choose a religious tradition, but to dismantle and reassemble it, with scraps of faith and practice from the past, the present, and the imagined future."[28]

The core of Ambedkar's "discovery" of Buddhism lies in his own rewriting of Buddhist precepts to achieve the goals of dalit emancipation; *The Buddha and His Dhamma* stands as his most complete exposition of an ancient tradition updated to suit the complex requirements of a modern, secular India. Richard Taylor's inspired comparison of Ambedkar's compilation of *The Buddha and His Dhamma* with his work on the Indian Constitution suggests how both documents were carefully reassembled, the first from selectively highlighted Buddhist precepts and the other from aspects of American, British, and Indian law, to express the religious and political life of the community.[29] While conversion to Buddhism, no doubt, is an important emphasis of the traditional text, Ambedkar makes it absolutely central to the reworked structure he gives the Buddha's teachings, which are carefully reorganized to fall into symmetrical parts covering not only the conversion of "sinful" people like Brahmins, criminals, and other fallen beings, but also that of women and oppressed social classes.[30] Ambedkar's reinvented Buddhism has long been a troublesome issue to traditional Buddhists, who find missing in his commentary some of the fundamental precepts of Buddhism, such as the Four Noble Truths; karma and reincarnation; the emphasis on monasticism; the otherworldly dimensions of time and space; and the notion of suffering as the product of ego attachments. Right at the outset, in his introduction, the Four Noble Truths come in for particularly strong attack by Ambedkar, who describes their resigned attitude to sorrow as a product of Aryanism, which gives people nothing more than a "gospel of pessimism" that expects them to endure the gross injustices of their present existence. Ambedkar eliminates these "Truths" altogether, believing that of all the obstacles to the acceptance of Buddhism by non-Brahmins, none was a greater stumbling block than the Four Noble Truths.

Out of the Buddhism of the classical texts Ambedkar reconstructs a pragmatic code book of social morality that offers what he believed classical Marxism also offered, but without the stable structure of identity that a social ethic, on the other hand, was able to provide. For example, in a somewhat whimsical essay called "Buddha or Karl Marx," Ambedkar defends Buddhism as a precursor to Marxism in a number of respects, notably its emphasis on the abolition of private property, its linking of suffering with social exploitation and poverty, and its antipathy toward an otherworldliness that sanctions the endurance of poverty.[31]

But in Ambedkar's reading, Buddhism parts company with Marxism in the latter's proven failure to change the moral disposition, even though it may succeed in altering the economic relations within society. For Ambedkar, the idea of "moral disposition" was closely intertwined with notions of rational choice, cultural identity, and self-renewal. And indeed, his great fear was that a secular and materialist response to factors of class and caste annihilated dalits' consciousness of their own past, besides inducing a cultural paralysis that held them back from actively claiming an identity for themselves. Ambedkar was critical of the dalit tendency to combine with peasant movements, but he was equally rejecting of Gandhi's insistence that they remain within the Hindu fold. Ambedkar's alienation from both the materialist rhetoric of dalit ideology and the accommodating gestures of Hindu social reformers has been read by some critics as embodying the classic disjunction between the positions of a "troubled insider" and a "struggling victim."[32]

The appeal of the Buddha's *dhamma* for Ambedkar was, again, its emphasis on the element of rational choice; the Buddha's mode of instruction was not to compel people to act in ways not of their own choosing, but to alter their *disposition* so that they would be prepared, through a combination of rationality, morality, and social consciousness, to take action out of reasoned volition. Ambedkar described religion as a means of "universalizing" social values that "brings them to the mind of the individual who is required to recognize them in all his acts in order that he may function as an approved member of the society."[33] The potential of a Buddhist ethic for dalit praxis captured Ambedkar's imagination as no other social philosophy had. The most subversive, "antinational" statement Ambedkar made at Yeola, where he first announced his decision to leave Hinduism, was his exhortation to his dalit followers that they regard their religious identity as something they had the right to choose, and not a fate to which they were irretrievably doomed. No other single statement of his roused Gandhi to anger in the same way, and he dismissed the claim that one may choose one's religious identity by retorting, "Religion is not like a house or a cloak, which can be changed at will. It is a more integral part of one's self than one's own body. . . . A change of faith . . . will not serve the cause which [Ambedkar and the untouchables] have at their heart, . . . especially when it is remembered that their lives for good or for evil are intervolved [sic] with those of caste Hindus."[34]

It is precisely the nature of this "intervolving" that Ambedkar sought to disentangle by converting to Buddhism and creating the basis for an alternative nationalist politics, which took into account the double deracination that non-elite Indians suffered as victims of both caste and colonialism. The clearest demonstration of what Christopher Queen calls Ambedkar's post-modern technique of dismantling and reassembling is found in his 1948 publication, *The Untouchables*. Quite unlike the work of a trained political scientist, Ambedkar's monograph on the origins of untouchability shows little inclination to demonstrate a scientific temperament; rather, drawing on a typology that recalls mythological description, it retells the story of untouchability as a product of religious conflict. Gail Omvedt makes the important observation that, while Ambedkar subscribed to certain Marxist descriptions of ideology and economic relations, he reversed the base-superstructure model to give primacy to the superstructure, of which religious factors were fundamentally important.[35] Instead of falling back on a theory of caste oppression as determined by economic disparities, Ambedkar interpreted religious difference as having an equally material effect in explaining the nature of social oppression. Buddhism's attraction for him lay in the originary link he established between the advent of untouchability and the spread of Buddhism. In his treatise, the untouchables are recast as "Broken Men" who converted to Buddhism in 400 A.D. and were ostracized by caste Hindus following the conquest of Buddhism by Brahmanism.[36] As Buddhists who showed no interest in venerating Brahmins or employing them as priests, these "Broken Men" were tyrannized by Hindus, and were further made to feel impure because they continued to eat beef after the practice had been abolished in Hinduism. The refusal by the "Broken Men" to return to Brahmanism when it triumphed over Buddhism, for which they were punished with the stigma of untouchability, creates for the dalits a history in which they are agents, and not merely victims buffeted by the forces of economic change. In believing that conversion to Buddhism would restore to dalits an agency that untouchability had eroded, Ambedkar brilliantly provided a religious framework for a politics of dalit renewal. Indeed, one of his main objections to Gandhi's offer to "purify" Hinduism of its discriminatory practices, in exchange for Ambedkar's commitment to stay within the Hindu fold, was that such an offer assumed untouchability was a problem internal to Hinduism and confined active agency to caste Hindus. Ambedkar's conversion to Buddhism aimed at challenging precisely this assumption; to the extent that it unsettled the complacency of Hindu reformers, who believed the initiative for social change lay exclusively with them, it was certainly successful.

Even more importantly, by reinserting into the narrative history of India the "central" chapter of the struggle for supremacy between Buddhism and Brahmanism, in which both caste Hindus and those known hence as un-

touchables were key players, Ambedkar fundamentally challenged the Indian National Congress's representation of the dalit political demands as
separatist, antinational, and therefore undermining of the struggle against
British colonialism. On the contrary, as he affirmed in a speech delivered
in 1944 before the Madras Rationalist Society, the ascendancy of Brahmanism held back the empiricist and epistemological advances made by
Buddhism toward laying the foundation for a "new and modern India,"
and it returned India to a more benighted scripturalism from which a truly
moral, political community could not be forged. Ambedkar's explanation
for the colonial subordination of India to England was precisely that the
closed system of Brahmanism prevented the consolidation of organic communities based on principles of justice and equality, which alone would
have been able to resist colonial aggressiveness. Indeed, the crowning
achievement of Ambedkar's writings was the identification of Buddhism
with enlightened nationhood—a historical possibility that clearly existed in
ancient India but was thwarted due to Hindu casteism. The theory that the
nation had failed to come into its own as a result of the tenacious hold of
Brahmanism enabled Ambedkar to turn to ancient Buddhism as the prototype of a rational, modern nation-state and, in the process, identify himself as a loyal Indian. In much the same way that Newman turned to
pre-Reformation Catholicism to recover the foundational structure of
Englishness, Ambedkar turned to an originary moment in Indian history—
the spread of Buddhism—to reclaim a redemptive cultural identity not only
for dalits but for all Indians.

But even while Ambedkar sought to rewrite Buddhism into a liberation
theology for dalits, it is also clear that Buddhism was made to carry added
cultural weight in order to establish the appropriateness of converting to
this faith rather than Islam, Christianity, Sikhism, or Jainism, the other possibilities Ambedkar had considered. Though all of Ambedkar's postures indicated an abiding and irreversible decision to sever himself and his fellow
dalits from all ties that bound them to Hinduism, he was never able to fully
unfasten the link that he believed existed between Hinduism and *India*. At
no time did he seriously entertain Islam or Christianity as real choices, and
his writings and speeches abound in references to these as foreign religions,
alien to India and further alienating to already deracinated subjects.[37] His
dismissal of Islam and Christianity as religions that threatened to "denationalize" untouchables by extending the hold of foreign powers spurned
transnational alliances as a mode of consolidating dalit power.

Apart from Buddhism, the only other religion that Ambedkar seriously
considered was Sikhism. But he also confessed that he was drawn to this re-

ligion primarily because it was "in the interest of the country" and untouchables would not then have to forsake Indian culture if they converted.[38] Preserving "Indian culture," "Indianness," and "Indian nationality" must surely appear a strange ambition in one who bitterly told Gandhi, "I have no country." But while Ambedkar's twenty-year study of comparative religions to decide which religion he would embrace was undertaken almost like a scientific project, and conducted very publicly, the tenterhooks on which he kept Hindu leaders for years gradually disappeared when even they realized Ambedkar's ambivalence in leaving not the Hindu fold, but the fold of Indianness with which Hinduism was so obstinately identified. When Ambedkar finally converted to Buddhism in 1956, most Hindus breathed a sigh of relief, because in their view Buddhism did not pose a threat or a challenge to the concept of a predominantly Hindu India, which Islam or Christianity certainly did. If Hindus were so little ruffled by Ambedkar's final act, it would suggest that the liberating potential of Buddhism for dalits had no such subversive force for Hindus, and the radical, revisionist possibilities of Ambedkar's conversion were neutralized by his difficulties in disengaging Hinduism from the concept "India." As an incomplete project, his conversion was unable to effectively negotiate the split between religious and national identity, despite its success in providing an ethics of cultural self-renewal.

A striking example of the contradictions in Ambedkar's thought is his position on temple entry. While there was already a significant split within modern Hinduism between the Gandhian idealization of the temple and the antitemple radicalism of Hindu thinkers like Tagore, which it would have been easy for Ambedkar to exploit, he was less interested in combining with the iconoclasm of the latter group than in demanding access to the very symbolic structure that dalits were fighting against—Hinduism. The intense energies that he poured into the temple-entry movement were so obsessional that it is clear at some crucial point the struggle for temple entry was conflated into an act of reclaiming a *cultural*, not religious, symbol that embodied nothing short of India. An inherent ambivalence, which generally informed his attitude to Hinduism, carried over into his fight to gain dalits entry into the religious space of Hindu worship, where, it has to be admitted, he was far less successful than when fighting a secular civil rights issue like securing access to public water.

Ambedkar's other great ambivalence lay in his attitude toward authority, particularly the authority of the state. On one hand, he was quite settled in the conviction that the secular Indian state, emerging from the ashes of colonialism, was incapable of providing a positive cultural identity to the underclasses, least of all by electoral means; nor did he believe that the problem of untouchability and caste discrimination could be solved through legislation or by getting representation in the legislature. His rejection of the state was complete insofar as he believed that untouchables would never secure their full rights within a political system dominated by a Hindu majority. Following the defeat of his demand for separate electorates for untouchables, Ambedkar turned his back on institutionalized social measures:

> Any electoral arrangement, I believe, cannot be a solution of the larger social problems. It requires more than any political arrangement and I hope that it would be possible for you to go beyond this political arrangement that we are making today [of joint electorates] and devise ways and means whereby it would be possible for the Depressed Classes not only to be part and parcel of the Hindu community but also to occupy an honorable position, a position of equality of status in the community.[39]

Elsewhere, in *States and Minorities*, Ambedkar deplored the fact that throwing off the British yoke did not result in a value-based democratic society committed to equality but merely perpetuated the political structure of hierarchical constraints introduced by British colonialism: "The soul of Democracy is the doctrine of one man, one value. Unfortunately, Democracy has attempted to give effect to the doctrine only so far as the political structure is concerned by adopting the rule of one man, one vote. . . . It has left the economic structure to take the shape given by those who are in a position to mould it."[40]

Ambedkar's conversion, along with the conversions of his followers, sounded the death knell for any hopes that the state would be an agent for social change. Yet, despite his loss of faith in the secular state as a potential ally in the lifting of disabilities under which untouchables had labored for centuries, one of Ambedkar's primary objections to Marxist philosophy was its belief that the crowning moment of world history would witness the withering away of the state. The fear of anarchy as a successor to the ultimate dissolution of the state so gripped Ambedkar that he found himself reasserting the need for some system of authority to ensure the continuing presence of moral laws. Though he may have blandly believed that "the only thing which can sustain [class struggle] after force is withdrawn is Religion,"[41] it is ironic that the position ultimately affirmed by him maintained that the social values universalized by religion could only be protected by the state. So that even as Ambedkar despaired of the state being the source of fundamental rights for untouchables, he turned to that selfsame state to provide the stable authority through which the nation's moral life would be ensured.

The ambivalence toward state authority that exists in Ambedkar's work reenacts a split between the *separatism* of his call for protection of dalits' rights and the *universalism* of his appeal for the dissemination of religious and social values, which the *dhamma* embodied for him. On the issue of political representation, Ambedkar never yielded to the suggestion that dalits would be given the right to full political participation under the rule of a Hindu majority, no matter how democratic the existing political apparatus. And in tracing the disenfranchisement of untouchables to an indifferent British government that, "in the manner of the Chinese tailor who when given an old coat as a pattern, produced with pride an exact replica, rents, patches, and all,"[42] Ambedkar was scathing in his indictment of a double colonialism at work. Some of Ambedkar's bitterest language is reserved for British rulers who, despite their reformist rhetoric, were never prepared to make the practice of untouchability a penal offense nor undertake the large-scale education of untouchables and place them in positions of authority.[43] By contrast, English-educated Indians, secular and cosmopolitan in their outlook, were disaffiliating themselves from their Hindu and Muslim belief systems while retaining their religious identities to organize themselves politically. Ambedkar's litany of continuing civil disabilities under the British, only now further aggravated by untouchables' having to pay taxes to the British for what Hindus refused to allow them to use, reveals the gross discrepancy between the British discourse of reform and Britain's accommodation of the hierarchical structure of Hindu society. It is no wonder that in his memorandum to the Round Table Conference, Ambedkar categorically demanded the total removal of all civil disabilities as the first right of citizenship, preceding all other electoral calculations or conferral of political power.[44] Ambedkar ripped apart the British ideology of partial assimilation of colonial subjects—those already secularized through English education, whose status as Hindus or Muslims had pre-emptively been neutralized rather than enfranchised, unlike the case in nineteenth-century England in which the secularization process was set in motion by the lifting of punitive restrictions against non-Anglican groups. The stalled enfranchisement of colonial subjects had its most deleterious effects on these untouchables, who remained consigned to the status of subjects rather than citizens long after the first concessions in self-rule.

After the disaster of the separate electorates, while Ambedkar now changed his tune to maintain that the dalits' right to equality was only realizable through their leaving the Hindu fold, to the point that he was willing to renounce whatever constitutional provisions were made for "scheduled castes" as certified members of Hinduism, his idea of nationhood, based on an overarching unity of the religious values of brotherhood, equality, and freedom (which he found in the *dhamma* of Buddhism), required a centralized, unitary state to prevent their being relegated to the possession of a separate religious minority. In this description, Ambedkar pointedly reminds his readers of the living scenario of its very opposite—the effect of Hindu casteism on the balkanization of communities, which are thus derailed from organizing themselves into a modernizing nation. Ambedkar's conversion to Buddhism, which shows all signs of having roots in a separatist impulse, is nonetheless the base from which a national community is sought to be reconstructed. This redefines rights not in terms of political franchise alone but primarily moral claims.

Where Ambedkar parted company with Gandhi on what seemed to be a shared objective was in the latter's conviction that untouchability was a Hindu problem that had to be tackled within the terms of Hindu social reform. For Ambedkar, the moral horror of untouchability could only be abolished by an alternative religious framework from which derived the social principles that recognized untouchability as a *moral* offense against India's historical mission as exemplar of rationality, justice, and right conduct—values ideally embodied in the figures of the Buddha and the emperor Ashoka. Ambedkar had earlier insisted on legislative measures against untouchability, and, while not abandoning it altogether, he now acknowledged that legislation did not alter the caste structure of Hinduism but merely established the limits of caste prejudice. If Ambedkar exhorted untouchables to leave Hinduism for cultural self-renewal, he conceived of that departure not as a withdrawal into an autonomous space, but as a prerequisite to reclaiming India as the nation from which untouchables had been severed by political disenfranchisement. As is evident, Ambedkar's nationalism struggled to release itself from the stranglehold of Hinduism and relocate national identity in alternative religious systems, for which, as I suggested earlier, a new historical mythology of Brahmanism, Buddhism, and "Broken Men" was pressed into service.

The construction of a moral community emerges as Ambedkar's most fundamental motive for conversion. As such, his departure from Hinduism cannot be said to be merely a reactive gesture. But the final goal of his conversion—the assertion of a "fundamental oneness of all things"[45]—enters into such a realm of abstraction that the vital link he seeks to establish between an ethics of social equality and a newly imagined modernized nation cannot altogether dispense with forms of authority derived from earlier political systems. He is firm in his conviction that political rights can issue only from a reconstructed community whose structural origin is neither the British system of limited representation nor the reformed system of Hinduism, purged of its casteist features. Indeed, one of Ambedkar's most radical gestures was to deny that the rights of untouchables would be adequately protected by a government characterized by structural continuity with previous systems of authority. However, while the *dhamma* provided the moral authority for the reclamation of full rights by untouchables, Ambedkar could find no means of disseminating the values of the alternative ethical system he envisioned for India as a whole, other than by utilizing existing forms of centralized state authority. This is not to say he conceived of a theocratic Buddhist state; rather, for the *principle* of Buddhism to be the democratic principle of the modern nation-state, Ambedkar was drawn back into the political apparatus of a parliamentary democracy in which such concepts as popular representation, electorates, and the franchise were already fraught with hierarchical constraints. The translation of moral laws into political rights, for which conversion functions as a trope, is more completely worked out as a strategic maneuver of dissent, which required Ambedkar to go through a separatist route to attain a nation committed to the universalist principles of justice and equality. That the principal architect of the Indian Constitution was obliged to traverse such a tortuous route to create the political character of his ideal nation-state suggests the vast gap between his vision and the collective aspirations that the written document was intended to reflect.

Notes

This essay is part of a longer work titled *Outside the Fold: Conversion, Modernity, and Belief* (Princeton University Press, forthcoming).

1. Simon During, for instance, provides a useful working definition of nationalism as "the battery of discursive and representational practices which define, legitimate, or valorize a specific nation-state or individuals as members of a nation-state." See "Literature—Nationalism's Other? The Case for Revision." In Homi Bhabha (ed.), *Nation and Narration* (London: Routledge, 1990), 138.

2. Peter van der Veer, *Religious Nationalism: Hindus and Muslims* (Berkeley: University of California Press, 1994), ix.

3. See Peter van der Veer, "Multiculturalism and Syncretism." Charles Stewart and Rosalind Shaw (eds.), *Syncretism/Anti-Syncretism* (London: Routledge, 1994).

4. Thomas B. Macaulay, "Minute on Indian education, February 2, 1835." G. M. Young (ed.), *Macaulay: Poetry and Prose* (Cambridge, MA: Harvard University Press, 1967), 729.

5. Israel Finestein, *Jewish Society in Victorian England* (London: Valentine Mitchell, 1993), 79–92.

6. See my "Coping with (Civil) Death: The Christian Convert's Rights of Passage in Colonial India." In Gyan Prakash (ed.), *After Colonialism: Imperial Histories and Postcolonial Displacements* (Princeton: Princeton University Press, 1994).

7. Rajni Kothari, "Rise of the Dalits and the Renewed Debate on Caste." In *Economic and Political Weekly* (June 25, 1994), 1589.

8. John Henry Newman, *An Essay in Aid of a Grammar of Assent* (Notre Dame: University of Notre Dame Press, 1979).

9. I am grateful to David Lipscomb for suggesting this phrase.

10. *The Letters and Diaries of John Henry Newman*, vol. 2, 128. Charles Stephen Dessain, ed. (Oxford: Clarendon Press, 1978). Also quoted in Ian Ker, *John Henry Newman: A Biography* (Oxford: Oxford University Press, 1988), 34.

11. *Ibid.*, p. 103; quoted in Ker, 83.

12. John Henry Newman, *Historical Sketches* 1 (London: Pickering and Co., 1889), 340; quoted in Ker, *op. cit.*, 82.

13. *Letters and Diaries of John Henry Newman, op. cit.*, 339; quoted in Ker, 109.

14. John Henry Newman, *Apologia Pro Vita Sua* (New York: Doubleday, 1956), 120.

15. See D. G. Paz, *Popular Anti-Catholicism in Mid-Victorian England* (Stanford: Stanford University Press, 1992), for a comprehensive discussion of the extent to which anti-Catholicism was at the center of political life during the nineteenth century, which Paz meticulously links to the Irish Question.

16. I am indebted to Sarita Echavez. See for these insights. See Lester R. Kurtz, *The Politics of Heresy: The Modernist Crisis in Roman Catholicism* (Berkeley: University of California Press, 1986), for a detailed discussion of Catholicism's response to modernity with its partial assimilation of the doctrine of evolution and scientific progress.

17. Stephen Thomas, *Newman and Heresy* (Cambridge: Cambridge University Press, 1992), 5.

18. The matter of terminology is evidently an important one, and the term for social groups, who in the past used to be simply referred to as "untouchables," has gone through a number of christenings. Gandhi's term "harijan," or children of God, was categorically rejected by Ambedkar as patronizing. In his own writings Ambedkar used the term "Depressed Classes," and subsequent commentary has agreed on the term "Dalit." For purposes of consistency I will use the word "dalit" to refer to untouchables, though I will revert occasionally to the term "untouchables" when it is specifically used in a text from which I may be quoting or paraphrasing, or to refer to the historical context in which the word was widely used.

19. B. R. Ambedkar, "What the Congress and Gandhi Have Done to the Untouchables." *Writings and Speeches* 9 (Bombay: Education Department, Government of Maharashtra, 1991).

20. C. Rajagopalachari, *Ambedkar Refuted* (Bombay: Hind Publications, 1945).

21. Dakshayani Velayudhan, ed. *Gandhi or Ambedkar, by a Harijan* (Madras: Gandhi Era Publications, 1945), 9.

22. B. R. Ambedkar, "The Untouchables and the Pax Britannica." In *Writings and Speeches* 12 (Bombay: Education Department, Government of Maharashtra, 1993), 146.

23. See Julian Saldanha, *Conversion and Indian Civil Law* (Bangalore: Theological Publications in India, 1981).

24. Gail Omvedt, *Dalits and the Democratic Revolution: Dr. Ambedkar and the Dalit Movement in Colonial India* (New Delhi: Sage, 1994).

25. Bhagwan Das, "Ambedkar's Journey to Mass Conversion." In Verinder Grover, ed. *B. R. Ambedkar* (New Delhi: Deep and Deep Publications, 1993), 609. See also Ravinder Kumar, "Ambedkar, Gandhi, and the Poona Pact." *Occasional Papers in Society and History*, no. 20 (New Delhi: Nehru Memorial Museum, 1985); and Dhananjay Keer, *B. R. Ambedkar: Life and Mission* (Bombay: Popular Prakashan, 1962).

26. V. R. Lakshminarayanan, "Dr. Ambedkar's Contribution to the Revival of Buddhism in India." In J. Parthasarathi (ed.), *Buddhist Themes in Modern Indian Literature* (Madras: Institute of Asian Studies, 1992), 40. Ambedkar converted on October 16, 1956, a day traditionally associated with Ashoka's conversion to Buddhism.

27. I do not have the space here to go into the fascinating details of Ambedkar's role in the drafting of the Indian Constitution, a discussion that is absolutely central to any consideration of his thought but requires a whole essay. Readers are advised to refer to volume 13 of *Dr. Babasaheb Ambedkar: Writings and Speeches* (Bombay: Education Department, Government of Maharashtra, 1994), for a complete record of his constitutional thinking.

28. Christopher Queen, "Ambedkar, Modernity, and the Hermeneutics of Buddhist Liberation." In A. K. Narain and D. C. Ahir, eds., *Dr. Ambedkar, Buddhism and Social Change* (Delhi: B. R. Publishing, 1994).

29. Richard Taylor, "The Ambedkarite Buddhists." In T. S. Wilkinson and M. M. Thomas, eds., *Ambedkar and the Neo-Buddhist Movement* (Madras: Christian Literature Society, 1972), 146.

30. B. R. Ambedkar, *The Buddha and His Dhamma*. In *Writings and Speeches* 11 (Bombay: Education Department, Government of Maharashtra, 1992).

31. B. R. Ambedkar, "Buddha or Karl Marx." In *Writings and Speeches* 3 (Bombay: Education Department, Government of Maharashtra, 1989).

32. D. R. Nagaraj, *The Flaming Feet: A Study of the Dalit Movement* (Bangalore: South Forum Press, 1993).

33. R. Ambedkar, "Away from the Hindus." In *Writings and Speeches* 5 (Bombay: Education Department, Government of Maharashtra, 1989), 409. Reprinted in B. R. Ambedkar, *Christianizing the Untouchables* (Madras: Dalit Liberation Education Trust, 1994).

34. Quoted in Keer, *op. cit.*, 255. See also M. K. Gandhi, *The Removal of Untouchability* (Ahmedabad: Navajivan Publishing House, 1954), 135–64.

35. Omvedt, *op. cit.*, 229.

36. B. R. Ambedkar, *The Untouchables: Who Were They and Why They Became Untouchables* (New Delhi: Amrit Book Co., 1948), 76.

37. See B. R. Ambedkar, "The Condition of the Convert." In *Writings and Speeches* 5. Reprinted in *Christianizing the Untouchables*.

38. Das, *op. cit.*, 609.

39. Quoted in Das, 595.

40. B. R. Ambedkar, *States and Minorities*. In *Writings and Speeches* 1 (Bombay: Education Department, Government of Maharashtra, 1979), 412.

41. Ambedkar, "Buddha or Karl Marx," 460.

42. B. R. Ambedkar, "The Untouchables and the Pax Britannica." In *Writings and Speeches* 12 (Bombay: Education Department, Government of Maharashtra, 1993), 145.

43. *Ibid.*, 146.

44. B. R. Ambedkar and Rao Bahadur Srinivasan, *A Scheme of Political Safeguards for the Protection of the Depressed Classes in the Future Constitution of a Self-Governing India, Submitted to the Indian Round Table Conference* (London: A. C. Phillips).

45. Ambedkar, "Buddha or Karl Marx," 460.

5

THE CONVERSION OF CASTE: LOCATION, TRANSLATION, AND APPROPRIATION

Nicholas B. Dirks

History is the subject of a structure whose site is not homogeneous empty time, but time filled by the presence of the now.
—Walter Benjamin

*I*F UNDER COLONIALISM CASTE BECAME THE FOUNDATIONAL BASIS of Indian society, caste itself was represented by colonial observers in vastly different ways. In the late eighteenth and early nineteenth centuries, caste was commonly seen as a harmonious social institution that legislated both the gradations of social rank and the divisions of labor that were fundamental to Indian society. As colonial power was consolidated in the late nineteenth century, British opinion was sharply redrawn, in part as a reaction to the rebellion of 1857, in part because of the intensification of Britain's reliance on India as the basis for its own claim to European power. Under the late colonial regime of knowledge and power, caste came to be seen as the primary sign of India's decadence, an institution defined by the other-worldly religiosity of a civilization that had long been incapable of either self-rule or material progress. When H. H. Risley—writing in 1909 just after the swadeshi movement had introduced the possibility of mass agitational politics as well as the specter of communal violence in Bengal—contemplated the political implications of the caste system, he confirmed British assumption by declaring that caste opposed nationality and would hinder the growth of nationalist politics. Caste was thus at once religious and political, an institution buoyed by the intransigent commitments of a decadent

Hinduism, and a resilient social form that expressed and contained the full range of social solidarities and political loyalties within Indian society.

Whether caste was praised or condemned, it was invariably defined as somehow essential to India, a transhistorical constant in Indian civilization. Theories could change; caste could not. Caste seemed necessary both for understanding and for rule. Shorn of history and politics, caste neverthe- less explained them both and sustained the colonial capacity to control them. If you could know a man by his caste, you could rule him that way as well. But despite the uniform fashioning of caste as useful for colonial rule, there were in fact major differences in the understanding and repre- sentation of caste, complicating the history of a monolithic colonialism and opening up spaces for contradiction and contestation. For if colonial discourses about caste can be functionally allied to colonial domination re- gardless of their actual content, we might also note that it is precisely the centrality of caste, and its linkage to discourses of rule, that made it so crit- ical to a great variety of other discourses concerning the history of tradi- tion, the nature of modernity, the character of social change, the position of women, the possibilities for democracy, the apotheosis of nationalism, the future of Hinduism, and the fate of Christianization, among many oth- ers. And on all of the matters there were major differences both within the most exclusive European enclaves of discourse and throughout the myriad worlds of colonial encounter.

Among the most important European voices in characterizing caste, de- scribing Indian society, and interpreting custom, tradition, ritual, and reli- gion, were those of European missionaries. Until the early nineteenth century, missionary activity was significantly curtailed by the East India Company's concern about keeping missionaries from disturbing local sen- sibilities, but Church pressure in England and the growing legitimation cri- sis of empire conspired to open India up to Christian prosyletization on a significant basis from the mid-1820s on. Less concerned about social order than moral transformation, missionaries tended to be more critical of In- dian society than official British opinion, identifying caste as the single greatest impediment to conversion, and Hinduism as the repository of bar- baric practice and moral depravity on a scale previously unknown in the civilized world. In general, although missionary opinion was varied and sometimes highly divided, missionaries tended to be more critical of caste than most other Western secular observers of India, even when they were substantially more sympathetic to India than those same observers.[1] Mis- sionaries frequently wrote detailed accounts of Hindu morality (or rather, the lack of it) and ritual practice, documenting everything from the mistreatment of women among the highest castes to the performance of human sacrifice among the jungle-dwelling tribal groups of central India. And missionaries often tried to put pressure on the British government to intervene more actively in Indian society, both to encourage the missionary efforts of the church and to use state power and influence to curb the most egregious abuses within Indian society. In the late nineteenth century in particular, missionaries used a variety of forms of publicity to bring reform agendas and concerns to the public eye, advocating everything from greater support for education to the need to abolish nautch dancing and hook swinging. And while missionaries played a role in social reform movements in India, missionary critiques frequently led to significant backlash on the part of social reformers, whose sharp reaction to missionary denunciation led them increasingly to distinguish social-reform projects from the nationalist movement. Ethnographies penned by missionaries circulated around local Church societies in England, providing ample grounds to alert English Christians to the difficulties confronted by missionaries, at the same time encouraging them to support the missionary venture as generously as possible.

If, in retrospect, missionary discourse seems problematic, sometimes even reprehensible, and if the history of missionary social concerns raises the contradictory relationship of modernity and colonial power, missionary concerns nevertheless were often echoed in social reform movements, and missionary discourses have occasionally had profound consequences for political as well as social movements, sometimes of a distinctly progressive kind. In this paper I will concentrate on the work of a particular missionary who worked in southern India, a man by the name of Robert Caldwell, who has now been canonized as one of the most prominent influences on the formation of the Dravidian movement. Caldwell, who wrote the most important grammar of Dravidian languages in the nineteenth century, proposing the autonomy and classical status of Tamil, wrote a great deal as well on caste, Hinduism, South Indian history, and the problems of Christian conversion. His influence has been important, if selective, and his work reveals the extraordinary complexities of tracing the genealogies of postcolonial knowledge in southern India today.

In evaluating the postcolonial effects of a colonial sociology of caste, it is important to attend to these contradictions and contestations, both because of the sometimes close genealogical connection between the postcolonial and the colonial, and because many of the older contradictions, though transformed, have been incorporated into contemporary discourses and debates about caste. Similarly, caste continues to be seen as one of the major impediments to modernity even as it is thought by many to survive as the sedimented marker of traditional privilege and oppression. The debate over the report of the Mandal Commission and its intended uses by V. P. Singh highlighted some of the contradictions in the contemporary politics of caste, creating conditions that made it possible—and frighteningly compelling—for right wing ideologues to assert that a newly defined notion of Hinduism might be less divisive than caste as a focus for national politics. Caste was turned into a symbol of traditional decadence, to be replaced by other forms of tradition—chief among which seem now to be the equation of Hinduness with Indian nationality and the celebration of Hinduism's extraordinary history of tolerance and incorporation—that will counter the mischievous use of caste by Congress and other pseudosecularists who have, so the charge goes, said one thing and done another.

If contemporary political discourse thus seems to echo many of the key features of colonial sociology and history, it is important to recognize that any attempt today to simply wish caste away inevitably finds itself in possible ideological alliance with forces of communalism that appear to make the myriad problems of the politicization of caste a relatively minor evil. Similarly, attempts to argue that caste, when harnessed to the discursive power of affirmative action policies, will become simultaneously stronger and more "colonial," may end up working against a variety of progressive impulses toward social legislation, even if those impulses at the same time become affiliated to populist politics of uncertain progressive pedigree. Through the maze of these now highly politicized debates, anthropology—and the allied study of the histories of colonial sociology, Indian religion, and social transformation—is now cast well outside the academy, for we must address the politics of the study of caste, even as we attempt sagely to evaluate the politics of caste itself. As debates become translated from one context to another, the politics of location and appropriation constantly seem to undermine our confident capacity to control the meanings we engage.

When turning our attention to the cultural politics of southern India, the possible alliance of discourses about caste with the terrifying proliferation of communalist sentiment, politics, and violence may seem less immediately dangerous than it does in most other parts of India. However, when we remember the particular history of Tamil politics, the dangers of casteist preoccupation and rhetoric seem altogether too clear. The kind of communalist discourse and politics that in much of the rest of India has surrounded the social identities of "Hindu" and "Muslim" has been inscribed in South India in the identities of Brahman and non-Brahman. On one hand, the non-Brahman movement has been the basis for, and site of, an extraordinary history of progressive politics, of contestation against cultural hegemony and social domination. However, on the other hand, there have been myriad concerns about the provincialization of South Indian politics, the way the non-Brahman movement has removed the south from participation in all-India debates and concerns, at times in terms of the explicit anti- or counternationalist implications of Dravidianism. And, while the south has kept itself relatively free of the anti-Muslim hysteria that has gripped so much of the rest of India, there are fears that a kind of nationalist backlash to the old Dravidian party (the DMK), whether driven specifically by the forces of Brahman hegemony or not (as charged by a number of Dravidianist critics in Madras), may ultimately fall under the enunciatory sway of the Hindu right. There are evident dangers when the voices of progressive politics seem—to most observers from outside the specific world of Tamil political discourse—to be mired in an overdetermined preoccupation with caste. Can a colonial/postcolonial preoccupation with caste provide adequate grounds for an emancipatory politics, not just in southern India but in the larger and more complex Indian nation today (and, conversely, does not the preoccupation with caste end up playing right into the hands of the forces of Hindu fundamentalism).

The problematic relationship between postcolonial politics and Orientalist forms of knowledge takes yet another form on the terrain I have just outlined, for it is now widely accepted that the foundations for these general assumptions about south India emerge not out of primordial tradition but rather from nineteenth-century Orientalist sources. Importantly, however, the most important source for general assumption comes not from official colonial discourse but from the writings of missionaries. The general conviction underlying much Dravidian radicalism—that the subjection of non-Brahman Dravidian peoples and cultures was based on the Aryan conquest of the Dravidian south—was in large part an invention of Robert Caldwell. Caldwell, who labored for fifty years in the Tinnevelly Mission, struggled against the hold of Brahmanic orthodoxy and caste consciousness, and like most other missionaries who had to justify the fact that they could only report conversions of the very lowest caste groups, was especially resentful of the Brahmans, who frustrated his efforts to proselytize. Caldwell developed a theory of cultural hegemony that was predicated on the ascription of foreignness, difference, and domination to Brahmans, who were affiliated with Aryan languages rather than Dravidian, northern India rather than southern, Brahmanic preoccupations with caste purity and ritual process rather than Dravidian receptiveness to devotional religion, and ultimately with racial attributions that, for the late nineteenth century, made the ultimate argument about difference. Much current scholarship—from nationalist history to general anthropology—continues to accept Caldwell's philological sociology of southern India, asserting that Brahmans and non-Brahmans occupied fundamentally different cultural spheres and that the roots of the anti-Brahman movement can be found in the social facts of south Indian adherence, in the absence of extensive Islamic influence, to primordial forms of Hindu hierarchy and social structure.

In this paper, I ask how we might evaluate a colonial tradition of learning and critique—one that was centrally embedded in the missionary project of conversion—that has provided the terms of a colonized discourse and associated politics that has laid claim to both some of the most progressive politics in India in the twentieth century and some of the most provincial and reactionary. I also ask about the contradictions inherent in tracing the genealogies of Tamil social discourses to Caldwell in particular, and missionary interventions in southern India more generally. Caldwell's antipathy toward Brahmans, both toward their social domination and their cultural hegemony, has secured a hallowed place in the citational structures and justificatory rhetorics of anti-Brahmanism up to the present day. At least two conspicuous features of Caldwell's discourse, however, have been either dropped or transformed. First, Caldwell's dislike of Brahmans was directly connected to his concern over Brahmans' resistance of conversion to Christianity and their considerable influence over lower social strata, who resisted as well: Brahmans, in other words, were the principal enemy of the Church in India. Second, raising a different kind of concern, Caldwell's rhetorical condemnation of Brahmans was part of a larger critique of caste altogether. Caldwell, and indeed the entire missionary movement in southern India in the mid to late nineteenth century, wrote against the iniquity of caste, frequently charging that until caste was abolished there would be no hope for either Christian conversion or social progress. While this condemnation of caste was in large part a condemnation of Indian society that participated in more general Orientalist critiques of Indian society, it frequently anticipated the kinds of radical critiques of caste that have been aligned with the most progressive movements in south Indian politics. One of the major breaks in the Dravidian movement surrounded E. V. Ramaswamy Naicker's concern about obliterating caste altogether, encouraging his followers, as a century before European missionaries had encouraged theirs, to engage in intercaste marriages and eschew all reference to caste in their everyday dealings with issues of ritual, devotion, marriage, commensality, and residence.

In tracing the history of missionary rhetorics of conversion, we must complicate the conviction of critical distance that seems so necessary in contemporary colonial discourse studies; the multiple histories of political appropriation ironically undermine the usual positions of critique. But at the same time, we need to attend very carefully to the deployment of missionary arguments about caste, for the rhetoric of conversion contained within itself a set of assumptions that were as problematic (and as curiously affiliated with our contemporary predicaments of location) as they were useful to other projects and groups in Tamil society. Charting the critical cartography of the politics of location—a necessarily reflexive and historicist enterprise—thus becomes central to this appraisal of missionary activities in southern India. And, as I shall attempt to show, the politics of location are inseparable from the politics of translation, thus invoking the questions brought to the study of language and history by nineteenth-century British missionaries, and those that frame the evaluation of the appropriations as well as transformations of this knowledge in the work of later political and cultural figures.[2]

Conversion, in other words, is not just a social process engaged in by groups such as the missionaries who sought to recruit followers into their own forms of religious practice and belief. Conversion in this paper becomes rather a more general trope for both translation and appropriation, a sign of the epistemological violence implied by myriad efforts to know, domesticate, name, claim, and ultimately inhabit "the other." Conversion is emphatically intransitive, a one-way street. As such, it is always a relationship of domination, even when the means of domination are much more subtle and even voluntary than in the more general colonial situation. We might recognize the dialectical logic conceived by Hegel in his characterization of the relationship between master and slave. The condition of domination for the master was the failure to recognize the self-consciousness of the other; the other was merely a means by which to procure the external validation of one's own self-consciousness. The predicament of the slave was domination by the master, but within that structure of domination was the possibility that both self and other could be recognized. In the end, the missionary could only recognize the other as heathen or as convert; conversion entailed a world of Manichean antinomy. But the slave could recognize the master as self; and perhaps it is this logic we can see play itself out in the appropriations made by colonial subjects of the rhetorics—the histories and anthropologies—of conversion once they were unleashed in the southern Indian environment. The histories of appropriation thus remind us of the myriad contradictions of the colonial encounter, all the while reiterating the violence of the past.

The Poetics of Conversion;
the Dialogics of Ethnology; the Politics of Philology

When Robert Caldwell first arrived in southern India, he found "the native converts sneered at by the governing race as 'rice Christians'; and disdained by the Brahmans and educated Hindus as a new low-caste, begotten of ignorance and hunger."[3] Caldwell first went to India in 1838 as a nonconformist missionary, but after a few years switched allegiances to the Church of England, working for the Anglican Society for the Propagation of the Gospel and toward the end of his life becoming a Bishop. Throughout his career he wrote yearly reports to the Mission Board back home, listing, as was common practice, the harvest in souls for each year, the ultimate index of missionary success. In the balance ledgers of salvation, the numbers not only remained frustratingly small and limited to specific areas but reflected the overwhelming fact that, for the most part, only lower-caste Nadars and even lower "untouchables" converted to Christianity in any systematic way. Caldwell thought and wrote extensively about the question of conversion, defending the Church against critics who maintained, first, that conversion by the poor and downtrodden was motivated only by material interests and was, as a consequence, inauthentic, and second, that the failure to convert Brahmans rendered the missionary enterprise an absolute failure.

Caldwell admitted that the lower castes initially came to Christianity for protection and material help, "the natural outcome of the circumstances in which they are placed."[4] He wrote, "I cannot imagine any person who has lived and worked amongst uneducated heathens in the rural districts believing them to be influenced by high motives in anything they do. If they place themselves under Christian instructions, the motive power is not theirs, but ours. . . . They will learn what good motives mean, I trust, in time—and perhaps high motives, too—if they remain long enough under Christian teaching and discipline; but till they discard heathenism, with its debasing idolatries and superstitions, and place themselves under the wings of the Church, there is not the slightest chance, as it appears to me, of their motives becoming better than they are."[5] But Caldwell used this assertion to predicate a more general theory of conversion, in which he held that conversion was more than the acceptance of a new religion—it was the more radical inculcation of new possibilities and predispositions, a readiness for new beliefs as well as new forms of knowledge and morality. The Church, like Christ, would take whoever would come, for whatever reason, and then endow them with the means and the conditions for a new kind of life.

Caldwell was aware that one of the principal motives for conversion, particularly among the agricultural classes, was the "desire of protection from oppression," a fact he found "natural and reasonable." But rather than alleviating the grounds for oppression, conversion often led to new forms of struggle and difficulty. Frequently, for example, landlords viewed conversion as an attempt "on the part of tenants-at-will to secure tenant right, or of people who have a tenant-right to make themselves proprietors." Newly converted Christians were accordingly often involved in long and bitter lawsuits, steeping them "in feelings of animosity against their opponents, who are also neighbors, and whom they ought to be endeavoring to convert."[6] Not only did this render problematic the notion that conversion was desired for its own sake, Caldwell worried that other motives could dominate the early lives of new converts, distracting both from the cultivation of Christian understanding and virtue as well as from the project of converting others.

Caldwell accepted that the task would be easier when more educated natives became converts to Christianity, and he resented the general antipathy and resistance of the higher classes. He noted, "Higher motives and a higher type of Christianity may be expected, and will be found, here and there, amongst educated converts to Christianity, especially amongst the young men that have been educated in our mission Anglo-Vernacular schools."[7] Like other missionaries in southern India, he celebrated those cases in which Brahmans converted to Christianity as instances of genuine theological triumph. But the triumph was ambivalent, the credibility of such conversion too often compromised by the gravitational force of theological difference and numerical improbability. Through the very frustrations of the missionizing process, Caldwell developed a serious appreciation of the relationship of knowledge and power, as well as of the ways in which cultural hegemony produced the terms on which knowledge and power would meet in India. In particular, he argued that despite vast differences among the indigenous population, "whatever their culture or want of culture—whether they are of high caste or low caste—the ideas and feelings of the entire mass have in the course of ages become so completely interpenetrated by the religion they all profess in common, and all classes, down even to the lowest, are so fast tied and bound by the iron fetters of caste, and so proud of these fetters, that the difficulties in the way of their conversion to Christianity are very much greater than those that stand in the way of the conversion of the ruder, but freer, aboriginal tribes."[8] Thus it was that Caldwell confronted the frustrations of his practice, and thus it was that caste was increasingly identified as the structural mechanism for, and ideological apparatus sustaining, the hegemonic sway of heathen obstructionism.

When Caldwell died in 1891, he was recognized not only for his extraordinary success in building up the Tinnevelly mission enterprise but also for his impressive scholarly writing, including ethnographic work on certain caste groups in the south; a detailed history of southern India; and a pathbreaking philological work on the history and structure of Dravidian languages. Caldwell's first major publication was an ethnographic work on the *toddy tapper* caste of Shanars who lived in the southern portion of the Tamil country and became one of the principal foci of Caldwell's proselytizing efforts.[9] The book provoked a largely negative reaction from the educated members of the Shanar caste, who were upset in particular with Caldwell's assertion that the Shanars were non-Aryan.

Caldwell had argued that one of the principal reasons for the large number of Shanar converts to Christianity was that they were not under the sway of Brahmanical religion, an argument he felt was supported by claiming the authentic and autonomous racial identity of Shanars as original Dravidians. He had written that some among the wealthier Shanars imitated the Brahmanical ideas and rites held by the "higher classes of the Tamil people" (p. 17), but argued that for the most part "their connexion with the Brahmanical systems of dogmas and observances, commonly described in the mass as Hinduism, is so small that they may be considered votaries of a different religion" (p. 13). He went on to anticipate the theory of Sanskritization, though in a far more critical light than M. N. Srinivas years later: "It may be true that the Brahmans have reserved a place in their Pantheon, or Pandemonium, for local deities and even for aboriginal demons; but in this the policy of conquerors is exemplified, rather than the discrimination of philosophers, or the exclusiveness of honest believers" (p. 13). Indeed, Caldwell used this recognition to assert the fundamental autonomy of Shanar identity through religious practice and racial origin as well as philological affiliation. He betrayed the usual missionary contempt for "native" religion, writing that "the extent and universal prevalence of their depravity are without a parallel. Where else shall we find such indelicacy of feeling, and systematic licentiousness" (p. 59). But he saved his sharpest criticism for Brahmans and Brahmanism, arguing that the cultural elite of Hindu India was much more responsible for their depravity than the lower classes, precisely because of their entitlement and education.

Indeed, Caldwell developed a complex sociology of religion in southern India, organized fundamentally around caste difference. While he noted that Brahmans have certain moral advantages over Shanars, he frequently condemned the effects of ritual discipline as either totally self-interested or lacking in sincerity. For example, while Brahmans have the custom of generosity, they give alms only because of the merit it accrues, not on account of compassion or brotherly love. And while Brahmans are educated and intelligent, they lack sincerity. As Caldwell noted, "The greatest of all obstacles to the spread of Christianity in India consists in the practice and love of lying which pervade all classes of the people. . . ." (p. 42)

The authenticity of Christian conversion, perhaps more than in any other social process, was judged by measures that could not be seen; thus, conversion was frequently evaluated in relation to the presence of possible instrumental interests, with the assumption that only when there was no interest could it be ascertained beyond doubt that there was genuine belief. It was of some residual satisfaction to Caldwell that he found the level of deceit higher as he went up the social scale; like many other missionaries, the lack of knowledge and the dependence of poverty was offset by the simplicity and sincerity of the lower classes who did convert. As Caldwell wrote, "But the longer I have observed the characteristics of the various castes, I have been the more convinced that as regards deceit, especially deceit in matters of religion, the Shanars must yield the palm to the high castes, and the high castes and all castes to the Brahmans. . . . Their lies are never so mature, so smoothly polished, so neatly dove-tailed, or uttered with so complacent a smile" (p. 42). Shanars could not dissimulate as could Brahmans, and when they disappointed or deceived, they did so merely because of their "procrastination, their indolence, and fickleness," not their fundamental duplicity. The insincerity of Brahmans also extended to their religious beliefs: "The follower of the brahmanical system professes to believe in 330 millions of gods, but in the majority of cases does not care a pin about any of them. . . . He never forgets his ablutions, his holy ashes, or any of the thousand and one ceremonies which sanctify his domestic life; but ordinarily he has not the smallest iota of belief in the divinities he so elaborately worships" (pp. 42, 43). Regrettably, Caldwell found that this very lack of sincerity hindered his efforts to convert Brahmans, who cared little about religious principle and yet obsessed constantly about ritual purity.

The religion of the Shanars had little to do with the religion of the Brahmans. As Caldwell argued, "In those extensive tracts of country where the Shanars form the bulk of the population, and the cultivation of the palmyra is the ordinary employment of the people, the Brahmanical deities rarely receive any notice" (p. 12). Caldwell asserted that "demonolatry, or devil-worship, is the only term by which the religion of the Shanars can be accurately described" (p. 12). Here, anticipating his later philological work, Caldwell noted an etymological basis for this separation: "Every word used in the Tamil country relative to the Brahmanical religions, the names of the gods, and the words applicable to their worship, belong to the Sanscrit, the Brahmanical tongue; whilst the names of the demons worshipped by the Shanars in the south, the common term for "devil," and the various words used with reference to devil-worship are as uniformly Tamil. . . ." (p. 25) Here Caldwell went far beyond the writing of other missionaries, betraying his deep, scholarly interest in origins, his Orientalist sense that only if Shanar religion, and by implication Tamil religion more generally, could be understood to have existed as a separate and autonomous system, could he genuinely believe that the power of Sanskritic inflection and Brahmanic belief might be undone. And for Caldwell, a theory of origins could best be demonstrated through linguistic analysis, with language as the only real sedimentary evidence of early history. Caldwell wrote that, "The fact of the terminology of devil-worship being purely Tamil throughout is to my mind a tolerably conclusive argument of the Tamil origin of the system. With reference to the social state of the Tamil people, it is clear that the origin of the words in common use will enable any one to determine what was introduced by the Brahmans, the civilizers of Peninsular India, and what existed before their arrival. All words relating to science, literature, and mental refinement, all that relate to an advanced civilization, and all words pertaining to religion, the soul, and the invisible world, are in the language of the Brahmans; whilst all words that relate to the ordinary arts of life, the face of nature, the wants, feelings, and duties of a rude and almost a savage people, are being exclusively Tamil, we are obliged to assign to this superstition a high antiquity, and refer its establishment in the arid plains of Tinnevelly and amongst the Travancore jungles and hills to a period long anterior to the influx of the Brahmans and their civilization of the primitive Tamil tribes" (p. 25). Thus, Caldwell the scholar was able to take heart in his lifelong effort to gain Christian converts among the lowly heathen Shanars of the southern Tamil country.

Caldwell argued further not only that demonolatry was unconnected with Brahmanism, it shared many features with the superstitions of Western Africa, "as a species of fetishism." After providing an account of devil worship (devil dancing, possession, etc.), he wrote that he had exhausted their "scanty creed" (p. 29). However, the one thing that could be said in favor of the bloody sacrifices that go along with devil worship is that they permitted some form of understanding of the Christian principle of sacrifice: "The fact of the prevalence of bloody sacrifices for the removal of the anger of superior powers is one of the most striking in the religious condition of the Shanars, and is appealed to by the Christian Missionary with the best effect" (p. 22). And yet, despite contrasting this approvingly with the incomprehension Brahmans exhibited toward Christian belief, Caldwell noted elsewhere that, "Devil-worship is . . . not only dissociated from morality but perfectly subversive of it. If the offering of bloody sacrifices conveyed to the minds of the Shanars any idea of their own demerit or of the necessity of expiation, the rite might be productive of moral benefit. . . ." (p. 37)

As for the progress of, and impediments to, conversion, Caldwell wrote: "It cannot be alleged of the Shanars, as of many other castes and classes in India, that they are fenced round by priestcraft and prejudice, and are apparently inaccessible to Christian influence. On the contrary, they are peculiarly free from prejudice, and peculiarly accessible. Without priests; without a written religious code; without sacred traditions; without historic recollections; without that aversion to Christianity as a foreign religion, which other classes evince: the chief obstacle to their evangelization is the density of their ignorance" (p. 71). At the same time, Caldwell wrote that this was not an ultimate barrier, that Shanars could grasp basic principles, that sometimes ignorance and illiteracy facilitated understanding since there were fewer obstacles in the way of belief. He also noted that the Shanars were compelled to convert, in any case, because of social pressure rather than individual enlightenment: "Partly through their indolent submission to custom, and partly through their inability to think for themselves, and their timidity, their habits of mind are 'gregarious' beyond those of any people I know. Solitary individuals amongst them rarely adopt any new opinion, or any new course of procedure. They follow the multitude to do evil, and they follow the multitude to do good. They think in herds. Hence individuals and single families rarely are found to relinquish heathenism and join the Christian Church. They wait till favourable circumstances influence the minds of their relatives or neighbours; and then they come in a body" (p. 69). Although the mass character of conversion seemed to fly in the face of Protestant notions concerning the individual nature of salvation, Caldwell, like most other missionaries, was fully aware of the social character of religious affiliation, though once again the level of individuation and agency is, for India, correlated negatively against the achievements of Brahmanic civilization, and in terms of a general condemnation of the intellectual and cultural capacities of the people among whom he worked throughout his life in southern India.

Despite his wide-ranging criticisms of Shanar religion, custom, and social position, Caldwell was taken by surprise when these same Shanars whom he sought to defend and convert reacted with such vehemence that he was forced to withdraw his book from publication after a series of riots against it took place. The reaction was principally caused by the Shanar elite's dislike of Caldwell's representation of their culture as quite divorced from Brahmanic civilization. Ironically, what once was the greatest sore point became, in the space of the next seventy-five years, the basis for Caldwell's most influential, and radical, contribution to Tamil political culture.

Caldwell did not abandon his central thesis, instead generalizing it to apply to all Tamil non-Brahmans. In his *A Comparative Grammar of the Dravidian or South-Indian Family of Languages*, first published in 1856,[10] Caldwell predicated many of his earlier assertions on far more systematically presented historical and linguistic arguments. He had already suggested some of his fundamental philological convictions in the book on Shanars. But now he extended this argument, proclaiming in his extraordinarily learned grammatical treatise not only the antiquity and autonomy of Dravidian culture but that the language Tamil, the "most highly cultivated *ab intra* of all Dravidian idioms, can dispense with its Sanskrit, if need be, and not only stand alone, but flourish, without its aid" (p. 49). He further held that Brahmans had brought Sanskrit with them when they moved from the north to the south, along with a strain of Hinduism that emphasized idol worship. As he wrote: "Through the predominant influence of the religion of the Brahmans, the majority of the words expressive of religious ideas in actual use in modern Tamil are of Sanskrit origin" (p. 51). Once again, the concerns of the missionary perhaps are nowhere more obvious than in this condemnation of Brahmanic religious influence, for in claiming the independence of the Tamils, he seemed also to claim their souls for Christian conversion.

Caldwell now clothed in impressive philological form his determination to prove the essential autonomy of Dravidian culture, language, and racial stock from the colonizing duplicity of Aryan Brahmans. He wrote that the Dravidians had occupied the southern portion of the Indian subcontinent some time before the Aryan invasion. It was only well after the invasion that they were subdued by the Aryans, "not as conquerors, but as colonists and instructors" (p. 109). As he wrote, "The introduction of the Dravidians within the pale of Hinduism appears to have originated not in conquest but in the peaceable process of colonization and progressive civilization. . . . All existing traditions . . . tend to show that the Brahmans acquired their ascendancy by their intelligence and their administrative skill" (p. 114). Caldwell further argued that "the Brahmans, who came in 'peaceably, and obtained the kingdom by flatteries,' may probably have persuaded the Dravidians that in calling them Sudras they were conferring upon them a title of honour." But in fact, Caldwell continued, the Brahmans, as representatives of the Aryan race, made the Dravidian groups accept the appellation of what in the north was reserved for the servile castes. Dravidians had even, Caldwell maintained, accepted the falsehood that Tamil was inferior to and dependent on Sanskrit, the language of the Aryan race and of Brahmans in particular.

Caldwell's argument was made by a combination of historical speculation and philological conjecture. In particular, he correlated the autonomous survival of Tamil with his estimate of the limited number of Aryan colonists who actually settled in the south. "If we should suppose that the Aryan immigration to Southern India consisted, not of large masses of people, but of small isolated parties of adventurers, like that which is said to have colonised Ceylon; if we should suppose that the immigrants consisted chiefly of a few younger sons of Aryan princes, attended by small bodies of armed followers and a few Brahman priests—the result would probably be that a certain number of words connected with government, with religion, and with the higher learning, would be introduced into the Dravidian languages, and that the literary life of these languages would then commence, or at least would then receive a new development, whilst the entire structure of their grammar and the bulk of their vocabulary would remain unchanged" (p. 577). Caldwell wrote that this was indeed the case, and that therefore it seemed reasonable to conclude that the Dravidians could throw off the shackles of the colonists. Here, he articulated his extraordinary recognition of how conquest and colonization could work through a subtle combination of flattery and intimidation. He also used his theories of history and language to disparage the position of Brahmans in South Indian society, directly challenging their cultural hegemony.

Caldwell's dislike of Brahmans was matched by his dislike of caste, a sentiment he shared with almost all the Protestant missionaries who worked in southern India in the nineteenth century. J. M. Lechler, writing from Salem in 1857, expressed a common conviction when he noted that, "the greatest enemy that opposes itself to us and the gospel is that absurdity of absurdity and yet most clever masterpiece of Satan—Caste."[11] W. B. Addis, writing in 1854, noted his conviction that "idolatry will disappear from India before the system of Caste from its inhabitants." Every missionary had hundreds of examples in which the appearance of conversion was sustained until caste intervened: "Caste is an evil that sometimes lies a long time dormant, but revives when the individual comes in constant contact with it, or family, or other circumstances conduce to such an effect."[12] Caste was consistently seen as the primary enemy of conversion.

Caldwell's generalized antipathy to caste, however, has been received in Dravidianist ideologies, principally in relation to the general critique of Brahmans, not as applying to caste divisions among non-Brahmans. Indeed, the critique of Brahmans has elaborated another kind of assumption in Caldwell's writing altogether; namely, that Brahmans and non-Brahmans were of different racial stock, that Dravidians were neither Indo-Aryans nor the original inhabitants of the subcontinent. Caldwell's articulation of the racial and historical basis of the Aryan-Dravidian divide was, in fact, perhaps the first European valorization of the Dravidian category cast specifically in racial terms, though he admitted the likelihood of considerable racial intermixture. At the same time, Caldwell was merely modifying conventional wisdom in his uncritical acceptance of an Aryan theory of race, in which Dravidians were seen as pre-Aryan inhabitants of India.

The Aryan theory of race, based as it was on William Jones's well-known "discovery" of the Indo-Aryan family of languages, had been developed by German comparative philologists in the 1840s and 1850s. It maintained that the speakers of Indo-European languages in India, Persia, and Europe were of the same culture and race.[13] While most Western writers on this subject ignored the racial equality this theory afforded Asian subjects of British colonial rule, Max Muller praised this common descent, though he lamented the demise of Indian civilizational genius in the medieval period. A number of Indian intellectuals used both Max Muller's praise and the general theory to claim equality and unity between Britons and Indians. Chief among these in the nineteenth century were Debendranath Tagore and Keshab Chandra Sen. Later nationalist leaders used "Aryan" less as a racial term than as a gloss for ancient Indian religious tradition. Dayananda Saraswati, Vivekananda, Ranade, and Annie Besant all urged in one way or another that the Aryan faith, which had united the north and the south in ancient times, be used once more to bring India together.

But in the Tamil country the theories of Aryanism, whether they linked or separated language and race, worked in most cases to do precisely the opposite. Frequently, British writers used the Aryan theory to justify a view of Dravidians as markedly inferior to Aryans. In the 1860s and 1870s, Henry Maine and Meadows Taylor emphasized the barbarity and superstition of the early Dravidians who "had infected ancient Hindu society and destroyed its pure Aryan features."[14] James Fergusson and R. H. Patterson took this argument one step further, arguing (in anticipation of Risley) that the caste system, with its built-in racial suspicion and endogamous taboos, made upper-caste Hindus more ambitious and progressive than they otherwise might have been, discouraging as it did marriage between Aryans and non-Aryans.[15] Small wonder, then, that Caldwell's grammatical writings were particularly influential, given that they were written in a spirit of praise and respect both for the Tamil language and for the cultural inheritance of the south. But Caldwell's influence has had an extraordinary career in Madras, exceeding in many ways the influence of any other European ideological formulation in the history of British colonial knowledge on the subcontinent. Partly this was because of the emphasis on language, which subsequently became appropriated and inscribed in the deification of Tamil around the cult of Tamil Tay (the mother goddess of Tamil).[16] Partly this was because, as I suggested above, Caldwell was the first to argue the dynamics and mechanisms of cultural imperialism, the operations of cultural hegemony itself. Despite the character of his condemnations of Shanar religion in his earlier writings, he managed to suggest that the autonomy of Dravidian religious practices was part of the same history that gave Tamil its foundational originality and Dravidian culture its civilizational integrity. But perhaps more than anything else, it was Caldwell's virulent anti-Brahmanism that made him the extraordinary figure he has become in the history of the Dravidian movement.

The Dravidian renaissance entailed a multitude of intellectual, religious, cultural, and political activities from the late nineteenth century on. While Caldwell made philology a privileged domain for scholarly investigations into the glories and autonomous history of Tamil, U. V. Swaminathan Iyer's "discovery" of Sangam poetic texts gave the Tamil country a classical literature of its own that could claim the antiquity, density, and poesy of any great classical civilization. Characteristically, the most dramatic activities in the "Dravidianist" movement found issues of language, and specifically Tamil, at their core. Sumathi Ramaswamy has recently argued that the importance of Tamil, and language politics more generally, to the history of Tamil cultural nationalism hinged on the capacity of language to be central to a wide variety of cultural and political movements, at the same time that language could be used to unite a wide variety of potentially divisive identities and groupings. But, as Ramaswamy makes evidently clear, the salience of Tamil also fed into the steady marginalization of Brahmans, and Aryanism more generally, from the core features of the Dravidian renaissance and its associated political movements. Despite the impressive character of the role of Brahmans in the Dravidian movement, e.g., such central figures as Swaminatha Iyer and Subramania Bharati, and despite, as Ramaswamy shows, the extraordinary rapprochement between certain areas of nationalist activity in the south and the key preoccupations of Dravidianism—including stressing Tamil literature and language, claiming a distinguished and autonomous Dravidian civilization, and asserting a distinct role for the south in the nationalist career of the Indian nation—Brahmans became increasingly inscribed as the internal other, the "Muslims" of the south.

If Caldwell could not have predicted that he would one day be affiliated with the rise of anti-Brahmanism on a major political scale in southern Indian politics, it was clearly his antipathy toward Brahmanic accomplishment that made him so appropriate a figure for Dravidianist appropriation. But it was also his central concern with language as the evidence for origins, as the basis for civilizational genius, as the medium for religious expression and experience, that marked him out as such a special figure. Caldwell's grammar, rather than his concerns with conversion and his dismissals of Shanar religion, survives as not only the most important European contribution to nineteenth-century Tamil intellectual history, but the most influential of all European constructions of South Indian culture and civilization.

Appropriations

The Dravidian movement took many forms, from the elite political negotiations and agitations of the Justice Party from 1916 through the 1920s, to the radical populism of E. V. Ramaswamy Naicker, who formed the social reformist Self Respect Movement in the 1930s and then established the Dravida Karakam in the 1940s, to the political normalization of Dravidianism in the 1960s and 1970s under the leadership of C. N. Annadurai and M. Karunanidhi. On occasion, Dravidianism exemplified the best of colonial nationalism by setting progressive social and political agendas; at other times, it popularized itself by sanctioning the dramatic rewritings of Sanskrit epics and religious traditions, it distinguished itself by advocating secularist and rationalist philosophies, it dramatized itself by pillorying Brahmans, Aryanism, Sanskrit, and Hindi, and ultimately it established itself through the consensus- and patronage-building politics of modern democratic India. E. V. Ramaswamy Naicker, or E.V.R., proposed the most radical forms of critique in the history of Dravidianism, using rhetoric that was as fiery as it was carefully modulated to suit particular occasions and concerns. E.V.R. maintained friendships with individual Brahmans while railing against Brahmanism; he championed subaltern political issues, organized intercaste marriages, designed new forms of secular ritual, only to also call for the destruction of the foreign agents of local domination: Brahmans, along with their language, religion, and ritual conceits. And in establishing the simultaneously progressive and xenophobic terms of Dravidian nationalism, E.V.R., along with many others in the movement, cited Caldwell's work as fundamental to understanding the history of Aryan imperialism and the foundational character of Dravidian self-reconstitution.

If it seems peculiar that Caldwell's Christian understanding of southern Indian society should be adapted to the purposes of an extreme form of secular ideology, it is even stranger that Caldwell's colonial view of Aryan cultural hegemony should have been so easily converted for the uses of a xenophobic nationalism that substituted Brahmans for British, Aryanism for modernity, Sanskrit or Hindi for English, and northern India for Europe. Thus, too, the conversion of meanings of caste from precolonial to colonial grammars participated in extraordinary processes of translation and appropriation. While Caldwell developed a peculiarly virulent critique of caste as a result of his frustration with confronting the apparent intransigence of caste hegemony and Brahmanical influence, he provided the terms for a critique of caste that were as radical as they were ultimately limited by the vilification of a particular social group. And this social group, namely Brahmans, could only be uniformly affiliated with the ideological apparatuses of foreign colonialism by appropriating the most specifically located critiques of Brahmanism by colonial missionization, a critique that, as we have seen, displaced its own frustrations with conversion onto a language of colonial hegemony that erased its own fundamental coloniality.

In tracing the myriad contexts as well as effects of Caldwell's work on Dravidian religion, language, and history, we learn about the hybrid transitivity between intention and effect, mimicry and mimesis, production and appropriation; about how the most extraordinary of all colonial enterprises—the attempt to convert the soul—can deploy philological, historical, and ethnological means that end up converting the very categories through which the soul itself can be (mis)recognized: e.g., Brahmanism and demonolatry, Hinduism and popular religion, learning and ignorance, sincerity and deceit, hegemony and resistance. The crime of conversion is thus the convention of colonialism, the displacement of the logic of translation from the instrumentalities of possession to the technicalities of truth, the deferral of the adequacy of translation from the inscrutibility of salvation to the intractability of sociology, the substitition of the context of conversion for the text of conversion itself. Retelling the political history of this paper reminds us of the violences that are committed against, and in the name of, identity, about how political utopia and desire become caught up in the violence and positivities of fundamentalism and official nationalism. In other words, we are confronted with the mystery and the travesty of translation.

The story of Caldwell and his grammar is, of course, centrally about translation. A grammar is a kind of metatranslation, a code book that unlocks and translates the structure of a language into universal rules, forms, and features. For the British missionaries who went to India in the nineteenth century, the project of translation was fundamental, for it was the project of bringing the gospel to the natives, of writing the Bible in native languages, of conveying universal truth in the particularistic settings of heathenism. By possessing a language, one could possess a people. But for Caldwell, the project of possession and translation involved creating a set of historical identities that both explained the difficulty of his own translation—namely, the goal of conversion—and was designed to create the conditions for a cultural liberation that would replace one hegemony with another, one form of flattery and conquest with his own. Caldwell's grammar was about the repossession and redeployment of language: the exorcism of certain Brahmanic religious possibilities and the celebration of new, racially purified identities that could now admit the instantiation of new utopias.

Conversion itself seems to be about the project of translation, the shifting of one context to another. Context, however, is no mere ornamentation, but the ground of intelligibility, the condition of possibility, that both defines and constructs the text. Caldwell's grammar was written not just about Tamil, but about the Tamil soul, which had to be freed from its particularistic moorings in order to be accessible to the universalizing rhetorics and ambitions of Christian colonization. The Tamil soul had been defined by Orientalist scholarship in terms of Brahmanical Hinduism, which Caldwell took great care to deconstruct; Hinduism was both conveyed and enforced by Brahmanical institutions, most significantly caste itself, which provided the basis for Brahmanical power at the same time it deployed that power through the hegemonic procedures so carefully delineated by Caldwell in his characterizations of history, language, race, and religion in southern India. But the identification of one form of hegemony obscured countless others. In one extreme, Shanar religious practice and sensibility could be degraded in order to create the conditions under which conversion and translation (or rather, the philological constitution of a language as historically autonomous and sui-generis), might be genuinely possible. In the other extreme, British colonial rule, and the relationship of the history of imperialism to the history of Christian missionization, becomes translated as the conditions under which the critique of Brahmanic domination can be made. Thus the appropriation of these Christian critiques in the service of secular anti-Brahmanism and counternationalist politics becomes yet another seemingly inevitable effect of the history of colonial/postcolonial translation.

These questions of (mis)translation, (mis)recognition, and (mis)appropriation double back and forth until we appreciate in new, more nuanced, ways the difficulties of writing about the identities signified by tropes of language, race, culture, history, community, and biology. The identification of a colonial history of constructing caste as fixed in primordial traditions of division and difference can be harnessed to Hindu nationalism as easily as it was once generated by colonial sociology; critiques of caste as the ground of cultural hegemony and social domination can be linked to secularist modernity as directly as they can be seen as the effects of the difficulties encountered by Christian missionization; the claims about the autonomy of racial, linguistic, and religious identities can be the cause for shame for one generation's cultural deprivation and for pride for another generation's cultural politics.

And so the politics of location, translation, and appropriation seem to underwrite this interrogation of the epistemologies of conversion in nineteenth-century colonial India at the same time these politics reflexively insist on the dangers of holding ourselves (however we define and wherever we locate ourselves) apart from the histories that we write about—the colonial misrecognitions of other times and places. We can no longer remain free from the problematic of conversion itself, nor suppress the contradictions of our own frustrations with converting a critique of colonial domination into an account of postcolonial liberation. We can no longer dismiss the sources and the mechanisms of discursive hegemony by simply proclaiming our own political engagement with a universalizing rhetoric of critique, distance, and demystification. We have before us the task of the translator, which, as Benjamin reminds us, accepts the possibility of translatability in terms of a language of truth that is most densely concealed in translation itself.

Notes

1. Duncan B. Forrester, *Caste and Christianity: Attitudes and Policies on Caste of Anglo-Saxon Protestant Missions in India* (London: Curzon Press, 1980), 7.

2. I mean to raise by implication a whole set of questions about the relationship between histories of colonial discourses and genealogies of anti/postcolonial influence. For ex-

ample, what is the relationship between missionary critiques of the practice of clit-oridectomy in East Africa in the early twentieth century and later critiques? What are the politics of location and translation here?

3. *London Times*, Obituary, October 19, 1891.

4. Quoted in *Reminiscences of Bishop Caldwell*, edited by his son-in-law, Rev. J. L. Wyatt, Missionary, S.P.G., Trichinopoly (Madras: Addison & Co., 1894).

5. Ibid.

6. Ibid.

7. Ibid.

8. Robert Caldwell, "The Languages of India in their relation to Missionary Work," a speech delivered at the Annual Meeting of the Society for the Propagation of the Gospel in Foreign Parts, April 28, 1875 (London: R. Clay, Sons & Taylor, 1875), 9.

9. *The Tinnevelly Shanars: A sketch of their religion, and their moral condition and characteristics, as a caste; with special reference to the facilities and hindrances to the progress of Christianity amongst them* (Madras: Christian Knowledge Society's Press, 1849).

10. Page numbers are from the 1875 edition (London: Trubner & Co., Ludgate Hill).

11. Archives of the Council for World Missions, South India. Housed in the Library of the School of Oriental and African Studies, London.

12. Ibid.

13. See the important new study of the development of ideas of race in relation to India in the nineteenth century by Thomas R. Trautmann, *Aryans and British India* (forth-coming).

14. See Joan Leopold, "The Aryan Theory of Race." *The Indian Economic and Social History Review* 7 no. 2 (June 1970): 281.

15. Ibid.

16. See the excellent dissertation by Sumathi Ramaswamy, *Engendering Language: The Poetics and Politics of Tamil Identity, 1891–1970*. Department of History, University of California, Berkeley, 1992.

6

MATERIALISM, MISSIONARIES, AND MODERN SUBJECTS IN COLONIAL INDONESIA

Webb Keane

Sound contrition and brokenness of heart brings a strange and a sudden alteration into the world, varies the price and value of things beyond imagination, . . . makes the things appear as they are.
  —Thomas Hooker, *Application of Redemption*

In the realm of ends everything has either a *price* or a *dignity*. Whatever has a price can be replaced by something else as its equivalent; on the other hand, whatever is above all price, and therefore admits of no equivalent, has a dignity.
  —Immanuel Kant, *Foundations of the Metaphysics of Morals*

*W*HEN CALVINISTS ENCOUNTER ANCESTRAL RITUAL in eastern Indonesia, they recurrently wrestle with problems of material value and that which is "above price," the human subject. The dilemmas posed for Calvinists by sacrifice, sacralia, and other forms of "idolatry" cast into sharp relief the ambivalent relations between Protestant spirit and material economy. Since overseas evangelization often overlays a contrast of present and past upon a parallel contrast of here and there, it also introduces a historical dimension into the relations of spirit and matter. The comparisons induced by religious conversion, like those arising in other colonial, ethnographic, or home-grown reformist contexts, provide a site for interpretive and evaluative reflection on culture as well as cosmos, reflections animated by a sense of moral and mortal consequences. The missionary seeks to change the convert's self-consciousness so that, in Hooker's words, things may appear "as they are." Evangelism is thus an assault, in part, on the explicit contents of what is construed as false knowledge. But the church also seeks to transform local practices, with implications that may exceed the range of explicit doctrine. Central to the Christianization of twentieth century Sumba (an island between Bali and Timor) is an effort to correct what appears to the missionary to be an illicit conflation of words, things, and persons. This process of disentangling is critical for the constitution of a modern subject (in at least some recensions) and its insertion into an emergent political economy, processes associated with Protestantism since Weber (1958; cf. Comaroff and Comaroff 1991). The process, however, can be a matter of ongoing and sometimes heated dispute, even among missionaries of the same church. In this paper, I will look at some of the difficulties they face as providing evidence of aporia that arise when a Protestant subject seeks to define itself by delimiting the functions and meanings of material objects.

Two sets of practices in particular serve in Sumba as potent synecdoches for the transformations of value and the subject, and occasion a high degree of controversy. Calvinists challenge *marapu* ritual (as well as Catholicism and Islam), both for what they take to be inauthentic language (formulaic prayer spoken "with open eyes" by priests) and for its apparent materialism (the ritual use of inalienable valuables, or sacralia, and sacrificial meat).[1] In drawing on both recent conversations with Sumbanese, and earlier writings of Dutch missionaries, I am not interested in adjudicating which accounts are ethnographically truer, nor in determining what lies on which side of a pre-existing cultural divide. Indeed, the latter project is increasingly problematic, as the work of missionization now lies in Sumbanese hands, and the current generation of Sumbanese Christians comes, in part, to interpret its own past through the interpretive frame provided by foreign missionaries (Keane 1995b). Rather, my interest is in problems raised by, and in, the encounter itself: I wish to show how the conjunction of pagan practices and Christian evangelism reveals and historicizes some common difficulties in distinguishing signs, objects, and subjects, and how these are to be assigned their proper values. In particular, I focus here on the problem of material objects, which seems to have been an especially destabilizing element in this cluster, and continues to trouble the present development-oriented government.[2]

The difficulties posed for the church by Sumbanese uses of valuable objects and animals are manifold. In practical terms, valuables circulate in a complex and expensive network of exchanges that so pervades social and economic life as to resist direct efforts at reform.[3] But these material practices also seem to raise in observers a degree of anxiety that exceeds mere practical considerations, and which, I suggest, arises at the intersection of theological iconoclasm with the founding assumptions of a modern political economy.[4] Traditions of iconoclasm—whether Christian, humanist, or Marxist—tend to view "fetishistic" or "idolatrous" practices with both contempt, as the mistaken and inappropriate elevation of inferior signs, and fear, as a threat to the powers and autonomy of the human subject (Mitchell 1986).[5] Such practices are especially problematic given their peculiar location at politically and emotionally fraught sites of conjuncture. As one writer characterizes Marx's use of the term, "the fetish is situated in the space of cultural revolution, as the place where the truth of the object as fetish is revealed" (Pietz 1985, 11). That is, the concept of fetish arises in a comparative context, as an observer's response to seeing *other* people attribute false values to objects.[6] While Marx appropriates the language of religion ironically to speak of political economy, we can follow the trope back to the questions of belief and value in which it originates, for, whether a matter of false gods or commodities, "fetish discourse always posits this double consciousness of absorbed credulity and degraded or distanced incredulity" (Pietz 1985, 14). But fetish discourse is seldom complacent in its incredulity. It is precisely because material things seem to be endowed with objective, culture-free values, in the eyes of both the bearers of a capitalist political economy and adherents of religious totalizations, that the encounter with others who evaluate things quite differently can be so troubling.[7]

Complaints and Accusations

When I first went to West Sumba, in 1985, it was the last Regency in Indonesia to still have a majority that claimed no adherence to a legally recognized religion (Hoskins 1987).[8] At that time, the balance—at least where I worked in Anakalang—was rapidly shifting, and when I returned in 1993, a Christian majority seemed to have emerged.[9] Today the coexistence of active ritualists (*marapu* people) and increasingly self-confident Christians produces tensions and resentments, but these are tempered by the fact that in social, economic, and political practice, members of both faiths are thoroughly intertwined. Christians and *marapu* people live together, work together, often intermarry, and are deeply involved in mutual exchange relations. In many cases, even brothers follow different faiths, with no apparent effects on the close cooperation they are expected to have. Although factionalism, contention, and feuding are rife, the fracture lines are rarely those of religion.

Sumba was incorporated into Dutch rule in the final burst of colonial expansion early in this century. Located off the main trade routes, drought-prone, thinly settled, infertile, and lacking a politically threatening Islamic presence, it had little to attract the ambitious, greedy, or geopolitically inclined, and remained the province of a handful of administrators and missionaries.[10] The island was given to the Orthodox Calvinist Church (Gereformeerde Kerk), and in 1902 made the responsibility of congregations in the provinces of Groningen, Drenthe, and Overijsel (van den End 1987, 7).[11] During the first decades, missionary activity was largely restricted to a few central locations in East and West Sumba.[12] In 1947, with independence, the Sumbanese Christian Church (Gereja Kristen Sumba) was formed (Kapita 1965, 45–46; van den End 1987, 34). The GKS retains close financial and advisory ties with the Netherlands to this day. In addition, there is a handful of Catholic missions run by German Redemptorists (Haripranata 1984; May and May 1980). Nonetheless, although Catholics compete for the remaining unconverted and are the object of some enthusiastic interdenominational backbiting, the most important contrast today, across most of the island, remains that between *marapu* and Orthodox Calvinist.

Despite my efforts at diplomatic neutrality, and in contrast to the general cooperativeness in practice that I have mentioned, I was often the recipient of partisan complaints about religious difference. A particularly long and vehement discussion arose in 1993, on my return visit to the village of Prai Bakul, an important center of *marapu* ritual.[13] I sat on the veranda with several men as they brought me up to date. They were especially proud of the fact that one of their *ratu* (*marapu* ritual specialists) had recently been elected head of the basic unit of local government, the Desa. This success, they boasted, was a tribute to the superior powers of their ancestor. The Desa Head added that none of his new colleagues bothered him about religion, since, after all, though we each have our own faith (an interpretation that is not, as it happens, officially sanctioned), they all share a single direction. After awhile, however, the conversation took a less complacent turn, as the Desa Head left and Umbu Delu began this complaint.[14]

How can those Christians claim to face God directly, and tell us our own drum was only made with human hands?[15] And they keep coming to my house to plague me. But after all, how do we get to God anyway? God created Adam and Eve. They in turn had Cain and Abel. Now they had children in turn and so on—how many centuries before arriving at my father? My father is in front. But now these Christians say "It's only God

which we face" But if not by way of my father, then how? . . . Christians
say "Only God, besides that there's nothing." Indeed, God made Adam
and Eve, all of humanity. God ordered them to replace God. Cain and
Abel, He handed it on to them after Adam and Eve were old. It descends
down to our parents. So the right comes from God to us—so we're God
now. But Christians say "That's useless."

At this point, Umbu Hiwa, a *ratu* in his fifties (and nephew of a Protestant
minister), took over, asserting his authority to speak of ritual knowledge,
and imposing his own canon of discursive coherence on the conversation:

> According to tradition, (this ancestor) was an ordinary human. We give
> rice and chicken to his spirit—not to gold, but to the ancestral spirit. We
> have gold so that he's there, as a reminder that our ancestor was rich. . . .
> The gold is in the house so we remember the spirit of our ancestor. It's
> like when you write things down in your book there, so you remember.

Here Umbu Delu interrupted:

> But *that* thing (i.e., the church) I call a subtle colonizer (Indo. *penjajah
> halus*)—every day you pay money. Give money to the minister, to the
> congregation. They say "If you don't give money, it's not under the com-
> mand of God." If you don't give them money, they won't read from their
> book. Pay that money. It's as if we buy it. But what are we buying? What
> we hear all our lives. It's the same too if we're sick—pay first. . . . Even if
> you pay, you'll still be dead in the end. When are we going to see the
> proof? They talk about hell—there's no proof of hell. The minister says
> whoever doesn't follow Christianity will go to hell. I was already a Chris-
> tian once, but they made me pay every day. Plus tithes every year. So I left
> the church. (I ask, what about the expense of sacrifices?) That's only once
> a year, and if there doesn't happen to be any, we give areca and betel, it's
> alright. But if there's no money in front of the minister, it's for nothing.

Umbu Hiwa intervened again:

> Let's compare religions. As for our proof, you can already see it—there's
> that gold. But the Christians don't have any proof. All they have is that
> book. . . . That's where we have our strength—*we* didn't make that gold.
> Each one of these houses has its gold, replacement of the name of the
> ones who brought it, so there's a sign that they really came here. But
> these Christians, all they have is a book. This book can be destroyed, or
> again its handiwork can fade. But as for the tomb of (our ancestor), we

can see it with our own eyes, we don't have to go far. . . . It's not easy to look at God, if it weren't for our ancestor who's at the side of God. We don't know God's place, only our ancestor does. We're not saying God doesn't exist—He exists (pointing upward). We say so, so do the Christians. . . . But *they*, they only *talk*, they say "These are my sins" while *we* use *materials*—like our ancestors did, they'd say "Give me a buffalo."

Then, having made his point, he reasserted the norm of acceptance, that there's really no difference, only the fact that humans have different opinions. Given that Prai Bakul is the center of a strongly *marapu* enclave, there was a certain element of self-confidence mixed in with the resentment. But similar notes were sounded elsewhere—for example, in the talk of Umbu Paji, who, having returned to the *marapu* after his first wife died, now saw himself as the holdout in his village after several waves of mass baptism:

It's like when you come here to visit: we roll out the mat for you to sit on. That's the base. That's what our gold is. It's just dead matter, but to say the name of God, you need a base. . . . Now those Christians say we make stones into God, but that's not so. The stone altar is where we meet. It's like if I promise to meet you, we need to have someplace to meet, right? How can we meet if there's no sign? . . . The Psalm says God exists everywhere—in the house, on the veranda, in the forest. Well, if this is so, how come when we pray (in these places) they tell us it's Satan? Take the Owner of the Land (*Mangu Tana*). Like when you arrive at someone's house and you call out (the greeting) "Hey, house-owner!" (*O mangu uma!*)—who's that? It's the person who made the house! So too, the Owner of the Land is the Creator. . . . The ancestors didn't know God because they didn't have the Bible. Only a Bible that isn't read, isn't written; that is, only gold. Now they say we when we pray at the spring we're praying to Satan. But it wasn't Satan who made that spring, it's God. So if we take water from the spring, why not give thanks? *We* didn't make that spring! So too in the secret room (i.e., the bedroom), they say it's wrong to pray there. But what goes on in that room is not the work of our own hands, such that children come to be created in the womb of women.

These conversations bring up many of the most prominent leitmotifs when *marapu* people talk about religions (I'll turn to the Christian side of the story in a moment). They do not challenge the truth-claims of Christianity—indeed, they cite the Old Testament in their own defense. The conflict lies instead in the nature of practices and their interpretation, involving both criticism of Christian and defense of *marapu* procedures. The challenge to Christians given above touches on three issues: mediation, language, and money. The defense of the *marapu* appeals to norms of deference, claims of realism and symbolism, and the rhetoric of the state. One possible resolution appeals to a concept of functional equivalence among religious practices that implicitly seeks to lay claim to a relativistic interpretation of religion and, (against most available evidence) state policy.[16]

The note of humility with which Umbu Paji closed is characteristic, for he was implicitly contrasting his own stance against the arrogance displayed by Christians in both their knowledge claims and liturgical practice. So, too, Umbu Delu started off by speaking of the Christian presumption to face God directly, rather than through the mediation of ancestors. The problem is in part a matter of knowledge: as Umbu Hiwa put it, we don't know where God is located. Christians lack proof for their claims that is as convincing as the *marapu* possession of material remnants of the ancestors. This is more than an epistemological dilemma, however. It is a statement about hubris. After all, *marapu* people don't challenge other Christian claims to knowledge, accepting the additions to ancestral history apparently provided by the Old Testament (for example, many people, even those most embittered and alienated by the new state of affairs, speak of ancestral valuables as coming from Babel). But the claim to be able to address God directly is a form of arrogance at variance with every expectation of respectful behavior in Sumba. Umbu Hiwa reflected this, saying that, unlike Christians, "we don't say his name." Or, as someone else put it to me in the heavily laden terms of state rationality, "After all, you don't communicate directly with the President in Jakarta, do you? You go through the Desa Head, the District Head, the Regent, and the Governor." What Umbu Delu and Umbu Hiwa were claiming for themselves was greater refinement, shown in their respect for deferential mediation.

The nature of this mediation is critical. In addition to seeking to face God directly, Christians just use talk; that is, they make no offerings. One sign of the arrogance of Christians is that they eat meat without prayers of invocation—they kill, *marapu* people often say, simply in order to eat meat. Doing so is doubly vulgar, as it emphasizes both the materiality of the animal and the willfulness of the action. In contrast, deference is expressed by displacement. *Marapu* rituals, however much they may seek desirable ends, such as wealth and fertility, are enacted as inescapable obligations arising from an origin beyond the wishes and intentions of the participants. The value of displacement is also embodied in ancestral valuables. This is why Umbu Delu was offended by the Christian claim that the drum named for the ancestor was made by human hands. The contrast between the God-given, or natural, and human production has long been a defining tenet of Christian attacks on idolatry.[17] One response to Christian attacks is to insist that the present drum (despite periodic ritual renewals) is consubstantial with that left by the ancestors. Note that Umbu Paji took up the argument of idolatry and implicitly turned it back on the Christians: we give thanks for that which was palpably not our own production. This echoes Christian claims that we owe thanks to God as the source of everything—and transforms the nature of *marapu* prayer from interactive request or cajolement to an expression of thanks. But a second attack on idolatry is that it mistakes the very nature of objects, and by worshipping them takes them to be subjects. Umbu Hiwa and Umbu Paji, both sophisticated apologists, had ready responses: they essentially accused the Christians of error, of mistaking symbols for substances. At least at the level of explicit propositions (actual practices suggest a more complex set of assumptions), they claimed to agree with the Protestant distinction between material and spiritual, and asserted that *marapu* objects are material signs of immaterial substances.

Umbu Delu's economic complaint (which others also stress) is especially interesting, because one of the recurrent claims by *Christians* is that *marapu* ritual is wasteful. About twenty years ago, one of the first Anakalangese to be ordained composed a song with a line that ran, "What good is prayer, the *marapu* words? (They) just use up the little chicks." In a similar vein, one man justified to me his baptism, in the mid-1960s, in terms of neither truth or ethics but practical expense. He figured the cash given to the church came out to less than all the chickens and pigs he sacrificed in his rice fields each year. Pak Pendeta, a retired minister, one of the first to go through the on-island Dutch theological school system, told me, in speaking of his evangelical efforts in the 1940s and 1950s:

> I'd ask them, why are they afraid of the *marapu*? Because they created us, and if we don't respect them, we'll get sick. I'd tell them, "Yes, that's true, we must be afraid. We're afraid because we can't *see* Him. So the ancestors used gold, gongs, spears, those humans—they became signs that Lord God is there—like a king or a *ratu*—people fear them because of their power. So now we don't need to pray. God doesn't want us to bring chickens anymore. God sent me so you can return to God—not that wood, not that rock. What saves us isn't wood, rock, cattle, but Lord Jesus.

He, like early missionaries, sees non-Christians as living in a state of constant fear. His representation of material media is similar to those of Umbu Hiwa and Umbu Paji in one respect: he sees them as replacements for something that is absent; that is, as representatives and signs of something else. It is only because that something else has no palpable form that material objects are needed. But now, with an encompassing account, carried in the words of the Bible, these substitutes are no longer necessary.

Devil Worship and Misrecognition

The interwoven themes of economy and of signs mistaken for real things (and vice versa) play their roles in a contemporary context of burgeoning state power, an ideology of development, and the accompanying pressures for rationalization of markets and institutions. They are also shaped, however, by church policies and terms of debate dating back to the early years of the mission. Confronted with what looked to some like a living Old Testament world, the Dutch were often at great odds amongst themselves as to how to interpret and respond to ritual practice. Much of their interest was in a perennial problem in Christian theology, the role of material objects in religion, brought to a focus by the practical need to make decisions about the distribution of offerings. Practical need was, however, already anticipated by prior scriptural knowledge, as expressed by one of the Mission Deputies:

> The wretchedness of paganism comes from the abominations which they commit and "the fear of the dead, with servitude to whom they are subjected all their lives" (Hebr. 2: 15). That wretchedness comes out more deeply in what the Scripture teaches us about the way in which the poor heathen seeks comfort and deliverance. For he brings offerings which he supposes he offers to the gods and actually he offers them to devils. . . . The Sumbanese know of the one great God, who rests and to whom little service is shown; moreover, he knows of deceased ancestors, who exercise great influence on the lives of men. He divides these into good and evil; the good intends well-being for their descendants and confers on them only favors, the evil bestows perdition upon men; they avenge themselves for the evil that was done to them in their earthly lives and for negligence of their memory. Now the Sumbanese seek to satisfy these evil spirits through offerings. Their idol-worship is therefore direct devil-worship. . . . The God of truth receives there not the least honor; there is likewise no recourse to be had to the only Helper in their need. In one word: that in the midst of all pagan wretchedness, this is the greatest, that one has no helper. Poor pagan! (H. Dijkstra, 1902. Den duivelen offeren. *Het Mosterdzaad* v. 21; in van den End 1987, 122–23).[18]

As in current debates, the problem here is not entirely one of truth. The European seems to find himself in the same universe as the Sumbanese, one that can indeed be identified in Old Testament prototypes. By Dijkstra's account, both European and Sumbanese know of God, and it seems both know of other invisible beings as well. Since the Sumbanese err not in their intentions but in misidentifying the recipient, the issue is not whether invisible beings populate the world but what their real natures are. The pathetic condition of the pagan is twofold: a matter of confusing devils with gods, and the resultant life of fear without help.[19] The practical outcome of false identification is misdirected practice: offerings have the wrong destination (a destination of whose existence Dijkstra seems to be in no doubt).

A more self-consciously scientific spirit presents itself in the report of a visit to West Sumba after some fifteen years of missionization.

> Lumbu Langa had a long time ago removed the marapu-stones (i.e., altars) from his garden, and as his maize was no less than that of his neighbors, he therein knew that it is evident that things go just as well without offerings. . . . And now the conclusion is obvious. That one makes offerings yields nothing, but is merely harmful, the misery of chickens and buffalo. And so as time goes by one becomes detached from the marapu. Naturally that says nothing about the positive, only that the old was broken. But it is indeed still the time to bring the Gospel. There exists the risk that otherwise men become indifferent, that they let go of the old without desiring the new. (J. F. Colenbrander, letter to the Sumba Mission Deputation, October 7, 1922; in van den End 1987, 218–19)

By presenting the Sumbanese as born scientists stumbling across an empirical demonstration, Colenbrander's narrative implies that they are following a natural relationship of causality between active subjects and an objective world. He also implies that the offering mediates nothing—it is reducible to its material form, chickens and buffalo, and thus to the economic calculation of losses. In addition, his worry reveals another important theme, that of functional equivalents. He can imagine a world without any belief at all, and sees in the new religion a functional substitute for something that is absent.[20]

In theological terms, an especially disturbing dimension of material offerings is the fact that they can be interpreted economically, still an important issue today. They are capable of diversion into alternative uses and value frameworks (Appadurai 1986; Thomas 1991). In contrast to verbal performances, their semantic meaning and social value are relatively underdetermined (see Keane 1994).[21] Furthermore, unlimited by clear distinctions between religious and secular action, the expenditure of sacrifices threatens, in missionary eyes, to become indefinitely excessive. This is brought out when D. K. Wielenga, writing for a mission-society journal, seeks an elevating comparison for the Sumbanese (and quietly assumes for himself the position of the Apostle):

> "You men of Athens, I perceive, are in every respect like religious men," so Paul was once forced to exclaim, seeing the "civilized" Athens so full of altars of numerous gods and goddesses that one built one there for the unknown God himself, as one was afraid to have forgotten one, whose wrath one might then unwittingly bear. And in Sumba, the "uncivilized" land, one stumbles, as it were, over the numerous offering stones. For he too is "in every respect like religious men." . . . So the men of Athens reach out the hand to the "poor uncivilized Sumbanese." . . . A Sumbanese, however, has quite little self-confidence. From his birth to his death, he lives in animistic dependence. Even the most simple and everyday actions are supposed to be dependent on the will of the supernatural powers. It is then also astonishing, the number of offering stones that one comes upon everywhere, different in structure and different in intention. One not only offers under all green trees and on all high hills, but also at each house and at each village and in each garden. (Wielenga 1910, 72–73)

Like Dijkstra, Wielenga emphasizes the affectual dimension, portraying a fearful native more deserving of pity than scorn. His real interest, however, is ethnographic, and he devotes the bulk of the article to describing *marapu* ritual, giving a wealth of detail that fleshes out the trope of excess with which he closes: "And so one has offering stones for the fish in the sea and the birds in the air and the wild animals in the fields and the forests. One stumbles over the offering stones. Poor Sumba, so sunken in idolatry and spirit worship!" (Wielenga 1910, 99).[22]

Whereas for Dijkstra the offering involves real intercourse with real others who are misidentified, for Wielenga the sacrifice is a material waste predicated on false ideas—there is no recipient, only objective matter. A third view, the logical underpinnings of which were already implied by Colenbrander, becomes over time increasingly central: offerings have no recipient, but they serve symbolic or social functions. The ambiguous status of material media provides the occasion for some evangelical irony, in Wielenga's account of a reconnaissance trip to West Sumba. There, he watches the sacrifice of a rooster. After the prayers have been said and the bird plucked,

> The children came back and brought along a tuft of the tail feathers. Umbu Pandji took it and stuck it above us in the roof amidst the alang-

alang (thatching material). That was for the *Marapu* of the house, that was his share of the slain animal. At which feathers he can see that one had not forgotten him.

"If I were the Marapu in this house here, I would rather the flesh than the feathers," I said.

"*What* did my lord say?"

"Well, that the *Marapu* here is already quite soon contented. We men will presently eat the flesh, and he must be lucky with but a tuft of feathers. Even the dogs are yet better off, for they still get the little bones and the pigs under the house will devour the intestines. No, you fellows trifle a bit with the Marapu!"

"But still he sees our good will; we have given to him, haven't we?"

"But when you brought a chicken to the king this morning and asked him for a favor, what did you do then? Perhaps the same thing, hastily killed and then put some feathers on a plate and give them to Umbu Timba, while taking the meat yourselves. I should certainly like to see the face of the raja then. I think that he would prettily abuse you and fling the plate with the feathers at your head."

"That is rather natural, but with our *Marapu* it is somewhat different. He is content with this. Such is the custom of old days here. It is a sign (*teeken*) that the guests have not forgotten him, the spirit of the house." (Wielenga 1908, 172–73)

The play of irony here lies in taking literally the materiality of the offering—that what *marapu* seek, for example, is actual gain and not gestures of deference—which provokes the response by Umbu Pandji that the offering is merely a sign. Wielenga, at least as he presents his tactics to the Dutch reader, moves between two possible forms of misrecognition. In Socratic style, he wishes to cast doubt on the ritual by displaying himself as mistaking a sign for the real thing.[23] He does not challenge the reality of the *marapu* but rather the appropriateness of the medium. At the same time, his irony is directed at the materialism of Sumbanese desires: they imagine *marapu* to be as covetous as they are themselves. This inappropriateness, however, is itself predicated on a greater misrecognition of lesser spirits for higher ones.

The Problem of Meat

It is relatively easy for converts to abandon altars and cease making offerings to gold, since in their apparently "religious" character they seem readily distinguishable from "practical" functions. Meat is another matter, because as food (unlike the token portions in Holy Communion), it is hard to categorize as lacking immediate practicality, and because as the medium of social feasting, it is difficult for people to escape the practices in which it plays a role. This gives rise to probably the most contentious and long-lived debate in the course of Sumbanese conversion, concerning the policy to adopt toward sacrificial meat.

Large-scale sacrifice and commensuality occupy an important part of Sumbanese ritual and social life. Most rituals require the killing and eating of at least a chicken or two, and at some events, such as funerals, scores of buffalo are dramatically slaughtered in the village plaza for distribution among many hundreds of guests. In parts of West Sumba, the feasting season is the stage for vigorous status competition. In major feasts, meat is distributed both raw and cooked, the latter consumed on the spot, the former apportioned among guests to take home. Hosts make great efforts to assure that everyone is given a share, and to be overlooked or to refuse one's portion are equally sharp offenses. To demand of converts that they withdraw from this commensuality is to threaten their participation in society altogether. In the early days of the mission, this did not seem to be a problem; in fact, what seemed to be in question was whether the Sumbanese would *permit* the Christian to take part.

> Also POS tried to penetrate more and more into Sumbanese life, although little was said of a direct mission campaign. So he told of a "prayer time" which was held by them and which he attended. . . . First, with certain ceremonies, the Marapu were given offerings consisting of cooked rice, roasted hens, buffalo meat, and betel with areca-nut. . . . It happens there very "informally" and one had no objection that the missionary also attended this ceremony. He himself was permitted to participate in the meal, which consisted of the offerings presented. (Wielenga 1926, 112)

According to Wielenga, however, when Colenbrander mentioned this event in a report, "a sister of the congregation in the fatherland" criticized this eating of sacrifices and a long controversy ensued. In arguing their cases, the partisans are in part concerned with questions of strategy, but also encounter the ambiguous status of material signs.

In 1914, Wielenga, who had been working in East Sumba, published an article called "On the Eating of Flesh Offered to Idols" (see van den End 1987, 196). He argued in pragmatic terms that the missionary should be permitted to eat sacrificial meat in order to maintain good relations with the Sumbanese. So important was feasting there that to refuse to participate would be to cut oneself off from them. The following year, Krijger, who ran the West Sumba mission from 1912 to 1922 (van den End 1987, 16–17), announced that he had forbidden his native evangelists to eat sacrifices. This public controversy led to a special assembly of missionaries in 1917. The key texts for this and all subsequent discussion of the issue are 1 Cor. 8 and 10, in which Paul warns against the temptations presented by others' idolatry:

> But I say, that the things which the Gentiles sacrifice, they sacrifice to devils, and not to God: and I would not that ye should have fellowship with devils. Ye cannot drink the cup of the Lord and the cup of the devils: ye cannot be partakers of the Lord's table, and of the table of the devils. . . . If any of them that believe not bid you to a feast, and ye be disposed to go; whatsoever is set before you, eat, asking no question for conscience' sake. But if any man say unto you, This is offered in sacrifice unto idols, eat not for his sake that showed it, and for conscience' sake: for the earth is the Lord's, and the fullness thereof: Conscience, I say, not thine own, but of the other: for why is my liberty judged of another man's conscience? . . . Give none offense, neither to the Jews, nor to the Gentiles, nor to the church of God (1 Cor. 10: 20–21, 27–29, 32, King James version)

The point is not any effect of meat itself, which is merely objective matter and bears no inherent consequences (1 Cor. 8, 8). Rather, the problem is the effect of being seen eating the meat of idolators *by others*. Others, lacking the knowledge that one has oneself, may succumb to temptation, their resolve weakened by one's own misconstrued example.

The assembly was inconclusive, as opinions were split and the matter left to case-by-case decisions (van den End 1987, 196). Meat continued to introduce a remarkable element of instability into mission practice; nearly a generation later, a different pair of missionaries replayed the initial conflict. Again, the debate reveals an interaction between theological interpretation and ethnographic contexts: the more tolerant view in each case is taken by the missionary with experience in East Sumba, where the competitive politics of meat are less pronounced. By 1930, converts in West Sumba were subject to discipline for accepting meat sent to them at home from a *marapu* feast, an act that was permitted in East Sumba. Justifying the prohibition, W. van Dijk, who had taken over in West Sumba in 1932, cited 1 Cor. to the effect that eating sacrificial meat must be shunned as a snare for new Christians, lest they be gathered back into the circle of idol worshippers (van den End 1987, 344, n. 1). Objecting to this was P. J. Lambooy, based in East Sumba from 1924–48 (van den End 1987, 17).

In 1932, when both men were on leave, they were called before the Board of Deputies to discuss the matter, but again the Board remained divided. Shortly thereafter, Lambooy defended himself to the Deputies. What Paul criticizes, he asserted, is participation in a sacramental communion with a god or goddess, through which the communicant receives new life.

> In Sumba, the killing and eating of animals has an entirely different meaning. There it is a food given to the deceased ancestors. Materialistic as the heathen is in his religion, he thinks of his deceased as still wanting nourishment. . . . At the end of the feast the praying priest may eat up (the liver presented to the dead). The rest of the animal is divided among those present. This last food is not having a communion with the ancestors through eating. The communion is only practiced through being present at the feast, . . . It is therefore not desirable for our Christians to go to the feasts and to participate therein. (P. J. Lambooy, letter to the Deputies of the Sumba Mission, 25 July 1932, in van den End 1987, 345)

He set participation in the feast itself in sharp contrast to the meat sent home with the guests after the same feast: "Therein is rightly expressed a demonstration of friendship or fellowship, but this has no meaning of sacramental communion with idols." (Lambooy 1932, in van den End 1987, 346). To forbid Sumbanese to eat meat that has been brought to the house "would be a great insult. One holds this as the breaking of all bonds and friendship," a strategic error, "to the great detriment of the spreading of God's Kingdom in Sumba." Instead, one must sort out religious and secular functions—something that Lambooy, anticipating later policies, attempted to perform by mapping different intentions directly onto different pieces of meat.

In the face of this continued controversy, the Deputies asked Colenbrander, who had returned to the Netherlands, to undertake a Biblical exegesis. His report supports Lambooy, but by drawing in part on a somewhat different principle: apparently following the libertarian strain in Orthodox Calvinist views of government (Wintle 1987, 59–60), he asserted that to restrict the eating of meat would be too interventionist:

> One must make distinctions between the meat at the offering meal itself and the meat that comes from it. . . . The former is obviously forbidden both for the risk that it will be an offense for another and for the risk of exposing oneself to the danger of a sphere where the evil power prevails. (J. F. Colenbrander, "Eten van offervleesch," 1932, in van den End 1987, 357)

In principle, there is nothing wrong in receiving this meat at home, however—that remains a matter for the individual conscience. He goes on to
compare this meat to the Holy Communion, for no one objects to giving
leftover bread and wine to the poor or sick, "because it is felt there there is
no longer the least connection with the table of the Lord." In conclusion,
having drawn a sharp distinction between matter and spirit, he returns to
the overriding principle:

> One must also in the Missionfield not go further than what the Lord said
> in His Word, not to rob the freedom which the Lord granted. In certain
> respects it is easier only to set this rule, that one should never eat any
> meat with which some pagan act has taken place. But then that would be
> a rule which God's Word does not give. (Colenbrander 1932, in van den
> End 1987, 357)

Indeed, by leaving persons free to deal with the dilemma, they are forced
to reflect on their actions. This antiregulatory stance, therefore, is not only
a matter of principle in its own right but serves as a means to further the
development of self-consciousness. The pressure exerted by *practices* can, as
it were, induce effects in the *subject*.

Yet in the end, the restrictive view won out, in a resolution delivered by
a Special Assembly of Missionaries in 1934:

> A Christian, through the accepting and eating of meat brought to the
> house (that comes) from animals slain according to pagan *adat*, of which
> he knows the source, has objective communion with the worship of the
> devil. Moreover, the accepting and eating of meat as mentioned above is
> (a) unworthy of the Christian, (b) dangerous for the Christian and the
> young Christian congregation, (c) contrary to the commandment of
> brotherly love. Also on the ground of all these considerations, the ac-
> cepting and eating of such flesh is in conflict with God's Word, for which
> reason . . . our Christians must hate and eschew such a thing from the
> heart. (Special Assembly 1934, in van den End 1987, 369).

This policy, which even van Dijk remarked was "really very harsh" (van
den End 1987, 344, n. 1), seems to reflect the increasingly isolated position
of S. J. Goossens, who by 1939 broke with the church altogether and
joined the Free Church (*Vrij Gemaakte Kerk*) (Kapita 1965, 31–32). Indeed, the policy remained unworkable without either Christian withdrawal
from social intercourse altogether or the cooperation of *marapu* people. The
former path was finally taken by Goossens's schismatics, who established a

closed compound in which not only the eating of sacrificial meat but also all other material media of sociability—tobacco, coffee, and betel—were eliminated. The latter path has become common as *marapu* followers find their numbers shrinking and thus become increasingly dependent on Christian support in rituals and other exchange events. By the 1980s, Anakalangese sponsors of large *marapu* rituals often omitted from the offering prayers one pig that would be fed to the Christian visitors.

The course of this debate replays problems faced, under the rubric of idolatry, by Christianity's encounter with paganism from the start, and of Protestantism's challenge to Catholicism as well.[24] More specifically, I wish to draw out three points here: the difficulty Christians encounter in clarifying the distinction between performative language and material object, the problem of social functionalism, and the ambivalently "modern" models of economic matter that result.

Exchange Value, Use Value, and Spirit

If the notion of economic rationality presupposes a subject that has a clear understanding of material objects, religious confusion over objects implies an earlier, irrational economy.[25] That *marapu* people are to be seen as lost in economic irrationality is abundantly clear from missionary perspectives and some Sumbanese representations of the past as well.[26] A typical passage comes from Wielenga's first visit to West Sumba. While it does not directly address ancestral ritual, the episode is revealing for the light it casts on the problem of value. Wielenga has arrived at a small port, where he meets Umbu Dong, a noble from the interior.

> He was a still inexperienced nature-child, his many years notwithstanding. A true child of the hills, gullible before the cunning Endenese (Muslim traders). And now he was in the process of doing so-called "business." He wanted to sell a month's worth of accumulated yellow dye-wood. He had already earlier received some goods as an "advance," but now would settle up. . . . And so, how many bunches would he provide? He had some thousand bundles lying above in the hills. And what now will he get for the thousand bundles? Our Umbu at this named: a chopping knife with an ivory handle, three rolls of white material, one roll of black material, one mamuli, and some more. We wrote it all down and came to the high assessment of about f. 90. Thus he must provide a thousand bundles of wood for f. 90 of goods. Now four bundles are the same as one *pikol*, the same as f. 4. That is according to Bartjes thus f. 1000. (Wielenga 1908, 257–58)

This is, of course, a familiar scene in colonial literature, in which the native is characterized by the inability to know the true value of things. The scare quotes that frame "business" and "advance" portray the activity itself as mere mimicry of the real thing, a stock figure in colonial perceptions (Bhabha 1987). Anakalangese today sometimes still represent their own ancestors as economically foolish, telling me that in the past people bartered like quantities for like, regardless of differences of quality. A sack of maize went for an equal-sized sack of sugar. Part of the subtext when Anakalangese tell such stories today is a display of aristocratic distain for haggling and calculation of which they often boast. But they also see the past as a time in which people were taken in by the very materiality of things and were unable to perform the symbolic operations embodied in money: exchange value was inseparable from the things themselves.

At the same time, while portrayed as unschooled in economic calculation, the Sumbanese also appear as thoroughly materialistic. For one thing, heathens ask the spirits for wealth. While the missionary must accept a certain amount of magical thinking in the early stages of Christianization as only natural, notes Kruyt, he must "deal severely with such demonstrations when he notices that the aim is to get personal benefit therefrom" (1924, 275). This is not merely a matter of means and ends; it has consequences for the very character of the subject. For example, when Wielenga tells the *raja* of Napu of the Ten Commandments, the latter responds that he already knows them.

> But when I said to him it would be good if you were to begin then with leaving these bad things behind, he asserted that it would not be possible. "For the human is so evil! How many buffalo have I already not been obliged to kill and how many offerings have I already not brought. But yet I go at it once again. Yes, a bad deed costs much, but luckily I am rich." He thus would say: Ah, when I but confess my fault to the gods and placate them with an offering, then it shall still turn out well. With paying and with gifts one comes far in this world, but also in the next. (Wielenga 1909, 41)

Here a perverse political economy stands in the way of moral redemption, for as long as one can buy one's way out, one requires no interior transformation. The link between Sumbanese materialism and their inability to know the true value of things lies in this conflation of that which is properly material, objects of value, and that which belongs to the soul.

Indeed, even the effort to give a sympathetic portrait of *marapu* life tends to present a political economy, if not of misplaced value, at least of excess. For example, U. H. Kapita, the Sumbanese assistant to the missionary linguist Onvlee, describes traditional Sumbanese life as a total cultural system. Children are trained from the beginning to serve the *marapu*, the purpose of marriage is to produce a next generation for the *marapu*, the work of planting and herding all aim to provide offerings: "It may be said that in all efforts of the Sumbanese, the principal goal is in order to get offering materials for Marapu" (Kapita 1976a, 102–104). Omitting any other function, such as keeping oneself fed, providing oneself with descendants, or acquiring power, Kapita writes as if in seeking the intersection of material and spiritual worlds the latter must either be everywhere or nowhere. But the Sumbanese stand accused of excess in opposing directions, for they at once recognize too many spirits in too many places, and, reflecting Colenbrander's worries that they might turn into free thinkers, are too materialistic.

In self-conscious contrast to this seemingly irrational past, the contemporary GKS aspires in its financial operations to the fully rational forms of a well-controlled institutional operation. Umbu Delu's complaint was to that extent accurate: Money is everywhere in church activities.[27] The ubiquity of cash and the economic calculation it suggests are, if anything, highlighted by the manner in which cash is collected—unlike ceremonial exchange, which is theatrically displayed, church collections are at once public and yet veiled. The black cloth collection sacks passed each Sunday in church are designed to conceal the donor's hand as it reaches in to drop a coin or bill. When collections are made at home, during prayer meetings or wedding parties, people are always careful to circulate a plate covered with a piece of cloth, under which the donor slips a discreet hand. And yet these transactions are then exposed in a public accounting of the most economic sort. In the announcements before the beginning of each church service, a member of the vestry reads off that week's accounting, giving the totals received in each collection sack and at each household gathering, naming the household heads in question. This may well serve as a public disciplining and incitement; it also situates the church within an order of rational calculation quite at odds with the deferential mediations of exchange. The act of giving, which takes center stage in ceremonial exchange, is suppressed in favor of the totaling of outcomes. Dwelling on final sums displays the usefulness and convertability of cash into resources, a sharp contrast to the ways in which exchange plays down use in favor of conventional symbolism and performativity. As the agent that renders accounts and the recipient of multiple donations, the church transcends any particular claims that the bonds of giving might impose.

The Dilemmas of Functionalism

To suppose that the media of pagan ritual themselves carry some sort of potency that threatens the convert risks crediting the putative content of pagan beliefs. Although the prohibition on eating sacrificial meat always threatens to slip from serving as a bulwark against the weakness of others into an acknowledgement of the power of the spirits themselves, as the Calvinist separation of material and spiritual takes hold, missionaries allow themselves to reevaluate the nature of ritual. The groundwork for a functionalist reinterpretation of Sumbanese practice was already laid, both in governmental policies of indirect rule (e.g. Riekerk 1934; Waitz 1933) and in the ethnographic training of missionaries (Brouwer 1912; Kruyt 1936).

Like missionaries elsewhere, those on Sumba weighed strategies for the "recreation or renewal" ("*recreatie of vernieuwing*" [Lambooy 1932, in van den End 1987, 341]) of local practices against the risks of syncretism.

> The giving of food to the dead and the dead-feasts can be renewed in a commemoration speech on New Year's Eve. Harvest feasts become thanksgiving days. On the social terrain lie practices such as contribution to the pagan priests, which becomes transposed into contributions to the church and the poor. . . . In funerals, animals may rightly be killed but only those which are necessary to provide food for those in attendance. The custom among the Sumbanese, to bring home the meat given to the spirits, is transposed into support for the poor. (Lambooy, "Zending en volksgewoonten op Soemba" 1932, in van den End 1987, 342)

To "renew" involves several things. One is to continue a material practice but reframe it in speech. Another is to redirect the flow of material goods to a recognizably practical function, such as feeding the guests at a funeral. In the first instance, the materiality of things is to be suppressed in favor of their reframing as symbolic expressions of something else, an immaterial intention. In the latter case, their materiality is to be foregrounded at the expense of any other interpretations. Both require vigilance against the propensity for objects to acquire unwanted meanings and effects. It is perhaps only in charity for the poor that an economic function (useful goods for those in need) and immaterial intention (the embodiment of an ethical spirit) can be combined.

It is the most ethnographically oriented of the missionaries, writing at a time when the eventual victory of the church was assured, who faces most directly the dilemmas of functionalism. Lois Onvlee was trained as a field linguist and worked as a Bible translator for many years on Sumba. In a lecture given in 1969, he returned to the question of sacrifical meat, commenting that nowhere has it led to more discussion than in Sumba (1973b, 144). His approach was to ask what it meant to accept meat in Sumbanese society. The overriding principle is this: "One kills no animal without reason. Ideally, killing only . . . because of the desire to eat meat does not occur" (1973b, 145). Thus, the first step toward a relativistic understanding of meat was to foreground intentionality over mere matter. This intentionality could be described in terms of functions, which Onvlee organized in relation to contexts in which meat played a role: to receive guests, in collective labor, at funerals, and in religious feasts. The analytic task was to separate out social (thus religiously neutral) from religious (thus pagan) functions. Although Onvlee portrayed these contexts as a progression from social to religious function, he observed that even in the first type, "host and guest both stand in relation to the invisible . . . part of society" (1973b, 146), while even the funeral, during which the animal was sacrificed to accompany the deceased to the afterworld, had the economic function of creating debts that guaranteed future contributions and the social one of affirming status. For a guest to receive inadequate acknowledgement in the distribution of meat was shaming. Here Onvlee made a curious aside, in an uncharacteristic departure from his careful ethnographic relativism: "As if I should be embarrassed for meat!" (1973b, 147)—a remark that seemed to force itself out, as if to say that, despite all his scholarly efforts, the sheer materiality of this social medium became suddenly too much for him to accept.

The real meaning of meat, Onvlee asserted, was located in both general social functions and specific intentions expressed in the words of the invocation. But, invoking Durkheim, Onvlee assumed that "culture is an integrated coherent whole; each part is understood to be in this whole and each alteration works on this whole (1973b, 133). As a result, *all* meat is a kind of offering, and all transactions of flesh, living or dead, have social functions (1973b, 148); thus, to forbid the accepting of sacrifices is to induce social isolation. In opposition to the 1934 prohibition against accepting meat, Onvlee wished to distinguish between rituals with religious functions and those that foregrounded the social and economic motive (1973b, 149–50). Yet the very holism of culture that he presumed rendered this distinction problematic. This is evident in the final section of the lecture, a discussion of feasting, in which he proposed that commensuality of some sort be retained as a sort of functional equivalent of what has been lost. Like Colenbrander, he was concerned that conversion "creates here an emptiness which asks to be filled" (1973b, 156).

Refunctionalized, material objects become forms of symbolic expression rather than media through which actions are performed; they become more representation than practice (see Keane 1995a). By reframing the rite, the voluntaristic yet disinterested character of action can be strengthened: "The feast then is no longer a necessity but a gift. Not in order to influence but to thank; not "supaja" (in order) but "sebab" (because) (1973b, 156–57). What this suggests is that in order for the will to be properly located, it must be clearly distinguished from the material objects that serve as its media, as well as from the its orientation toward simple material gain. One way to do this is to restructure what had been itself a form of *action* into an *expression* that responds to the actions of an other.

Yet what is most striking in the rhetorical structure of this concluding segment of the lecture is the repetition, five times on a single page, of the assertion: "The world wherein one lives has become fundamentally other." This refrain suggests a sense of loss greater than the somewhat insubstantial hope that new functional equivalents can be found. It was in this moment of rhetorical flourish that Onvlee appeared most strongly to recognize the implications of his holistic view of culture. He expressed this sense of loss in the face of modernity in another essay, "The Significance of Livestock on Sumba" (1980). He quoted at length lines supposed to have been sung by a lord's horses when he sold them for export in the late nineteenth century (1980, 197–99), voicing his own lament at modern forms of alienation in words attributed to the very possessions themselves. Here Onvlee, an heir of Mauss (1990), stressed inalienability, not to excoriate economic irrationality but to celebrate an integrated premodern world. This has effects on the subject's capacity to act, however, for

> A person cannot do whatever he pleases with his possessions. Possessions have their rules and prohibitions (*hida hàrina*), and breaking these rules is dangerous because possessions react to such trespasses. A person may be the master of his possessions, but his possessions exert an influence on him to which he must respond. (1980, 203)

The power of objects, as it were, extracts something from the subject, much as the horror of idolatry is that it will drain the humanity of its practitioner (Mitchell 1986, 190).

The article closed on a note of lament:

> Possessions on Sumba . . . must be seen in terms of broad social and religious relationships. These relationships are now breaking down. . . . As the Sumbanese come increasingly to regard their possessions in an eco-

nomic sense, I can only hope that they will view these goods in the proper context, without which these possessions could become a dangerous and threatening power. I can only hope that the Sumbanese people will find a new control over their possessions—one that will provide a new context and a new respect (Onvlee 1980, 206–207)

Here the theme of the willful subject and the threat posed by the material object has, in a sense, come full circle. It is no longer idolatry that threatens the humanity of the ritualist, but something that starts to look like a commodity fetishism supplanting social relations.

The Christian's assurance of victory permits a moment of nostalgia for a holistic world. This nostalgia seems as well to express a more troubling recognition, that the secular world of economic calculation emerges precisely from the very separation of subject and object for which the mission has striven. If "primitive" fetishism threatens the subject by attributing agency to possessions—recall Wielenga's comment that the Sumbanese, lacking self-confidence, live in animistic dependence (1910, 72)—the emerging economic regime threatens to awaken in objects dangerous new powers as commodities.[28] As the conversations above suggest, the remaining *marapu* people also resist the transformed role of objects. When they accuse Christians, who slaughter without offering prayers, of self-centered greed for meat, they are portraying a parallel alienation in which self-assertive subjects set objects into free circulation, unconstrained by ancestral obligation. Dwelling on different loci of agency, Christian and *marapu* alike accuse each other of willfulness and lack of deference. Looking at the individual assertiveness embodied in Christian practices, *marapu* people are unimpressed by doctrinal claims of respect for the Lord. Convinced of the deluded character of fetishism (and holding a stake in existing political hierarchies), colonial missionaries are similarly unimpressed by *marapu* understandings of agency, and overlook the ways in which valuable objects articulate a spiritual model of power with a mundane political economy, material quantities with spiritual qualities.

Conclusion: Personal Intentions and Unspeakable Things

Throughout the colonial period and to an extent even today, Christians have rarely been in a position to change local practices at will. Both theological inclination and practical realities drove the church continually to explain itself, compelling *marapu* people to explain themselves as well.

Although the conversations were always between unequals, at no time was either side in full command of the terms of discourse. In addition, the entanglement of *marapu* and Christian discourses reflects the double problem that missionization faces, especially when it is internal to a single society. The church must now ask both how it can win over the unconverted and how, once converted, the converts should behave. Nonetheless, the disabilities faced by *marapu* people and Christians differ in characteristic ways. Christian talk about heathen practices displays anxieties beneath the self-assurance, while *marapu* people are continually put in the position of responding and rationalizing. While *marapu* people retain their most important practices, the need to justify themselves has forced them increasingly to assume the dualistic and functionalist terms presumed by Christian discourse. When Umbu Pandji defended himself against Wielenga's challenge over giving only feathers to the *marapu*, he was already accepting a distinction between the material and the symbolic. The same distinction persists when *marapu* people speak of ancestral gold as being a mat, reminder, proof, or site for meeting the spirits. *Marapu* people also seek to appropriate the language of functional equivalents (the purification *ratu* is like Christ, chicken entrails are like the Book), but in doing so leave themselves vulnerable to the claim, voiced by Pak Pendeta, that Christianity provides a more encompassing language into which their local speech can be translated. Conversely, the practical economy of material practices continues to entangle Christians in operations, such as marriage exchange and feasting, whose presuppositions and economic requirements exceed the limits of doctrine—indeed, of what can be put into words at all.

A final anecdote, not from Sumba but from another feasting society on Sulawesi, an island to its north, captures the dilemmas encountered in the attempt to specify the meanings of material objects. Torajan Christians, balking at having to present the customary shoulder cut of meat to the headman, offered instead to give him a different cut of meat on the grounds that the shoulder cut was pagan, but the substitute gift still bore the *secular* display of deference. The headmen complained to the authorities, and finally the Governor, considering it riskier to alienate the elite than offend the converts, ruled that as long as the chiefs would swear to receive the meat merely as an honorific, the practice could continue (Bigalke 1981, 233–34).

These Christians appeal to the logic of functional equivalence along two dimensions, for as food, one cut of meat is pretty much equivalent to another, and as a symbolic gesture, one act of giving may be equivalent to another. But, imputed intentions aside, neither objects nor gestures are equivalent for the chiefs in material or symbolic terms. The case cannot be resolved by separating the economy of material things from the intentionality of immaterial subjects. The meat is not reducible to either a material good or a symbolic expression. Now consider the Governor's effort to fix the meaning of the act through an oath, which supposes the verbal oath to exhaustively and accurately represent the speaker's beliefs and the meanings of the transaction. Even if that model of speech were adequate, it still fails to grasp the character of material exchange. The oath is meant to bring the intentions of the recipient into line with the already-stated intentions of the donors, but this only works if the performative act itself has no meaning beyond the respective intentions. Yet the original objections of both donors and recipients, which emphasize the actual cut of meat, suggest that the effects of the gift cannot be fully grounded in individual purposes.[29] Leaving aside the matter of "pagan symbolism" (apparently an expression reflecting the Dutch assumption that objects merely express immaterial meanings—which, as statements, can thus can be evaluated as true or false), the Governor's solution still fails to take seriously the fact of the meat itself. In supposing that the intentions of donor and recipient could fully constrain the meaning of the gift, the oath solution overlooks both the economy by which the meat actually enters into circulation and the fact that the gift is embedded in a social field that exceeds individual interpretations and goals. The difficulty that "pagan" exchange presents is in part that the value of things cannot be established by appeal to desires, uses, or intentions, and these in turn cannot be fully defined by what can be said.

Pietz argues that the concept of fetish arises at points at which contrasting value systems meet and the obviousness of material things is challenged. The Christian missionaries attempt to control the semantic and economic underdetermination of objects by pinning down their functions and meanings, and assuring that these can always be put into words. Thus, Lambooy tries to map different functions, sacred and secular, directly onto different pieces of meat. Following reasoning similar to that of the Governor for the Toraja, Goossens and many contemporary Sumbanese try to situate the function in performative speech, to prohibit the meat over which the invocation is spoken. To an extent, this reflects actual ritual pragmatics, in which the powers of words and things are complementary and mutually dependent. But these solutions seek to isolate the offering from the full performance, the economy, and the exercises of power of which it is part. Moreover, the solutions reflect, and ultimately help reproduce, a model in which words and things are radically unconnected, and in which the range of ties between persons and possessions is obscured. In this model, objects bear obvious and universal uses yet lack meaning, while the purpose of

words is limited to expressing intentions located within the speaking subject. This reflects a modern subject's position in the world of circulating and
useful things, but it has not succeeded in containing the elusive ability of
words and things to carry both values and meanings that exceed the purposes of their transactors.

Acknowledgments

This paper was written during a period of leave provided by a National
Endowment for the Humanities Fellowship for University Professors, and
draws on a 1993 field trip funded by the Southeast Asia Council of the As-
sociation for Asian Studies and archival research supported by the Wenner-
Gren Foundation. Versions were presented at the Symposium on
Conversion at the University of Amsterdam, the Ethnohistory Seminar at
the University of Pennsylvania, and the Program in the Comparative
Study of Social Transformation at the University of Michigan. I am grate-
ful to all who participated in those discussions, especially the respondents,
Ann Matter, Liam Riordan, and Rafael Sánchez, and to Marilyn Ivy,
Adela Pinch, and Talal Asad for their careful readings of the manuscript. I
owe a special debt to Umbu Kanna Dapanammung, Umbu Pila Ngala
Deta, and Bapak U. S. Kadiwangu for their generosity and insights.

Notes

1. Strictly speaking, the word *marapu* refers to spirits of the earliest ancestors, but has come
   into general use in Sumba to refer to the entire ritual system and its practitioners. In using
   the awkward expression "*marapu* people," I follow the common Sumbanese practice.

2. I want to stress the deep interdependence of material and verbal practices for constituting the subject. Indeed, the Protestant tradition of iconoclasm entails a coordinate
   tradition of linguistic reform (e.g. Bauman 1983; cf. Rafael 1988). However, this interdependence raises so many complexities that I will be primarily concerned with the
   material side of the relationship (for more on the language side of this problem, see
   Keane 1994, 1995a, 1995b).

3. Regardless of the participants' religious affiliations, highly formalized and often very expensive exchanges involving gold, cloth, metal items, ivory, pigs, horses, and buffalo are
   critical to Sumbanese social relations, local status politics, and economic organization.
   In the eastern part of the island, where asymmetric marriage alliance is favored, the
   focal point is marriage exchange (Forth 1981, Kapita 1976a, Keane 1991, 1994), while
   in much of West Sumba competitive feasting takes center stage (Hoskins 1993). Across
   the island, the principles of exchange dominate even the minutiae of everyday interactions, (Onvlee 1973a). The system of exchange articulates with retention of inalienable

valuables, the "*marapu* portion," which concretize both the identity and powers claimed by each clan (for the relations among exchange, retention, value, and power, see Munn 1983). Although the *marapu* portion has lost some of its physical potency in the eyes of many Christians, it remains important for claims to legitimate status.

4. In Weber's account (1958), Protestantism eschews "idolatry of the flesh" because the sensuous is the point of entry for corruption. For Kant (1959, 53), the distinction between things and humans is between means and ends. Objects can have a price insofar as they are interchangeable with other objects in relation to an end that lies beyond them, while humans are ends in themselves.

5. In discussing Marx, Mitchell draws on Max Müller: While the idol is considered by its worshipper to be a *symbol* of something else, the fetish is seen as *itself* supernatural (1986, 190). Note that this implies an epistemological distinction, for while the outsider might see *both* as varieties of false practice, the *practitioner* cannot in good faith do so. The "fetishist" or "idolator," who might agree with the "outsider" as to the symbolic status of the "idol," is in principle excluded from a position that would recognize the fetish as no more than a fetish. In the following discussion, I will not attempt to distinguish between these two concepts. My interest is in the entire complex of problems raised for Christians by non-Christian uses of material objects. As will be seen below, both missionary and indigenous discourses slide from one to the other view of non-Christian practices, as predisposition and strategic advantage dictate. For "fetish" as a technical term, the Dutch on Sumba probably followed the influential missionary ethnographer A. C. Kruyt, who defines it as the attribution of powerful "soul substance" (*zielstof*) to unusual objects (1906, 199–201).

6. I draw on Pietz in particular for his emphasis on the historicity of the *idea* or discourses of "fetishism" (cf. Ellen 1988; Sebeok 1991). Such discourses are marked by their doubleness: they require both a fetishist and an outside observer in whose eyes the fetishist is trapped in misrecognition. This approach draws attention to the critical or anxious responses that this doubleness induces.

7. Given the role of emotions and subjectivity in much of the literature of conversion (e.g., James 1982), this focus may seem excessively intellectualist. It has been my experience, however, that when both Christian and non-Christian Sumbanese talk about conversion, they are usually undramatic, rational, and rarely touch on emotional questions—in part, a reflection of a general Sumbanese reticence about most forms of emotional expression and lack of interest in the language of interiority. The style of missionization also contributes to this rationalism. Describing the Reformed (Hervormde) mission in Sumatra in the late nineteenth century, Kipp writes "entry into this community . . . was not an emotional rebirth but a rational process. Converts expressed a desire to be Christian, were schooled in basic understandings, examined, and then baptized" (Kipp 1990, 23). Missionaries were taught to preach "without the use of dogmatic terms such as sin, conversion, regeneration, redemption, atonement, and others of a similar kind" (Brouwer 1912, 232). If anything, this style was probably even stronger in Sumba, since it was evangelized by the Orthodox Calvinist Church (Gereformeerde Kerk) which alone required its missionaries to have university degrees (Brouwer 1912, 226; van den End 1987, 27).

8. The state recognizes five religions (Islam, Hinduism, Buddhism, Catholicism, and Protestantism), national ideology (Pancasila) declaring Indonesians to be monotheistic believers (Kipp and Rodgers 1987). All others are relegated to the politically suspect

position of those who "do not yet have a religion" (Indo. *belum beragama*), or the more neutral census category "other" (Indo. *lain*). Into the latter falls 63.6 percent of West Sumba's population of 262,813, according to the 1986 census (Kantor Statistik 1987). Such figures, of course, reflect neither the numbers of unbaptized Christians nor those among the baptized who continue to join in ancestral ritual. An important impetus for conversion was the association of nonaffiliation with Communism, even in the relatively isolated Sumba (see Webb 1986a), during the violent birth of the New Order regime (1965-66). For the effects of the state on non-Christian religions, see Bowen 1993; Geertz 1973; Hefner 1985, 1993.

9. The conversations with which I begin occurred in Anakalang, an ethnolinguistic domain located in West Sumba, but linguistically, and in many respects culturally, closer to East Sumba. The missionary writings to which I then turn bear less specific provenances, but are usually meant to apply to the entire island.

10. The sandalwood for which Sumba was once known was pretty much gone by the nineteenth century, and the only other important exports were horses, and slaves. In 1930, at the height of the colonial presence in West Sumba, the (not entirely consistent) census reports a population of 32 Europeans compared to 107,877 Sumbanese (*Volkstelling 1930*, 123, 137, 173).

11. Gereformeerde Kerk, literally "Reformed Church," is variously rendered in English to avoid confusion with the larger and more mainstream Nederlandse Hervormde Kerk (Dutch Reformed Church). The former arose as conservatives seceded from the liberalizing Hervormde Kerk in the nineteenth century. By 1899, the Gereformeerde claimed 8.18 percent of the Dutch population (to the Hervormde's 48.61 percent), and was strongest among artisans, small farmers, skilled laborers, and small tradesmen (Wintle 1987, 3, 59). In the face of the colonial policy of dividing territories among different missions, the Catholic Societas Verbi Divini claimed a right to enter on the basis of a previous mission from 1885 to 1893 (Haripranata 1984). Despite the strong objections of some local officials (e.g. Waitz 1933, 41), they were allowed to operate but were restricted to a certain number of places. Since independence, the SVD has been replaced by the Redemptorists with an expanded operation. More recent additions are a single, self-isolating settlement of Calvinist schismatics of the Free Church in East Sumba, and small congregations of largely ethnic Chinese town dwellers of the American-based Bethel Church.

12. After sporadic efforts to establish a mission on the island from 1881 on, the Deputaten voor de Zending op Soemba was organized in 1902, sending D. K. Wielenga in 1904. Within the first three years, his house was torched twice and he himself was seriously wounded in a spear attack. Accounts differ as to when the first baptism occured, ranging from 1915 (Webb 1986b, 20) to 1928 (Deputaten 1965, 44). By 1932, there were only 755 adult members of the Orthodox Calvinist church in West Sumba, out of a population of approximately 107,800 (Waitz 1933). This slow and careful progress can be contrasted to more exuberant activities elsewhere: a single missionary of the Protestant Church of the Indies claimed to have baptized 5000 persons on his first brief visits to Mamasa, Sulawesi (Bigalke 1981, 143). In recent years, the pace in Sumba has quickened considerably. During my first stay in Anakalang, I heard of one mass baptism involving over 100 people, and one report from around the same time claims 10,000 were baptized across West Sumba in two months (van Helsma 1987, 7). For the history of the Orthodox mission to Sumba, see Deputaten 1965; Kapita 1965; 1976b;

Luijendijk 1946; Meijering et al 1927; Rot-van der Gaast and van Halsema 1984; van den End 1987; and the writings of Wielenga, e.g., 1926 (updated in 1949).

13. I have altered the names of this village and of living Sumbanese.

14. Unless otherwise noted, quotations are based on notes I made during the conversations.

15. The reference here is to a large drum that hangs in his clan's ancestral house and bears the same name as the founding ancestor. This and the gold referred to later in the conversation are both components of the "*marapu* portion" (*tagu marapu*), inalienable valuables said to have been brought by the ancestors and normally kept hidden in ancestral houses. They are handled only under cautious prohibitions during occasional rituals.

16. The appeal to relativism seems to have three sources. One is the sociological specificity of ritual powers, such as clan ancestors, commonly found outside of the totalizing claims of "world religions." Thus, Livingston attributes to a Kwena "rain doctor" an appeal for mutual respect: as we don't despise your knowledge, you shouldn't despise ours (Comaroff and Comaroff 1991, 210). A second source might be the direct influence of the Dutch. Their training early in this century included the principle, albeit for strategic ends, that "a missionary must learn to respect the national and spiritual life of other peoples" (Brouwer 1912, 237), and several missionaries developed a strong interest in ethnography (Wielenga's voluminous ethnographic writings include three local-color novels). One *ratu*, when marshalling for me his many arguments against the strong pressure being put on him to convert, claimed that the missionary linguist Onvlee had told him never to abandon his faith. A third source seems to be a very selective reading of state ideology, which speaks (for example, in Article 29 of the 1945 Constitution) of religous tolerance. This last source is especially problematic, since *marapu* ritual is not recognized as a "religion" and there is some dispute as to whether it sufficiently recognizes a single God.

17. Pietz traces the word "fetish" back to the *facticius* of early Christian theology, whose referents include both superstitious materialism (versus the immateriality of spirit), and the willful alteration of the natural body (1987, 26). When Augustine, speaking of the defeat of desire, contrasts the chaste to the eunuch, he argues that only the former truly embodies a virtuous soul. The difference lies in the expression of the (immaterial) will as opposed to merely material operations (1987, 28).

18. All translations from the Dutch are my own.

19. The theme of fear persists to the present, as can be seen in Pak Pendeta's comments, given above. One former *marapu* priest, who entered Catholicism between my first and second visits to Sumba, said somewhat scornfully of another priest who refused to convert that he was afraid of lightning. He added, "Now that we have that metal (lightning rods) to put on top of buildings, we don't need to fear the *marapu* any longer."

20. Compare the view of the influential missionary Kruyt, who warns against acting too harshly against what he sees as a necessary first stage of "superstitious Christianity," lest the missionary, "by attempting to drive the people to be more spiritual that they are capable of being may promote their becoming free-thinkers and atheists" (1924, 271–72). Like Colenbrander, Kruyt imagines the loss of a set of beliefs, if not replaced with another, leads to some sort of a null set. However, to equate this absence with free thought seems to require an additional supposition, which might lie in his description

of heathens as fundamentally materialistic (1924, 266), and thus, perhaps, in particular danger of sliding into western styles of materialism.

21. Prayers help specify the otherwise ambiguous meanings of sacrifices (Valeri 1985, 52). Nonetheless, offerings, both as silent material objects and as elements in a total ritual performance, should not be reduced to a single set meaning, for they can represent "the deities, the sacrifier, their relationship, and the results required" (Valeri 1985, 67).

22. Note that in early Christian theology, the quality of excess is a defining feature of *superstitio*, which refers to "that religious sensibility which produced exaggerated or excessive, and hence superfluous, cult practices" (Pietz 1987, 29).

23. In playing with the distinction between sign and substance, he is, of course, echoing a central concern of iconoclasm. The problem recurs not only between Christian and pagan and then between Protestant and Catholic, but even within the Reformation. Protestantism challenged the mediating powers claimed by the Catholic church, in part by denying the act of transubstantiation within the Mass. For Calvin, whose position lies between Luther and the even greater iconoclasm of Zwingli (Niesel 1956, 215–24), the material ingredients of the sacrament have no inherent efficacy but serve as outward signs of the verbal promise made by Christ: "If the visible symbols are offered without the Word, they are not only powerless and dead but even harmful juggelry" (*Corpus Reformatorum*, quoted in Niesel 1956, 213). The Word does not in itself require embodiment, but in the face of the weaknesses of human faith, the tangibility of material things helps provide certainty. For a Pre-Reformation view, see Asad 1993, 154–55.

24. Early Dutch Calvinist travelers explicitly identified African fetishes with Catholic sacramental objects (Pietz 1987, 89). In contemporary Sumba, many Protestants claim that images of the Virgin Mary are no better than the gold and offering stones of *marapu* ritual; some also claim the foundations of Catholic churches are strengthened with the burial of sacrificed children.

25. The concept of fetish was first formulated by early travelers to West Africa, for whom the most prominent aspect of value-bearing objects was "the impersonality of their mode of being and operating and their perceived transcultural significance" (Pietz 1987, 40). That is, the practical value of a gun or a bolt of cloth is the same regardless of what you believe about them—one aspect of the impersonality of goods against which Mauss (1990) defines gift exchange.

26. In missionary writings, the economics of sacrifice seem to have evoked much less discussion than the spiritual dimension. In contrast, today the state is more concerned with the economic problems raised by Sumbanese practices. Feasting is seen as a serious problem of waste, and several efforts have been made to limit it (cf. Volkman 1985).

27. Cash is still hard to come by in much of Sumba. Most people support themselves in subsistence agriculture and husbandry. Anakalangese obtain cash from wage-earning relatives or through petty trade in the semi-weekly market. According to Desa census figures in the mid-1980s, less than twelve percent of Anakalangese households, largely those of schoolteachers or minor civil servants, had regular access to wages. However, even they still derived most of their livelihood from agriculture.

28. The general sense that goods can act in evil ways upon the body and mind is quite common, and is expressed, for example, by Rousseau in the Second Discourse on Inequality (cited in Hugh-Jones 1992, 42).

29. Insofar as even purely verbal performatives are public acts that always bear a socially conventional dimension that permits them to be used "out of context" or "insincerely," they cannot be fully and conclusively grounded in the intentions of the individual speaker (Derrida 1982).

References

Appadurai, Arjun. 1986. "Introduction: Commodities and the politics of value." In Arjun Appadurai, ed., *The Social Life of Things: Commodities in Cultural Perspective*. Cambridge: Cambridge University Press.

Asad, Talal. 1993. "On discipline and humility in Medieval Christian monasticism." In *Genealogies of Religion: Discipline and Reasons of Power in Christianity and Islam*. Baltimore: Johns Hopkins University Press.

Bauman, Richard. 1983. *Let Your Words Be Few: Symbolism of Speaking and Silence among Seventeenth Century Quakers*. Cambridge: Cambridge University Press.

Bhabha, Homi K. 1987. "Of mimicry and man: The ambivalence of colonial discourse. In *October: Anthology*. Boston: MIT Press.

Bigalke, Terance W. 1981. A Social History of "Tana Toraja" 1870-1965. Unpublished PhD. Dissertation, University of Wisconsin, Madison.

Bowen, John R. 1993. *Muslims Through Discourse: Religion and Ritual in Gayo Society*. Princeton: Princeton University Press.

Brouwer, A. M. 1912. The Preparation of Missionaries in Holland. *The International Review of Missions* 1: 226-39.

Comaroff, Jean and John Comaroff. 1991. *Of Revelation and Revolution: Christianity, Colonialism, and Consciousness in South Africa* 1 Chicago: University of Chicago Press.

Deputaten 1965. *Rapport inzake de Zending op Soemba aan de Zendingssynode van de Gereformeerde kerken in de Provincies Groningen, Drenthe, en Overijssel en de Altreformierte Kirche in Niedersachsen*. Groningen: J. Niemeijer.

Derrida, Jacques. 1982 (1977). "Signature event context." In Alan Bass, trans., *Margins of Philosophy*. Chicago: University of Chicago Press.

Ellen, Roy. 1988. Fetishism. *Man* (NS) 23: 213–35.

Forth, Gregory. 1981. *Rindi: An Ethnographic Study of a Traditional Domain in Eastern Sumba*. The Hague: Martinus Nijhoff.

Geertz, Clifford. 1973. "Internal conversion in contemporary Bali." In *The Interpretation of Cultures*. New York: Basic Books.

Haripranata. H. 1984. *Ceritera Sejarah Gereja Katolik Sumba dan Sumbawa*. Ende: Arnoldus.

Hefner, Robert W. 1985. *Hindu Javanese: Tengger Tradition and Islam*. Princeton: Princeton University Press.

———. ed. 1993. *Conversion to Christianity: Historical and Anthropological Perspectives on a Great Transformation*. Berkeley: University of California Press.

Hoskins, Janet A. 1987. "Entering the bitter house: Spirit worship and conversion in West Sumba." In Rita Smith Kipp and Susan Rodgers, eds., *Indonesian Religions in Transition*. Tucson: University of Arizona Press.

―――. 1993. "Violence, Sacrifice, and Divination: Giving and Taking Life in Eastern Indonesia." *American Ethnologist* 20: 159-78.

Hugh-Jones, Stephen. 1992. "Yesterday's Luxuries, Tomorrow's Necessities: Business and Barter in Northwest Amazonia." In Caroline Humphrey and Stephen Hugh-Jones, eds., *Barter, Exchange and Value: An Anthropological Account*. Cambridge: Cambridge University Press.

James, William. 1982 (1902). *The Varieties of Religious Experience: A Study in Human Nature*. New York: The Modern Library.

Kant, Immanuel. 1956 (1785). "Foundations of the metaphysics of morals." In Lewis White Beck, trans., *Foundations of the Metaphysics of Morals and What is Enlightenment?* Indianapolis: Bobbs-Merrill.

Kantor Statistik. 1987. *Sumba Barat dalam Angka 1986*. Waikabubak: Kantor Statistik Kabupaten Sumba Barat.

Kapita, U. (Oe.) H. 1965. *Sedjarah Pergumulan Indjil di Sumba*. Pajeti: Lembaga Penerbitan Kristen.

―――. 1976a. *Masyarakat Sumba dan Adat Istiadatnya*. Waingapu: Panitia Penerbit Naskah-Naskah Kebudayaan Daerah Sumba Dewan Penata Layanan Gereja Kristen Sumba.

―――. 1976b. *Sumba di dalam Jangkauan Jaman*. Waingapu: Panitia Penerbit Naskah-Naskah Kebudayaan Daerah Sumba Dewan Penata Layanan Gereja Kristen Sumba.

Keane, Webb. 1991. Delegated Voice: Ritual Speech, Risk, and the Making of Marriage Alliances in Anakalang. *American Ethnologist*. 18: 311–30.

―――. 1994. The Value of Words and the Meaning of Things in Eastern Indonesian Exchange. *Man* (NS) 29: 605–629.

―――. 1995a. The Spoken House: Text, Act, and Object in Eastern Indonesia. *American Ethnologist*. v. 22: 102–124.

―――. 1995b. Religious Change and Historical Reflection in Anakalang, West Sumba. *Journal of Southeast Asian Studies*. v. 26: 289–306.

Kipp, Rita Smith. 1990. *The Early Years of a Dutch Colonial Mission: The Karo Field*. Ann Arbor: University of Michigan Press.

Kipp, Rita Smith, and Susan Rodgers, eds. 1987. *Indonesian Religions in Transition*. Tucson: University of Arizona Press.

Kruyt (Kruijt), Albertus. C. 1906. *Het Animisme in den Indischen Archipel*. 's-Gravenhage: Martinus Nijhoff.

―――. 1924. The Appropriation of Christianity by Primitive Heathen in Central Celebes. *The International Review of Missions* 13: 267–75.

―――. 1936. *Zending en Volkskracht*. 's-Gravenhage: Boekhandel en Uitgeverij voor Inwendige en Uitwendige Zending.

Luijendijk, P. J. 1946. *Zeven Jaar Zendingswerk op Soemba (1939-1946)*. Groningen: J. Niemeijer.

Mauss, Marcel. 1990 (1950) W. D. Halls, trans. *The Gift: The Form and Reason for Exchange in Archaic Societies*. New York: Norton.

May, Ernst L., and Felicia May, eds. 1980. *Die Insel Sumba: Macht und Mythen der Steinzeit im 20 Jahrhundert*. Bonn: Hofbauer Verlag.

Meijering, M. et al. 1927. *Tot Dankbaarheid Genoopt: Gedenkboek ter Gelegenheid van de 25-jarigen Zendingsarbeid op Soemba vanwege de Gereformeerde Kerken in Groningen, Drente en Overisjel*. Kampen: J. H. Kok.

Mitchell, W. J. T. 1986. *Iconology: Image, Text, Ideology*. Chicago: University of Chicago Press.

Munn, Nancy D. 1983. "Gawan Kula: Spatiotemporal Control and the Symbolism of Influence." In Jerry W. Leach and Edmund Leach, eds., *The Kula: New Perspectives on Massim Exchange*. Cambridge: Cambridge University Press.

Niesel, Wilhelm. 1956 (1938). Harold Knight, trans. *The Theology of Calvin*. Philadelphia: Westminster Press.

Onvlee, L. 1973a (1933). "Na Huri Hàpa." In *Cultuur als Antwoord*. Verhandelingen van het KILTV, 66. 's-Gravenhage: Martinus Nijhoff.

———. 1973b (unpublished lecture 1969). Woord en Antwoord, Zending en Adat. In *Cultuur als Antwoord*. Verhandelingen van het KILTV, 66. 's-Gravenhage: Martinus Nijhoff.

———. 1980 (1952). "The Significance of Livestock on Sumba." James J. Fox and Henny Fokker-Bakker, trans. In *The Flow of Life: Essays on Eastern Indonesia*, ed. James J. Fox. Cambridge, MA: Harvard University Press.

Pietz, William. 1985. The Problem of the Fetish, I. *Res* 9: 5–17.

———. 1987. The Problem of the Fetish, II: The Origin of the Fetish. *Res* 13: 23–45.

Rafael, Vicente L. 1988. *Contracting Colonialism: Translation and Christian Conversion in Tagalog Society under Early Spanish Rule*. Ithaca: Cornell University Press.

Riekerk, G.H.M. 1934. Grensregeling Anakalang, Oemboe Ratoe Nggai. Typescript, no. H975 (2), Koninklijk Instituut voor Taal-, Land, en Volkenkunde, Leiden.

Rot-van der Gaast, A. T. and W. B. van Halsema. 1984. Kerk-zijn temidden van Veranderingen: Verslag van een Bezoek aan de kerken van Sumba en Timor. Typescript, Hendrik Kraemer Instituut, Oegstgeest.

Sebeok, Thomas A. 1991. "Fetish." In *A Sign is Just a Sign*. Bloomington: University of Indiana Press.

Thomas, Nicholas. 1991. *Entangled Objects: Exchange, Material Culture, and Colonialism in the Pacific*. Cambridge, MA: Harvard University Press.

Valeri, Valerio. 1985. Paula Wissing, trans. *Kingship and Sacrifice: Ritual and Society in Ancient Hawaii*. Chicago: University of Chicago Press.

van den End, Th., ed. 1987. *Gereformeerde Zending op Sumba: Een Bronnenpublicatie.* Alphen aan den Rijn: Raad voor de Zending der Ned. Herv. Kerk, de Zending der Gereformeerde kerken in Nederland en de Gereformeerde Zendingsbond in de Ned. Herv. Kerk.

van Helsema, W. B. 1987. Kerk van het Kruis? Verslag van een Bezoek aan de kerken van Sumba en Timor, 3-24 Oktober 1987. Typescript, Hendrik Kraemer Instituut, Oegstgeest.

Volkman, Toby Alice. 1985. *Feasts of Honor: Ritual and Change in the Toraja Highlands.* Urbana: University of Illinois Press.

Volkstelling 1930, Deel V: Inheemsche bevolking van Borneo, Celebes, de Kleinen Sunda Eilanden, en de Molukken. Batavia: Department van Landbouw, Nijverheid en Handel, 1934,

Waitz, E.W. F. J. 1933. Bestuurs-memorie van den Gezaghebber van West Soemba. Typescript, Algemeen Rijksarchief, The Hague.

Webb, R. A. F. Paul 1986a. The Sickle and the Cross: Christians and Communists in Bali, Flores, Sumba, and Timor, 1965-67. *Journal of Southeast Asian Studies* 17: 94–112.

———. 1986b. *Palms and the Cross: Socioeconomic Development in Nusatenggara.* Townsville: James Cook University of North Queensland.

Weber, Max. 1958. Talcott Parsons, trans. *The Protestant Ethic and the Spirit of Capitalism.* New York: Charles Scribners Sons.

Wielenga, D. K. 1908. Soemba: Op Reis (Van Pajeti naar Memboro). *De Macedoniër* 12: 167–74; 257–69.

———. 1909. Soemba: De Dooden en Levenden, V. De Kip die Gouden Eieren Legt. *De Macendoniër* 13: 41–45.

———. 1910. Soemba: Offersteenen. *De Macedoniër* 14: 72–80.

———. 1926. *Onze Zendingsvelden, V: Soemba.* 's-Gravenhage: Zendings-Studieraad.

Wintle, Michael. 1987. *Pillars of Piety: Religion in the Netherlands in the Nineteenth Century.* Hull University Press Occasional Papers in Modern Dutch Studies, no. 2. (Hull): Hull University Press.

7

SERIAL CONVERSION/CONVERSION TO SERIALITY: RELIGION, STATE, AND NUMBER IN ARU, EASTERN INDONESIA

Patricia Spyer

*R*ECENTLY, UNDER A PALM TREE somewhere in the south Moluccas, a retired policeman posted to Aru in the mid-1970s spoke to me of the waves of conversion that swept the islands at this time.[1] Aru was no different in this regard from many other parts of Indonesia. In the wake of the communist purges that accompanied Suharto's rise to power in 1965 and 1966, persons stigmatized as "not yet having a religion" (*belum beragama*),[2] and thus subject to suspicion as possible communists, converted to one of the five world religions recognized by the government—Islam, Protestant Christianity, Catholicism, Hinduism, and Buddhism (Kipp and Rodgers 1987; Webb 1986). A more immediate impetus of this archipelagowide process in Aru were the national elections of 1977, and, specifically, the determination on the part of government bureaucrats in the island capital, Dobo, that all Aruese participate fully in this critical ritual of New Order rule.[3] According to a logic premised on a double conversion—both to a world religion and to citizenship—participation in the elections necessitated the possession of a citizen's identity card, which in turn demanded of a person that he or she declare his or her religion (*agama*).

This essay takes off from the mutual implication of religion and state in Indonesia to explore how, in Aru, an insistence on a rhetoric of number and accounting in diverse narratives and storytelling moves, traces the contours of a discursive space in which interpretations of conversion and the elections that compelled them collude in the making of persons and their proper places within Suharto's New Order regime. My aim will be to investigate one dimension of the complex and ongoing process of Aruese conversion:

the significance of "the avalanche of numbers" (Hacking 1990)—and the practices in relation to which they have to be reckoned—that confronted me on a recent visit to these islands. Through selected examples I hope to convey a sense of the immense wave of numbers currently inundating this sprinkling of islands in the easternmost reaches of the Indonesian archipelago. Against this background I will consider more closely the account of one Aruese man who in comparing his position as *adat*, or "traditional," official in a small Aruese community to that of a Catholic priest, had repeated recourse to what is best understood as a kind of language of bookkeeping. In tallying the rising numbers of women and men who sought him out during recent *adat* performances to undo, as it were, the consequences of the "sins" they had committed in these same settings, this man thereby claimed an important constituency for himself. If, in so doing, this *adat* official aimed to set himself off against his self-proclaimed professional counterpart, the local Catholic priest, he also belied another aspect of conversion in contemporary Indonesia—including, in certain important respects, his own. As a claim staked in a miniature battle of numbers, and, as I will show, in the rhetorics and poetics deployed therein, this man's account is already shot through with the marks of the ongoing serialization of social life as one crucial aspect of the discursive and political production of persons as subjects and as citizens of Suharto's Indonesia.

I use the term "serialization" broadly to refer to the interrelated dimensions of the process by which homogeneously defined and bounded units are created, units such as "religion," "citizen," or even *adat* dance (Spyer, 1996), which at least for the practical purposes of rule are regarded as alike, interchangeable, and enumerable; in short, as belonging to a series of like sorts. For the purposes of my argument, the distinction sometimes made between finite and infinite sets is irrelevant. Thus, in this essay, I apply seriality equally to what might be called the finite set of religions, or *agama*, of which, as noted above, the government recognizes five, as well as to the category of citizen that in theory, at least, is infinite. Finally, if I ascribe to the general view that seriality is one important inflection of a much larger conversion to modernity, I, along with many others, also insist on the possibility of myriad and diverse modernities, on a critique of an essentialized and reified understanding of the state, and on a notion of the political as complexly and multiply located, as continually made, transformed, disputed, and redefined in discursive practices as those that are the concern of this essay. Here I primarily consider four clusters of intersecting and related practices discursively shaped and entailed within serialization in Indonesia: the constitution of citizens defined on the basis of their affiliation to one of the five recognized *agama*s, the accounting of converts by the Catholic mission, the national program of development, and a phenomenon that I have termed serial conversion.

The Missionary-in-the-Rowboat and Other Modernities

Together with the account of the *adat* official whose "conversion" has been prefigured above, and the sea of numbers that describes its general context, this essay also takes off from some comments made to me by the retired policeman left stranded at its opening on a south Moluccan shore. Franciscus X., as I will call him, to echo another religious beginning in Moluccan history, had been actively involved in the conversion of Aruese, and, along with others, had in the mid-1970s engaged in the fierce fight for local converts that pitted advocates of Islam, Protestant Christianity represented by the GPM (*Gereja Protestan Maluku*, or the Protestant Church of the Moluccas), and Sacred Heart Catholicism against each other.[4] Historically, Islam had been the great enemy in the Netherlands East Indies—indeed, so much so that the mutual exclusion of *agama*, or "religion," on one hand, and that which is opposed to it as the residual domain of *adat*, or "custom," delimiting the traditional, tribal, and markedly local on the other, is to a large extent a legacy of colonial policies aimed at containing the spread and influence of Islam (van Doorn 1994; Fox 1988; Mahadi 1987). If Islam presented itself in the nineteenth century as a formidable opponent of some of the most important Catholic mission stations in Maluku, notably that of the Kei Islands adjacent to Aru,[5] it must also be emphasized that competition between Protestants and Catholics—both at this time and later—never lagged far behind (Schreurs 1992). During the time of the mass conversions in Aru in the 1970s, the battle between Catholics and Protestants is commonly said to have been the most vicious of all. It seems to have played itself out especially among government officials who were themselves primarily from the neighboring south Moluccan islands of Kei and Babar and the provincial capital of Ambon, and among their Aruese followers.

In a letter to his Bishop in Ambon, one Dutch priest went so far as to characterize the conflicts over converts between the Catholics of his own Sacred Heart Mission—with whom we will be most concerned in this essay—and the GPM Protestants as "miniature wars of religion" (D. *godsdienstoorlogjes*) (Pater E., letter of May 31, 1979). More generally, correspondence between Dutch priests based in Dobo and their Bishop, dating from the period of conversion itself as well as the years immediately thereafter, conveys a profound sense of ambivalence toward the manner in which the conversions took place. While sincerely deploring the coercion and violence involved in converting the archipelago, they also—to raise another ghost of Dutch national history—found themselves in a position of embarrassment vis-à-vis potential riches (Schama 1987). Since the Sacred Heart first began its work in Aru in the 1950s, the recalcitrance of the natives toward religion and the stubbornness with which they held to their own ways had been a persistent theme in the letters traveling back and forth between Ambon and Aru. Thus, notwithstanding serious misgivings about the methods of local bureaucrats, members of the police, and military personnel in compelling adherence to their own particular religion, the Catholics had no intention of being left behind in the struggle for Aruese souls. Both the descriptions by church officials of the frenzy of the mass conversions of pagan Aruese, especially in the months leading up to the elections, as well as the celebratory enumeration in mission documents of new Catholics made in Backshore or eastern Aru villages suggest the energy with which the Sacred Heart flung itself into the fray.[6]

In our interview, Franciscus X. reiterated the tension and violence of these times, at one point even asking me not to record something he had just said and adding *in English* a warning: "Very dangerous." Yet when he came to speak of Aruese within all of this, he summed their attitude up with a phrase that took me aback: "*berlumba-lumba.*" In Maluku Malay, *berlumba-lumba* describes the play of porpoises as they frolic in and out of waves, in so doing moving in rapid succession from one place to another. For Franciscus, speaking from a position of authority seen in retrospect and from the relaxation of retirement, the phrase captured a tendency among Aruese toward what I will call—insisting on a certain sense of the ominous within this particular play—serial conversion. A phenomenon that crops up in missionary correspondence as well as in the stories of Aruese villagers, *berlumba-lumba* refers to a pervasive pattern in these tumultuous times according to which both male and female islanders would switch from one religion to another, in some cases moving through all three local options until—at least for the time being—settling on one.

Rather than reducing this sense of randomness in choice and conviction to either the requirements of a policeman's gaze, which would necessarily conjure unruliness (such as that of a crowd or mob) in order to announce the arrival of law and order, or to an originary culture in which Aruese happen to be always already nomadic, shifting, and mobile, and world religions unimportant, I will juxtapose this narrative with another that—as already intimated—speaks less of serial conversion than conversion to a kind of seriality. Despite crucial differences in the situations of their use, their poetics, and their politics, the two can arguably be seen as enmeshed in a dialogue with each other. Both speak a language of seriality and multiplicity and in a rhetoric of repetition and number; in so doing, each answers to the discursive needs of conversion, or, more broadly, religion, within a certain modernity. By thus locating conversion within the unfolding of a particular kind of modernity, I aim to complicate the teleology implied when conversion is seen simply as one more step taken within a predictable trajectory and toward the making of a certain kind of subject. Focusing on the state dimension of institutionalized discourses and technologies risks precisely, however, reinstating one or another version of this same teleology. From the start, therefore, it is important to realize that such things take on their own particular tendencies, genealogies, even obsessions across a given national landscape as they are refracted and produced in varied forms of knowing, doing, and believing.

One simple instance of this has already been touched upon in the preceding pages—namely, that the five religions upheld by the Indonesian government rarely—if ever—represent the actual choices of *agama* as these present themselves to persons and collectivities throughout Indonesia's vast archipelago. This small but basic point is at times overlooked or at least not spelled out by scholars of Indonesia when in their writings on religion they merely reproduce the official list. For pagan Aruese in the 1970s, for instance, there were realistically three *agamas* from which they could choose: Islam, GPM Protestantism, and Sacred Heart Catholicism—that is, *agama* scaled down in correspondence with regional and historical specificities as well as—and probably more importantly—in direct relation to the religious composition of the local officialdom (both civil and military), which stood behind and largely orchestrated the conversion of the archipelago. Not surprisingly, with the hindsight of knowledge brought to these islands by the recent introduction of national television, some Backshore Aruese wonder today why their own choice of *agama* at the time had been so restricted—why, more precisely, unlike themselves, the Balinese, as they see it, were permitted to remain "Hindu," a term that in Aru applies to what on certain limited occasions these islanders conceive of as their former "religion." Or what of the tale told to me by a high-ranking dignitary of the Catholic church, concerning an overzealous catechist who explained the government policy regarding the necessity of having a religion to a group of Moluccan pagans as a straightforward decision between either Islam, glossed simply as a prohibition on the consumption of pork, or Catholicism, defined more favorably in the eyes of the local population as the absence of this same prohibition?

The problems besetting a mere abstract appraisal of state policies and discourses regarding *agama* become all the more glaring—at least in the eastern parts of Indonesia and presumably in most other parts as well—in the case of two other religions that are sometimes appended to the familiar list of five—Judaism and Confucianism. Granted, neither Judaism nor Confucianism—as world religions conventionally understood—present as such any definitional problems that would prevent them from being considered an *agama* and therefore included on Indonesia's official list (see below). Nonetheless, Judaism is hardly a realistic option for potential converts, while Confucianism poses special problems as primarily a "Chinese" religion. In addition to the chain of associations that frequently links Confucianism to "Chinese" and "Chinese" to Communism, the textual orientation of Confucianism is already enough of a problem in light of the prohibition on the use and display of Chinese ideograms and the official ban on the public worship of Chinese religions, both of which have been in place since 1967. In actuality, "religion" among the majority of Chinese in Indonesia was never Confucianism as such but revolved, and in many places continues to revolve, around the commemoration of ancestors in the context of specific festivals like Chinese New Year and the Day of the Dead, as well as in other, more everyday practices (cf. Tan 1991). In his discussion of the post-1965 conversions in the Lesser Sundas, Webb quite rightly singles out both pagans and Chinese as "those who became Christians to save their lives" (Webb 1986, 108). Much the same could be said of Aru, where every Sino-Indonesian trader I know was either Catholic or Protestant, the majority having converted in the wake of the horrors of 1965.

As with *agama* and the need to track its significance as a salient category of Indonesian citizenship in those discursive practices through which it is repeatedly elaborated and produced, so too with serialization and the enumeration with which it characteristically goes hand in hand. Asad argues, for instance, regarding enumerative practices, that these had quite a different role in colonial versus metropolitan societies—an observation that, in turn, implies a somewhat different history for such things in postcolonial places (Asad 1994). To give just one example, the taking of censuses was much more an affair of the colonies than of the European colonizer nations at home (Appadurai 1993; Cohn 1987a; Hacking 1990, 17). And as with the nations of Europe, in which the obsessions and bureaucratic idiosyncracies of each particular country could be read off of their accumulated numbers (Hacking, ibid), the application of ennumeration presumably differed from one colony to the next as well as across the expanses of a given colonial territory—from, let's say, Java to Aru. Clearly, the avalanche of numbers descending on Aru today was already prefigured in multiple ways during the colonial period: in the mapping of different Aru "landscapes" throughout the latter half of the nineteenth century as a process that transformed this alleged "terra incognita" into a well-defined colonial possession by the first decades of this century; in the introduction of a capitation tax in 1908 (Baron Quarles de Quarles 1908, ARA, The Hague); in the registration of Aruese for inoculation campaigns against polio and other diseases; in the taking of censuses; in the accumulation of trade statistics, and so on. Only recently, however, have the consequences of enumerative practices such as these become most apparent in Backshore Aru. This circumstance I attribute largely to the central role of numbers in articulating Suharto's national program of development; to the large-scale collection of statistics in the islands by the Sacred Heart Mission—including most crucially the numbers of Aruese converts and their births, marriages, and deaths, or the other types of figures with which the Catholics commonly pepper their periodic reports to the Propaganda Fide in Rome; and especially to the intensity and vigor with which these different parties have applied themselves to enumeration.

If, in this instance, these distinct discourses articulated typically through numbers can be said to have converged and partially developed in tandem, it is equally important to realize that they can also act upon and interfere with each other. Such, as we will see, is the case of a discourse pertaining to the collection of sea products for trade and the accounting of debts that bind Aruese to Sino-Indonesian traders. The rather obvious point to be gained from this is that at any given time any given discursive space is constructed out of many different strands. Once localized, however, such discourse already begins to take on its own "history of accrued meaningfulness," a history that in the case considered here enabled a certain collaboration between religion and citizenship (Stewart 1991, 403). Yet even if this collaboration, following my argument, is facilitated by and through a discourse of numbers, and even if such discourse can be shown to be pervasive and insistent at this moment in Backshore Aru, its status and significance at present remains uncertain. To evaluate them both would entail carefully distinguishing between recent, unevenly distributed and variable forms of domination—of which a rhetoric of number appears to form a crucial component—and a more thoroughgoing hegemony (Guha in Mani 1992, 394). This, however, is not a concern of the present essay.

At any rate, the attempt in raising the more general problem of modernity will be to avoid the kind of missionary-in-the-rowboat model (Cohn 1987b) in which conversion figures as the recurrent trope of a before-and-

after story in which persons and their places (Thomas 1992; Young 1990)—
on whatever side of this divide they find themselves positioned—are clear-
cut and ready-made, the kind of argument in which the world, as it were,
also becomes "Catholic," or, for that matter, numerical, overnight. If one
might argue that the insistence on seriality and number in Aru is merely the
prelude of a modernity *writ large*, and one with which we are all too familiar, the following example should give us some pause, suggesting that
modernity itself can only be multiply configured. Let us dwell for a moment on the tick-tock of the clock whose hours were struck by miniature
British soldiers in the onward march of "a history of the colonization of
consciousness and the consciousness of colonization" in South Africa, with
which the Comaroffs open their important book (Comaroff and Comaroff
1991, xi). I could not help but recall this clock, measuring out one "historical process in the making" on this last trip to Aru when I sat with an
Aruese teacher in the front "guest" room of his house in a village adjacent
to Bemun. Given the ticks and tocks of no less than eleven clocks in this
front room that punctuated our conversation, it was indeed hard not to.
One clock in particular stands out in my recollections: a vividly colored
scene of the Last Supper on which was superimposed a pair of thin, coppery hands and twelve coppery hour marks to indicate the measure of one
or another thing. Such proliferation begs a number of questions: What is
one to make of these multiple ticks (and tocks)? Do they all measure out
the same world historical time or can such seriality itself pose a challenge
to a certain kind of ennumeration? How to figure, for instance, religious affiliation, or locate, count, and constitute a congregation when its members insist on repeating their own conversion as a serial process that cuts
across several different religions? Or, as some might argue, should we see
the Last Supper as simply a prelude to McDonald's? In short, can we *place*
this excess of eleven clocks?

As for my method in exploring these different questions, it will in some
respects mimic the play of *lumba-lumba* itself and touch on a number of different places as I move throughout the remainder of this essay. The essay is
meant therefore to be exploratory, to sketch out a space for further investigation and to raise more questions than it attempts to resolve. Its impetus
comes in part from the realization that the kinds of analyses often proposed
for conversion do not apply in Aru. This is neither a case of "on les croyait
chrétiens" only to discover beyond the signs and props of a Christian decor
a deeper, recalcitrant paganism (de Certeau 1971),[7] nor of fully fledged religious subjects—whether Catholic or Protestant—who are continuously
summoned to speak and practice their own interiority as the privileged site

of conviction, choice, and communion—in short, of belief (Foucault 1978). Nor, as I suggested above, would it be plausible to locate Aruese on some sort of mission-made road in between, for the peoples with whom I worked in the southeastern parts of the archipelago defy such categorization. If, for example, one were to evaluate the degree of Christianization among them according to conventional criteria such as their grasp of Church doctrine, their observance of the sacraments, their knowledge of religious holidays, or their church attendance, then one could arrive at only a negative conclusion. As with other peoples who claim allegiance to one or another religion but may not always be regarded as bonafide practitioners by others, such a situation does not, however, in my view, imply that Christianity merely overlays a more deep-rooted pagan existence. Although following some descriptions this might be the case, it is equally true that for Bemunese today, and even for those villagers who at the time most resisted conversion, having a religion (*agama*) and being Catholic are all-important determinations.

All this is expressive of a complex situation in which one has to minimally take into account the weak institutionalization of the Catholic church in most of Aru, together with the overriding importance for the Suharto government of *agama*. I will treat each of these contributing factors in turn, beginning with a brief overview of the history of the Catholic mission in Aru. The first reports of "service trips" to Aru lasting anywhere from a few days to a month or more and made by mission personnel from the first MSC station in Maluku in Langgur, Kei, date from 1949 and become increasingly frequent in the 1950s. These early writings from the incipient mission station in Dobo speak forcefully, repetitively, and at times desperately of the difficulties of the place, of the trials of establishing a place for the mission in the islands, and especially of the hardships of moving from place to place in an archipelago cross-cut by large sea channels, edged by treacherous shallows on its eastern side, as well as subject to the dramatic seasonal shift of the monsoon winds. As if that were not enough, travel in this early period inevitably meant depending upon the comings and goings of local craft, whether the canoes and plank-built sailboats of Aruese or the somewhat larger vessels owned by the traders. By August 1958, we encounter a letter written by a certain Bishop Grent describing the various tasks to be carried out by the new Dobo priest (Mgr. Grent, letter of August 8, 1958), in which clearly at issue was still very much "the extension of God's kingdom into a new terrain" (letter of September 30, 1958). Among the primary tasks laid out in the letter addressed to the new priest was, not surprisingly, the spread of faith both in the capital, Dobo, and in

Aru villages, including, in the case of the latter, a "thorough visit" (D. *grondig bezoek*) at least twice a year to those villages with a mission school.

By the 1970s, especially under Father van Lith, who had a most active hand in the conversion of Backshore Aru, such visits were not only thorough but also more frequent. Although this is probably an exaggeration, and hardly plausible given the vicissitudes of the weather, one man claimed that during this period Father van Lith came to the Backshore as often as once a month on tournee accompanied by his Keiese skipper, Amerika, and on one of the two mission "Hope" motorboats (*Harapan* I or II). At any rate, it is at this time that the ground for conversion was laid—a period that Bemunese usually recall with reference to the lotteries for Dutch clothes sponsored in the village by van Lith (and organized in the usual manner of lotteries, with *numbered* tickets representing the lots to be won— in this case, articles of clothing),[8] to the much appreciated injections and other care of the sick van Lith provided—often free of charge—and in the face of the conflict with the neighboring village of Longgar over the founding of a mission school in Bemun.[9] If both the period preceding and following the mass conversions of the mid-1970s was an extremely active one, visits of the priest or of mission brothers to the Backshore were, in my own experience, sporadic and, with the exception of the major holidays, usually impossible to predict. Even during my last visit in early 1994, it appeared that the presence of the mission continued to make itself felt primarily through the village school and in more or less regular church activities that were, however, irregularly attended by most of the community. The running of the church and related activities rests on the shoulders of only a few people, mostly men, who teach in the school during the week, run the church service on the weekend, officiate at funerals, and guide the schoolchildren in the preparation of religious readings, songs, and dances to be performed on the major church holidays.

Not infrequently, these men, who were all from neighboring Kei—or those islands on which the MSC can claim a longstanding and solid constituency—complained to me about the laxity of the local population regarding *agama*, the low church attendance outside of holidays, and the limited enthusiasm generated by mission plans to make Bemun, one of only two Aru villages boasting a wholly Catholic population, into an important parish center. For these men, therefore, the link between the school and the church was all-important because it ensured that at least a majority of the schoolchildren, accompanied by their mothers, would attend the Sunday service. In this regard, the mission's prediction that children would be those most likely to serve as "the best propagandists" of the new religion seems in some respects to have borne out (unsigned MSC report on the Tanimbar Islands, 1953). Indeed, apart from a few men from Kei who were either married to Bemunese women or employed as divers on the motorboats of local traders, the very youngest members of the community were those who commonly made up its congregation.

. . . And Then There Were Five

Were it not for the Suharto government's policy toward *agama*, the above would suffice as a general picture of the rather tenuous state of religion among Backshore Aruese. Everything already said, however, is offset by the New Order's stance toward *agama* and the codification of "religion" within the national doctrine of Pancasila, or the five principles declared in 1985 to be "the sole basis" (*azas tunggal*) of the state as itself a *Negara Pancasila* or "Pancasila State" (van Langenberg 1990, 123). Important as well in this regard is the complicated relation of both *agama* and Pancasila to the national program of development and, more generally, to notions of progress, moral direction, and modernization. In the briefest of terms:

> Beginning in elementary classrooms, texts and lectures convey the idea that *agama* is progressive (*maju*) and a requisite of good citizenship. By an implicit logic of opposites, the official endorsements of *agama* make those persons without *agama* appear to be disloyal national citizens, uncommitted to the values of Pancasila, not to mention intellectually and morally backward (Kipp and Rodgers 1987, 23).

Note that *agama*, significantly, is not further specified with reference to a particular religion. Itself an idiosyncratic amalgam of "a Sanskrit derived-term, a 19th-century European conception of specific "world religions," and "an Islamic view that all proper religions must minimally have a prophet, a scripture, and a belief in one God" (Fox 1988, 806), *agama* figures in the Pancasila state ideology as the first of its five points, or *sila*: the belief in one Supreme Being (*Sila Ketuhanan yang Maha Esa*). Neither a religious state in the sense of prescribing a specific religion for its citizens nor a secular one insofar as it sees itself as "having the responsibility to ensure that its citizens follow an acceptable religious faith as an obligation of citizenship" (Stange in Adnan 1990, 449), the Pancasila state is best regarded as a variant of what van der Veer has characterized, with respect to Hindus and Muslims in South Asia, as religious nationalism (van der Veer 1994).

Put simply, Pancasila under Sukarno, and specifically its first point, was formulated largely with the double-edged intent of excluding the possibility of an Islamic state, while at the same time aiming to appease those who most subscribed to it (Adnan 1990, 451; Morfit 1981, 844). The substitution in the wording of the first *sila* of the more neutral Tuhan for the Islamic Allah for "God" offers a concrete example of the highly ambiguous moves this stance produced. While all along the Pancasila has been subject to redefinition as it has been called upon to negotiate the precarious line between religion (especially Islam) and state in Indonesia, one thing is for sure: Under Suharto, Pancasila has lost the sense of revolutionary impetus and historical dynamism it had under Sukarno (Morfit 1981). Along the lines of the national program of development for which ensuring order and a certain status quo guaranteed by the military is more crucial than social change, Pancasila has become "an extraordinarily static ideology" (Morfit 1981, 84) and one, moreover, with pronounced "religious" overtones (Bambang Pranowo 1990, 493). Among the most important of the recent reworkings ensuring this ideology's sacral character, as well as what some regard as the final blow to those in favor of an Islamic state (Adnan 1990, 466), was the 1978 implementation of the Pancasila Moral Teaching in school curricula and in "refresher" courses designed for civil servants, together with Pancasila's subsequent elevation to the "sole basis" (*azas tunggal*) of all political parties and social and religious organizations. What is more, any fundamental dissent from this "sole basis" of the nation-state or from the principles of the national program of development is regarded as subversive.

In Aru—a kind of last place on earth not only in Indonesia but even in the provincial context of the Moluccas—the importance of *agama* for the Suharto government may be further exacerbated by a stance that the Bishop himself characterized as "more Catholic than the Pope," attributing it to government officialdom on the periphery. This probably explains the special zeal to convert the overwhelmingly pagan population that in the 1970s took hold of Dobo bureaucrats, or the more recent privileging of religion above all else in local development projects that are themselves part and parcel of the national program guided by Indonesia's self-styled "Father of Development," President Suharto.[10] An official from the Dobo development office vividly illustrated for me the centrality of *agama* in the local implementation of this first among national programs. Speaking of a majority of Aru communities that as "villages left behind" (*desa tertinggal*) qualify for substantial subsidies, this official gave the example of a hypothetical Aru village that had decided to spend its funds on asphalting roads when its mosque or church turned out to be in a state of disrepair. "What good are streets," he asked, "if *agama* is not observed?" More generally, as stated above, the importance of *agama* is derived in the first instance from a simple equation between having a religion and admission to citizenship. Yet beyond this, as we will see, it says something more about the very mode that citizenship takes in a place like Indonesia.

In order to understand how this might be the case, I turn now to the Backshore community of Bemun, which under strong pressure to convert and after considerable to-and-froing on the part of some of its members between alternative religions (*berlumba-lumba*) opted as a whole for Catholicism converting in three waves, beginning in 1976 and ending in 1977, in the week immediately prior to the national elections. In what follows, I consider how conversion has come to be storied by some Bemunese and explore a few of its implications in Backshore Aru.

The Catholic Cassowary

Ostensibly, the *adat* specialist holding the office of "Stern" in this small southeastern Aru village of approximately 350 inhabitants was not speaking of conversion when we talked one morning in February 1994 over coffee in his kitchen. Rather, he had taken it upon himself to fill me in on the events that had marked the staging of Bemun's annual Cassowary performance since my departure from the village in March of 1988 (something that parenthetically underscores the historicity of such performances). Rapidly, however, as we will see, this briefing turned into a tale of numbers, with the *adat* specialist himself inserted into the tally in the role of overworked "priest." As for Bemun's annual *adat* performance, suffice it to say here that the practical implications of the ritual for this community of pearl divers and collectors of sea products revolves around the celebration of an autochthonous Cassowary spirit as the emblem of the quintessentially "Aru" identified with certain extraordinary powers. To this day, the spirit is regarded by Bemunese as the source of the pearl oyster harvest of the up-coming season. He is said to measure out and modulate the rhythms of the tides and the movements of the winds, and it is his "killing" that marks the transition from the east to the west monsoon, thereby producing trade as well as much that enables Bemunese to engage within it.

Although triggered by specific incidents, it is not altogether surprising to me that the Stern felt compelled to speak on this particular morning about Bemun's annual performance. He was, among other things, merely re-asserting his special claim to the Cassowary as his ground of authority vis-à-vis me and the wider Bemun community. At the same time, such talk confirmed an understanding more generally held by Bemunese that my project was intimately linked with their own passions for this privileged and highly problematic bird. On this morning, however, the Stern spoke as much of conversion as of cassowaries—a convergence I consider quite novel in the setting, although the slippage from one to the other—from, let's say, *adat* to *agama* and back—was already anticipated in the mid-1970s in the context of conversion itself.

Talk of the tension of those times, of being accosted on all sides by the proponents of different faiths, of being propitiated, plied with commodities, and of feeling coerced, commonly describes how—notwithstanding such concerted efforts to compel the direction of the community's conversion(s)—alternative *agama*s were weighed by Bemunese, both individually and collectively, against the village's annual *adat* celebration. The Cassowary's own baptism, as allegedly the first among Bemunese to convert to Catholicism, figures prominently in such talk. Some villagers also invoke the image of a broad and resplendent beam of light spotted by several Bemunese on the evening preceding one of the community's group conversions. A great shaft splitting the night sky, it is said to have illuminated precisely that place where once a year and at the end of his celebration, a palmfrond Cassowary is 'killed' at the center of successively widening rings of villagers. Others sometimes recall the dream of a Bemunese woman in which the Cassowary appears as double in a mini-series of two that represents simultaneously a gendering, thereby suggesting, once again, that seriality can be subject to different takes, that it may play itself out in a polyvocality that engenders talk that, as here, enabled one woman to imaginatively link herself to the most important figure in a male-dominated performance. In the dream a kinsman of the woman sits before the altar of Bemun's church clutching under each arm a cassowary (one male and one female) as these are baptized in what looks like an uncanny fusion of conversion and marriage, or those Catholic rites most familiar to Bemunese. Such familiarity suggests that the talk in which cassowaries and conversion insistently come together evidences later elaborations, an observation that is sustained by, for instance, the reported widespread fear of ancestral repercussions accompanying Bemun's first celebration of Palm Sunday, in the late 1970s. According to the catechist, and as reiterated by many villagers, the trouble with this early observance of the church holiday centered on the prominent display in the procession planned around the village of the same "white" palm fronds used in the annual making of Aru's Cassowary and paraded in his performance down the very same pathways. In short, the prevailing idea then seems to have been the strict avoidance of any overlap between, or even convergence of, *adat* and *agama*, or, somewhat differently, "aru" and "malay," although an explication of the shifting, complex contrasts and crossings of this latter pair would require more space than I have been allotted here.

Let me limit my comments, therefore, to noting that if such avoidance continues to underwrite the mutual relations of *adat* and *agama*, not to mention "aru" and "malay," the Cassowary himself appears less scrupulously assigned to a given place. Increasingly, he seems to serve as a kind of shifter, undergoing his own successive conversions across "aru," *adat*, and *agama*. The emergence of this pattern is not altogether surprising insofar as the autochthone's own annual reception into the community—beckoned forth from the forested interiors of the island that are associated with both Bemun's past and the primitiveness that government propaganda identifies with its former "forest" and nonsedentary existence (Spyer, forthcoming b; cf. Tsing 1994)—can be easily construed as a conversion. So, too, the bath taken by Bemunese at the conclusion of their annual performance works much as a baptism back into their ordinary, everyday lives, an association that women and men themselves at times make when recalling their own, and especially the Cassowary's, conversion.

Even more important, however, than this kind of enabling resonance in explaining the Cassowary's promiscuous religiosity is, I believe, the extent of mission intervention in codifying a particular connection between *agama* and *adat*. What is continually reiterated by schoolteachers, catechists, visiting church personnel, and more and more by Aruese themselves, is not only the importance of *adat* but its equal, albeit different, place alongside *agama* in community affairs. Thus, the Keiese catechist, who was also one of Bemun's schoolteachers, always insisted to Backshore men and women as well as in private to me that *adat* and *agama* necessarily go hand in hand, that they mutually support each other and fulfill different but complementary functions—invoking, in short, the kind of language that one would more readily apply to a couple. During a conversation on one of my periodic visits to Ambon, the Bishop himself emphasized the critical and beneficial role of *adat* in maintaining traditional social structures and kin relations. Somewhat similarly, several villagers also remembered on separate occasions how Father van Lith had told them that Bemun could never "cast off" its *adat*, which they, at any rate, took to mean as their annual Cassowary celebration. If some Bemunese also recalled a sermon given by another Dutch priest in which he cast the Cassowary as a mere bird, which once dead was very much and truly dead, mission correspondence shows evidence of a more generally concerted effort to use *adat* in the process of evangelization by setting it by *agama*'s side. This happens most notably when a couple is ideally married in succession according to *adat* (*nikah adat*) and *agama* (*nikah gereja*) procedures. The move to make a pair or draw a parallel between *adat* and *agama* is also prefigured in that other church rite with which, as already pointed out, Bemunese are most familiar: Once baptized, an Aruese assumes in addition to her "Aru" name (B. *ngaran gwerka*) a "Catholic" one (B. *ngaran katolik*) as well.[11]

In Bemun the relations between *adat* and *agama*, Cassowary and Catholicism, are very much in flux and subject to intense negotiation. Within this flux, however, what seems most salient at the present time is less the substitution by which *agama* comes to replace *adat*, or, more commonly, something construed as the "old" religion, although the demarcation of a "before" and an "after" is certainly effective in some rhetorical contexts, than the construction of a copresence—sometimes amiable, other times uneasy—of *agama* and *adat*. And whether or not the Cassowary, as locally claimed, headed the procession of Bemunese making their way to the church to be baptized in much the same way that he leads them singing and dancing around the village during his own celebration, the following account more than hints at such a connection. At the same time, it attests most strikingly to that other conversion at issue here: namely, conversion to seriality as one important inflection of a larger conversion to modernity.

The Stern's account of Cassowary performances held during the period of my absence lasted almost three hours and ended with an analogy between his own position and that of a priest, which was only qualified with the assertion that of the two, his task was by far the more taxing. Not unlike the devotional recitation of a rosary in its mnemonics and repetition, the Stern composed his story by stringing together a multitude of little stories, each triggered by the name of a person in the village and followed by the "reason" (B. *ken sebab*) constituting this person's transgression in the context of the performance, its consequences for herself or for others, and, in conclusion, a number: that of the plates the Stern had offered at his altar as a payment on the person's behalf. Such offerings ranged from a single to a dozen plates (B. *mangkok lusin eti*), which in turn were often subdivided into separate payments destined for places presided over by distinct *adat* specialists. Sometimes, where applicable, an additional number was added to the first if the person's continued ill health or troubles had made another payment necessary, or, in the most extreme cases, a "doubling" of the initial offering.

The first "nodule" in the string of stories concerned a young woman on whose father's behalf four plates had been offered the previous evening. To convey a sense of what these miniature stories are like, although they vary considerably in length, complexity, and the seriousness of the situations they evoke, I present here a brief summary of the one with which the Stern began.

In the opening of the story, the Stern introduced the protagonist as a transgressor by locating her and her "reason" at a specific moment in the annual performance, something that at the same time allowed me and others in the kitchen to gauge the import of what she had done. "The hunters were already at Gwaur Jalen [mention of this site suggests that the performance had been underway for at least 40 minutes and prohibitions such as that against wearing "malay" as opposed to "aru" dress were already in force] when B's mother spotted B at the far end of Bemun wearing a skirt and blouse. The Stern went on to relate how the young woman's mother admonished her, telling her to refrain from participation in that year's performance since by presenting herself as "malay" through her attire at such a late moment in its unfolding she had, as it were, already missed the boat. Due to what appeared to be the cumulative effect of this initial transgression, the girl's resistance to her mother's warning and her laxity even thereafter in changing her clothes, the young woman's father, as so often happens in this setting, paid for his daughter's mistake.[12] On that very same day somewhere in the forest during the hunt of the Cassowary, B's father was speared in the back of his neck by another hunter.[13] After a number of detours and interruptions, the Stern summed up the story with the payment he had made at the time: one plate for B's father, one for B, and another for B's husband, who as a hunter was also at particular risk during the performance.

The recollection of a name functioned as a mnemonic device that allowed the Stern to recall the details of each person's story at the same time that it generated an increasingly long list of villagers whose transgressions and individual circumstances were loosely linked by either a "now I'll tell you about so-and-so" or "this one is done; now here's another." What seemed to matter in all of this were not the events of a given year's performance—years were, in fact, rarely mentioned—but rather the sense of sheer accumulation. This sense, in turn, derived additional force from the extensive repetition in the poetics of the account, the repeated enumeration of the offerings made, and the fact of numbers themselves, which in their cool precision create the effect of pure quantity (cf. Appadurai 1993, 323). This impression is also borne out by the Stern's insistence at various moments in his account, especially toward its conclusion, on the amount of offerings he had made and on how truly exhausted he had been after one or another of his community's recent annual performances.

Since the (provisional) ending of this loosely-strung-together story actually goes on for some time, I will not be able to present it in full here. I begin where the Stern moved from the account of an individual person to the analogy between himself and a Catholic priest:

> It's the same as a priest, you acknowledge your wrongdoings to him, you tell him your sins. I am like that but this is even more so. I also got it; I couldn't sleep for two or three weeks so now I don't drink coffee. So I took a plate and made an offering for myself. The guardian spirits were mad and I didn't sleep for two or three weeks. We did a divination and got it [i.e., the reason he was not able to sleep], then a plate [was offered]. Until now I've been alright but my wife, they've tied a rope around her neck, I've been making offerings for her continuously [he was refering to the lump on his wife's throat and attributing it to Bemun's guardian spirits who were upset at the quantity of sins produced by Bemunese and punishing the Stern and his wife as *adat* officials for this surplus] . . . if it was just one person, it would be alright but this was lots of people, lots of people fooling around, saying things they shouldn't have said . . . hé, *setengah mati*, I was really *setengah mati* [literally half-dead] . . . if it had been children it would have been alright but it was adults so I got it, its my responsibility . . . before you knew it someone else would appear [to say they had committed some transgression and to ask the Stern to make an offering] . . . if it had been children. After the celebration was all over then they would come and say "when I was in the forest I touched water" and then I would make an offering and it would be alright . . . (At this point the Stern paused, only to begin again with a gesture toward the altar in the front room of his house) . . . look at all those plates . . . peoples wrongdoings, these past years . . . the Prow's house is the same—an excess of plates. . . .

This kind of excess—albeit not made problematic—has come up before in the form of the army of clocks ranged in the front room of an Aruese teacher's house. If the clocks seemed—at least for their owner—a cause for celebration (they were, indeed, presented to him and his wife by various well-wishers on the occasion of a kind of housewarming for their new residence), the excess of plates and the counting of sins to which the carefully stacked piles of porcelain bear witness registers an important complaint. Through it one can just about make out the roar of "the avalanche of numbers" and, more precisely, the increasing pervasiveness in Backshore life of the kinds of technologies and practices in relation to which numbers have to be understood. Articulated in a language of numbers, the Stern's tale— quite literally an account of his own congregation—alludes to another form of reckoning that more often than not is seen as a burden by Bemunese. I refer here to the debts of divers tallied against the pearl oysters turned in by them to the Sino-Indonesian traders who operate the island stores. Through a complicated series of transactions involving traders, divers, and the latter's female undersea spirit partners, these oysters are, in turn, converted into white porcelain plates that are presented to the divers' "sea wives" as a payment for their assistance in procuring shells. To this discourse of commerce and commodities the Stern is also clearly indebted in his calculation of those villagers indebted, as it were, to him (as opposed to the Catholic priest)—if you recall, the greatest sin demands a payment of a *dozen* white plates.[14]

In addition to a surplus of sins and plates, on another occasion the Stern, being simultaneously bemused and amused by what he called "this new crying religion in Dobo" (a form of Pentacostalism recent to Aru), offered his opinion that there were of late too many religions in the world. I hasten to add that if all the above appears to set numbers and their excessive proliferation squarely in the realm of *adat* and *agama* (not to mention trade), Bemunese are not unaware of the more direct significance of numbers for the state. Development, for quite important reasons, as we will see, characteristically enters the village in the form of numbers—as so many sacks of cement, or chickens, or new hybrid, extra-sturdy coconut palms allocated to each household, or inversely, as so many cement houses still to be built to deprive the government of its sense that Bemun has somehow "been left behind." Finally, there is also the perceived interest of presidents in the serial production of persons. Thus, one story that circulates in Bemun has it that following World War II the "President" of Japan conceived a plan meant to augment his country's population (which, as the loser, had been decimated in the war) through an intensive program of controlled copulation. A ship with scores of men and women on board was set out to sea with the sole purpose of circling around while its passengers engaged themselves over and over again in the important business of procreation. A doctor whose only task it was to repeatedly administer "shots of strength" (to the men) accompanied the ship, which would stop at periodic intervals to drop off pregnant women and take fresh ones on board.

A Spectacle of Statistics

Let us return again to the feeling of *setengah mati* so prominent in the Stern's account and provoked by the excess of plates piling up on the altar in the front room of his house. *Setengah mati* was invoked on another occasion in relation to priests and numbers when a man in his thirties recalled the moment when the majority of villagers took the step to convert to Catholi-cism. Using an expression that conveys simultaneously mass, direction, and a certain haste, and which is usually applied to fish and sometimes other an-imals, he characterized the procession of Bemunese heading towards bap-tism as moving in a school [like fish] (B. *dai rumin dabane*) Little did he know how apt this metaphor was. In a letter detailing one of the main practices used by the mission to pave the way to conversion, "the Apostolate of Schooling" (Schreurs 1992, 216), a sister in charge of the first batch of Aruese sent to school in Langgur in the mid-1960s (including this man's elder sister and one of his maternal uncles) concludes by saying that "we will all pray to the Great Fisherman so that this first catch may provoke many subsequent catches" (Sister T., letter of April 1967). Laughing, the man added that "they" [the Bishop and the priest at the officiating end] were re-ally *setengah mati* with all these people showing up at once. Such a feeling was, indeed, reiterated by the Bishop himself, who spoke to me of the rush to convert, the numbers of people this had involved, and the expediency with which he and the Dutch priest stationed in Aru had decided to fuse, in many cases, two of the seven sacraments of the Catholic church—baptism and confirmation—perhaps in an effort to overdetermine the act of conver-sion itself. With a clear sense of amusement at the recollection, the Bishop mimicked the movement with which the priest would thrust yet another Aruese he had just baptized toward himself to be confirmed. In passing, he also mentioned how tired they had been after those long days in which scores of villagers filed by to be baptized and/or confirmed, and, as if by way of explanation, how they had feared that if Aruese were not made Catholic one day they might very well be made something else the next.

Numbers also tend to overwhelm persons in two important respects in a report written by the Bishop about the historic "Confirmation Trip" of September 1976 (Sol manuscript). Describing the prelude to this trip, when the only priest in the islands, Father van Lith, was forced to become "a second Franciscus Xaverius," converting more than 800 persons all over Aru within the space of a few months, the Bishop emphasized the severe cramps the missionary suffered in his legs from the journey—made largely on foot—through extensive portions of the archipelago. In an interesting twist to this passage, which in its emphasis on the trials of the trip and the heroism with which these were overcome recapitulates a well-established missionary genre (Comaroff and Comaroff 1991, 172–78), the Bishop con-cludes with a fragment from one of van Lith's own letters: "The return went much better, I strutted like a cassowary"—a striking figure that some-how converts the missionary into a local hero. In the same report, numbers also overwhelm persons by displacing them in its pages, up until the final one that again summarizes the historic importance of the "Confirmation Trip" by reverting to a kind of language of bookkeeping:[15]

> It was a historic trip: Approximately 1000 persons had given themselves up to be incorporated into the church of which approximately 900 were baptised, either by Father van Lith or Father Esserey. From January through September 1976, 1800 heathens were baptized, now in November this has already risen to more than 2200. Fifteen churches have to be built. More than 15 catechists have been put to work for at least two years. A whole package of projects, around 15, were set up which in all kinds of areas would promote construction and development.

Numbers in such reports are not gratuitous, and even a casual perusal of some of the mission documentation will allow a veritable "spectacle of statistics" to emerge from its pages (Pepon Osorio in Bhabha 1993). Across the globe, those stationed in various Catholic mission fields established by members of different European nations periodically translated their successes into numbers sent to the Propaganda Fide in Rome, as well as deployed in the interest of a more commonplace propaganda at home. Similarly, a recent detailed history of the MSC in Maluku, written by a missionary, tends to assess or at least summarize the progress of the mission by providing the numbers for a given year. A more graphic rendition of this same history unfolds across a succession of dated scenes, beginning with the arrival of Francis Xavier and then (after a gap of more than 300 years) working its way through the highpoints of 100 years of MSC in Maluku, detailed in relief on a cement wall bordering the mission park built on the site where a Bishop and a score of priests and brothers were executed by the Japanese in July of 1942. I should add that this preoccupation with numbers is not peculiar to the MSC, nor is it limited to Catholic missionization (Hall 1992, 248–49) or even to the heyday of missionization from the mid-nineteenth to the early twentieth century (Po-chia Hsia 1994).

Whether one is dealing with state or church (or a complex mix of the two, such as in Indonesia) it is crucial to realize from the start that, generally speaking, numbers, statistics, and the range of enumerative practices with which they are associated are, following Hacking, "much more than a matter of representation." They are instead highly effective tools for political interventions of the most far-reaching kind (Hacking 1990, 76). In Asad's assessment, "what matters is that the figures and the categories in terms of which they were (are) collected, manipulated, and presented belong to proj-

ects aimed at determining the values and practices—the souls and bodies—
of entire populations" (Asad 1994, 77). Another important thing to realize,
already implied in this quote from Asad, is that enumeration also entails the
creation and definition of categories or classes that can serve as the units of
reckoning (cf. Appadurai 1993). *Agama* in this sense is ready-made (albeit
continually retooled), fulfilling precisely this role in contemporary Indonesia.

While the genealogy of *agama* under Dutch colonial rule is more relevant here, it is nonetheless interesting to note that, more generally, following a critical shift in the history of religious practice in seventeenth-century
Europe, religion has been a recurrent category used to establish the boundaries of groups and to mobilize their members for practical purposes (de
Certeau 1988, 25–27). Opposed to pagan practices, *agama* under Suharto
conveys ideas of moral progress; opposed to communism it represents the
order imposed by the New Order, as well as the ordering of the population
into manageable and mobilizable units that, above all, are unified in their
common recognition of a single God-head enshrined in the principles of
Pancasila. In this crucial respect they are held to be safeguarded from something that the government fears most: the specter of a "formless organization," a description that also sometimes serves as a synonym for communism
(Budiman 1990). Significantly, enumeration and, specifically, the use of
comparative statistics in government reports not only buttresses but even
helps to bring about the moral and material "progress" that is guided by Indonesia's Father of Development, Suharto. Indeed, as Asad has persuasively
argued, the very concept of progress is to a large extent the product of statistical practices that themselves form a crucial part of "the great process of
conversion we know as 'modernization,' " and that are already familiar to us
from the mission reports sent to Rome as documents of a more literal
project of conversion (Asad 1994, 79).

A rhetoric of number and accounting, explored in the workings of
several different discursive formations in this essay, facilitated and thereby
contributed to a collusion in the 1970s between practices of religious
conversion and national elections in Aru.[16] This is because the numerical
glossing of persons in both these instances establishes their abstract ex-
changeability vis-à-vis one or another universal equivalent—whether
God, the State, or commerce—and has more to do with allegiances that
are enforced and can be assessed than with internalized beliefs and convictions. Or, as it was put somewhat differently and certainly more
bluntly by an official whom I questioned about the link posited between
"having a religion" and participating in elections: "If a person can follow the command(s) of God (*perintah Tuhan*), he can follow the com-

mand(s) of the state (*perintah Negara*)." In short, religion functions in Aru and more generally throughout Indonesia as a means to the end of citizenship. In this respect, under the Suharto regime it comes close to its Latin etymology, *religare*, or "to bind (over and over) again," that is, to what is first and foremost a practical process. By extension, this interpretation allows us to place the mimicry of the Stern in regarding himself as a kind of overtaxed priest. If my suspicions are correct, then such mimicry is not in any obvious way subversive but rather a way of inflecting, and only then perhaps deflecting, in one particular context, the very mode in which citizenship is made in Indonesia.

Notes

1. Research in the Aru Islands, Southeast Moluccas, was sponsored by the Lembaga Ilmu Pengetahuan Indonesia (Jakarta) and by the Universitas Pattimura (Ambon). Recent field research in Aru (Jan-Feb.1994) was supported by the Southeast Asian Council for the Association of Asian Studies and the Luce Foundation Small Grants for Isolated Scholars, as well as the Netherlands Foundation for the Advancement of Tropical Research (WOTRO). Funding for doctoral research carried out between 1986 and 1988 was provided by a Department of Education Fulbright-Hays Dissertation Fellowship and by the Wenner-Gren Foundation for Anthropological Research. The Institute for Intercultural Studies provided support for three months of archival research in the Netherlands and for a preliminary field trip to Aru in 1984. I would like to thank all of these institutions for their generous support of my work. In addition to the version of this essay presented at the International Conference on Conversion held at the Research Centre Religion and Society in June 1994, I also presented versions at the meetings of the European Association for Social Anthropologists in June 1994 in Oslo, Norway, and in the Department of Anthropology, Johns Hopkins University, in November 1994. I would like to thank the members of these different audiences for their comments and suggestions. Special thanks are also due to the missionaries of the Sacred Heart for their generosity in sharing with me their knowledge, documentation, and observations concerning the mission process in Aru. In particular, I would like to thank Bishop Sol, Father van Lith, Father Segers, and Father Scheurs, as well as the mission archivist in Tilburg, Father Akeboom. Finally, with appreciation, I acknowlege here Peter van der Veer's helpful editorial comments, my colleague Gerd Bauman for his careful reading of a penultimate draft, and Rafael Sánchez for accompanying me on a return trip to Aru and for the contribution of his insights and understanding.

2. In this essay, I will refer to words and phrases from three languages: Bahasa Indonesia, the national language of the Republic of Indonesia; Dutch, the language of the former colonizers; and Barakai, a South Moluccan language spoken by approximately 2,500 people on the island of the same name in southeastern Arn. Indonesian will be left unmarked; Dutch and Barakai preceded by a 'D.' and 'B.' respectively.

3. For an insightful analysis of the 1982 national elections in Solo (Central Java), see Pemberton 1986; cf. McVey 1993.

4. The Missionarissen van het Heilig Hart form the Dutch province of the M.S.C., or Société des Missionaires du Sacré Coeur, which was founded in 1854 and extended to the Netherlands in 1894 (Comité 100 jaar MSC 1954; van Weerdenburg msc n.d.). Franciscus X. is, of course, the Jesuit Francis Xavier (1506–52), or Franciscus Xaverius, as he is more commonly known in the Moluccas. One of the first companions of Ignatius of Loyola, Xavier spent several months in the Central Moluccas in 1546 and 1547, at which time he converted thousands of persons (de Graaf 1977; Neill 1964). Although a member of the Order of Jesus, Xavier serves as a kind of eponymous ancestor for the Dutch Missionaries of the Sacred Heart in the Moluccas. A large statue of the Jesuit stands in front of the Cathedral in Ambon, facing a mission-run kindergarten across the street that is also named after him.

5. Of course, as one mission history points out, the colonial government often encouraged missionization as a kind of "dam" against what it saw as a wave of Islamic expansion. Given that this was the explicit intention behind the invitation extended to the MSC in 1886 to found a mission station in the Kei Islands, it is not surprising that precisely here they found such opposition in Islam (Schreurs 1992, 172).

6. There is another side to this as well. In harboring few scruples as to the preparedness of persons for conversion, Protestant and Catholic churches throughout the archipelago were instrumental in saving the lives of those vulnerable to accusations of Communist sympathies. As Webb observes, however, "this is no way precludes the churches, Christian charity aside, from the suspicion that they were sometimes not loathe to increase their membership at the expense of Muslims and atheists" (Webb 1986, 109). Thus, if church officials in some respects looked away when evaluating potential converts, they also kept their eyes out for those who—as in one case described in Aru— being "overly fond of a bit of pork" (*te veel van het varkentje houden*) might be enticed away from Islam (Pater L., letter of June 1, 1979).

7. A good example of this perspective in relation to Indonesia is Webb's "The Sickle and the Cross: Christians and Communists in Bali, Flores, Sumba and Timor, 1965–67." In addition to the tension frequently found within a given mission due to the need, on the one hand, to produce vast numbers of converts, and the concern, on the other, about guaranteeing the authenticity of such conversions, the accusation of the superficiality of conversions was often used by one group of missionaries to undermine and criticize the work of another (Neill 1964, 163). A similar idea of the "real" versus the "statistical" in religion underwrites Geertz's distinction between *santri* and *abangan* Muslims in Java (Geertz 1960).

8. I am grateful to my colleague Gerd Bauman for pointing out the intimate relationship between lotteries and numbers, which caused me to consult my notes on the clothing lotteries held in Backshore villages.

9. Longgar had a school run by GPM Protestants since 1921, which some Bemunese attended. For an analysis of a conflict between these two villages that in part articulated itself along the lines of a religious difference occasioned by the two schools—see Spyer (forthcoming b).

10. As McDonald puts it, "The accession of the Suharto Government changed Indonesia's operational model from 'Revolution' to 'Development' " (McDonald 1980, 68).

11. The phenomenon of constructing parallelisms that frequently lend themselves to temporalization crops up widely in the literature on conversion (cf. Hoskins 1987). Graham gives a wonderful example from Flores in which the "new" religion is more or less

spliced onto something configured as the "old" indigenous religion, or the so-called *agama asli* conceived as "analagous to the biblical Old Testament: honourable in its time and place, but now superseded by the New Testament and the knowledge of Christ it contains" (Graham n.d.). This temporalization informed the organization of a procession that in tracing a trajectory from the site of the demolished temple of the "old indigenous religion" to the Catholic church enacted the supposed transition from the "old" to the "new," from a "before" to an "after."

12. During Bemun's performance, a causal relationship is at work according to which the actions of women and, to a lesser extent, children in the village have direct implications for the successes, failures, and accidents of the communal hunt engaged in by Bemunese men in the forest. Hence the expression in the Barakai language that was also put forth in this context: "The forest gets it" (*gobole artom*).

13. At this point, much was made by members of the Stern's family also listening that morning of the amount of blood that gushed forth from the wound, and of how the Stern's daughter had to tend to it since the fact of performance precluded a visit to the "malay" *Puskesmas* (*Pusat Kesehatan Masyarakat*), or Community Health Center, several hours away by boat. Although others in the kitchen could easily recall which men had carried the wounded hunter back to the village, there was considerable uncertainty about whose spear had in fact caused the wound. Since agency in these matters is always located elsewhere—with guardian spirits who monitor the performance and who, in turn, intervene in reaction to actions of Bemunese—such a lapse of memory is not surprising.

14. Although it is not possible to speak of a thoroughgoing aesthetics of numbers such as has been described for parts of Melanesia (Strathern 1992), the contemporary appeal of numbers in Backshore Aru may also draw on older lineages. Of relevance here would be the long history of trade and commercial relations in this region in which various forms of reckoning have been employed (for an interesting example see Riedel 1886, 269), as well as the "Nine" and the "Five" moiety system widely mentioned for Aru in nineteenth-century sources. At least in other parts of the Moluccas in which these same moieties were found, the numbers by which they were known informed the patterning of special social activities (Valeri 1989).

15. In his piece on Ignatius of Loyola, Barthes refers to the bookkeeping nature of sin to describe the self-perpetuating obsessional character of Loyola's *Exercises*, in which the redeeming accounting of errors produces new errors, and thereby the renewal of the need to account (Barthes 1976).

16. Regarding those state practices especially pertinent to the history of statistical representation, Asad mentions national election polls, market research, social security legislation, and markets for consumer goods (Asad 1994, 74).

References

Adnan, Zifirdaus (1990) 'Islamic Religion: Yes, Islamic (Political) Ideology: No! Islam and the State in Indonesia', in Arief Budiman (ed.) *State and Civil Society in Indonesia*, Monash Papers on Southeast Asia 22, Monash University: Centre of Southeast Asian Studies.

Appadurai, Arjun (1993) 'Number in the Colonial Imagination', in Carol A. Breckenridge and Peter van der Veer (eds) *Orientalism and the Postcolonial Predicament*, Philadelphia: University of Pennsylvania Press.

Asad, Talal (1994) 'Ethnographic Representation, Statistics and Modern Power', *Social Research*: 55–88.

Bambang Pranowo, M. (1990) 'Which Islam and Which Pancasila? Islam and the State in Indonesia: A Comment', in Arief Budiman (ed.) *State and Civil Society in Indonesia*, Monash Papers on Southeast Asia 22, Monash University: Centre of Southeast Asian Studies.

Baron Quarles de Quarles, A.J. (1908) 'Memorie van Overgave van het bestuur over de Residentie Amboina van den aftredende Resident', July, 311, Algemeen Rijksarchief, The Hague.

Barthes, Roland (1976) *Sade, Fourier, Loyola*, trans. Richard Miller, New York: Hill and Wang.

Bhabha, Homi K. (1993) 'Beyond the pale: Art in the age of multicultural translation' in Ria Lavrijsen (ed.) *Cultural Diversity in the Arts*, Amsterdam, Royal Tropical Institute.

Budiman, Arief (1990) 'Introduction' in Arief Budiman (ed.) *State and Civil Society in Indonesia*, Monash Papers on Southeast Asia 22, Monash University: Centre of Southeast Asian Studies.

Cohn, Bernard S. (1987a) 'The Census, Social Structure and Objectification in South Asia', in Bernard S. Cohn *An Anthropologist Among the Historians and Other Essays*, Delhi and London: Oxford University Press.

———. (1987b) 'History and Anthropology: The State of Play', in Bernard S. Cohn *An Anthropolist Among the Historians and Other Essays*, Delhi and London: Oxford University Press.

Comaroff, Jean and John (1991) *Of Revelation and Revolution: Christianity, Colonialism, and Consciousness in South Africa*, Vol I, Chicago: University of Chicago Press.

Comité 100 Jaar MSC (1954) *Memoriale: hundred years msc all over the world*, Tilburg: Comité 100 Jaar MSC.

de Certeau, Michel (1971) 'Le Danger de l'Insignificance', *Spiritus* 12,44:86–90.

———. (1988) *The Writing of History*, trans. Tom Conley, New York: Columbia University Press.

de Graaf, H.J. (1977) *De Geschiedenis van Ambon en de Zuid Molukken*, Franeker: T. Wever B.V.

Foucault, Michel (1978) *The History of Sexuality*, New York: Vintage Books.

Fox, James J. (1988) Review of Rita Smith Kipp and Susan Rodgers (eds) *Indonesian Religions in Transition*, *American Ethnologist* 15,4:806–7.

Geertz, Clifford (1960) *The Religion of Java*, Chicago: University of Chicago Press.

Graham, Penelope (n.d.) 'Moralities in conflict: forging minority religious identities within the Indonesian state', paper presented at the Meetings of the European Association of Social Anthropologists, Oslo, Norway, June 1994.

Hacking, Ian (1990) *The Taming of Chance*, Cambridge: Cambridge University Press.

Hall, Catherine (1992) 'Missionary Stories: Gender and Ethnicity in England in the 1830s and 1840s', in Lawrence Grossberg, Cary Nelson, and Paula Treichler (eds) *Cultural Studies*, London: Routledge.

Hoskins, Janet (1987) 'Entering the Bitter House: Spirit Worship and Conversin in West Sumba' in Rita Smith Kipp and Susan Rodgers (eds) *Indonesian Religions in Transition*, Tucson: University of Arizona Press.

Kipp, Rita Smith and Rodgers, Susan (eds) (1987) *Indonesian Religions in Transition*, Tucson: University of Arizona Press.

Mahadi (1987) 'Islam and Law in Indonesia' in Rita Smith Kipp and Susan Rodgers (eds) *Indonesian Religions in Transition*, Tucson: University of Arizona Press.

Mani, Lata (1992) 'Cultural Theory, Colonial Texts: Reading Eyewitness Accounts of Widow Burning', in Lawrence Grossberg, Cary Nelson, and Paula Treichler (eds) *Cultural Studies*, London: Routledge.

McDonald, Hamish (1980) *Suharto's Indonesia*, Australia: Fontana Books.

McVey, Ruth (1993) 'Redesigning the Cosmos: Belief Systems and State Power in Indonesia', *NIAS Report* 14, Copenhagen: Nordic Institute of Asian Studies.

Morfit, Michael (1981) 'Pancasila: The Indonesian State Ideology According to the New Order Government', *Asian Survey* 21:838–851.

MSC Archives, Correspondence concerning Aru, 1949–present, Missionhouse Ambon, Indonesia.

Neill, Stephen (1986) *A History of Christian Missions*, revised for the second edition by Owen Chadwick, Hammondsworth: Penguin Books, Ltd.

Pemberton, John (1986) 'Notes on the 1982 General Election in Solo', *Indonesia* 41:1–22.

Po-chia Hsia, R. (n.d.) 'The Jesuits in China: Stories of Conversion', paper presented at the Research Centre for Religion and Society, University of Amsterdam, October 1994.

Riedel, J.G.F. (1886) *De Sluik- en Kroesharige Rassen tusschen Selebes en Papua*, The Hague: Nijhoff.

Schama, Simon (1987) *The Embarrassment of Riches: An Interpretation of Dutch Culture in the Golden Age*, Great Britain: Fontana Press.

Scheurs, P.H.G. (1992) *Terug in het Erfgoed van Franciscus Xaverius: Het herstel van de katholieke missie in Maluku, 1886–1960*, Tilburg: Missiehuis MSC.

Sol msc., A., Bisschop van Amboina (n.d.) 'Rapport van vormreis september 1976 op de Aroe-eilanden', unpublished manuscript.

Spyer, Patricia (1996) 'Diversity with a Difference: *Adat* and the New Order in Aru (Eastern Indonesia)', in *Cultural Anthropology* 11,1.

——. (forthcoming b) *The Memory of Trade*, Durham, NC: Duke University Press.

Stewart, Kathleen (1991) "n the Politics of Cultural Theory: A Case for "Contaminated" Cultural Critique', *Social Research* 58,2:395–412.

Strathern, Marilyn (1992) 'Qualified value: the perspective of gift exchange' in Caroline Humphrey and Stephen Hugh-Jones (eds) *Barter, Exchange and Value: An Anthropological Approach*, Cambridge: Cambridge University Press.

Tan, Mély G. (1991) 'The Social and Cultural Dimensions of the Role of Ethnic Chinese in Indonesian Society', *Indonesia*, Proceedings of the symposium held at Cornell University.

Thomas, Nicholas (1993) 'Colonial Conversions: Differences, Hierarchy and History in Early Twentieth Century Evangelical Propaganda', *Comparative Studies in Society and History* 34,2:514–551.

Tsing, Anna Lowenhaupt (1994) *In the Realm of the Diamond Queen: Marginality in an Out-of-the-Way Place*, Princeton: Princeton University Press.

Valeri, Valerio (1989) 'Reciprocal Centers: The Siwa-Lima System in the Central Moluccas' in David Maybury Lewis and Uri Almagor (eds) *The Attraction of Opposites: thought and society in the dualistic mode*, Ann Arbor: University of Michigan Press.

van der Veer, Peter (1994) *Religious Nationalism: Hindus and Muslims in India*, Berkeley: University of California Press.

van Doorn, J.A.A. (1994) *De laatste eeuw van Indië: Ontwikkeling and ondergang van een koloniaal project*, Amsterdam: Uitgeverij Bert Bakker.

van Langenberg, Michael (1990) 'The New Order State: Language, Ideology, Hegemony' in Arief Budiman (ed) *State and Civil Society in Indonesia*, Monash Papers on Southeast Asia 22, Monash University: Centre of Southeast Asian Studies.

van Weerdenburg msc, H. (n.d.) *MSC*, Tilburg: Missiehuis Tilburg.

Webb, R.A.F. Paul (1986) 'The Sickle and the Cross: Christians and Communists in Bali, Flores, Sumba, and Timor, 1965–67', *Journal of Southeast Asian Studies* 17,1:94–112.

Young, Robert (1990) *White Mythologies: Writing History and the West*, London: Routledge.

8

MODERNITY AND ENCHANTMENT: THE IMAGE OF THE DEVIL IN POPULAR AFRICAN CHRISTIANITY

Birgit Meyer

Introduction

While Christian discourses of conversion concentrate on an intrapersonal shift of religious allegiance and conviction, social scientists have long conceptualized conversion in terms of increasing rationalization and disenchantment (*Entzauberung*). This view of conversion, of course, draws upon Max Weber's (1978) work on religious change and on the conditions for, and implications of, people's turn from "traditional" religions[1] to one of the world religions. Hefner recently summarized Weber's understanding of religious rationalization. World religions differ from traditional religions by "1) the creation and clarification of doctrines by intellectual systematizers, 2) the canonization and institutionalization of these doctrines by certain social carriers, and 3) the effective socialization of these cultural principles into the ideas and actions of believers" (1993, 18). A fourth point of importance in the framework of this essay is that in his work on Protestantism, Weber (1984) suggested that the internalization of this variant of Christianity would eventually lead to the disenchantment of modern society. All this, of course, is an ideal-type description. There is ample evidence, especially from non–Western contexts subject to Western missionaries' activities but also from Western popular Christianity, that the actual praxis does not necessarily meet the ideal type.

Weber himself was aware of this. In his work, one can note a tension between the ideal-type course of religious development and the practical-historical manifestation of religion in everyday life.[2] It seems to me that many students inspired by Weber, especially those introduced to him through

Parsons, fail to note this tension and understand his work merely in terms of his ideal-type abstraction.[3] The following quotation dealing with Christianity is of particular interest for this problem:

> The path to monotheism has been traversed with varying degrees of consistency, but nowhere—not even during the Reformation—was the existence of spirits and demons permanently eliminated; rather, they were simply subordinated unconditionally to the one god, at least in theory. The decisive consideration was, and remains: Who is deemed to exert the stronger influence on the interests of the individual in his everyday life, the theoretically supreme god or the lower spirits and demons? If the spirits, then the religion of everyday life is decisively determined by them, regardless of the official god-concept of the ostensibly rationalized religion [1978, 415–16].

In this fascinating passage Weber points to the gap between official theological theory, with its monotheistic orientation, and people's actual religious praxis,[4] with its emphasis on demons. The rationalization implied in world religions on the level of theological doctrine thus does not need to imply the closure of the doctrine and the disenchantment of the world in lay believers' praxis. It is exactly this tension—a tension Weber only indicated but did not work out—that I wish to explore in this essay. It may be located between the ideal-type description of Protestantism in terms of the belief in God professed by modern theologians and taken for granted by social scientists on one hand, and the popular praxis of demonology or diabology that focuses on the works of Satan and his agents on the other. Thus, rather than inferring the characteristics of Protestantism from the claims of its theologically trained proponents, I will investigate how a historical encounter between missionaries and Africans gave rise to a peculiar African version of missionary Pietism.

This essay deals with the activities of the *Norddeutsche Mission* (NMG), a German nineteenth-century Pietist mission society among the Ewe on the so-called Slavecoast (now southern Togo and southeastern Ghana). In the first years after its arrival in 1847, the mission society had little success, and had above all to lament its young missionaries' untimely deaths from tropical fevers. However, after the establishment of British and German colonial rule over Goldcoast and Togo, the group of converts among the Ewe, who lived in both colonies, grew steadily: In 1890 the church had about 700 members, and in 1914 it counted almost 11,700. When as a result of Germany's involvement in the First World War the NMG was forced to withdraw from the field in 1916, it left behind an institutionalized mission church, the Ewe Presbyterian Church, that became formally independent from the mother society in 1922; from then on, church affairs were run by native workers. It is the aim of this essay to throw light on the conversions occurring in the course of the mission's activities among the Ewe between 1847 and 1916. I will try to provide insight into the political, socioeconomic, and religious implications of conversion by way of studying believers'—both missionaries and Ewe Christians—ideas regarding the turn to Christianity.

My main concern in this essay, then, is the relationship among conversion, modernity, (dis)enchantment, and the image of the Devil. I will argue that Pietist missionaries' and Ewe converts' image of the Devil lay at the base of a popular form of African Christianity that entailed both the modernization and the enchantment of the converts' world.

The Pietist Missionaries

Nineteenth-century Germany was characterized by substantial economic, social, political, cultural, and religious changes that brought about the gradual transition from traditional corporative and agrarian forms of life to increasingly modern, democratic, and industrial ones. The nineteenth-century Christian Awakening, which was inspired by seventeenth- and eighteenth-century Pietism, faced the field of tensions that resulted from these changes in its own specific way. In the framework of this movement, many missions were founded all over Europe, which aimed at the conversion of all non-Christians inside and outside their own society (Gray 1981; Neil 1975, 251ff). One of these missions was the *Norddeutsche Missionsgesellschaft* (NMG). Whereas its Board consisted of pastors and wealthy traders who were convinced that global "fair trade" (*redlicher Handel*) and the spread of the Gospel went hand in hand (cf. Tell & Heinrich 1986), its missionaries were recruited from the lower classes. The greater part of the missionaries originated from southern Germany, especially from Württemberg, which was known for the vitality of its Pietist tradition.

The nineteenth-century Pietist Awakening, which brought back the focus on the inner life, was a conservative movement triggered by, and responding to, the socioeconomic, political, cultural, and religious changes affecting all German states. Although the movement was part of the Protestant church, it vehemently opposed both the routinization of church life and the modern, post-enlightened liberal Protestant theology that tried to reconciliate faith with modern science. The Awakening was popular among people who saw their economic and social position threatened by industrialization and urbanization (Scharfe 1980, 135). The missionaries of the NMG, who usually had no more than basic education and had been trained to work as farmers, craftsmen, or petty traders, upheld the Pietist ideal of life and work in a well-ordered rural setting. Many of them were driven out of the rural-life context against their wills, and the experience of the rural way of life being threatened by modern developments was one important motive for the wish to become missionaries among the "heathens" who still seemed unaffected by modern life.

Pietism offered these people a means of orientation that was of great help in determining their attitudes toward the modernizing world. Their world view is condensed in the popular lithograph, "The Broad and the Narrow Path" that could be found in the homes of many nineteenth-century German Pietists.[5] This lithograph illustrates how walking Satan's Broad Path, which leads pilgrims through such places as a public house, a ballroom, a whorehouse, a theater, and a hotel with a republican flag, spells pleasure on earth but will result in infernal destruction in the Hereafter. By contrast, those who follow God's Narrow Path, which entails abstinence from worldly pleasures, will be rewarded with salvation and eternal enjoyment in the Heavenly Jerusalem. According to the lithograph, temptations include sexual pleasure, alcohol, gambling, and other forms of entertainment that money could buy and in which an increasing number of people indulged in the course of industrialization and urbanization.

According to Pietist thinking, however, the Devil did not merely operate through the world of modern consumption but also through traditional popular religion, which was still very much alive in Pietist surroundings. The Awakening developed not only in response to, and as part and parcel of, modern changes such as industrialization, urbanization, and rationalization, but also in the confrontation with popular peasant religion. In nineteenth-century Württemberg, a belief in spirits and so-called superstitious beliefs and practices had remained common among the peasant population. There were people accused of witchcraft, as well as other persons known as black magicians or sorcerers who could bring about wealth or health for some and harm for others through their magic (cf. Bohnenberger 1961).[6] As members of the Catholic or Protestant church, many people consulted these sorcerers. The Pietists, though of course inclined to resist these popular practices, still lived in this context and had to define their position against them. As we shall see further on, the missionaries' position at home did not, in this respect, differ much from their position among the Ewe in

Africa. Pietists considered Satan to be the force behind the popular beliefs and practices dealing with spirits, thereby subordinating popular religion to Pietism without having to dismiss it as irrational "superstition" in the way mainstream theologians such as Schleiermacher[7] would have done. The spirits of popular religion were thus integrated into the Pietist religion by being denounced as agents of Satan.

Locating the Pietist religion within Germany, the NMG formed part of a conservative minority movement focused on restoring Christian values to the family, faith, and lifestyle—especially against the background of possible increased consumption—that had been eroded in the course of the nineteenth century. Though antimodern in outlook, the Pietist Awakening was a phenomenon of its time (cf. Van Rooden 1990). Its emphasis on individual self-control and its sober, ascetic ethics fit well into the evolving capitalist economy. Moreover, the denial of "worldly" pleasures made it easier for people to accept their lack of prosperity and poor working conditions. Nevertheless, while these ethics corresponded to modern conditions, the missionaries were not consciously modern, rational people, up to date with their time, but rather people who defined themselves as resisting the modernity and rationality professed by rational and liberal theologians, philosophers, democrats, and socialists. The Awakened Pietists can thus be described as "modern conservatives." Many missionaries wanted to realize their dream of returning to the good rural life; simultaneously, they became agents of change who contributed to the global spread of a modern political and economic configuration. We shall soon see how their somewhat paradoxical modern conservativism gave rise to contradictions in the African context that they were unable to resolve.

Conversion and "Civilization"

The Ewe in Premissionary Times

To appreciate the impact of the NMG on Ewe converts, it is useful to briefly sketch premissionary Ewe society. The Ewe, who lived on the coast and in the inland of what was then called Slavecoast, were actually constructed as one "people" through the mission's linguistic and ethnographic work (Westermann 1936) and its translation into real policies by colonial administrators. The inland Ewe, among whom the mission started its work and who concern us in this essay, lived in various small states ruled by the king of Peki because in 1833 they had defeated the neighboring Akwamu,

who had hitherto dominated them. The configuration of Ewe states, however, never formed an integrated empire comparable to that of the Asante
but consisted of fragile alliances between individual states that often strove
for mutual independence (Amenumey 1986; Asare 1973). The inland
economy relied on subsistence agriculture and, to some extent, cotton
trade with Africans and Europeans. Land, the prime base of production,
was owned by patrilineages. All patrilineal family members were to make
use of the family land without anyone owning it personally. The production of food and clothes depended on the cooperation of husbands and
wives. Those who had managed to become prosperous were expected to
help and support their poorer relatives and other needy people. These co-
operative principles were embedded in a gerontocratic organization of authority (cf. Spieth 1906). That the cooperation of patrilineal kin, husbands
and wives, the rich and the poor, and the acceptance of the authority of the
elders was the norm does not, however, imply that people always behaved
accordingly. On the contrary, in practice these norms gave rise to all sorts
of conflicts in these relationships. We shall soon see that colonization and
missionization brought about changes affecting everyone's position. As a result of these changes, the relationships between siblings and cousins, husbands and wives, the rich and the poor, and the young and the old would
eventually transform, and this would break up the material need for, and
moral obligation of, cooperation and obedience.[8]

The Christian Village and Congregational Life

When the first missionaries started their work among the Ewe in 1847, the
NMG could not limit itself to purely religious activities. Though at home
the missionaries belonged to a conservative movement, in the African context they paradoxically became the first agents of "civilization" and modernity with which the Ewe were confronted. They always followed the same
missionizing strategy: Propagating "civilization"[9] through missionization,
they instigated the establishment of Christian villages (called Kpozdi—i.e.,
"on the hilltop")[10] with a school, church, and small houses for nuclear families. They taught people basic literacy in the Ewe language and propagated
hitherto unknown skills such as carpentry, masonry, and teaching. After the
area inhabited by Ewe "tribes" had been pacified and colonial rule established in the first decade after 1884, the NMG also propagated the cultivation of cash crops such as cotton, coffee, and most importantly cocoa,
which became the main export crop from 1900 onward. Although for the
mission all these activities were rather ordinary (and not particularly mod-

ern) and fully in line with the Pietist ideal of a rural way of life, they appeared as an alley toward "civilization" and modernity to the Ewe. Before we pursue this tension, it is useful to describe congregational life in some detail.

The missionaries set down new rules of conduct for Christians that matched the Pietist lifestyle but differed considerably from the Ewe's previous way of life. The first congregational order (*Gemeindeordnung*) was formulated by the missionaries and assistants in 1876 and revised in 1909.[11] The submission to the congregational order was equated with obedience to God (translated as *Mawu*); Christian life de facto boiled down to the observance of rules that, ideally, were internalized.[12] Membership in the Christian congregation was confined to a person "who is baptized on the name of the Trinity, who lives according to the Gospel, and who obeys the order valid in our congregations."

Every Sunday the congregation had to attend church. Before taking Holy Communion, members had to see the head of the congregation, who could deny them participation if their behavior had been inappropriate for a Christian. Christian marriages were performed after having been announced twice in church service. If a previously "heathen" couple converted, their marriage was confirmed. Noisy marriage celebrations and shooting guns were absolutely forbidden. The mission prohibited childhood betrothals and polygamous marriage, which were common in traditional Ewe society, but accepted the marriage of a Christian and a "heathen" partner. Divorce was only possible if the dupe of the partner's adultery insisted. The mission expected Christian couples to share table and bed, and disapproved of wives leaving their husbands alone for a long period of time because this would entice adultery. A Christian's property was to be inherited by the close relatives—that is, the partner and children. Christian children should "not go naked as those of the heathens did, rather a feeling of sense of shame and discipline should be awakened in and demanded from them" (ibid.). In the case of death, Christians had to make sure that "clothes, jewelry, objects, cowries . . . were not put into the grave of the deceased." "Heathen lamentations" and noise had to be prevented, and after the burial in the congregational cemetery there could be no funeral meal. The sick could never be treated with "heathen" medicines, but had to "trust in the Lord" instead.

In the "outward life," Christian behavior was supposed to be honorable, virtuous, simple, ordered, and sober. The men were to learn a profession, avoid incurring debts, and abstain from spending money on imported rum. Earthly goods were a "blessing from the Lord" that was to be neither squandered nor treated with avarice. The Christian's true home (*Heimat*) was heaven. Among the "heathens" they were to walk with care without neglecting their obligation to submit themselves to the political authorities. In line with Romans 13 they had to obey the government—that is, the British District Commissioner as well as the traditional chiefs.

The whole Christian congregation was to watch over the "purity of behavior and doctrine." A person who violated the Christian regulations was admonished first and, if the inappropriate behavior was repeated, excommunicated. Punished were all those who

> had committed severe faults such as relapse into heathen sin, idolatry, participation in heathen feasts and ceremonies or other rude sins such as adultery, fornication, theft, fraud, cramming, boozing, squandering, obstinate irreconcilability, abuse of relatives, cruelty, etc., and who had become causes of public annoyance (ibid.).

This order was read to the congregation once or twice a year. Next to this institutionalized repetition of rules, the indigenous teachers were supposed to provide practical examples of true Christian life.

The missionaries devoted a lot of energy to their training. Between 1871 and 1900, twenty of these students were even sent to the missionaries' home base in Westheim (Württemberg) (Schreiber 1936, 249ff), where they were to learn the virtues of Pietist family life.[13] These German-trained teachers became the central exponents of a Pietist lifestyle. They met regularly at conferences and discussed topics such as the improvement of Christian family life. Their material culture—that is, the architecture of their houses as well as their furniture, household utensils, and clothes, and the way they organized family matters, provided the model for a Western way of life. Commanding a high status in the new colonial hierarchy, teachers were much admired and copied by "ordinary" Christians. Although the mission work would have been impossible without these native intermediaries who proclaimed the Christian message in the most remote villages, the missionaries denied the teachers an equal status.[14] Even after ordaining some of the teachers as pastors, the missionaries still adopted a paternalistic stance toward them and regarded them as not fully matured. This frequently led to conflicts between missionaries and native workers. When the missionaries left the mission field in 1916, the teachers became the leaders of the independent Ewe church that was officially founded in 1922.

It is ironic that whereas at home the missionaries belonged to a religious movement criticizing the outwardness and ritualization of the orthodox churches, among the Ewe they founded congregations wherein outward behavior and submission to the church order were overemphasized. The history of the mission among the Ewe illustrates how religiously moved missionaries sparked a process that brought about the very outwardness and superficiality of religious life they abhorred at home.

Socioeconomic Motivations for, and Consequences of, Conversion

Originally, few Ewe were inclined to convert. With the establishment of colonial rule and the political and economic ramifications it entailed, however, more and more people were attracted to the new way of life. It was evident that the Christians were the group able to profit most in colonial society. An answer to why so many Ewe converted can be found in an essay by the native mission teacher Hermann Nyalemegbe. According to him, people turned to Christianity for the following reasons: healing through the medical care of Christians; sorrow about the death of a child, assumed to be the work of gods (trɔ̃wo, sing. trɔ̃); a marginal position in the non-Christian community; the comparatively cheap Christian burial and the fact that Christians feared the dead less than the heathens did; the Christian clothes and the white marriage; the conversion of the partner; the fact that Christians neglected taboos and did not die from them; and the work of the Christians and their wealth.[15] Though this essay was qualified as "superficial" (oberflächlich) by the missionary Ernst Bürgi, who was in charge of the mission teachers, in my view it leads right to the heart of the matter.

Indeed, the Christian religion was attractive because it offered the material means to achieve a prosperous and relatively high position in colonial society. Though the mission's relationship with both the German and British colonial administration was not free from tensions, the missionaries themselves were proud of their important contribution to the colonial project of bringing "civilization" to the Ewe.[16] Especially from 1900 onward, cocoa cultivation was taken up by many inland Ewe (both Christian and non-Christian), who thereby were able to earn a lot of cash. The eagerness to cultivate cocoa gave rise to land conflicts between and within lineages, and to individuals attempting to purchase land privately. Soon virtually all farmland was under cultivation—a development that, in the long run, had disastrous effects on the environment. The increased cultivation of cocoa perfectly fit colonial interests: It not only provided the home countries with raw material but also increased the native demand for European goods.

But the mission did not only offer opportunities to achieve wealth, it set new directives for its distribution. In an essay about the question of whether most Ewe Christians understood "the real meaning of Christian life," the teacher E. Buama wrote about the Peki Dzake congregation in 1909:

> Many heathens have many things, and their families are troubling them [so] that they cannot keep what they save. This caused some to be Christians; thinking that being Christians all of their properties will be saved.[17]

The mission's emphasis on the Christian family thus implied that for a wealthy Christian there was no need to share property with his wider family. Christianity thereby contributed to the undermining of the old moral obligation of the rich to assist needy members of the wider family.

Though proud of their contribution to "civilization," the missionaries, in line with their beliefs, considered material achievements "outward" things that had to be paralleled by an individual "inner" development. Their stance toward "civilization" was paradoxical: Whereas they considered it a prerequisite for Christianization, they detested it at the same time because it made the Ewe focus on the outward rather than the inward aspects of the Pietist message. From a Pietist point of view, all the reasons for conversion given by Nyalemegbe, although implying a rejection of non-Christian religious practices, were outward and materialistic. For the missionaries it was not sufficient to leave the old religion because Christian rites were "nicer" and cheaper, Christians were free to violate taboos, or the medical treatment provided by the missionaries incidentally proved to be more successful than traditional medicines.[18] However, the main attraction of Christianity lay in these very material advantages. Therefore, Nyalemegbe's essay is not "superficial" at all, but rather an adequate assessment of the situation. It shows that, contrary to the missionaries' perspective, the Ewe did not reduce religion to a state of the mind but closely connected it with material life. To them, it was not just a matter of belief but also a set of practices linking the ideal and the material.

Unfortunately, the church statistics do not tell us anything about the numerical relationship between men and women and the age of their members. However, from the missionaries' written accounts and my own investigations, I conclude that the mission started as—and for long remained—mainly a male enterprise.[19] In 1892, the missionary Jacob Spieth complained about the low standards of the teachers' wives, who—in his view—prevented their husbands from leading a Christian family life (*Monatsblatt der Norddeutschen Mission*[20] (MB) 1892, 11). It seems that whereas especially young men were open to change, the women in general remained attached to the old religion and way of life much longer. This posed problems for young Christian males, who found it very difficult to find Christian spouses and often had to marry non-Christian girls who might convert to their husbands' religion after some time.

It is not surprising that the mission was much less attractive for women than for men—it did not offer women the possibility of improving their economic situation by their own labor. In line with their conservative Pietist norms and values, the missionaries simply did not appreciate economically independent women. This also had consequences for the performance of the marriage rites. Whereas traditionally a bride received a fixed amount of gifts from her groom, Christian marriage, which was imagined as a link between individual partners, was devoid of this practice, thereby depriving the wife of personal property. Yet the mission's emphasis on the nuclear family also implied benefits for women. If a husband indeed took the responsibility of feeding his wife and children, the woman was relieved of taking care of her children materially. Another benefit lay in the inheritance rules. Whereas traditionally a widow did not inherit her husband's property and his brothers obtained his movable things, the Christian order decreed that women and children got all belongings of the husband and father (cf. MB 1907, 34ff). Moreover, if a man married just one wife instead of several, he may have been better able to take care of her and the children. If a Christian husband lived up to these expectations, it may have been beneficial for a woman to convert. However, if he did not, from an economic point of view it was better for the woman to stick to traditional ways. It is thus impossible to judge unequivocally whether the mission was beneficial for women. This would depend on her familial situation.

In more narrowly religious respects, Christianity was less attractive for women. Only men were allowed to be pastors, teachers, and evangelists. In traditional religion, by contrast, women played an important role, for in the inland only women were possessed by the gods and functioned as their speakers. Through the turn to Christianity, women lost this spiritual function. Another reason for women not to convert was their responsibility for their children's health. Despite some occasional successes, against many sicknesses the mission could not offer remedies that were as good as, or even better than, those of the traditional priests. Since the mission forbade Christians to use such medicines, many women hesitated to convert. Compared with men— especially young men who could still undergo training—women could take much less material and spiritual advantage from turning to Christianity.

In short, the church mainly consisted of people—most of them young and middle-aged men—willing to participate in the economic opportunities that occurred as a result of the concerted economic impulses of the missions, traders, and administrators, and to limit the distribution of the riches earned through this participation to the nuclear family. They were a new social class of people attempting to go with their time and profit in colonial society. But this was not reason enough to be accepted into the Christian congregation. The decision to convert cannot be reduced to purely economic considerations. Indeed, as we shall see below, disappointment with the efficacy of the old religious practices also played an important role.

Conversion and Traditional Religion

"Heathendom" and the Devil

The missionaries considered it their main task to lead the Ewe "back" to the Christian God. They endorsed the nineteenth-century Protestant myth of the evolution of heathendom (Fabri 1859, 39ff), which stated that all descendants of Noah's cursed son Ham had turned into Devil worshippers. Thus, the Ewe were classified as belonging to the general category of "heathens" and assigned a place in the history of mankind: Separated from the God they had originally worshipped and serving the Devil (translated as *Abosam*) in the meantime, their customs and language had degenerated over the course of time. It was the task of the mission to lead them away from Satan back to the Christian God.

By diabolizing Ewe religion, the missionaries constructed Pietism and the former in terms of oppositions: Whereas they emphasized belief, the Ewe relied on rituals. Whereas they would not offer sacrifices, the Ewe would involve the gods and spirits in a relationship of gift exchange. Whereas God revealed himself through the Bible, the Ewe communicated with Satan's agents through dance and possession. Whereas Pietism's agents were male, the Ewe relied on priestesses in addition to priests, and the former expressed the voice of the gods. In the variant of Christianity advocated by the NMG, there was no room for any of these things. The missionaries thus represented traditional religion as Pietism's Other. They defined the two religions in terms of radical difference and denied Ewe Christians their previous expressive forms of worship.

In order to lead the Ewe away from Satan and back to the Christian God, the missionaries took to the investigation of Ewe language, history, and customs. They chose one Ewe dialect (the Anlo-variant spoken on the coast) as standard, turned it into writing, and translated the Bible and other Christian literary products. They trained indigenous assistants and let them preach the Gospel everywhere in the area inhabited by the Ewe. By preaching and teaching in standard Ewe, and through the formulation of Ewe history and customs, the mission aspired to turn the various separate Ewe "tribes" into one "people" united in the Ewe mission church.[21] Thus, the NMG's religious activities indeed aimed at the achievement of the characteristic features of religious rationalization described by Weber: Through their linguistic and ethnographic investigations, the missionaries were able to translate the Pietist doctrine into the Ewe language, thereby providing the Ewe with a canonized and institutionalized message. By educating Ewe assistants, they formed indigenous social carriers able to bring these doctrines home to their people. By imposing a church order, they intended to socialize converts into proper Christian life. However, one can wonder how much the missionaries actually achieved the closure and institutionalization of the doctrine among the Ewe, and how far the socialization of the Ewe converts into the new church order went. It seems to me that, above all through their emphasis on the Devil, whom they associated with all non-Christian religions, the missionaries themselves hindered the full achievement of these aims.[22] Indeed, as we saw above, by considering popular peasant religion a domain of demons, Pietism itself does not fully match Weber's ideal-type decription of Protestantism: it enchants rather than disenchants the world. By laying emphasis on the Devil, not only popular religion at home but also traditional Ewe religion were declared real rather than superstitious, and became part of the Christian discourse in a transformed way. This is what I shall try to show in the remainder of this essay.

Ewe Converts Turn Away from Traditional Religion

To fully understand the implications of conversion, it is necessary to study both people's dissatisfactions with the old and their quest for improvement in the framework of the new religion. In this section we shall assess which negative experiences with traditional religion made Ewe convert to missionary Pietism.

The majority of conversion candidates were people who had played no special role in the framework of Ewe religion and merely had sought a *trõ's* or *dzo's* [magic/medicine] protection in case of need. Many of them converted because they were tired of serving a *trõ* without profiting from it. For instance, a man from Peki-Avetile complained:

When my first child was sick, I offered the family-god Abia a goat; the child, however, died. For the second child I even bought three goats, but it also died. No less than twenty-five goats the god Abia has received from me. This, however, did not make my heart happy, but rather emptied my hand and made my heart poor. Now my eyes are opened to recognize Christ; with him there are no goats and chicken. Salvation from sin and death is only with him; for he loves us, although we are in the dark (MB 1902, 36).

Many people had similar problems and were disappointed by both the power of the *trõwo* and *dzo*. Indeed, "the main reason . . . which causes the heathens to start something new, lies in the paltriness of their idols and fetish-strings, as well as in the experience of the priests' fraud" (MB 1902, 36). The change of religion thus basically was a deliberate turn away from the old.

Occasionally, even priests turned to Christianity. In such cases, all paraphernalia related to *trõ*-worship would be burned and the priest would openly reject its service. Spieth, for instance, described the case of a priestess of the Peki-*trõ* Fofie, which had possessed her and turned her into its priestess against her will. The service of Fofie, which demanded expensive food sacrifices and forbade her to work in the field and to leave her compound, was costly and tedious, though she gained some money from consultations at the same time. Eventually she became a Christian. In the night after her decision to convert, she had a vision:

A big European had a book in his hand. The teacher was sitting at his right, and a male hideous creature, only dressed with a loin-cloth, was sitting at his left. The European had opened the book, read, and in the end said "No." Upon this the teacher shouted against the hideous creature, which, as a result, got up and fled. Then she fell asleep (1908, 12. Original in German, translation BM).

This vision casts the priestess' wish to leave her old god in a symbolic battle between Christianity, represented by the European and the Ewe teacher (certainly both dressed in coat and tie), and the old religion, represented by the sparely dressed creature. Her own decision was confirmed by the fact that the European found her name in God's book of life, so that the teacher could chase away the old god. Conversion was frequently cast in similar dream images that emphasized the superiority of the book religion, whose followers enhanced it by their own individual decision, over that of the traditional possession cults, whose followers were chosen and possessed by the *trɔ̃wo* against their own will. The issue of sin and internal change, however, was virtually never raised in the framework of this imagery, which emphasized the turn away from the old, "uncivilized" form of worship.

Another important consequence of, and thus attraction to, conversion was that Christians no more had to comply with the *trɔ̃wo's* taboos. Many of the *trɔ̃wo* were conservative in that they forbade people to make use of modern objects. For many people it was attractive to leave these taboos behind and be "civilized"; that is, undisturbed by such constraints. Other *trɔ̃wo* did not allow trees to be felled on their land. By declaring that the *trɔ̃wo* were devilish powers that no more had to be obeyed, Christians were free from submitting themselves to the constraints laid upon people by these powers.

However, the mere will to escape from old constraints was not enough to be accepted as a church member. There was a time span between the initial willingness to be a Christian and a person's acceptance into the mission church. In order to become a member, a person had to follow baptismal lessons. After this course, which was given by a native assistant teaching the basics of Protestant doctrine and morals, each candidate was interrogated by a missionary who then decided whether the person was to be accepted. In this context, the candidates had to confess their involvement with "heathendom" and their moral trespasses, such as non- or extramarital affairs. The NMG did not strive to baptize as many people as possible, but submitted each candidate to careful selection. In many cases, aspiring Christians were refused because they were not yet considered mature (e.g., MB 1896, 11); that is, they did not sufficiently match the mission's ideal of conversion.[23]

To the missionaries, ideal conversion resulted from a feeling of total sinfulness and entailed a complete change of a person's inner state and, as a next step, behavior. The missionaries continuously lamented that many just repeated what they had heard in the lesson, without seeming to have internalized the message.[24] Moreover, rather than having a notion of sinfulness, the candidates mainly complained about the traditional priests' inability to bring about health and protection, and about the fact that in the framework of *trɔ̃*-worship they could not be masters of their own lives. The historical documents abound with missionaries' criticisms that most Ewe lacked the "inner" dimension of conversion, that there was no real change in their heart, as the Ewe term newly coined to designate conversion, *dzimetɔtrɔ̃* ("turn in the heart"), suggested. However, the missionaries' uncertainties and complaints about the converts' inner state should not blind us to the fact that conversion actually was a radical step. As we have seen above, it did not only imply the full neglect of traditional religious practices but also the separation from groups to which the converts had hitherto belonged. Now their Christian identity was stressed above that of their being part of particular families, clans, towns, and states.

Since there was no way for the missionaries to look into people's minds, all those dissociating themselves openly from the old religion and adopting the Christian church order had to be accepted as members. People, for whatever reasons had initially driven them to the baptismal class, could become church members if they took up the missionaries' discourse and renounced the Ewe religion as "heathendom." Indeed, the rejection of traditional religion as satanic and backward was considered the hallmark of conversion by both Ewe Christians and missionaries. Spieth summarized this succinctly in his essay on conversion: "If we could ask the almost 6000 Christians of Ewe-land from where they come, they would all reply: 'We come out of the dark, where we stood under the power of Satan'" (1908, 1. Original in German, translation BM). Ewe Christians thus adopted the diabolization of the Ewe religion preached to them by the missionaries. The missionaries, however, were not all too happy with the popularity of this view. To them, conversion amounted to more than the mere turn away from old religious concepts and practices and the adoption of a Christian lifestyle.

"Pagan Survivals"

As the Devil played such a crucial role in the missionaries' world view, it is not astonishing that he did even more so in the Ewe's, and that through him the pre-Christian religion became a building block of their Christian understanding. The Ewe Christians seem to have perfectly grasped the central dichotomy of the Pietist world view continuously communicated to them, and applied it to their own situation (cf. Meyer 1992). This enabled them to dissociate themselves from the old religion, which they considered pagan and backward. It perfectly fit their spatial and social separation from the other people, and emphasized that the former looked down on the latter and considered themselves more advanced. In this sense, the diabolization of traditional practices reified as "heathendom" was a symbolic means of the new elite to define itself as different.

However, diabolization did not only entail the possibility of people dissociating themselves from "heathendom" but at the same time its confirmation as truly existent. This was how Ewe Christians experienced the non-Christian religion. In the same way as for the missionaries, for them the old gods and ghosts, which were now conceptualized as agents of the Devil, were actually present. But in contrast with the missionaries, most Ewe Christians had experienced their presence in their own lives, which had attracted them to Christianity. This even applied to the second- and third-generation Christians, many of whom still believed that the traditional powers were real. After all, though Christianity became more popular, in the period described in this essay the non-Christians still by far outnumbered the Christians. Thus, even after the turn to the Christian God, the traditional religious practices remained a reality from which Christians had to dissociate themselves continuously (and this, after all, was what the congregational order demanded). It was the basis against which, and hence also with which, Ewe Protestant identity was defined.

It seems that the missionaries were startled by the success of their own argumentation. Although they themselves had diabolized pre-Christian Ewe religion, Ewe Christians' understanding of the Devil went too far for them. The missionaries diabolized the old religion in order to denounce it as backward "heathendom." They found that once people had accepted that the old religion was a work of Satan, they were to leave it behind to fully concentrate on the Christian God and realize their personal sinfulness. Christians should no more think about the old gods.

Ewe Christians, however, continued to fear the same powers as the non-Christians. And like non-Christians, Ewe Christians understood sin, or *nuvõ*, primarily as something endured rather than committed by themselves. This is not astonishing given the fact that the Ewe term *nuvõ* (i.e., "evil thing") did not at all convey the Pietist notion of sin. Most Ewe Christians did not adopt the Pietist feeling of internal sinfulness but partly stuck to the old understanding of evil. In line with traditional concepts of evil, Ewe Christians found that evil was expressed through sickness and other forms of life destruction, and considered it a result of inappropriate behavior in a relationship, not as an individual state. If they violated the church order, they denied their personal responsibility and stated that it was the Devil who had tempted them to commit these sins (cf. Meyer 1992, 108).

However, in contrast with the non-Christians, Ewe Christians also considered the attempts to deal with traditional powers by way of sacrifices brought through intermediating *trõ*-priests, and by way of protective or counter-*dzo*, as evil. In my view, this shift was not all that surprising and spectacular because it was in line with traditional ideas about the relationships between human beings and spirits. The fact that Ewe Christians refused to bring them sacrifices turned the ancestors, *trõwo*, and other spirits into powers threatening to bring about evil in order to call their servants back again. For Ewe Christians, the only way to escape from such powers was to be on the other side—that is, to be no more sharing place and time with them, and to claim that God was more powerful than Satan.

As I have shown elsewhere (1992, 104–105), *Abosam* did not only refer to the old religion in general but also designated witchcraft in particular. Indeed, the existence of witchcraft was confirmed by the term *Abosam* itself.[25] According to Spieth, who unfortunately did not pay much attention to the phenomenon,[26] witchcraft (*adze*) was one of the most feared powers in Ewe land. It was the witches' "dearest longing . . . to make somebody poor. If he becomes rich, they destroy him. If he has children, they kill them all. Secretly they destroy everything he has" (Spieth 1906, 300). The Ewe understood witchcraft as a life-destroying activity undertaken by a jealous person envying richer family members; traditionally, the best remedy against the threat of witchcraft was to share one's riches with one's (poorer) relatives. By claiming to be more powerful than traditional spiritual entities, missionary Pietism seemed to offer protection against witchcraft by liberating the Christians from existing family ties. This was one of the reasons for the mission church's attraction. After all, as we have seen above, some people became church members because they did not want to share their riches with their families.

The missionaries did not appreciate the existence of the belief in witchcraft and other gods and spirits, which they considered to be a superstitious "heathen" survival. Although they themselves turned all traditional spiritual entities into demons by denouncing them as agents of Satan, the Ewe Christians' continued belief in the existence of witchcraft went too far for them. In this reluctance to thematize specific occult powers, we confront Pietisms' double stance toward the Devil, which was their basic category to dissociate themselves from the "world" but about whose machinations they were afraid to speak too much.[27] However, for many Ewe Christians the old powers were still too alive and real to be neglected in their discourse. To the dismay of the missionaries and some assistants, they kept talking about them. Thus, *Abosam* gave the Ewe's Christianity a new particular meaning through which it differed from the missionaries'. The reason for this lay on one hand in the perspective propagated by the missionaries themselves, and on the other hand in the peculiar position of the Devil in the Pietist doctrine triggering speculations and associations about the badness of the world. Thus, Ewe Christians enthusiastically took up the freedom to imagine the actions of the Devil in the framework of Pietism's imagery space that was offered them by the missionaries. This countered the closure and fixity of the doctrine.

"Backsliding into Heathendom"

As long as no mishap occurred and a person fared well, participation in the church activities was enough.[28] However, when Christians faced severe problems they were unable to solve, they often did not consider the practices entailed by missionary Pietism as sufficient. In such cases, "backsliding into heathendom"—an expression emphasizing the spatial and temporal difference constructed to distinguish Christianity and "heathendom"—occurred. This reveals the existence of uncertainties about Christians' new way of life. As long as everything went well, they could feel independent and refuse to share their riches with the members of their extended family; in case of mishap, however, many Christians rediscovered the importance of the family. For many converts, the wider family still was too important to simply be left behind. This also had to do with the fact that farming land, still to a great extent, was allocated by the lineage head, and also that Christians had to consult him in order to get access to the predominant base of production. Since the lineage was still largely providing the base of (agricultural) production, it is not surprising that missionary Pietism, with its emphasis on individuality, gave rise to contradictions between and among people.

However, it was not only the independence from their families that made some Ewe Christians feel insecure. In their experience, missionary Pietism lacked effective means to counter evil. Christians not only also fell sick, they also lacked the practical means to search recovery. Having "slid back" to the old ways, a former Christian woman from Tsibu stated:

> I had believed that, being a Christian, one would no more fall sick; but I see now that the worship of God and idolatry is one and the same thing, for wherever one is, one falls sick and dies. Therefore I have gone back" (MB 1890, 10).

The following, typical case further clarifies the issue:

> One of our female congregation members is no longer in the congregation. And she is a wife of a certain *trõ*-worshipper. It happened that she got pregnant by her husband, and as she got pregnant, she feared that something would happen to her in this her pregnancy or that she would

give birth once again to a child that would not live. So she went to *dzo* people and they tied pregnancy *dzo* strings for her. As they put them around her neck, she was hiding these things done [for her], so that people should no more see it. It happened such that I, the teacher, myself saw it on her neck when she was still hiding it. When I called her because of these things done [for her], she replied that human beings had more power than *Mawu*, the almighty. She said that she had been pregnant as often as three times and no pregnancy had been successful. And when she became pregnant, only sickness came into her and nobody made medicine for her. Therefore she herself went to the *dzo* people and they did these things for her. And I, the teacher, told her: "Have you forgotten *Mawu* or do you not know that *Mawu* is the medicine maker?" She replied that [as a Christian] she had nobody who made medicine for her and if she did not allow these things to be done for her [by the "heathens"] then she would just die. And I asked her again: "Are you not a Christian?" She replied to me that she herself had desired and agreed to be baptized and she herself had left it [Christianity] . . . She would not come back to us again (Waya 1909).[29]

This case clearly reveals the flaws of missionary Pietism if compared to traditional religion. We don't know when and why this woman converted to Christianity. The only thing we do know is that when after three miscarriages she was pregnant again, she was disillusioned about the capacity of Christianity to help solve her problem. This case again makes clear that people imagined the Christian God on the basis of existing concepts and still expected religion to *work*. Doubts about the *effectiveness* of Christianity in retaining people's health were expressed in many other cases. Against this background, it is not surprising that "backsliding into heathendom" occurred much more among women than men. Though some of the latter, of course, also "relapsed," the men's main offense was the violation of the Pietist sexual morals. The occurrence of "backsliding into heathendom"— and such cases are amply documented—shows that most Christians, especially women, did not share the missionaries' proclaimed neglect of rituals at the expense of mere belief, and retained an understanding of religion as a practical affair. They kept this stance even when they turned to Christianity, for they often did so for the very same reasons that made others return to the traditional priests.

Thus, there was a paradox inherent in the Ewe mission. On one hand, the mission intended to abolish the old religion; on the other hand, it was indispensable in order to demonstrate the meaning of Christianity. In this context the Devil was a key figure, because through him the gods and other spiritual beings remained real powers. Hence, the old religion was never abolished but only looked upon from a distance and through a particular filter. Since it remained part of Ewe Christians' discourse, its power was acknowledged. This implied that the non-Christian religion, though considered satanic, remained an alternative to Christianity. When spatial, social, economic, and symbolic separation from the "heathens" and mere belief in the Christian God did not prove to be protective enough to prevent serious mishap, and when prayers did not provide satisfying remedies, Ewe Christians abandoned the mission's dictum that the traditional religion was "evil," and returned to the traditional priests to counter the evil that had befallen them with sacrifices to the angry *trõ* or by *dzo*.

Conclusion

What can this case teach us about conversion as a theoretical concept? In his important work on conversion in Africa, which has dominated debates for years, Horton (1971, 1975) understood the replacement of old spirits by the High God as the most important feature of people's switch to Christianity. According to him, next to a feeling of community, traditional African religions provided people above all with knowledge to explain, predict, and control in the framework of the microcosm in which they lived. However, once people became integrated into wider contexts, the local gods could no more provide sufficient knowledge, and people tended to turn to world religions. For Horton, the weakening of the microcosm thus went hand in hand with the attribution of less power to local gods, and enhanced the adoption of a High God considered to be in charge of the macrocosm as a whole.[30] It is not my intention to fully discuss Horton's conversion thesis here.[31] I will, rather, comment on certain points relevant in this context.

In the case presented in this study, conversion to Christianity evidently went along with people's integration into a global political and economic configuration. It even appeared that people purposely and consciously converted to Christianity to escape from old constraints and to actively profit from the new opportunities brought by colonialism. A conceptualization of traditional societies as conservative and against passing the threshold to capitalism and modernity, as it was, for instance, put forward by Taussig (1980), therefore has to be dismissed as too romanticist (cf. Parry 1989). However, we saw that this does not imply that people uncritically accepted the new situation. Hence, I agree with Horton's argument that conversion occurs in the framework of the shift of people's identity from a microscosmic to a macrocosmic level. Moreover, I share his view that conversion does not entail a completely new way of thinking. Indeed, we have seen that after the turn to Christianity, Ewe converts stuck to the traditional pragmatic approach of religion—that is, they expected religious beliefs and practices to be effective, and criticized missionary Pietism in this light. Yet, the conceptualization of traditional religion as dynamic and open and of conversion in terms of continuity (rather than in terms of radical change, as the Christian model suggests) should not blind us to the fact that the turn to Christianity amounted to more than the mere adoption of another new cult. Converts were definitely aware that missionary Pietism was a new, exclusive affair. They opted for the change entailed by their conversion, and this also affected their way of thinking. So far, my view is more or less in line with Horton's.

My main critique of his theory on conversion pertains to his undue emphasis on the High God. For the Ewe, conversion entailed a socioeconomic and a religious dimension, which, as we have seen, were interconnected. In this context, it is important to realize that the adoption of the belief in the High God went hand in hand with the adoption of the image of the Devil, who was considered the Lord of the old gods and spirits and who defined the boundary between Christianity and traditional religion, but integrated the latter into Christian discourse at the same time. Though Horton occasionally remarked upon the fate of the previous gods in the framework of world religions—he stated that people "came to regard the lesser spirits as irrelevant or downright evil" (1971, 102)—he did not realize the importance of these beings in the minds of African Christians. In his view, sooner or later, people would stop believing in their existence. However, as we have seen in this essay, Ewe Christians eagerly took up the missionaries' dualism of God and Satan and the diabolization of "heathendom." Thus, the image of the Devil played a central role as a mediator between boundaries. This concerned not only the mediation between traditional and Christian religion in the narrow sense but also the mediation between traditional and modern ways of life entailed by people's integration into a global political, economic, and religious configuration.

The exclusive focus on God may be due to the fact that at the time Horton wrote his articles on conversion, there was little research done on the encounter of missionaries and Africans. Students of African Christianity took modern theologians' neglect of the Devil for granted and simply conceptualized conversion as a turn toward the High God[32]—not, at the same time, as a turn away from (and thus, on another level, to) Satan. Nevertheless, there are indications that all over the African continent, and even all over the world, conversion to Christianity went along with the diaboliza-tion of traditional religions.[33] This casts new light on the discussion on con-version in Africa. Therefore, I propose that in order to grasp the peculiarity of African Christianity, it may be of fundamental importance to concentrate on the "dark" side of the Christian religion that structured the world view of both Western missionaries and African converts. This seems to be crucial for a better understanding of the genesis of local variants of Christianity.[34] Indeed, in my view, the focus on the image of the Devil in African Chris-tianity can help reveal what Comaroff and Comaroff called "the highly vari-able, usually gradual, often implicit, and demonstrably 'syncretic' manner in which the social identities, cultural styles, and ritual practices of African peoples were transformed by the evangelical encounter" (1991, 25).

These conclusions are relevant in addressing the main concern of this essay: the relationship between conversion, modernity, (dis)enchantment, and the image of the Devil. As far as our case, the Ewe's encounter with Pietist missionaries between 1847 and 1916, is concerned, conversion did not bring about what professional theologians and social scientists used to expect: Conversion to Christianity does not necessarily lead to rational-ization and disenchantment. It seems to me that this is not confined to the case studied here. In the context of Pietist (but also pentecostally oriented) missions, whose missionaries themselves approach the world in terms of the dualism between God and Satan, new converts tend to adopt a variant of Protestantism emphasizing the image of the Devil and transforming tra-ditional gods and ghosts into "Christian" demons. By integrating "the world" and "heathendom" into the Christian universe of discourse, the complete closure and systematization of the doctrine, and people's effective socialization into the Christian religion's ethics, are thwarted: By directing people's attention to demons and providing temptations, "the Devil" con-tinuously endangers the purity of the doctrine and Christian lifestyle. This gives rise to a popular, "syncretistic" variant of Christianity centered on demonology.

But what makes for the attraction of the image of Satan? Or, put in Weber's terms, why do spirits and demons exert such a strong influence on the interests of the individual in his everyday life? Ewe Christians' obses-sion with the Devil has to be explained against the background of the fact that the politics and economy of colonial society were partly out of tune with the new Christian religion. Though Christianity offered an alley to-ward "civilization," it did not bring about the actual modernization of tra-ditional society. Christian converts, though professing individualism, actually still were involved in the traditional way of life. Above all, they could not fully renounce their extended families: With regard to economics, they were unable to dissociate themselves completely, because land was still allocated by the lineage heads. And in times of need, there was no other agency than the family to turn to for help. Moreover, in many respects Christianity could not compete with the more practically oriented traditional religion. Through the image of the Devil, Ewe converts were able to deal with the religion and way of life they wanted to leave behind and from which they could not fully dissociate at the same time.[35] Satan was "good to think with" about the ambivalence entailed by adopting the new ways and leaving the old. In talking about Satan and his demons, they could even thematize hidden desires to return to the old, without actually doing so. The image of the Devil and his demons thus enabled them to reflect upon their problems with the "civilized" state they strove for and found problematic at the same time. And if things seemed unresolvable in the framework of missionary Pietism, they could still, and perhaps temporarily, "slide back," for Christianity's Other was still there.

In short, the Ewe had an ambivalent stance toward modernity, which was attractive and problematic at the same time. The vehicle for expressing this ambivalence was the image of the Devil and his demons, which were continuously referred to but denounced at the same time. This image did not only enable Ewe Christians to thematize—to take up an expression used by Comaroff and Comaroff (1993)—modernity's malcontents, but also its attraction. Thus, the confrontation of traditional religions and Christianity, and new converts' quest for "civilization" and modernity, did not entail the disenchantment of their world. Rather, as has been shown by several authors, there may have occurred a rise of demons in the course of the transformation of traditional societies into modern ones (e.g., Taussig 1980; Thoden van Velzen and T. Van Wetering 1988, 1989). These images provide people with the possibility to reflect upon and fantasize about the problems and opportunities of their integration into a global modern political economy.

Notes

I want to thank Gerd Baumann, Bonno Thoden van Velzen, Peter van der Veer, and Jojada Verrips, as well as the participants of the "International Symposium on Conversion" (Amsterdam, June 13–15, 1994) for their comments on earlier versions of this essay. The historical material used in this essay has been assembled in the archives of the *Norddeutsche Missionsgesellschaft* (*Staatsarchiv Bremen*, Germany). This research would not have been possible without the financial assistance of the Amsterdam School for Social Science Research and the Netherlands Foundation for the Advancement of Tropical Research.

1. I am aware that "traditional religion" is not quite accurate as a term because it lumps together different forms of religious expression that have in common only that none of them achieved the status of "world religion" and remained more confined in time and space. However, alternative terms such as "local religion" have the same limitations.

2. Another, related tension in Weber's work is the one between nineteenth-century Hegelian philosophy and a sociological approach that sees actors as bringing about historical change (cf. Hefner 1993: 10–11). Weber thus tended to present the rise of world religions as a passage through stages that was going on beyond human action, whereas at the same time he attributed religious change to particular historical agents like priests and, in the case of the rise of world religions, prophets. Weber resolved this tension between evolution and history by the compromise that the unfolding of world religions would be realized through particular historical agents.

3. This can, for example, become clear from Hefner's (1993) review of the American reception of Weber by Parsons, Bendix, and Geertz and himself, wherein Weber is reduced to his ideal-type conceptualizations.

4. In the German original text, Weber wrote "*Praktisch* aber kam und kommt es darauf an" [1985: 255, emphasis mine]. This was translated with "The decisive consideration was and remains." In my view, the elimination of the term "praktisch" (i.e., practically or in praxis) from the English translation is unfortunate, because in this way the contrast Weber suggests between theological theory and believers' everyday praxis is less evident.

5. In Württemberg, Charlotte Reihlen's version of this lithograph from 1866 was very popular. For the history of the theme of the Broad and Narrow Path in Christian iconography cf. Knippenberg (1981), Rooijakkers (1993: 18–26), Scharfe (1990).

6. Moreover, in nineteenth-century Württemberg many customs and *rites de passage* were still performed by peasants (ibid.). For a description of nineteenth-century popular religion in the neighbouring Schwaben cf. Pfister (1924), and for Germany in general cf. Buschan (n.d.) From these sources it becomes clear that popular religion and culture was very much alive in rural areas in nineteenth-century Germany.

7. Schleiermacher, the most influental representative of German liberal theology, contributed to the destruction of traditional Christian diabology in Protestant theology with his work *Der christliche Glaube* (first published in 1830). He found that "the representation of the devil, as it developed among us, is so unmaintainable that one cannot expect anybody to be convinced of its truth" [1861: 209—original in German, translation BM].

8. For a more detailed description of the premissionary situation see Meyer (1995: 49ff).

9. The Ewe term for "civilization" became ŋku vu; that is "open eye." After the Asante war, which had upset the old order, an increasing number of Ewe longed for ŋku vu and asked the mission to open schools. In striving for ŋku vu, the Ewe took up the central term in colonial discourse, thereby opening themselves up to the civilizing offensive of Western agents aiming at the domination of the colonized. It was the Ewe's first step into the "long conversation" (Comaroff and Comaroff 1991) with Western agents.

10. The missonaries preferably built their stations on a hill, because there they considered the climate healthier than down in the villages. In this way, *Kpodzi* became the Ewe ex-

pression for Christian village. *Kpodzi* does not only denote the spatial but also the symbolic difference between the "heathen" and the Christian village. Even if there were no hill on which a Christian village could be built, it was called *Kpodzi*, thereby expressing its high state of development.

11. In 1933 the first church order (*Kirchenordnung*) for the Protestant Ewe-church in Togo and Gold Coast appeared. The difference between the church order (the German translation appeared in 1935) and previous congregational orders is that the former contains long passages about church organization and the hierarchy of its organs. Missionary B. Gutmann, who is famous for his propagation of an authentic African Christianity with African forms of expression, criticized this church order because it imposed a European Presbyterian form of organization upon an African Church. Moreover, he found that it was too little based on the Gospel and that the hierarchical order was overemphasized. Mission-inspector Schreiber defended the church order against this critique. He made clear that the NMG understood the Christianization of the Ewe as "a sharp break with their previous religion and thus in many respects also with their customs (*Volkstum*)." Making use of a war metaphor, he presented the church order as a "fight" or "field-service" order that was appropriate under the conditions prevailing at that time in that space (Schreiber 1937: 4—original in German, translation BM). The congregation orders of 1876 and 1909 can be found in Stab 7, 1025, 43/2 and 43/4.

12. Since in this respect, the orders of 1876 and 1909 are virtually identical, in the following I refer to the earliest version. The translations from German are mine.

13. In the mission archives, I found almost no documents giving insight into these teachers' stay in Germany.

14. Writing the history of these teachers would require another paper. Such a history could be based on documents written by this group. Take, for instance, the case of the teacher Albert Binder, a native of Peki Tsame. On his return from Germany in 1892, the mission only provided the white mission workers with cabins on the boat, whereas the black teachers had to travel "like animals" and to eat the leftovers. In his life history, Binder, who had never talked about the matter out of shame, wrote about how deeply hurt he was by this offensive treatment. At the same time, he assured that he knew it was not the work of God but an idea of human beings (Stab 7,1251, 1/30, life history Binder, pp. 37–38). Whereas most missionaries used to conceptualize the Ewe Christians as "children" and themselves as "fathers," Binder as well as some other native assistants rejected this asymmetrical order and emphasized the egalitarian aspect of the Christian religion. Other assistants, however, fully ackowledged the religious superiority of Pietism and the economic superiority of the Whites, and submitted themselves to the mission's authority.

15. Stab 7, 1025, 5/31, *Aufsatz Nyalemegbe zur Lehrerkonferenz Agu-Palime*, 22.3.1916.

16. Originally, the NMG did not present itself as a national mission society. But when Togo became a German colony in 1884, the NMG accommodated to the new political and economic circumstances and cooperated as best as possible with the government officials. In 1912, mission inspector Schreiber summarized the benefits of the mission of the colonial administration and vice versa. Whereas the NMG had provided pioneer services by studying the Ewe language, bringing about the Ewe's confidence in white people, training them in modern professions, and teaching them to respect the government, the colonial administration had "opened up" the interior and developed remedies against tropical diseases (cf. Tell & Heinrich 1986: 227–28.) Similarly, the Pietist trader Vietor praised the achievement of the mission. He emphasized that the mission had enhanced

the economic capacity of African farmers by stimulating individual entrepreneurs (1912). Elsewhere, he boasted: "Furthermore the mission provides the most important services to the colonies. It turns lazy polygamists living from the work of their wives into industrious farmers and workers. It increases people's needs and educates them according to the word of the Scriptures "Submit yourselves to the government" to loyal citizens" (Vietor quoted in Weißflog 1986: 276. Original in German, translation BM). For a critical evaluation of Vietor's ideas see Weißflog 1986.

17. Stab 7, 1025, 5/31, Essay Emmanuel Buama, 23–10–1909, original in English.

18. However, against most diseases the traditional medicines were more effective. Until the end of the nineteenth century, when Western tropical medicine made a big step forward through the discovery of chinine as a prophylaxis against Malaria, the missionaries had unscientific medical ideas. They stuck to "humoralpathology" that explained sickness as a result of an unbalanced relationship between bodily fluids and demanded as therapies blood-letting and purging (Fischer 1991). Their medical ideas thus were not superior to those of the Ewe, and less well adapted to tropical circumstances.

19. In an account on the Peki congregation, Spieth stated that the greatest group of Christians were children, followed by young men, and old men (MB 1892: 12). He did not even mention women.

20. The MB are written in German. This and all following translations from the MB are mine.

21. For a more detailed investigation of the construction of the Ewe as a people cf. Meyer (1995: 99ff).

22. Another factor complicating the transmission of the doctrine lay in the necessity of translating it into the Ewe language. In the Christian Ewe discourse, terms did not only refer to the *signifié* intended by the mission but also to previous meanings. Translation thus severely limited the systematization and closure of the doctrine (cf. Meyer 1994).

23. The editor of the MB referred approvingly to a statement made by the inspector Josenhans from the *Basler Mission*, that the best missionary was the one who was slowest in baptizing. The editor complained that the Methodist missionaries on the coast were baptizing people too quickly. By contrast, the NMG emphasized quality above quantity (MB 1899: 80).

24. According to Spieth, the Ewe's desire for atonement (*Sühnebedürfnis*) was still more or less indirect and revealed itself through the dissatisfaction with traditional religious practices (Spieth 1903).

25. *Bonsam* is the Akan term for sorcerer. To the Ewe it was synonomous with *adze*.

26. In his handbook he presented a report about *adze* among the Ho-people (1906: 544–45) and short statements about *adze* by other informants (ibid.: 682, 724, 832, 850, 906). In his book on the Ewe religion he devoted three pages to this phenomenon (1911: 299 ff). According to Spieth, the Ewe's concept and practice of witchcraft originated with the Yoruba.

27. Cf. Meyer (1995: 17ff).

28. Whereas the missionaries denied that attending church had a ritual aspect and continuously preached that Pietism was nonritualistic, Ewe Christians tended to see much more in the few rituals provided.

29. Stab 7,1025–56/8: 181–83.

30. For a critique of Horton's association of traditional religion with the local one cf. Ranger (1993). Indeed, as I show elsewhere (Meyer 1995: Chapter 3), the British administration actively prevented the rise of translocal cults in the Gold Coast.

31. Over the course of time, it has been criticized by several scholars (e.g. Fisher 1973; Hefner 1993: 20ff; Ifeka-Moller 1974; Ikenga-Metuh 1987: 13–16).

32. There is a great deal of literature regarding "African ideas about God" (e.g., Booth 1979; Dickson & Ellingworth 1970; Dzobo 1976, 1981; Kibicho 1978; Parrinder 1950; Ryan 1980; Schoenaker & Trouwborst 1983; Smith 1950), and almost none regarding African ideas about the Devil.

33. Regarding Africa, e.g., Fasholé-Luke 1978: 620; Fernandez 1982: 227ff; Kirwen 1987: 37ff; Kuper 1947: 127; Lienhardt 1982; Peel 1990: 351ff; Shorter 1973: 131; Sundkler 1961: 112, 189, 103–104). Regarding the New World, e.g., Cervantes 1994; Ingham 1989; Taussig 1980. Regarding Asia, e.g., Burt 1994: 264–65. See also the contributions in this volume by Jolly, and Keane. Especially in the study of African Christianity, the role of Satan in people's imagination has hardly been addressed. Most merely mention that converts regard the non-Christian religion they left behind as satanic without elaborating this point theoretically. In my view, there is need for more detailed case-studies on African Christians' ideas about evil.

34. In his reflection on what happens to the old religion once the Christian world religion becomes a social framework, Peel (1978: 451) mentioned the denunciation of deities as devils and the incorporation of elements of the old religion as two different possibilities. The case of the Ewe makes clear that these two possibilities do not exclude each other, but can occur at the same time.

35. It is important to realize that Ewe converts really strove to leave behind the old ways. Many authors reflecting upon the role of Christianity in Africans' incorporation into a global political and economic system (e.g., the much-discussed monographies by Fernandez 1982; Comaroff 1985) fail to explain why people were attracted by this new religion. Representing colonialism merely as a force overwhelming hitherto traditional people, these authors seem to take for granted the victimization of the colonized and represent modernity as basically negative. Moreover, though they recognize African Christians' obsession with evil forces, they do not devote attention to the enchantment entailed by this obsession. I, of course, do not want to deny that colonialism attacked "traditional society," but it has to be emphasized that Africans were not mere victims but also agents in this process, and strove to improve their situation as much as possible. They were, in other words, involved in a process of alienation from the old and of appropriation of the new. I hope to have shown in this essay which prominent role images of demons played in this process.

References

Amenumey, D. E. K. 1986. *The Ewe in Pre-Colonial Times. A Political History with Special Emphasis on the Anlo, Ge and Krepi.* Ho: E. P. Church Press.

Ardener, E. 1970. "Witchcraft, economics, and the continuity of belief." In M. Douglas, ed., *Witchcraft. Confessions and Accusations*, 141–60. London: Tavistock Publications.

Asare, E. B. 1973. *Akwamu—Peki Relations in the Eighteenth and Nineteenth Centuries*. University of Ghana: Unpublished M.A. Thesis.

Bohnenberger, Karl. 1961. *Volkstümliche Überlieferungen in Württemberg*. Unter Mitwirkung von A. Eberhardt, H. Höhm, und R. Kapff. Photomechanischer Nachdruck aus den Württembergischen Jahrbüchern für Statistik und Landeskunde 1904ff. Stuttgart: Silberburg Verlag.

Booth, N. S. 1979. "God and the gods in West Africa." In N. S. Booth, ed., *African Religions*, 1959–81. New York: NOK Publishers International).

Burt, Ben. 1994. *Tradition and Christianity. The Colonial Transformation of a Solomon Islands Society*. Chur: Harwood Publishers.

Buschan, Georg. 1922. *Das deutsche Volk in Sitte und Brauch. Geburt, Liebe, Hochzeit, Familienleben, Tod, Tracht, Wohnweise, Volkskunst, Lied, Tanz und Spiel, Handwerk und Zünfte, Aberglaube*. Unter Mitwirkung von M. Bauer, R. Julien, R. Mielke, H. J. Moser, O. Schwindrazheim. Stuttgart: Union Deutsche Verlagsgesellschaft.

Cervantes, Fernando. 1994. *The Devil in the New World. The Impact of Diabolism in New Spain*. New Haven and London: Yale University Press.

Comaroff, Jean. 1985. *Body of Power, Spirit of Resistance: The Culture and History of a South African People*. Chicago: University of Chicago Press.

Comaroff, Jean and John Comaroff. 1991. *Of Revelation and Revolution. Christianity, Colonialism, and Consciousness in South Africa* 1. Chicago: University of Chicago Press.

Comaroff, Jean and John Comaroff, eds. 1993. *Modernity and Its Malcontents. Ritual and Power in Postcolonial Africa*. Chicago: University of Chicago Press.

Dzobo, N. K. 1976. The Idea of God Among the Ewe of West Africa. Unpublished Manuscript.

———. 1981. The Indigenous African Theory of Knowledge and Truth; Examples of the Ewe and Akan of Ghana. *Conch* 13: 85–102.

Fabri, F. 1859. *Die Entstehung des Heidenthums*. Barmen.

Fasholé-Luke, E., R. Gray, A. Hastings, and G. Tasie, eds., 1978. *Christianity in Independent Africa*. London: Rex Collings.

Fernandez, James W. 1982. *Bwiti. An Ethnography of the Religious Imagination in Africa*. Princeton: Princeton University Press.

Fischer, Friedrich Hermann. 1991. *Der Missionsarzt Rudolf Fisch und die Anfänge medizinischer Arbeit der Basler Mission an der Goldküste (Ghana)*, Herzogenrath: Verlag Murken-Altrogge.

Fisher, Humphrey J. 1973. Conversion Reconsidered: Some Historical Aspects of Religious Conversion in Black Africa. *Africa* 43(1): 27–40.

Gray, Richard. 1981. "The origins and the organization of the nineteenth century missionary movement." In O. U. Kalu, ed., *The History of Christianity in West-Africa*, 14–21. Hongkong.

Hefner, Robert W. 1993. "World building and the rationality of conversion." In R. W. Hefner, ed., *Conversion to Christianity. Historical and Anthropological Perspectives on a Great Transformation*, 3–46. Berkeley: University of California Press.

Horton, R. 1971. African Conversion. *Africa* 41 (2): 86–108.

———. 1975. On the Rationality of Conversion. Part I & II. *Africa* 45 (3): 219–35, 373–99.

Ifeka-Moller, Caroline. 1974. White Power: Social-Structural Factors in Conversion to Christianity, Eastern Nigeria, 1921–1966. *Canadian Journal of African Studies* 8 (1): 55–72.

Ikenga-Metuh, Emefie. 1987. "The shattered microcosm: A critical survey of explanations of conversion in Africa." In K. Holst Petersen, *Religion, Development and African Identity*, 11–27. Uppsala: Scandinavian Institute of African Studies.

Ingham, J. M. 1986. *Mary, Michael, and Lucifer. Folk Catholicism in Central Mexico.* Austin: University of Texas Press.

Kibicho, S. G. 1978. "The continuity of the African conception of God into and through Christianity: A Kikuyu case-study." In E. Fasholé-Luke, et.al., eds., *Christianity in Independent Africa*, 370–88. London: Rex Collings.

Kirwen, M. C. 1987. *The Missionary and the Diviner. Contending Theologies of Christian and African Religions.* New York: Orbis Books.

Knippenberg, W. H. Th. 1981. "De brede en de smalle weg." *Brabants Heem* 33 (2/3): 106–111.

Kuper, Hilda. 1947. *The Uniform of Colour.* Johannesburg: Witwatersrand University Press.

Lienhardt, G. 1982. "The dinka and Catholicism." In J. Davis, ed., *Religious Organization and Religious Experience.* ASA Monograph 2, 81–85. London: Academic Press.

Meyer, Birgit. 1992. "If You are a Devil, You are a Witch and if You are a Witch, You are a Devil." The Integration of "Pagan" Ideas in the Conceptual Universe of Ewe Christians. *Journal of Religion in Africa* 22, no. 2: 98–132.

———. 1994. "Beyond syncretism. Africanization through translation and diabolization." In C. Stewart/Rosalind Shaw, eds., *Syncretism/Anti-syncretism*, 45–68. London: Routledge.

———. 1995. Translating the Devil. An African Appropriation of Pietist Protestantism. The Case of the Peki Ewe in Southeastern Ghana, 1897–1982. University of Amsterdam: Dissertation.

Mittheilungen/Monatsblatt der Norddeutschen Mission Hamburg 1840 ff & Bremen 1851 ff.

Neill, Stephen. 1975. *A History of Christian Missions.* First Published 1964. Harmondsworth: Penguin Books.

Norddeutsche Mission. 1935. *Kirchenordnung der Evangelischen Ewe-Kirche in Togo, West-Afrika.* Bremen: Verlag der Norddeutschen Missions-Gesellschaft.

Parrinder, E. G. 1950. "Theistic beliefs of the Yoruba and Ewe peoples of West Africa." In E. W. Smith, ed., *African Ideas about God. A Symposium*, 224–40. London: Edinburgh House Press.

Parry, J. 1989. "On the moral perils of exchange." In Parry, J. & M. Bloch, ed., *Money and the Morality of Exchange*, 64–93. Cambridge: Cambridge University Press.

Peel, J. D. Y. 1978. "The Christianization of African society: Some possible models." In E. Fasholé-Luke, et. al., eds., *Christianity in Independent Africa*, 443–54. London: Rex Collins.

———. 1990. The Pastor and the *Babalawo*: The Interaction of Religions in Nineteenth-Century Yorubaland. *Africa* 60 (3): 338–69.

Pfister, Friedrich. 1924. *Schwäbische Volksbräuche*. Augsburg: Dr. Benno Filser Verlag.

Ranger, Terence. 1993. "The local and the global in Southern African religious history." In R. W. Hefner, eds., *Conversion to Christianity. Historical and Anthropological Perspectives on a Great Transformation*, 65–98. Berkeley and Los Angeles: University of California Press.

Rooijakkers, Gerard. 1993. De brede en de smalle weg. Vermaak en zaligheid in Noord-Brabant: een problematisch duo. In: J.A.F.M. van Oudsheusden, et.al (Red.), *Ziel en zaligheid in Noord-Brabant*, 18–39. Vijfde verzameling bijdragen van de vereniging voor de Nederlandse kerkgeschiedenis. Delft: Eburon.

Ryan, P. J. 1980. "Arise, o God!" The Problem of "Gods" in West Africa. *Journal of Religion in Africa* 11 (3): 161–71.

Scharfe, Martin. 1980. *Die Religion des Volkes. Kleine Kultur- und Sozialgeschichte des Pietismus*. Gütersloh: Gütersloher Verlag.

———. 1990. Zwei-Wege-Bilder. Volkskundliche Aspekte evangelischer Bilderfrömmigkeit. *Blätter für württembergische Kirchengeschichte* 90: 123–44.

Schleiermacher, Friedrich. 1861. *Der christliche Glaube nach den Grundsätzen der evangelischen Kirche*. Fünfte unveränderte Ausgabe. Band 1. Berlin: Georg Reimer.

Schoenaker, H. & A. Trouwborst. 1983. Het godsbegrip in de etnografische berichtgeving van de missie en zending in Oost-Afrika. In: J. M. Schofeleers, et. al., eds., *Missie en ontwikkeling in Oost-Afrika; een ontmoeting van culturen*, 24–39. Nijmegen: Ambo.

Schreiber, A. d.W. (Hg.). 1936. *Bausteine zur Geschichte der Norddeutschen Missionsgesellschaft. Gesammelt zur Hundertjahrfeier*. Bremen: Verlag der Norddeutschen Mission.

Shorter, A. 1973. *African Culture and the Christian Church*. London: G. Chapman.

Smith, E. W., ed. 1950. *African Ideas about God. A Symposium*. London: Edinburgh House Press.

Spieth, Jacob. 1903. Das Sühnebedürfnis der Heiden im Ewelande. Bremen: Verlag der Norddeutschen Missionsgesellschaft.

———. 1906. *Die Ewe-Stämme. Material zur Kunde des Ewe-Volkes in Deutsch-Togo*. Berlin: Dietrich Reimer.

———. 1908. Wie kommt die Bekehrung eines Heiden zustande? Bremen: Verlag der Norddeutschen Missionsgesellschaft.

Sundkler, B. 1961. *Bantu Prophets in South Africa*. Second Edition. London: Oxford University Press.

Taussig, Michael T. 1980. *The Devil and Commodity Fetishism in South America*. Chapel Hill: The University of North Carolina Press.

Tell, Birgit & Uwe Heinrich. 1986. Mission und Handel im missionarischen Selbst-
verständnis und in der konkreten Praxis. In W. Ustorf (Hrsg.), *Mission im Kontext. Beiträge zur Sozialgeschichte der Norddeutschen Missionsgesellschaft,* 257–92.
Bremen: Übersee-Museum.

Thoden van Velzen, H. U. E. & W. van Wetering. 1988. *The Great Father and the
Danger: Religious Cults, Material Forces, and Collective Fantasies of the Surinamese
Maroons.* Dordrecht: Foris Publications.

———. 1989. Demonologie en de betovering van het moderne leven. *Sociologische
Gids* 36: 155–86.

van Rooden, Peter. 1990. The Concept of an International Revival Movement
around 1800. *Pietismus und Neuzeit. Ein Jahrbuch zur Geschichte des neueren
Protestantismus,* 155–72. Bd. 16.

Vietor, J. K. 1912. Die wirtschaftliche Leistungsfähigkeit des Afrikaners. In: Bre-
mer Missionsschriften Nr. 36, *Der Afrikaner, seine wirtschaftliche Leistungsfähigkeit, geistige Befähigung, religiöse Veranlagung. Vorträge auf dem II. Deutschen
Kolonial-Missionstag zu Cassel,* 1–10. Bremen: Verlag der Norddeutschen Missions-Gesellschaft.

Weber, Max. 1978. [1922] *Economy and Society. An Outline of Interpretive Sociology* 1.
G. Roth and C. Wittich, eds., Berkeley: University of California Press.

———. 1984. [1920] *Die Protestantische Ethik. Eine Aufsatzsammlung.* Heraus-
gegeben von Johannes Winckelmann. Gütersloh: Gütersloher Verlagshaus,
Gerd Mohn.

———. 1985. [1922] *Wirtschaft und Gesellschaft. Grundriss der verstehenden Soziolo-
gie.* Fünfte, revidierte Auflage, besorgt von Johannes Winckelmann. Tübingen:
J. C. B. Mohr.

Weißflog, Stefan. 1986. J. K. Vietor und sein Konzept des leistungsfähigen Afrikaners. In W. Ustorf (Hrsg.), *Mission im Kontext. Beiträge zur Sozialgeschichte der
Norddeutschen Missionsgesellschaft,* 293–306. Bremen: Übersee-Museum.

Westermann, Diedrich. 1936. *Volkwerdung und Evangelium unter den Ewe.* Bremen:
Verlag der Norddeutschen Missionsgesellschaft.

9

DEVILS, HOLY SPIRITS, AND THE SWOLLEN GOD: TRANSLATION, CONVERSION AND COLONIAL POWER IN THE MARIST MISSION, VANUATU, 1887–1934

Margaret Jolly

Introduction

In his preface to the 1988 edition of *Contracting Colonialism*, Vincente Rafael notes the semantic propinquity of the Spanish words *conquista* (conquest), *conversión* (conversion), and *traducción* (translation). Conquest is not only the forcible occupation of territory but the act of winning another's voluntary submission, even love. Conversion, literally the act of turning a thing into something else, or more specifically of effecting a change in religious practice, also implies a restructuring of desires. To be converted in this sense is to give in by giving up what one wants, in favor of the desires of someone else. Finally, conversion can mean something like translation, to express in one language what has been previously expressed in another (1988, xvii). Rafael goes further to suggest that the relationship between this trio of terms in the context of Spanish colonial rule in the Philippines also suggests the way in which translation and conversion simultaneously institute and subvert colonial rule (1988, xv).

I find Rafael's approach to the problem of Christian conversion inspiring, highlighting as it does the dialectics of force and persuasion, of interest and desire, and the way in which contests of power in the colonial context saturate the processes of translation on which conversion largely depends. I privilege these problems in this study of the Marist mission in the islands of Vanuatu (previously the New Hebrides). Like Rafael, I emphasize the centrality not only of the translation of words or of cosmological concepts but of practices embodying contesting ideas of sacred potency, most poignantly in the processes of dying and death.

Vanuatu (see Map 1), like the Philippines, is today a pervasively Christian country, but unlike the Philippines it is not predominantly Catholic. The Marists in Vanuatu were opposed not just by heathen resistance or evasion but also by rival Protestant groups. Indeed, the Protestants—the London Missionary Society, the Reformed Presbyterian Church, and the Melanesian Mission (high Anglicans) preceded them into the group from the 1840s and were arguably more successful, especially in the proselytizing of the southern islands. The Marist mission moved into the northern islands of Vanuatu in 1887, expressly at the invitation of French settlers and commercial interests, to combat the northward expansion of the Protestants from Scotland, Novia Scotia, New Zealand, and Australia. The rivalry between Catholic and Protestant missionaries "to gain souls" was inseparable from the struggle between the imperial powers of France and Britain for land, labor, trade, and strategic interests in the group.

This tiny archipelago in the western Pacific thus became the unfortunate site of two contending imperial powers and from the early twentieth century a joint colonial rule, or Condominium. The ensuing colonial state was both ineffectual and confusing, and was early labeled the "Pandemonium" government. But although this taunt was echoed with relish by independence activists from the 1970s, for ni-Vanuatu (the indigenous people) the Condominium proved a tragic farce. Vanuatu was proclaimed an independent state in 1980, in the face of French and secessionist subversions, but stills bears the traces of a metropolitan division between Anglophone and Francophone, Protestant and Catholic. Though linguistically and denominationally divided, the postcolonial state seeks unity in imaging a public culture that is indubitably Christian. Here, Christian theology was not implicated in a violent nationalist struggle as in the Phillipines (Ileto 1979) but was peacefully proclaimed the foundation of the nation. Witness the state motto: *Long God Yumi Stanap*—In God We Are Independent. Christian conversion was effected in a colonial conquest, but Christianity is today lovingly embraced as essential to "independent" existence.[1] So perhaps here, too, Christianity may be seen to both "institute and subvert" colonial rule. It is in this colonial and postcolonial context that I offer this study of the Marist mission. But first let me reflect

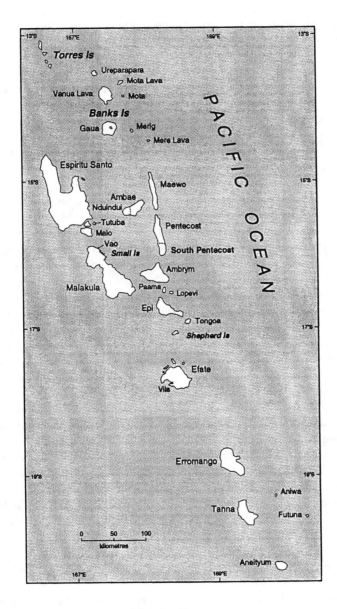

Map 1: Vanuatu

more generally on the problems of perceiving conversion as conversation and on the politics of translation.

Conversion as Conversation

Much recent writing about conversion treats the process as a dialogue, as a conversation between missionaries and their potential converts. Viewing conversion as a process of mutual translation has proved fertile (cf. Clifford 1980; Dening 1980; Douglas 1989), but we must be careful not to presume this is a cozy chat between equal interlocutors (cf. Barker 1990). The metaphor of conversion as a conversation can be overdrawn, obscuring important dimensions of power in such translations—the hierarchies posited between languages, the problematic relationship between orality and textuality, and the way in which, apart from the overt messages communicated, the covert structure of the conversation itself is constituted and speakers differentially empowered.

First, it is clear that most missionaries, regardless of ethnicity and epoch, construct a hierarchy of languages between the presumably "universal" languages of Latin, French, or English and those local languages we describe as "vernacular." Rafael (1988, 28–29) depicts how Dominican priests simultaneously vaunted proselytizing in the vernacular, be it Castilian or Tagalog, and the power of classical Latin as a universal language, superior to both in the clarity of its grammatical structure and the stability of its rules (immutable because all its original speakers were dead!). Thus, the problem of translation from the viewpoint of the priests was not a mutual accommodation of meanings, in which the arbitrary relationship of signifier and signified, and a space between languages, which defied translation, was admitted. Rather, the presumption was that God's truth, though it could be conveyed in other languages, was most lucidly expressed in Latin: priests translated and interpreted the grammars of vernaculars through the lexical and grammatical grids of Latin. Strange distortions resulted—for example, reference to Latin case or tense structures, where no such cases or tenses pertained. Such a Latinate lens clouds Catholic missionaries' views of Austronesian[2] languages from the sixteenth century to the early twentieth, from the Phillipines to Vanuatu.

Sometimes missionaries seem to have presumed that the languages they learned did not really exist as proper languages until they recorded them, wrote them down, and constructed grammars.[3] Local languages thus were often rendered inferior and inadequate. Missionary linguists typically did not grant the semiotic equality of languages. The act of translation by missionary linguists was therefore, according to Rafael, not to erase linguistic boundaries but to reinscribe them within a framework of divine transactions. Translatability became an index of the spread of God's Word (1988, 28).

Thus, the very process of translation entailed a hierarchy of languages, from the missionary viewpoint. Those whom they attempted to convert did not necessarily succumb to this view, but indigenous perceptions of their own spoken languages were challenged and sometimes subverted by the process of writing. The process of a "vernacular" being written down by missionary linguists and of translations of Biblical texts, of catechism and hymns, into local languages, is a paradoxical one. It seemingly inscribes the worth of local languages and epistemologies by educating people in literate knowledge in a language they use in everyday speech, a process some have proclaimed emancipatory.[4] I would view it rather more ambiguously.

We have also to consider who translates, who learns, and what knowledge is gained through literacy. When missionaries translated and transcribed local languages, they did so in a way that was partial. Certain words were elided, and some concepts, especially those pertaining to ancestral religion, were translated in ways that suppressed some connotations while amplifying others, thus distorting the indigenous meanings circulating in conversation. The codification of oral tradition as text often impoverished indigenous genres and privileged the creativity of the author over the audience. It rendered the written word more canonical (witness the respect given to versions of myths early recorded in mission texts). And in "writing down" local languages, particular languages or dialects were situated above others, as lingua franca.[5]

Although missionaries might have lamented the backwardness of indigenes in failing to develop a script, and indeed local people might have sometimes entertained fantastic ideas about the power of the written word, this did not imply for either that the written word was hegemonic. Rafael (1988, 31) argues to the contrary that the men of the book in Luzon believed the power of the spoken word was more telling, and that the very process of speaking the word of God was in itself efficacious.[6] Reading aloud from the Bible or the catechism thus transparently conveyed God's word, and in listening to it human beings recognized their debt to the creator. The Comaroffs report a similar theory of language on the part of the nonconformists in Africa.[7]

Such messages were often ignored or rudely rejected, but the Comaroffs make the crucial point that it is not just the messages at issue but the very structure of the speaking situation. Besides the overt content of the conversation, dominated by substantive mission messages in sermons, lessons, and didactic dialogues, they perceive a covert quieter struggle over the very terms of the conversation.[8] In the Comaroffs' view, it is initiated by the invading colonists on their terms. Although I ultimately concur with stressing colonial dominance in the process of conversion in Vanuatu, the power of missionaries is not hegemonic (cf. Guha 1988). This is not just because their power was faltering, uncertain and contested, but also because, as was true in the Philippines and South Africa, ni-Vanuatu appropriated Christianity to themselves, and Christian beliefs and values became an important predicate of their later rejection of colonial rule (cf. Douglas 1995).

In my story of the Marist mission in Vanuatu, I start by insisting on the salience of silence, the centrality of not hearing, not talking, and not reading as a way of resisting the power of the word of God. This is perhaps unsurprising, because hearing, listening, and believing a message are intimately connected in indigenous epistemologies, as much as in certain Christian conceptions (cf. Otto 1992, 153ff). Monty Lindstrom has reported for Tanna (1990, 145–46) that those who were indifferent or opposed to the sermons of early Protestant missions either ran away or tried to drown them out by making a racket beating clubs on logs or trees. Those opposed to the mission also buried biblical texts and songbooks, or spat during services.[9] In the encounter between indigenes and the Marists in the north, similar tactics were used. Indifference or resistance was marked by refusing to listen, by refusing to talk, and especially by manifesting boredom or incapacity when missionaries tried to learn the vernacular.

The Politics of Closing the Mouth

First, a few suggestive passages from the letters of several priests, all written to Monsigneur Doucéré between the years 1907 and 1916, but from diverse locales on Santo, Ambrym, and Efate. "Port Olry people are naturally reluctant to help. It is enough if they see you write down something on a piece of paper for their mouths to close" (PMB57 Roux to Doucéré, Port Olry, Santo, July 21, 1907). Their "natural reluctance" is not explained, but perhaps derives from a sense of the appropriative power of the written word and its link to the incursions of labour recruiters, planters and representatives of the rival colonial powers. Roux explains that he had hoped to have Henri, who spoke French, teach him the vernacular, and in the course of these language lessons to convert Henri to Catholicism. But Henri was unwilling either to be his language teacher or to convert. Roux's lament was echoed by several others. Strock, writing from Sesivi two years later, reports that he was trying to learn the language as a distraction from loneliness and dire depression, but that "everyone whom he asks to teach manifests boredom, pretended not to know the language, French, or English well" (PMB 57 Strock to Doucéré from Sesivi, Ambrym, March 3, 1909). And later, Strock writing from Port Sandwich reports, "No more language lessons with Baikou. Could he be afraid that I will learn the language? I'll learn by myself" (PMB 57 Strock to Doucéré from Port Sandwich, Malakula, April 8, 1910).

This was an idle hope. Given that these languages were not yet written ones, and that there was no extant dictionary or grammar, learning a vernacular was very difficult without a native teacher or routine exposure to conversations in the local language. Not teaching the vernacular was simultaneously a means of inhibiting the missionaries' knowledge of local practices and idioms, and of reducing the impact of their evangelical words. But such reluctance was also manifested in a refusal to converse even in those lingua franca that were available, English or French and, most important, the local pidgin, *bislama*. Thus, in response to the Monsigneur's queries as to why he never writes about the local people, Romeuf confided that he had little contact with them and that they refused his attempts at conversation. He speculates that someone must have ordered them not to talk and to limit their relations with the missionaries, for "even in chance meetings, if one wants to strike up a conversation—even the most trite—people try to escape, to escape in fact as soon as a few sentences are exchanged. Well at least there are no arguments with them" (PMB 57 Romeuf to Doucéré, Port Sandwich, September 8, 1916).

Ironically, in the next sentence Romeuf does document an argument with them, not expressed in words but in the embodied combat of local resistance to missionary occupation of land. The mission appropriation of land for the station had been recently disputed by local people; despite this, Romeuf insisted that his contract workers (from another island), employed to work coconut and cotton plantations, complete a boundary fence. That those whose land was being occupied may have preferred not to chat, or, more broadly, that ni-Vanuatu may not have been well disposed to strangers given contemporaneous shellings of resistant villages by war ships, seemed not to occur to Romeuf as a compelling explanation for their silence or avoidance.

Tattevin and Translation

I do not want to overdraw the significance of this refusal to talk, because in many places Marist missionaries early drew local people into conversation, managed to learn local languages, and record them in writing, and through this process began the slow and faltering process of Christian conversion. Moreover, like the Protestants who preceded them in the southern islands, they translated Biblical texts, catechisms, lessons, and hymns into local languages. Exemplary in this respect were priests like Suas and Tattevin who became astute linguists and ethnographers of the several places in which they had postings. I consider both in some detail, but will in this section focus on Father Elie Tattevin (a priest who was a long-time resident of Baie Barrier in South Pentecost—see Map 2). Here I did anthropological field work from the 1970s, primarily with *kastom* (traditionalist) people who, despite the effects of colonization and Christianity, proclaimed their continued adherence to their ancestors' ways and indigenous religion.

Before my fieldwork,[10] it was Tattevin's texts of Sa myths in the vernacular, with accompanying French translation, that provided me with the only written source of the local language. I was later to discover, long after I had composed my own slip-file dictionary and made a few conjectures about the grammar, that there was a moldy manuscript of a dictionary and a grammar in the cupboards at Baie Barrier mission, presumably left there by Tattevin in the 1920s. Even if the latter seemed to render the language more like Latin than an Austronesian language, I was heartily impressed by his ethnographic and linguistic capacity. More problematic were his attempts to render local mythological personae and religious concepts as equivalent to those of the universal Catholic religion.[11]

Like many other Marist priests, Tattevin assiduously sought indigenous equivalents for the notions of God, spirit, sanctity, or sacred power. These were, of course, not just different words for the same concept but radically different concepts. The slippage between the ancestral and the mission uses of such "equivalents" is the space of a colonial contest.

First, let us take the persona, the being that Tattevin translates as God— Barkulkul, literally "the Great Big One" or "the swollen one."[12] The Barkulkul who emerges from the indigenous narratives is no doubt very powerful, but even in his swollen form uncomfortably fills the category of "God" in Catholic theology. Barkulkul appears in the first and primordial *dun*, (Sa origin myths) along with his five brothers. They slide down a coconut tree from the sky to the earth. Since there are no women, they have been born by parthenogenesis. Without a breast to suckle, they drink co-

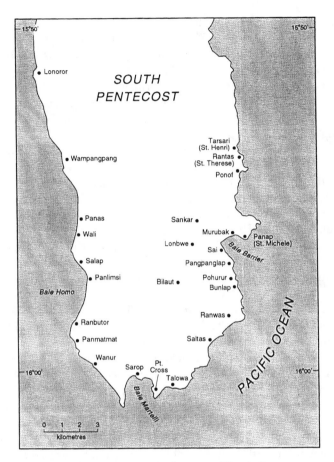

Map 2: Contemporary Settlements of South Pentecost

conut milk to survive. Barkulkul is constituted as the most powerful, the eldest, "the one who emerged first," who castrates the youngest brother to make the first woman, Sermorp, or Broken Chestnut.

As well as being credited with the creation of sexed difference, Barkulkul also creates many other natural and cultural things, but he is not the exclusive male author of the world. The basic topography of earth preexists him, although his mythic movements (and those of later ancestral beings, male and female) helped to create rivers and the sea. Yet other important creations emanate from the bodies of coeval and later male creator beings—

warfare and weapons from his brother Melesia, yams from the body of Sin-git, pigs from the testicles of Wahgere. Barkulkul's power emerges thus as akin to that of a *loas*[13]—efficacious in making crops grow, causing pigs' tusks to circle, attracting fish to his line, and seducing women—a priest or (using Tattevin's gloss) a magician rather than the sole primordial creator. The time of his being on earth is thought to have been a paradisical, Edenic epoch—when magical efficacy rather than work prevailed, leisure and dancing were paramount and life was eternal.

This epoch was terminated when work and death ensued. The origin of death is, as in Christian theology, linked to sexual knowledge and sin. But unlike the Old Testament story of Adam and Eve,[14] Barkulkul is rather more intimately implicated, as a jealous husband who commits fratricide because of his wife's adultery. His wife, Sermorp, has sex with his brother Marelul, and though he does not confess, diagnostic signs reveal Marelul to be the adulterer. Barkulkul kills his brother in a yam garden and buries him as a long yam is planted—deep down in the earth. He then departs this world for the northeast; those who remain behind are condemned to be mortal.

Although sex, sin, and death are closely linked in Christian theology, it is (despite Gnostic interpretations) hardly the jealous wrath of God as husband that creates mortality. God, though punishing of sin, also offers the future promise of immortality if believers are free from sin or in a state of grace. Barkulkul offers no such promise, first because all human beings live on as spirit regardless of their behavior in this world, and second because Barkulkul has no such direct relationship to the living. The presence of God in this world is perceived very differently. Barkulkul is a past if palpable presence, evinced in a very material way in the world but no longer controlling it. Thus, the imprint of his buttocks can be seen where he long ago sat down to rest on a rock near Bunlap. But in indigenous religious practices at least, his presence is not daily manifested in material signs nor felt as an intimately omnipresent holy spirit. There is nothing akin to prayers or incantations directed to him to try to influence his continuing engagement with the world. He is rather experienced as a being distant in space and time, as an originary rather than an omnipresent creator (cf. Lane 1965, 266).

An intimate omnipresent spirit exists, but this is not an aspect of the one God (like the Holy Spirit) but a proliferation of ancestral beings, or *adumwat* (cf. Keesing 1982). How might this concept relate to Christian notions of spirit, soul, and devil? *Adumwat* are the spirits of both long-departed ancestors and, potentially, those of the more recent dead. When a person dies, the spiritual aspect of his or her body (*manun*) is thought to depart, to leave the corpse and to hover around villages, gardens, and the sea—on the routes of its daily movements. Though invisible, the spirit is not ethereal; it is embodied.[15] *Manun* also means shadow or reflection, and this suggests that it is a kind of derivative body, an illusory reflection of the true living body. Immediately after death, it is a highly dangerous and malevolent being—proximate to the living and wandering aimlessly.

Mourning and funerary feasting are supposed to ensure that the dead person's spirit does not linger but rather departs at the appropriate time. At twenty days, the spirit body ideally should run down the mountain range and into the mouth of a cave on the southern tip of Pentecost, into Lonwe, the land of the dead. Although subterranaean, this is not a hell, but akin to heaven, where regardless of what one did in life, there is, like the originary epoch of Barkulkul, no work to do—just eating, dancing, and sleeping. Wafting through this village there are no rotting smells of corpses, but the perfumes of sweet-smelling leaves that excite and signify sensual pleasure.[16]

The spirits of the dead become firmly secured in Lonwe by the respect of their living descendants, manifest in particular by the sequence of funerary feasts, culminating at 100 days. Those who are most respected and honored turn into *adumwat*. This parallels in the present those events of the past, when ancestors first settled and cultivated the soil. The spirits of the earliest ancestors of specific descent groups are thought to still reside in the place they first cleared—sites visibly signaled by groves of virgin bush called *ut loas*.

The power of such ancestors, like those of the more recent dead, is ambivalent. They can help or harm, make fertile or sterile. Thus, ancestral *adumwat* pleased by the ritual attention of their descendants will cause their gardens to grow, their pigs to fatten, and their children to be many and healthy. If, on the other hand, their descendants neglect them, their crops will wither, their pigs will be scrawny and sickly, and children will sicken and die or worse, not even be conceived.[17] In this malevolent form, such ancestral spirits are called *adumwat ensanga* (literally bad spirits), or alternatively, *tegar*.[18]

. Sometimes the anger of these *aduwmat* is so great that they actually possess the body of the living, causing sickness, even death. Epilepsy, asthma, and a litany of other diseases can be attributed to *adumwat*. Such possession requires careful divination to establish which spirit is attacking and for what reason, in order to effect its removal. This is done by the diviner uttering incantations over water in a bamboo tube, spraying the water over the victim and then rushing off, hopefully with the exorcised spirit captured within. If the victim recovers, this is evidence of succesful diagnosis and treatment; if the victim worsens or dies, it is presumed that the diagnosis was incorrect.

It was clearly tempting for Catholics to identify these ancestral spirits as ghosts or devils, especially since their effects were most obvious to them in sickness and death (rather than health or growth) and their removal clearly paralleled processes of exorcism long practiced, though controversial, among Catholics. And this was how Tattevin translated the concept. This particular translation—*adumwat* as ghosts or devils—was clearly partial in both senses of the word. First, it obscured the positive dimensions, the creative powers of *adumwat*, by crediting only their malignant aspect. Second, by assimilating this congeries of ancestral spirits to the Catholic concept of the Devil, it stressed not only their essential negativity in the perpetual struggle with the forces of life, growth, and goodness but intimated their defeat. They were in terms either of Manichean opposition or a more orthodox Catholic theology ultimately defeated by the power of God. But third, this translation created difficulties in translating related terms—for soul, sanctity, and sacred power.

If *manun* were ideally transmuted into *adumwat* and the *adumwat* were not just ghosts but probably devils, how was Tattevin to recuperate the soul and its capacity for salvation? The Catholic project, no less than the Protestant, required a person who could recognize their sin, confess, and transform into a good, believing Christian (although the former stressed forgiveness and the latter transformation). The indigenous *manun*, potentially the soul, was by this translation doing the devil's work. Moreover, the indigenous notions of sanctity and sacred power that Tattevin chose to deploy were also grossly tainted by the very ancestral powers routinely equated with devils.

In Sa, there were two potential candidates for the translation of sacred—*loas* and *kon*. Although they have slightly different meanings and contextual uses, both are derived from ancestral power. *Loas* denotes people who are ancestrally endowed with the power to hurt or heal—it is the term applied to the priests of agriculture, weather, war, and childbirth, i.e., female midwives. *Loas* also denotes places endowed with the danger and sanctity of the first settlers, who are called *ut loas*. Tattevin regularly translated this word as "magician" or "sorcerer" in both his translations of myths and in his dictionary glosses. This translation simultaneously elides the "holiness" in *loas* by labeling these practices magical rather than religious, and stresses its destructive manifestations in sorcery and war magic rather than the creative forces it can equally denote—facilitating birth, curing, causing to grow. He thus assimilates the meaning of *loas* to that of *abile*, those living human beings who ensorcel, through various forms of destructive magic using food leavings, bodily wastes, or the manipulation of stones.

Kon, on the other hand, he translates as holy, sacred, and taboo. But in indigenous religion this is also a state that is ambiguous, sacred, and dangerous. However, unlike *loas*, it is typically attained by a process of sacrifice in life. Canonically, this is the power that men and women attain by the sacrifice and exchange of pigs in graded society ritual, a process thought to honor and approach the state of ancestral being. This state, like *loas*, has both a positive potential to make things grow or to destroy. A man who had taken some of the highest titles was so holy, that though he excelled as a gardener, a pig herder, and a curer, most of his children died in infancy. A woman who was extremely *kon*, but whose husband had not sacrificed comparable pigs, was said to have unintentionally "killed" him with her holiness. Being *kon* is a state of efficacy conferred by the ancestors, but power is achieved by successive acts of sacrifice to them, not hereditarily given.

It may be that Tattevin's preference for *kon* over *loas* was related to this difference in meaning. Perhaps the latter term befitted a stress on the convert's choice for Christ, rather than one that was predetermined. Whether his choice was so theorized or was simply the serendipitous result of separating out good from bad, religious from magical, the holy from the devilish, I cannot say. But the consequences of this separation were very important. This separation entailed the recognition of ancestral powers, but only in their negative devilish mode. Moreover, such powers as were credited were subdued or subjugated by the power of God. The Church thus assumed the language of ancestral potency, as it simultaneously tried to deprive it of its power. The church was thus *im kon*—the sacred house, the communion, the *anian kon* (the sacred food).

These novel denotations entailed a semiotic as much as a material struggle over rival spaces and structures of sanctity in the patterns of ancestral religion (cf. Jolly 1989). In particular, they set up a struggle between two forms of collectivity—the men's house, or *mal*, and the church. The *mal* was markedly *kon*, it was a space to which men gained entry as a result of sacrifices to the ancestors—in infancy, at circumcision, and especially in the process of killing pigs (see Jolly 1994). Men at such times were so holy that they could not return home to the *im* (household dwelling). If they slept with their wives, it would kill them (the wives, that is!) The men's house was an exclusivist male dwelling, a collective space distinct from the *im*, where male and female dwelled conjugally. The sacred fires, *ap kon*, which were lit in both *mal* and *im*, were central to daily commensal segregations by rank and gender. The food cooked on them for grade-taking ceremonies was *anian kon*, sacred food. Thus, the full significance of naming the church *im kon* becomes clearer. Although avowedly a sacred space, *kon*, it is an *im*, a space for men and women, not a *mal* for men alone. And the *anian kon*, or communion, partaken of there is available to all who believe and not just to those who are able to eat sacred food because of their rank or gender. Christians today celebrate these facts about their unrestricted commensality in church and domestic contexts as against the restrictions still prevailing in *kastom* communities. Much more might also be said about the continuities between Christian ideas of the sacrifice of Christ's body, including the partaking of the host in communion and ancestral sacrifices of pigs and persons, and the communion with the ancestors effected through consumption of their flesh (cf. Clark 1989).

I cannot pursue this here, but rather conclude by stressing how Tattevin's partial and motivated translations were taken up by local Catholics (cf. Meyer this volume). The accommodation he effected between indigenous and exogenous concepts persists, although it might be argued that the potency of the ancestors imputed by Catholics today is greater than he was willing to credit, and their status as devils less certain.[19] By using indigenous terms to demarcate the new sacred spaces and objects of Christianity, Marist priests like Tattevin did more than extend Catholic notions of the sacred to island churches. By appropriating an indigenous word, *kon*, and insisting that its true meaning lay beyond ancestral spaces, a struggle was declared. Similar processes of partial translation and appropriation occurred throughout the archipelago. Such acts of translation simultaneously endow the holy with local value and threaten to eclipse that local value in the name of a holier holy.

I now want to move beyond this detemporalized, disembodied analysis of words and concepts to resituate such rival concepts in conversations, events, and embodied practices. We need to witness concepts in use, not just in the practices of the church but in the broader process of explaining the manifestations of sacred power in daily life. This has been done consummately in some contemporary ethnographies of Pacific Christianity (e.g. Barker 1990; Burt 1994; Clark 1989; White 1991), and I do not attempt to imitate such studies here. It is also possible to reconstruct from documentary sources earlier configurations in the struggle between the ancestors and God. Despite their partial view of this process, the correspondence and the journals of the Marist missionaries provide us with ample evidence of this. They document interactions with ni-Vanuatu and report events in which there is a patent contest between the powers of the ancestors and of the Christian God. Although we are dealing with a history

written in French, there is still much that can be deduced from the ap-
palling scrawl of these Marist missionaries about indigenous perceptions,
agency, and how previous generations of ni-Vanuatu both accommodated
and resisted Christianity. These stories differ from both the oral and the
written accounts of conversion told now.[20] Because the latter are told from
the endpoint of ultimate conversion, they have a more teleological trajectory, which can erase the uncertainties, the oscillations, and the contestations of the process. Most of the descendants who tell such stories are
committed Christians, a few like my friends on South Pentecost are recalcitrant heathens *(kastom* people). The ways they relate their histories of
conversion are motivated by these different presents. Contemporary Marist
sources suggest, far from a triumphal process of conversion, that missionary
presence was combatted and resisted, that the coming of the light was a
very slow and faltering dawn. This is most poignantly evident in the process
of dying and death, and in the struggles over its causes, meanings, and significance. Across the northern islands of the archipelago, the Catholics of
this period were battling death—not just as an epidemiological but as an
etiological struggle between Christian and ancestral understandings of sacred power (cf. Douglas 1994: 355ff).

Ancestral and Christian Aetiologies of Death and Disease

Death stalks relentlessly through the history of the early Catholic mission
in Vanuatu. The missionaries themselves are very often morbidly ill or
dying.[21] Their high rates of morbidity and mortality are almost matched by
the frequency with which indigenous people throughout the archipelago
were succumbing to disease and death in this period. Regularly, the journals
and letters attest not only to the omnipresence of indigenous diseases—fever
(malaria), filariasis—but also to the ravages of introduced disease—dysentery, measles, influenza, and venereal disease—which raged as major epidemics through the mission communities. Norma McArthur (1974)
implicates the earlier Presbyterian missionaries in the southern islands as important vectors in the spread of such diseases. Moreover, the concentration
of mission populations into stations, schools, and dormitories, and their
coastal location, close to fresh water and often near swampy ground, provided ideal breeding grounds for the spread of both indigenous and exotic
diseases. Although populations in these northern islands did not plummet
quite so dramatically as on the islands of Aneityum and Tanna, decades earlier both missionaries and local people alike shared the view that they were

in danger of dying out. Thus Roux, writing from Tolmaco on Santo, reported that in his population of converts there were no children and that all those born in the last seven years had died. At one point he even proclaimed that there was no future for the mission for "the population is condemned" (PMB57 Roux to Doucéré, Tolomaco, May 28, 1910).[22] Given both the sheer amount of dying and its shared religious salience, it is hardly surprising that death was the prime occasion on which the contest and negotiation between missionary and indigenous understandings of sacred power was most fiercely enacted. There are innumerable examples scattered throughout the Marist correspondence; I will consider just two. But let me first reflect on the fact that missionaries were seen both as the source of illness and death and the source of healing and of life (cf. Douglas 1989, 1994, 1995). The ambiguity of their sacred power was thus assimilated into local ideas about high-ranking people, priests and sorcerers; that is, they had the power to help or hurt, to kill or cure. The complexity of these twin convictions is evident in this observation of Romeuf from the small island of Atchin in 1896.

> Some people forbid me to come to their village, for they think I am bringing death here. They hide their sick ones, especially if they are children. Recently I was fetched to chase devils away. I went, and they brought me to the front of the house where the devils were. In fact they were in the next house eating a dying baby, whom nobody let me see. Two days later I went through the same place, the baby was dead and buried (eaten by the devils). Next time I'll do my utmost to find these devils (PMB 57 Romeuf to Doucéré, Atchin, April 21, 1896).

Romeuf satirizes the credulity of the Atchinese, but appears rather credulous himself, authoring himself as one able to exorcise and to cure, if only he is allowed closer. The ambivalence and fear of local people is apparent—they let him approach but not too close. Probably they believed that the baby had been attacked not by devils but by *mats*, or ancestral spirits (the equivalent of *adumwat* in Atchin). A later letter from Roux on Santo makes even more apparent the association between conversion and a conviction that the missionaries can heal.

> All the villages before so opposed to the fathers are now well disposed. They also come to us if they are sick. We are not good doctors, but sometimes even sugared or bitter water will do the trick. The natives' imagination is so powerful it can make them cured as well as dead (PMB57 Roux to Doucéré, Tolomaco, February 2, 1910).

That the priests had the power to kill and cure[23] was a quite reasonable conclusion under the circumstances, but one drawn from slightly different evidence than we might adduce from our appreciation of the importance of intimate exposure to germs and viruses in infection and contagion, and of the vulnerability of a population that lacked immunity to introduced diseases. The aetiologies of both ni-Vanuatu and the Marist priests alike saw disease and death as ultimately derived from sacred forces. Although ni-Vanuatu might credit death to a recognized illness, accident, violence, or simply old age, behind these visible causes always lay a notion of sacred power—as to why ancestral protection was withdrawn or became malignant, or why a human sorcerer had been able to penetrate the victim's ancestral armor to cause disease or death. Similarly, although these Marist missionaries were familiar with some of the medical science of the period, they also interpreted death or survival as a sign of sacred power witnessed in the world—albeit in their case, God's will.[24]

Thus, in the processes of diagnosis and cure, there was a contest of meanings about whose sacred power prevailed. Many ni-Vanuatu believed that the holy water of baptism could kill, and many also believed that the drinks of sugared or salted water administered by the missionaries could cure. Lest I seem to be stressing "the natives' credulity" as Roux does, I should say that such beliefs were paralleled by Marist beliefs that were not dissimilar—the crucifix, holy water from Lourdes, and statues of the Virgin or the saints were credited with powers verging on the miraculous. It was not just the powerful imagination of the natives (which can "make them cured as well as dead") but the contending, equally powerful, and sometimes florid imagination of the priests. Disease and death always entailed a combat between such rival imaginaries. Let me first consider the near-death experience of an indigenous man.

Baptism on the Death Bed

In the first years of the Marist mission, most converts were either small children or adults "rescued" in extremis on their deathbeds. The missionaries were constantly in pursuit of dying souls to save, and quite regularly admonished people for secreting the sick or preventing them from visiting the dying.[25] Around 1907–1908, at Port Sandwich, mission children were deployed to assist in finding the dying. Given this fervent desire to rescue the dying, it is not surprising that the Catholic Church was perceived as the church of death, in contradistinction to the Protestants. Thus, Roux reports

from Tolmaco that after he performed two baptisms in extremis and also vis-
ited the sick, the natives "think him better than the Protestant minister who
doesn't seem to care about the dying ones" (PMB 57 Roux to Doucéré,
Port Olry, Santo, August 21, 1908). Indeed it appears that the water of holy
baptism was itself seen as the agent of death, being called by ni-Vanuatu in
several places the water of death (for example, *wa na matan* in South Pentecost (cf. Douglas 1995).[26] The following deathbed story reported by Suas,
suggests both the persisting power of this belief and also the centrality of
such scenarios in conversion. Writing to Doucéré from Lolopwepwe on
Ambae, Suas tells the story of the near death of his old enemy, the pagan
Banke. Fifteen years before, Suas had intervened in a fight between him and
Manuel, a Christian convert, and since that time Banke had been covertly
trying to damage the mission. Then on January 22, 1926, Banke "made" his
six-year-old son sacrifice pigs in order to consecrate him as a pagan. Banke
fell gravely ill the next day and was on the verge of death when he sent for
Suas to baptize him. Suas, though at first doubtful, went, and as the entire
village stood around the dying man in his hut, Banke, still lucid, implored,
"Father, I'm going to die, as you see. Baptize me." Suas replied, "Why didn't
you ask for it before?" Banke retorted, "I was healthy before, but today I'm
dying. That's not the same." Suas enunciated his conditions for baptism—if
Banke died, his wife and children had to come to the mission; if he survived, he had to come with his entire family to attend catechism. Suas then
baptized him and left. He admits to Doucéré that he prayed Banke might
die, for if he survived he was likely to renounce these promises and thus be
damned. But Banke survived and kept his word, coming to mass with his
family and other pagans fifteen days after his baptism, and had until two
months after the incident not missed one ceremony. Suas was clearly surprised but also gratified: "At least they won't call baptism the water of death
anymore" (PMB 58, Suas to Doucéré Lolopwepwe, Ambae, March 23,
1926, dialogue translated from transcription of original in French).

Banke's conversion was a belated coup for Suas, in his sojourn on
Ambae. Although in Vanuatu there were not the group conversions following chiefs, that were typical of Polynesia[27] after powerful traditionalist elders
converted, or, alternatively, when they died after a wrangle with missionaries—this was often a critical turning point in local processes of conversion. Early in most Marist missions, the majority of the converts were
children, youths, and women. It was often suggested by the missionaries
that their parents, their elders, or their male kin, respectively, were trying
to hold them back or restrain them. Indeed, both Protestant missionaries
and Catholic priests often consciously deployed the dissatisfactions and re-

sentments created by the unequal relations of young and old, of women and men, in order to gain converts. This was both self-serving and self-deluding rhetoric, however, since many of the children, youths, and women at the mission station were, in fact, there with the consent of their families—either having been formally adopted or, in some cases, given to the mission, in return for what I elsewhere call "child price" or "bride price" (Jolly n.d.). Moreover, in this period such converts regularly returned to their villages when times got bad, when epidemics spread, when food was short, when the mission was subject to violent attack by pagans, or when the priests were either asking too much work or paying too little for it. They also often returned home when large ceremonies ensued, such as those for the yam harvest, for male circumcision, or for the ceremonies of the graded society. Those who controlled such rituals, all of which entailed sacrifice to the ancestors, were held to be and probably were the greatest opponents of the mission. They were men like Namal at Port Sandwich, Banke at Lolopwepwe, or Mariek at Namaram, a Marist station on Pentecost to which I now move.

The Priest and the Subversive Catechist:
Father Suas and Stefano Teviri, Pentecost, 1903–1904

Second, I turn to some extraordinary earlier events, also involving Father Suas, at the missions of Melsisi and Namaram. This not only entails a contest with the pagans or the Protestants but an internecine struggle within the mission that had dire implications for the broader processes of conversion. This is what Monnier dubs the "war" between the missionary, Father Suas, and the catechist, Stefano Teviri, an indigenous man who had returned from plantation work in Fiji, where he and many other laborers from Pentecost had been converted to Catholicism. Suas perceived Stefano as subverting his authority. What fascinates me here is the way in which the contest between them is again played out through threats of disease and death. Suas had moved from Olal on Ambrym only five months before, and over this period initiated what he saw as a slow process of reform. This primarily entailed reversing the influence of the indigenous catechist, Stefano.

In November 1903, Suas reported that Stefano was making war against pagans, and that he was refusing to obey him. "He knows his strength and he wants to command here; either he'll command or there won't be any mission." He suggested to Doucéré that he (Suas) had better go or the mission would be lost. An enclosed letter from Stefano catalogued the issues in contention—that Father Suas abandoned Stefano, that he destroyed the chapel, that there was no catechism. He also alleged maltreatment of women and of children. He accused Suas of beating a "backsliding" woman in the church and of sending women away, saying they should not be married to pagans but to educated men in Port Vila. He alleged that Suas treated the mission children like slaves, sending them to Malakula, Santo, and Vila without their parents' approval and that this led to the latter abandoning the new religion. He also claimed that Suas threatened to burn the houses and kill the pigs of those parents whose children did leave the mission. He concluded by claiming that many villages were holding meetings and deciding to give up Catholicism, and that catechists were fleeing elsewhere (PMB 57 Suas to Douceré, Melsisi, November 2, 1903).

In an earlier letter to Douceré, Suas also reproduces the text of a letter from Stefano, translated from the "vernacular" into French. His opening words are resounding: "I, Stefano, will speak for all the catechists. We cannot bear your rules anymore." He proclaims that he refuses to do what the priest orders him, for dangerous consequences will follow. This is a reference to the fact that the catechists refuse to go to the villages since people there do not want them and will kill them: "Already seven catechists have died 'poisoned' (i.e., ensorcelled)." He contends that the previous father allowed that catechists should only go to their own villages, where food would be given them by trusted close kin. Only when all villages have become Christian should catechists be free to move around, Stefano reasons. He continues

> We wanted to tell you this yesterday, but you answered badly, that we should grow our own food. Food takes time to grow and what about eating meanwhile? We all work for Catholicism, and if we have spiritual riches we must bear material poverty, which we do, unlike you priests who are paid and who freely receive food sent to you from a foreign place. Yet we ask nothing and bear it. Why cannot we follow the rules given by the previous father, for they were fruitful, and he used to comfort us with good words. But our new father shows us only sternness and spite. He also refuses to confess us. What if one of us died suddenly unconfessed? This hurts us greatly.

The letter goes on to complain that Suas fails to listen to advice from the villagers and from the council of the catechists. It ends by threatening to call a conjoined protest meeting of Catholics, Protestants, and pagans. Suas submits to his supervisor, Douceré, that this letter is "all lies," and warns that unless he supports him rather than Stefano, the latter will become "even more rude and audacious." Stefano later resigned in Suas' absence, but the contest continued in rival interpretations of a sequence of deaths and epidemics.

At Namaram it was reported that everybody had left the mission after Father Tayac's death. An old man, Mariek, had sacrificed pigs in order that the father drown. Tayac drowned, but the old man went unpunished; thus, claims Suas, others were encouraged. Mariek sacrificed more pigs, the anuses of which were painted red in order to signify his desire to bring disease—most likely dystentery—to the mission. Again he succeeded: dysentery came and everybody left. Stefano refused to help punish the guilty. Suas argued that even if such threats were ineffective, people must be punished or they would desert the mission. He urged Doucere, "You must call the warship, otherwise it's the end of the mission and after Namaram it would be Melsisi and Loltong's turn." Indeed, dysentery continued in Namaram, spread to Melsisi, and was followed by another epidemic Suas took to be typhoid. It seemed that the missionary was losing the epidemiological contest. But then Stefano himself sickened (PMB 57, Suas to Doucere, Melsisi, May 17, 1903) and predictably became more compliant, even helping to build the new chapel. By July, however, Suas' fortunes had reversed, the crisis had deepened, and Suas wrote to Doucere, reproaching him for his inaction,

> You did not ask for the warship. My predictions have come true. Namaram and Loltong are gone and Melsisi pagans, encouraged, have already hurt seven of our students. Five are dead, including a catechist and two injured, and this in only two days. Today they threaten to come here and destroy everything, the missionary first. I'll probably be dead when you receive this letter.[28]

Suas lived to fight a few more battles, including the continuing saga with Stefano, which I cannot detail here.[29] But by late July 1904, Suas declared that Stefano seemed to have accepted defeat and was sending him fish every Friday. What caused this reversal was not the arrival of the warship, nor even Doucere's forceful intervention on behalf of Suas. Rather, the brute facts of who was dying and who was surviving seem critical in missionary gains and losses. The epidemics had abated; Stefano himself became sick; the Christians succeeded in pitched battles with the pagans. We witness throughout this sequence of events the pervasive effects of a contest over the meaning of death. The fact that Tayac was drowned and that dysentery and typhoid were spreading was taken as a sign of the power of ancestral priests and the vulnerability of the Catholics. Later, when Father Ezekiel died, Stefano accused

Suas of both killing him and failing to avenge his death. The language is of threat, counterthreat, and of vengeance, manifest in violent deaths in war and homicide, "accidental" deaths like drowning, or death through disease (is it poisoning/sorcery or God's will?). But then when the epidemics recede and deaths abate, the power of the mission grows. This is a sign not so much of their coercive powers of warships or the persuasive power of their words but of the triumph of their sacred power over the local priests.[30]

Conclusion

This brief exploration of the Marist project of conversion in Vanuatu suggests the importance not just of translating words and concepts but of translating rival aetiologies of life and death. The epidemiological conditions were clearly conducive to such a contest—the proliferation of mysterious deaths in a succession of several introduced epidemics. The outcome of the combat between the powers of the ancestors and of God was evident in the differential survival of the "heathen" and the "mission" party. Even if missionaries tried to disclaim responsibility for either killing or curing,[31] this contradicted local views that all death was motivated (by living sorcerers/priests or ancestral spirits) as well as their own beliefs in extrahuman agency in this world (cf. Douglas 1994). The Marists strongly believed in God's will; they also sometimes believed that they were vulnerable to sorcery attack, refusing gifts of food because they suspected they were "poisoned."

In understanding the centrality of death in the process of conversion, we need also to ponder the new meaning that conversion gave to Christian life. It required generations of ni-Vanuatu, like islanders elsewhere in the Pacific, to detach themselves from their past, to resignify ancestral powers and sites as diabolic and destructive, and to embrace the new powers of the church not just as more efficacious but as bringing light and life in lieu of darkness and death. White recounts how indigenous conversion narratives from Santa Isabel in the Solomon Islands employ an imputed antithesis between the "now" characterized by love, togetherness, and happiness and the "before" typified by hatred, fighting, cannibalism, and misery. Although such an extreme contrast is not found in all such narratives, most render it as a transformation from a time of darkness to a time of light (White 1991, 8–9).[32]

It has been suggested that, throughout the Pacific, such images of the forces of light overtaking darkness were especially compelling, not just because they meshed with indigenous idioms but because they also imaged the colonial racial hierarchy (cf. Keesing 1992, 228–38). When Pacific Christians use these tropes of darkness and light, it is thus tempting to see this as a terrible persistence of the negativity of devilishness and blackness that white missionaries imputed. Is this merely a case of the "subalterns being deeply implicated in their own subjugation"? (Keesing 1992, ibid; cf. Meyer, this volume)

But there is both corollary and complication to this trope. Pacific Christians no longer see themselves as in the dark—they are in the light, unlike their pagan neighbors (such as the Kwaio of Malaita or the *kastom* villagers of South Pentecost). Conversion narratives often merge a story of collective and personal transformation, in the strong conviction that the new life is a better life. There is a complication too, in that the powers of the past, the forces of darkness, are not thought to have been totally vanquished. Thus, as in many parts of the Pacific, the islanders of Santa Isabel do not believe that God has completely eclipsed the ancestral religion. White considers that ancestral and Christian powers are still in contest, that although European missionaries tried to discredit the efficacy of ancestral agencies, indigenous catechists and converts were more likely to admit them. Paradoxically, even in continuing attempts to demonstrate the superior efficacy of God by banishing "devils" or neutralizing the power of "ghosts," the efficacy of ancestral agencies is still admitted (1991, 38, 53–56).

Thus, what emerges is a more complicated configuration wherein the contest between Christian and heathen, God and Satan, is not now between the colonizer and the colonized but within the collectivity and the subjectivity of the Pacific Christian. In narrating the negativities of their ancestors—their capacities for sorcery, violence, and cruelty—Pacific Christians are often also alluding to the present potential for devilishness in themselves (see White 1991).

Moreover, although Christian projects required converts to attach negative values to their ancestral past, declaring this sinful or savage, Christianity also provided the language for a challenge to colonial domination. This is obvious in the words of the catechist Stefano to the priest Suas, in his play and parody on the conventional Christian aphorism about material poverty enabling spiritual riches—you (priests) have both material and spiritual wealth, we (indigenous catechists) have neither material or spiritual wealth; we do not even have the right to confession. The racial hierarchy of the mission was blatant and was early challenged by Pacific converts. In many places, this provided a model for broader challenges to colonial rule, which frequently deployed the language of Christianity. Biblical images, the more emancipatory words of Jesus, the promised millennium, pervaded not just expressly Christian movements but other anticolonial movements such as those labeled "cargo cults."

Finally, let me return to my beginning. Rafael suggests that such questions of translation and conversion open up new ways in which to consider the emergence of nationalist consciousness in the Philippines (1988, xix). The experience of Filipino nationalism and the anticolonial movements against the Spanish and then the Americans have been much more bloody than those that have emerged in the Pacific up until now.[33] They have also drawn heavily on Christian imagery of redemption and sacrifice and, more recently, the emancipatory promises inherent in the concept of "rebirth." In Vanuatu, as in most of the Pacific, anticolonial movements and nationalist struggles have on the whole been less fierce, but Christian beliefs and values have been equally compelling in providing both the language and the resources to challenge colonial rule. Moreover, we increasingly hear the whites who brought the light criticized for their lack of Christian commitment. Ni-Vanuatu today espouse Christianity as indubitably theirs, not a derived form marked as Pacific, indigenous, or vernacular. And indeed, in many Pacific villages the need for reversing the flow of missionary messages is entertained, and the future scenario of Pacific peoples going forth to promote Christian renewal in Australia, in Europe, even in America, is imagined.[34]

Acknowledgments

This paper would have been impossible without the research assistance of Rachel Bloul and Annegret Shemberg. Thanks also to the Australian Research Council, Macquerie University and the Australian National University for material support. Thanks to our editor Peter van der Veer for providing an excellent context in the conference on conversion in Amsterdam, to other participants in that and to Bronwen Douglas, Christine Durea, Ton Otto, Matthew Spriggs and Nicholas Thomas and Michael Young for comments and criticisms, not all of which I have been able to address here.

Notes

1. See Young (n.d.) for a consideration of the link between narratives about missionary arrival and conversion and narratives about the nation and independence.
2. This is a large language family that includes most of the languages of the insular Pacific, coastal PNG, and of insular S. E. Asia.
3. This is patent in the translation work of the Inglises and the Geddies, two Presbyterian missionary couples on Aneityum in southern Vanuatu in the 1850s (Jolly 1991, Gard-

ner 1993). John Inglis simultaneously vaunts the capacity of the vernacular to express Christian concepts and declares it inchoate, prior to missionary codification, in his declaration that the missionaries "found a language . . . floating indistinctly . . . on the lips of the native. . . . They formed an alphabet; they found out the meaning of the words; they discovered their true pronunciation; and they ascertained the grammatical structure of the language. And the result is that we have a language at our command, both copious and exact, capable of giving utterance to every thought and idea" (Inglis 1882: xiii, cited in Gardner 1993: 23).

4. Sometimes this view underlies moves for education in the vernacular rather than in English or pidgin, for example. It also informed the views of some liberation theorists, including Paulo Freire in his *Pedagogy of the Oppressed* (1972), although his view of the emanicipatory potential of literacy is very complex and nuanced.

5. For example, Roviana in the Western Solomons; Motu in Papua New Guinea; the eastern variant of Fijian, which became Standard Fijian in Fiji; Raga and Mota in Vanuatu.

6. "Speech filled with the 'celestial doctrine' of God is received by the priest and retransmitted orally. The ear is conceived as the privileged zone of exchange between God and His people, His message is mediated by the mouth of the priest" (Rafael 1988: 31).

7. "Hardly had they parked their wagons when they began to preach from them in a gesture which became emblematic of the early mission at large . . . their faith in the persuasive power of the Word was so literal that, at first, they paid no attention to the manner in which their orations were being translated and understood" (Comaroff and Comaroff 1991: 2).

8. They perceive this not just as a struggle over words but over space and resources, especially water. They detail fascinating convergences between African and Biblical views of water, as signifying not only wealth but blessedness. Their discussion of the politics of water and the struggles over irrigation are scintillating (1991: 206ff).

9. Apparently the same tactic is still used on Tanna today—by making the speeches of one's political or religious opponents inaudible or inconsequential one renders them ineffective (Lindstrom 1990). Christine Dureau reports a similar identification between "listening" and "knowing" in the Western Solomons and notes the habit of fundamentalist preachers in town preaching loudly late into the night (personal communication, February 1995).

10. At the time of this fieldwork primarily with *kastom* people (that is traditionalists or heathens) there was some antagonism between them and their Christian neighbors, who included Catholic, Melanesian Mission, and Church of Christ adherents. I know less than I should about the local and contemporary uses of Christian concepts by the various denominations. My evocation of indigenous religion refers to beliefs and practices current then—which were neither as uniform nor as unchanged from Tattevin's time, as this vignette suggests (see Jolly 1994).

11. I do not mean to here convey the endorsement of the idea that Catholicism is transparently "universal" and ancestral religions "local." Of course, every particular manifestation of Islam or Christianity has a local as much as a global aspect and ancestral religions in both Africa and in the Pacific were arguably far more extended precolonially than they were to become (see Ranger 1993).

12. This translation was summarily criticized by Capell, who was of a different Christian persuasion. "[T]here is a belief in a superior being named Barkulkul or Barkolkol,

whom Fr Tattevin seems rather too ready to identify with the great World Spirit" (1938: 57). The Protestants by contrast often retained the English word 'God' according to Co-drington, because of "the enormous difficulty . . . of finding an adequate native ex-pression in any one language" (cited in Hilliard, 1974: 34; cf. Adams, 1984, 61–64).

13. I have translated this variously as priest or magician. Tattevin translates it consistently as magician or sorcerer. It is used in terms such as *loas na yil, loas na dam, loas na bwet, loas na tsingin,* and *loas na isin* to mean, respectively, priests of the sun, yams, taro, war, and women, i.e., a midwife. But it can also be used adjectivally to convey the idea of sacredness or danger, as in *ut loas,* a grove associated with first emergence or settlement of ancestors, and which is left uncultivated (see text and footnote 17 below).

14. Douceré was suspicious of these close parallels and raised the question as to whether the indigenous myths had been influenced by Biblical stories. Suas forcefully rebutted any such conjecture apropos this very myth, both as recorded on North Ambrym and on South Pentecost. "About this famous sun and moon theory built on the Barkolkol and Bougliam legends. If it were Pentecost (Tortali and Ul), I could understand something, but not see the usefulness as the text very clearly proves the tradition of the Earthly Par-adise, the temptation and fall of woman and her punishment. As for the Ambrym leg-end I cannot see the role of the sun and moon there. I wrote in the past 'Barkolkol who created everything cannot be but the Supreme Being.' I still hold by this in spite of all these theories. The tradition of the temptation and fall of man through women is so obvious there that it could be imitated from the Bible, which is not the case. You know I was the first Catholic missionary on Ambrym, arriving only three months after the first Protestants. And the elders who told me this legend said it was coming from their ancestors. It is their legend, not a Bible imitation. I am surprised you even asked con-firmation. I am surprised that scientists should feel the need for sun and moon theo-ries when the truth is so clear" (PMB 57, Suas to Douceré, Lolopwepe, January 20, 1913, emphases in original). Though the Barkulkul (Ambrymese, Barkolkol) cycle is no doubt indigenous rather than exogenous oral tradition, the creation stories are per-ceived today as related, but sometimes in opposition rather than derivation. Many tra-ditionalist (*kastom*) Sa speakers who told me versions of this myth prefaced it by contrasting it with the story of Adam and Eve, and in particular the tale that Eve was created from Adam's spare rib. They asserted that theirs was the true story of the origin of sexual difference and of death, and that the Bible story was false.

15. For this stress on the embodiment of spirit I am grateful to the insights of Richard Eves, exemplified in a chapter of his doctoral thesis on the body, gender and spatiality on the Lelet Plateau, New Ireland (Eves 1994).

16. I should stress at this point that this conception of the afterlife is not universal even in the northern islands of Vanuatu. Indeed, Capell (1938) demonstrates the great diversity of conceptions, although he situates them within a diffusionist framework. Deacon wrote of Sakau on Santo that their sky-dwelling creator being, Yetar, distinguishes between the good, those who have not killed who live on as spirit, and the bad, those who have killed, whom he eats. Layard reports very complicated beliefs for Vao, apropos the link between behavior in this world and the afterlife, entrance to which is guarded by a de-vouring female ogre. In some islands, then, there were incipient notions of Heaven and Hell, even if these were not spatialized as a skyworld and an underworld, respectively.

17. There are very strong sanctions against cultivating these sacred groves. During the first month of my fieldwork, a woman who, at her husband's urging, started to plant yams

in an *ut loas*, gave birth to a deformed baby who lacked an anus and died within a few days. This tragedy was directly attributed to their trespassing in this area.

18. I cannot resist noting here the similarity to the term *tagaro*, which in North Pentecost and East Ambae is the term for a primordial creator being from the sky, similar to Barkulkul. Whether these are cognates and are further cognate with Tangaroa who features in Polynesian myths is a subject of research by Austronesian linguists.

19. This is what Ben Burt (1994) argues in his book on Christianity and tradition on Malaita, Solomon Islands. He suggests that the morality ascribed by the Kwara'ae adherents to the South Seas Evangelical Church is more relative and contextual, and that ghosts, spirits, and even Satan are not so much intrinsically bad as failed or discredited alternatives to God (1994: 265). Compare White (1991) on Santa Isabel, also in the Solomons. Christine Dureau (1994) notes that Christians on Simbo, Western Solomons, tend to see their ancestors as "good sinners," distinct from those who persist in paganism, having heard who are "bad sinners." This then runs contrary to any simple theory of the "diabolization" of pre-Christian gods or spirits.

20. I am not implying that the contemporary documentary sources are better or worse than later oral traditions, only that they are importantly different. For an extended consideration of indigenous conversion narratives, see White (1991). He sees such stories of first contact with missionaries and their bringing peace and the light as the dominant mode of sociohistorical memory on Santa Isabel, Solomon Islands. These stories are not just told but sung and performed, and are as much a way of authoring the self and constructing the good Christian person as they are of constituting collective identity. White also notes that although indigenous narratives of conversion stress the agency of locals, and of chiefs in particular, they also heroize and amplify the power of the missionaries more than do the documentary accounts by the missionaries themselves (White 1991: 172).

21. The story that emerges from these letters is not one of triumphant conversion but of failure, lack of material and human resources, solitude, ill health, depression, despair, and omnipresent death. In most of these letters, these themes recur with agonizing regularity. The letters that flow between the Monsigneurs—first Fraysse and then Douceré in Port Vila and Father Regis in France—are a litany of laments about those fathers and brothers who are too "ruined" for active service. There are constant references to the ravages of malaria, dysentery, measles, and influenza, and the catastrophic effects of cyclones, earthquakes, and volcanic eruptions. After one tour of the mission stations, Douceré proclaimed that "bad health is the rule," and suggested that the first rule in the New Hebrides be that two people do the work of one (PMB52 Douceré to Regis, Port Vila, November 24, 1907).

22. Such high rates of infant and child mortality on mission stations is echoed from many places. Roux reports a similar situation in Big Bay on Santo, as does Strock on Port Sandwich (PMB 57 Strock to Douceré, Port Sandwich, June 30, 1910). (PMB57 Roux to Douceré, Tolomaco, February 2, 1910).

23. See also several incidents reported by Roux from Tolomaco in 1910 (PMB 57 Roux to Douceré, Tolomaco, February 2, 1910).

24. The Comaroffs also remark on this conjunction of scientific and religious aetiologies in Protestant missionary medical discourse in Africa (1991:206ff) and, indeed, in their wider theories of causation. They reproduce a delightful passage from Livingstone (1857: 25,

cited in Comaroff and Comaroff 1991: 210–211) in which a "rain doctor" and a European missionary, a "medical doctor," debate who controls the rain. As they note, Livingstone, in crafting this conversation, credits them equal ontological ground and suggests a parallel by calling them both "doctor." This they see as unique at the time, for most missionaries failed to see such symmetry, that a rain doctor "no more manufactured rainfall than did a clergy man praying to God" (1991: 210). This seems also to have been lost on the Marists. Thus, we have a sequence of entries in the journals of Pionnier from Port Sandwich in Malakula (PMB 53). On November 6, 1895 he writes that there is a drought and almost no water left, and that he has had recourse to St Antoine, who should work better than "the pagan rituals of the rainmaker Namal". The drought continued for months, "the rain seems ready to fall at any time but it always starts raining somewhere else" (January 3, 1896). But whereas it was clear to him that the rainmaker was a liar or an imposter, Father's faith in St Antoine endures undiminished; the saint's failure is because his power is being blocked by the Devil (January 2–3, 1896).

25. A few scattered illustrations will suffice. Jamond reports for Melsisi on Pentecost that there were 56 children baptized on January 13 and 14th, 1900, with 3 dying adults (PMB 53). Pionnier reports many such baptisms in Port Sandwich, For example, on February 25, 1893 he is told of a sick man in Boungarere, willing to accept baptism, whom he instructs partly in *bislama* and partly in the vernacular, and who the next day "received his reward," (i.e., died, PMB 53). But there are also many incidents when he hears of sick or dying people, but they are secreted. On one such occasion, Pionnier observes the "natives lie with an admirable naivete" (PMB 53 August 18, 1894). Moreover, even if the priests did make it to the dying person, there was rarely acceptance. Pionnier reports showing a crucifix to a sick man, who covered his eyes in order not to see it (PMB 53 April 24, 1895).

26. Bronwen Douglas has similarly reported for Grande Terre on New Caledonia that many Kanak were afraid of converting to Christianity since they believed the holy water of baptism could kill (1995: 64). At one level, this belief seems to simply derive from the fact that many of the early converts were in fact made on the death bed, in extremis. Those who were so baptized were very likely to die soon, and thus the water would be seen as effecting or hastening that death. But there perhaps is in Vanuatu also a link with indigenous divination in which "blessed" water was sprayed over a victim to diagnose and exorcise an attacking ancestral spirit (see above).

27. See Mathew Spriggs (1985) for considerations of this problem in the conversion history of Aneityum in the south. "A school in every district" was what the Presbyterians recommended, because of the small size of the polity and the localized power of chiefs. However, mass conversions have been reported elsewhere in Melanesia; for example, by Christine Dureau for Simbo in the Western Solomons (1994). She suggests that the rapid and almost total conversion to Methodism that occurred on Simbo just after pacification at the turn of the century was a response to the seeming abandonment by ancestors. Earlier an island that prevailed in local headhunting raids and in exchanges both of indigenous and imported goods, Simbo was "pacified" with humiliating ferocity and speed by the British navy. It shelled villages and destroyed the canoes and the canoe houses associated with the headhunting complex.

28. Suas also suggests that the Protestants at Waterfall may have been urging the pagans to oppose the Catholics, and threatens to circumvent Douceré by writing directly to the commandant of the warship (PMB 57 Suas to Douceré, Melsisi, November 2, 1903).

29. I find it an interesting irony that he applies to Suas the usual critique of indigenous cat-echists by whites—that is, that they are too zealous.

30. It is not just the pervasive facts of disease and death that are paramount but the discur-sive force of the medical metaphor in portraying other struggles. As well as this trope pervading his discussion of the struggle with the pagans, the Protestants, and insolent local converts, Suas uses the language of disease to refer to rival colonial influences. Thus, the widespread desire for labor recruiting in 1907–1908 he also proclaims as a mania, an "epidemic," which has claimed three "victims" from the Melsisi mission (PMB 58).

31. As did the Presbyerians on Aneityum in the south. Douglas notes how Geddie in par-ticular refrained from proclaiming that epidemics were God's punishment, and tried to disclaim any responsibility for curing. In this circumstance, it seems that the mission-aries were credited both with powerful sorcery and its antidote (Douglas 1989). See also Adams (1986: 116–49) for a superb treatment of the measles epidemic on Tanna.

32. White also notes the subtleties and ambiguities in such narratives. For example, someone who is a direct descendant of a heathen chief, who first resisted a missionary, dwelt on his chiefly power rather than his propensity for killing and cannibalism (White 1991: 156–59).

33. This is not to discount the bloodshed and cruelty of some colonial massacres and cam-paigns, such as those reported by Keesing for Malaita (1992). Nor do I intend by this comparison with Rafael and the Philippines to equate the Catholicism of Dominicans and Jesuits of the sixteenth century onwards to nineteenth- and twentieth-century Marists. The differences are as great as the commonalities privileged here.

34. This was mooted at a sermon I heard in a Methodist church in Koro Levu, western Viti Levu, in Fiji in October 1988. Christine Dureau has more recently heard similar sug-gestions in Simbo in the Western Solomons. It should be noted, though, that there is presently a second wave of conversions in the Pacific, as many are converting from the more orthodox denominations of Catholic, Anglican, Presbyterian, and Methodist to forms of "revivalist" or Pentecostalist Christianity, being promoted by missionaries from North America in particular and to B'ahai faith. This testifies yet again that the power of the "devils" has not yet been eclipsed.

References

Adams, R. 1984. *In the Hand of Strangers. A Century of European Contact with Tanna, 1774–1874*. Pacific Research Monograph 9, Canberra: ANU Press.

Barker, J., ed., 1990. *Christianity in Oceania: Ethnographic Perspectives*, ASAO Mono-graph No 12. Latham: University Press of America.

Barker, J. 1992. "Christianity in Western Melanesian Ethnography." In J. Carrier, ed., *History and Tradition in Melanesian Ethnography*. Berkeley: University of California Press, 144–73.

Barker, J. 1993. " 'We Are Eklesia': Conversion in Uiaku, Papua New Guinea." In R. W. Hefner, ed., *Conversion to Christianity: Historical and Anthropological Perspec-tives on a Great Transformation*, Berkeley: University of California Press, 199–230.

Burt, B. 1994. *Tradition and Christianity: The Colonial Transformation of a Solomon Is-land Society*. Chur and Reading: Harwood Academic Publishers.

Capell, A. 1938. "The Stratification of After-world Beliefs in the New Hebrides." *Folklore* 71: 19–36.

Clark, J. 1989. "Gods, ghosts and people: Christianity and social organisation among Takuru Wiru." In M. Jolly and M. Macintyre, eds., *Family and Gender in the Pacific: Domestic Contradictions and the Colonial Impact*. Cambridge: Cambridge University Press, 170–92.

Clifford, J. 1979. "The translation of cultures: Maurice Leenhardt's evangelism, New Caledonia 1902–1926." *The Journal of Pacific History* 15: 2–20.

Comaroff, J. and J. 1991. *Of Revelation and Revolution: Christianity, Colonialism and Consciousness in South Africa* 1. Chicago and London: University of Chicago Press.

Dening, G. 1980. *Islands and Beaches: Discourse on a Silent Land, Marquesas 1774–1880.* Melbourne: Melbourne University Press.

Douglas, B. 1989. "Autonomous and Controlled Spirits: Traditional Ritual and Early Interpretations of Christianity on Tanna, Aneityum and the Isle of Pines in Comparative Perspective." *The Journal of the Polynesian Society*, 98(1): 7–48.

Douglas, B. 1994. "Discourses on Death in a Melanesian World." In D. Merwick, ed., *Dangerous Liaisons: Essays in Honour of Greg Dening*. Melbourne: University of Melbourne, History Department, 353–78.

Douglas, B. 1995. "Power, Discourse and the Appropriation of God: Christianity and Subversion in a Melanesian Conext," *History and Anthropology*, 9(1): 57–92.

Dureau, C. 1994. "Mixed Blessings: Christianity and History in Women's Lives on Simbo, Western Solomon Islands." Doctoral thesis, Anthropology. Macquarie University, Australia.

Eves, R. 1994. "Seating the Place: Magic and Embodiment on the Lelet Plateau, New Ireland (Papua New Guinea)." Doctoral thesis, Anthropology. RSPAS, The Australian National University.

Freire, P. 1972. *Pedagogy of the Oppressed.* Harmondsworth: Penguin Books.

Gardner, H. 1993. " 'By the Foolishness of Preaching': Representations and Messages on the island of Aneityum (Vanuatu), 1848–1859." BA honors thesis, history. La Trobe University, Australia.

Guha, R. 1988. "Dominance without hegemony and its historiography." In R. Guha, ed., *Subaltern Studies VI: Writings on South Asian History and Society*. Delhi and Oxford: Oxford University Press, 210–309.

Hilliard, D. 1974. *God's Gentlemen: A History of the Melanesian Mission, 1849–1942.* St. Lucia: University of Queensland Press.

Ileto, R. 1979. *Pasyon and Revolution: Popular Movements in the Philippines, 1840–1910.* Quezon City: Ateneo de Manila University Press.

Jolly, M. 1989. "Sacred spaces: Churches, male clubhouses and households in South Pentecost, Vanuatu." In M. Jolly and M. Macintyre, eds., *Family and Gender in the Pacific: Domestic Contradictions and the Colonial Impact*. Cambridge: Cambridge University Press, 213–35.

Jolly, M. 1991. " 'To save the girls for brighter and better lives': Presbyterian missions and women in SouthernVanuatu, 1848–1870." *The Journal of Pacific History*, 26(1): 27–48.

Jolly, M. 1994. *Women of the Place: Kastom, Colonialism and Gender in Vanuatu.* Chur and Reading: Harwood Academic Publishers.

Jolly, M. n.d. *Engendering Colonialism: European Visions of Women in Vanuatu,* ts. in preparation.

Lane, R. 1965. "The Melanesians of South Pentecost, New Hebrides." In P. Lawrence and M. Meggitt, eds., *Gods, Ghosts and Men in Melanesia.* Melbourne: Oxford University Press, 250–79.

Keesing, R. M. 1982. *Kwaio Religion: the Living and the Dead in a Solomon Island Society.* NewYork: Columbia University Press.

Keesing. R. M. 1992. *Custom and Confrontation: The Kwaio Struggle for Cultural Autonomy.* Chicago: University of Chicago Press.

Laracy, H. M. 1976. *Marists and Melanesians: A History of Catholic Missions in the Solomon Islands.* Canberra: ANU Press.

Lindstrom, L. 1990. *Knowledge and Power in a South Pacific Society.* Washington: Smithsonian Institution Press.

McArthur, N. 1974. "Population and prehistory: The late phase on Aneityum." PhD thesis, prehistory. RSPacS, Australian National University.

Monnier, P. 1988a. *L'Eglise Catholique au Vanuatu, Cent Ans de Mission 1887–1987:* Biographies, PortVila: Archbishop's House.

Monnier 1988b. *Les Lettres du Père Suas,* PortVila: Archbishop's House.

Otto, T. 1992. *The Politics of Tradition in Baluan,* PhD thesis, Anthropology. RSPacS, Australian National University.

Rafael, V. 1988. *Contracting Colonialism: Translation and Christian Conversion in Tagalog Society Under Early Spanish Rule.* London: Cornell University Press.

Ranger, T. 1993. "The local and the global in Southern African religious history." In R. W. Hefner, ed., *Conversion to Christianity: Historical and Anthropological Perspectives on a Great Transformation.* Berkeley: University of California Press, 65–98.

Spriggs, M. 1985. " 'A School in Every District': The Cultural Geography of Conversion on Aneityum, SouthernVanuatu." *The Journal of Pacific History* 20: 23–41.

Suas, P. J. 1911–12. Myths et légendes des indigènes des Nouvelles Hébrides, (Océanie) *Anthropos,* 6: 901–910, 7: 33–66.

Tattevin, E. 1915. "A l'ombre des ignames: Myths et légendes de l'île Pentecôte, *Les Missions Catholiques,* 47: 213, 226–27, 236–37.

Tattevin, E. 1919. "Sacrifices et superstitions chez les canaques." *Annales de la Propagation de la Foi,* 91: 263–70.

Tattevin, E. 1926–27. "Sur les bords de la mer sauvage." *Revue d'Histoire des Missions* 3: 370–413; 4: 82–97, 407–29, 557–79.

Tattevin, E. 1929 and 1931. "Myths et légendes du sud de l'île Pentecôte." *Anthropos* 24: 983–1004; 26: 489–512, 863–66.

White, G. 1991. *Identity through History: Living Stories in a Solomon Islands Society.* Cambridge: Cambridge University Press.

Young. M. W. n.d. "Commemorating missionary heroes: Local Christianity and narratives of nationalism." In N. Thomas and T. Otto, eds., *Narrating the Nation in the Pacific*, ts. under review.

Unpublished Sources

Pacific Manuscripts Bureau, consulted on microfilm at Mitchell Library Sydney.

PMB 52 Roman Catholic Mission New Hebrides. Records Account of Mission at Pentecost by Father J. B. Jamond, SM.

PMB 53 Roman Catholic Mission, New Hebrides. Journal of the Mission at Port Sandwich, Malakula, 1889–99 by Father J. N. Pionnier, SM.

PMB 57 Roman Catholic Mission, New Hebrides. Records, 1894–1932 (Letters of Father Z. Strock, SM etc.).

PMB 58 Roman Catholic Mission, New Hebrides. Records, 1898–1932 (Letters of Father J. B. Suas, etc.).

10

COMMENTS ON CONVERSION

Talal Asad

So What Is Conversion?

Why do people convert? This seems an innocent question. Anthropologists have not only raised it but responded to it with interesting answers. In his edited volume *Conversion to Christianity*,[1] R. W. Hefner provides a useful overview of many of these answers. Populations become Christian or Muslim for different personal reasons and under a variety of social conditions. Hefner has outlined the debates about the proper explanation of such conversions.

But the question is not entirely innocent. At any rate, it is based on assumptions that are at least as interesting as the answers. John and Jean Comaroff have pointed to some of them in their admirable study *Of Revelation and Revolution*, and I will discuss their contribution in a moment. There's another point worth thinking about: religious conversion appears to need explaining in a way that secular conversion into modern ways of being does not.

There was a time when conversion didn't need explaining. People converted because God had helped them to see the truth. (This is still good enough for the religious.) Nonreligious persons today often think of the shift into modern life in a similar way. They want to know what is involved in living a modern life, not why people are motivated to become modern. Like the truth, modernity seems to justify itself. Religious conversion is usually thought of as "irrational," because it happens to people rather than being something that they choose to become after careful thought. And yet most individuals enter modernity rather as converts enter a new religion—as a consequence of forces beyond their control. Modernity, like the convert's religion, *defines* new choices; it is rarely the result of an entirely "free choice." And like the convert's religion, it annihilates old possibilities and puts others in their place.

Resisting Conversion

Writing about nineteenth-century missionary activity in southern Africa, the Comaroffs note that the term "conversion" carries a commonsense European connotation,[2] and they ask whether its use doesn't oversimplify the real process it purports to describe:

> How well does it grasp the highly variable, usually gradual, often implicit, and demonstrably "syncretic" manner in which social identities, cultural styles, and ritual practices of African peoples were transformed by the evangelical encounter? How well does it capture the complex dialectic of invasion and riposte, of challenge and resistance, set in motion among the likes of the Southern Tswana? Here, after all, was a politics of consciousness in which the very nature of consciousness was itself the object of struggle. (p. 250)

These concerns are to be found in the writings of many anthropologists and historians. They are genuine enough, and the Comaroffs are right to alert us to them. But there is another question that also needs asking: The transformations may be slow, erratic, incomplete, but what kind of epistemic structures emerged from the evangelical encounter? When we read of "syncretism," we are alerted to a multiplicity of origins of a new amalgam. And we are consequently led to inquire whether its syncretic character means that it is related in the same way as an amalgam to the European and African origins of its constituent elements.

On an earlier page, which deals with customs and beliefs relating to Tswana rainmaking, the Comaroffs tell us something of the asymmetry of origins: "In being drawn into that conversation, the Southern Tswana had no alternative but to be inducted, unwittingly and often unwillingly, into *forms* of European discourse. To argue over who was the legitimate rainmaker or where the water came from, for instance, was to be seduced into the modes of rational debate, positivist knowledge, and empirical reason at the core of bourgeois culture." (p. 213, emphasis in original) They are right, of course, to go on to insist that this did not mean that Tswana life was now patterned on European Christianity.[3] But it is important to recognize the profound displacements produced by the "conversion process," both in the specific Christian sense and in the associated sense of induction into modern life. That displacement cannot be grasped by tracing the origins of an amalgam.

To begin with, what is now identified as the *object* of struggle in the Tswana setting—consciousness—has a specific Western genealogy, partly rooted in the

Christian concept of "conscience." As self-awareness, or internal reflection (Hamlet's "Thus conscience does make cowards of us all"), consciousness becomes politically contestable only when it is represented publicly as the sign of an authentic identity. We cannot know how African converts *really* thought and felt, but we know something of what they said and did. To the extent that "consciousness" is a discursive object, talk about it belongs to bourgeois culture. To the extent that that object becomes *politicized*, we have a bourgeois activity. Therefore, the existence of "a politics of consciousness" in southern Africa rests on an epistemic structure that makes it thinkable and doable, a space that is continuous with modern European history and is thus something that represents a major conversion of African possibilities.

Put another way, the question is not merely whether, and if so to what extent, African subjects were converted. It is certainly not whether they were completely subjected to an external molding force. The prior question is what new possibilities for constituting themselves these subjects now encountered. Given that there was now a possibility of recognizing themselves as *authentic*, what part did this new fact play in their constitution? The possibility that one may be falsely conscious of oneself—and that such a possibility can itself become the object of public dispute—is not the same as the possibility of resisting the missionary's attempt to coerce one into becoming another kind of person: *His* idea of a good Christian. The changed epistemic structure brought about by the conversion to modernity articulates a range of new possibilities not adequately captured by the simple alternatives of passive reception by subjects or active resistance by agents, of unoriginal reproduction or synthetic originality. The *politics* of consciousness, like the politics of personal identity of which it is part, is an entirely modern Western possibility. The *self-conscious* selection and integration of new elements into that identity (which many anthropologists refer to as syncretism or hybridity) is central to that possibility. That is to say, the centrality of self-constructive *action* is due to a specific epistemic structure.

Conversion to the Better Life

Whereas the Comaroffs regard the concept of conversion as having a commonsense European connotation, some historians say that it is essentially Christian. "It is a confusion of categories," writes Morrison, "to use the word *conversion* as though it were an instrument of critical analysis, equally appropriate to any culture or religion. The word has a profound mystical sense in the West for which some great religions and languages of the world have no equivalent. Even in the history of the West, it has displayed different connotations at different moments. Thus, the word is more properly a subject, rather than a tool of analysis."[4] However, if one wishes to avoid the danger of confusing word with concept and concept with practice, it would be better to say that in studying conversion, one was dealing with the narratives by which people apprehended and described a radical change in the significance of their lives. Sometimes these narratives employ the notion of divine intervention; at other times the notion of a secular teleology.

The concept of conversion within the Christian tradition as a whole includes an intransitive and a transitive aspect at the same time, with the latter represented as an act of divine mercy. Long before Foucault, Augustine knew that power could be both productive and repressive. "Power"— *potens*—is at once torment and ability. For Augustine, therefore, belief in the Truth follows only through the operations of divine power.[5] The master narrative of the Old Testament is the story of divine chastisement and divine direction of his chosen but erring people, a story that implies and is completed by the Truth of the New Testament.

In the transitive sense, conversion is a process of divine enablement through which the intransitive work of becoming a Christian, of attaining true consciousness, can be completed. But that divine function has also been aided by human institutions that impose the conditions necessary for liberation from false consciousness. The Church in this world has an essential task to secure the Truth through human power.

In the modern era, European theologians have taken the close connection between imperial expansion and the spread of Christianity to be an embarassment and a scandal because the aims and conditions of empire appear to be essentially secular. They claim that theology must continually address the nature of human power, "which reaches its widest range of potential good and evil under the form of imperialism."

Max Warren, for example, argues that despite its negative effects, imperialism has functioned "as a *preparatio* for God's good will for the world." In secular terms this means that "the legacy of permanent good things such as legislation, political improvement, the development of European-style cities, cohesion of states, and the breakdown of isolation" are among the providential consequences of imperialism.[6] This makes modernity the common destination for the world willed by God. Missionary conversions to (West European) Christianity become a part of that destiny, as well as a means of fulfilling it. In Warren's theological formulation, the significance of conversion as a *secular* movement, at once transitive and intransitive, emerges in all its historical complexity.

What we distinguish today as secular history and religious history are closely connected in a single genealogy. For medieval Europeans, *saeculum* was the period of time within a Christian history between the Fall and the Last Day; in early modern Europe, "the secular" becomes a space beside "the religious." In the Enlightenment, *saeculum* is transformed into the domain of "purely natural" human action, now opposed to a domain of "supernatural" belief. Eventually, the concept of the social becomes rooted in "the secular" as the space of human action pure and simple, and "the religious" becomes subsumed by it as a social phenomenon to be characterized in terms of that ontological space. To act in that space is now the condition of being human, regardless of whether one's beliefs and motives are "religious" or not.

The question of imposed conversion, and of the limits to securing belief through coercion, is thus intertwined with the great theme of global progress on the one hand and that of religious toleration on the other. Both are connected with the political theories and practices that were initiated in Western Europe in the seventeenth century and that were fed into the nineteenth- and twentieth-century movements by which the world has been modernized.

Practical and Moral Limits to Conversion

I want to make some points about the doctrine of religious toleration in the early modern state in order to think about the connection between external ("secular") force and internal ("religious") belief.

It is not always recognized that this doctrine was associated with two epistemological changes: claims relating to religious Truth acquired the new status of private belief, and the concept of *practices* was partly subordinated to the concept of *propositions*.[7]

In a fascinating article on the Lockean theory of toleration, the political scientist Kirstie McClure reminds readers that in his early writings, Locke defended politically imposed rites by making a sharp distinction between the mind as the locus of faith and the body's activity as mere externality.[8] The prince's insistence that his subjects practice the same ritual ceremony should not therefore—so Locke maintained—be intolerable to them. In this early position, Locke represented *conscience* as "nothing but an opinion of the truth of any practical proposition, which may concern any actions as well moral as religious, civil as well as ecclesiastical." As such, he argued that if the principle of conscience were to be conceded as a basis for rejecting civil jurisdiction, all political authority would be undermined.

But in his later work, Locke concluded that the attempt to resolve the problem of religious conflict and coercion by means of theological formulas must fail, because every practical judgment by one person employing such a formula was bound to be regarded as scandalous by someone else. Locke there abandoned his reliance on a theological vocabulary and set up a new, "non-religious" principle for distinguishing between acts in which the magistrate might legitimately intervene and those in which he had no authority to do so. This was the now-famous principle of harm to life, limb, or property. All acts that resulted in such harm could be identified unanimously and therefore with certainty. Since no agreement could be reached on whether particular ritual practices resulted in harm to the soul, such acts could not be allowed to become objects of political judgment and control. Thus, politics dealt with the domain of "objective fact," religion with that of "subjective consciousness."

Locke's emphasis on human uncertainty regarding religious belief essentially refers to the simultaneous existence of several irreconcilable assertions (each based on conviction) about harm. Jurists of Roman and canon law in the sixteenth and seventeenth centuries dealt with conflicting assertions by assigning fractional measures (called "probabilities") to each type of evidence. Judicial "conviction" was reached in such situations by the calculation of "probabilities."[9] However, for Locke, the political mode of resolving uncertainty was inadmissable wherever the harm in question was itself subject to uncertain claims—as in claims that one's soul would be harmed by being forcibly subjected to "scandalous" rituals and doctrines. The result was the liberal theory of religious toleration, which—as McClure rightly points out—renders (religious) *difference* into (cultural) *diversity*, and prohibits private and public agents from attempting to coerce others into or out of existing religions.

McClure wants to reinstate the importance of irreconcilable *difference* via the notion of personal "identity" within a modern concept of society. By insisting that harms to personal identity belong in the domain of social fact (a new kind of knowledge) and not in the domain of subjective belief (the old notion of opinion), she hopes to restore *difference* to the political domain in which compulsion can now be practiced on a principled basis. But her reasoning at this point appears to me faulty on several counts: (1) The representation of seventeenth-century religious convictions "as what we today might understand as *identity*" is a misleading secular anachronism; (2) the knowledge produced by contemporary social science does not constitute a new kind of facticity but a new space of argument; and (3) that there are now conflicts over what constitutes "subjective" harm certainly makes for a new kind of politics (identity politics), but this politics provides no criteria for judging between conflicting claims to difference. For seventeenth-century sectarians, it was neither politics nor self-authenticating claims about harm to identity but divine authority that provided those criteria.

Of course, Locke's theory is a *normative* one. But every normative theory carries certain social, psychological, and theological assumptions about the world to which it is meant to apply. To that extent, the theory is also *descriptive*. The liberal theory of religious toleration that traces its origin to Locke is therefore an account of the limits of historical possibility in which empirical and moral elements are combined.

According to Susan Mendus,[10] Locke propounded his theory of toleration on the basis of the psychological principle that belief can never be determined by the will. However, this principle belongs to a modern psychology that was beginning to emerge in seventeenth-century Europe. In the Middle Ages, a contrary doctrine prevailed. Thus, for Thomas Aquinas, drawing on Aristotelian psychology, belief could indeed be willed.

"To 'will,' in Greek thought," writes G. Vesey, "is not to exercise an independent mental faculty called 'the will'; it is to adopt a favorable attitude to some specific object . . . For Descartes, on the other hand, there are 'operations of the will' on a par with those of the intellect, the imagination, and the senses. Descartes may even have introduced this concept of the will, and willing, [into general currency]. . . . Descartes evidently thinks of thoughts as having a perceptible or phenomenal character. An 'idea' is a thought *qua* perceptible. In this he was followed by John Locke, who called a person's perception of the operations of his mind 'reflection.' . . ."[11] This new psychology inaugurated the modern discourse of "mental or psychological phenomena," and, hence, a way of identifying "religious belief" as a phenomenon of "consciousness" together with other internal phenomena.

It was this psychology that allowed Locke to insist that the Prince's attempt to coerce religious belief—including belief in the salvational implications of religious practices—was irrational. All that imposition could secure was an insincere profession of faith and therefore *an incomplete conversion*. Of course, the Prince might have reasons for imposing conformity on his subjects other than concern for their salvation—such as upholding law and order—that would not render his coercive efforts necessarily irrational. Nevertheless, Mendus maintains that "rationality" had a strong moral value for the Puritan tradition to which Locke belonged, and that he therefore regarded religious intolerance not only as impractical but as morally wrong.

The presumption that political attempts to coerce belief are irrational because impossible has been the focus of modern debate, summarized in part by Mendus. Her own view is that Locke was right to make that presumption, and she defends him against his critics on this point by making what she regards as a crucial distinction *within* the convert's consciousness—a difference between *sincere* and *authentic* belief. This allows her to argue that an externally imposed attempt at conversion may, at most, obtain *sincere* belief, not an *authentic* one.

But the conditions cited by Mendus—beginning with the so-called "acceptance" condition—are, I think questionable. Thus, her claim that the alternatives of deliberate reticence (not saying what one really believes) and insincerity (affirming what one doesn't believe) must always exist as possibilities in order to determine whether a belief is really sincere, seems to me not clear enough. The *possibility* must surely be more than simply an abstract logical option; it must relate to an act that could, within a specific religious context, be properly performed. But if that is so, then the Christian act of "bearing witness in public" would have to be identified as "sincere but inauthentic," because for the Christian it excludes the possibility of deliberate reticence or insincerity. Mendus would have to describe Luther's declaration ("I am a prisoner in conscience to the Word of God. I cannot retract and will not retract. To go against the conscience is neither safe nor right. God help me. Amen.")[12] as sincere but inauthentic. This doesn't seem correct, however. Everyone is familiar with situations in which it seems to be morally impossible not to say what one believes. One feels *compelled* to speak out in the only way possible. Should the absence of the possibility of reticence in such situations be taken to mean that the belief is inauthentic? If that is so, then "authenticity" here seems to be no more than a way of valorizing *the absence of moral passion.* The distinction between "sincere" and "authentic" belief thus reflects a particular liberal inclination.

Mendus goes on to insist that "the irrationality of coercing belief, even indirectly, is akin to the irrationality of brain washing: It can certainly be done, but it does not generate the right kind of belief or, more precisely, it does not generate a belief which is held in the right kind of way."[13] This seems to me unhelpful for three reasons: first, because *indirect* coercion is precisely not akin to "brainwashing"; second, because brainwashing is not "irrational" if it does what it sets out to do; and finally, because it is not clear why the magistrate (the holder of political power) in any and every society would wish to distinguish an "authentic" belief from one that is merely "sincere" among his subjects.[14]

The general point I am making here is that arguments like those of McClure and Mendus on Locke's theory of toleration articulate some of the assumptions about the practical and moral limits to forcible conversion. But they do not pay adequate attention to the historical conditions—including changing psychological discourses—that construct those limits.

Conversion and Agency

That leads me to a question with which I want to conclude my comments: Why does it seem so important to us to insist that the converted are "agents"? Why do we discount the convert's claim that he or she has been "made into" a Christian?

One aspect of "agency," of course, is the old Protestant doctrine of individual responsibility. Individuals are agents because they are responsible for their own souls.[15] That was a central doctrine for Puritans like Locke. The secular concept of agency is also connected to the spirit of capitalism. It invokes the mutually dependent figures of the entrepreneur and the consumer, or, more abstractly, the functions of initiating and choosing. Liberalism has worked these figures into its individualist theories of politics and morality.

Modern definitions of agency typically operate to render a world of "accidents" into a world of moral and legal responsibility (i.e., "necessities"). We tend to think of responsibility as being intrinsic to the way an action binds cause and effect. To abbreviate that structure, to deny that certain responsibilities necessarily apply to the performance of an act, is to define a particular kind of agency.

The paradigmatic agent is the human individual. Modern law also constitutes collections of humans as agents, making it possible thereby to hold the collectivity—as distinct from its individual members—liable for certain "accidents." But although legal fictions such as corporations are said to be agents, animals that we can see and touch are never agents—at any rate, not in our modern, disenchanted world. "Consciousness" is not an essential property of agents, certainly not of corporations. Even activity is not such a property. If a mother's failure to act has consequences, she is liable as an agent regardless of "consciousness"; a "child," on the other hand, may act, and do so consciously, but is not therefore an agent in the sense of someone who can be held legally or morally responsible. Similarly, we describe chemicals, bacteria, or machine parts as agents or active elements when we wish to attribute causal force to them. The point is that agency is not a universal property, nor is it a transcendental quality. "Agency" operates through a particular network of concepts within which the historical possibilities and limits of responsibility are defined.

In brief, what is not always made clear in narratives of conversion employing the concept of agency is what theoretical work that concept is doing. What are the culturally specific properties that define agency? How much agency do particular categories of person possess? For what and to whom are agents responsible? When and where can attributions of agency be successfully disowned? Can non-humans be agents?

Too often, the assumptions we bring with us when talking about the conversion of people in another epoch or society are the ideological assumptions in and about our modern condition. Conversion is regarded by moderns as an "irrational" event or process, but resort to the idea of agency renders it "rational" and "freely chosen." Everyone has agency; everyone is responsible for the life he or she leads. The doctrine of action has become essential to our recognition of other people's humanity. Suffering, we think, does not serve to mark humans off from other animals. And that distinction is crucial for those who want to justify conversions to modernity.

Notes

1. R. W. Hefner, ed., *Conversion to Christianity: Historical and Anthropological Perspectives on a Great Transformation* (Berkeley: California Univ. Press, 1993).

2. Earlier, the Medieval historian Karl Morrison maintained that the concept of conversion was unique to Western culture, and especially to the Christian tradition that helped shape that culture from the twelfth century on.

3. There is some lack of clarity on this point, however. When they write that "increasingly, then, the argument over such issues as rainmaking became a confrontation between two cultures, two social orders, in which each had a palpable impact upon the other," (op. cit., 213) the Comaroffs are confusing the local adaptations made by the ~~missionaries in~~ order to seduce more Tswana into their fold with the abstractions called "cultures" and "social orders." They cannot mean to say that the legal, moral, and religious principles of life in Europe were altered by an infusion of Tswana discourses.

4. K. F. Morrison, *Understanding Conversion* (Charlottesville: Virginia Univ. Press, 1992), xiv.

5. See Augustine of Hippo, *Confessions*, Eighth Book, XII: 30.

6. Cited in Neil Gunson, "The Theology of Imperialism and the Missionary History of the Pacific." *Journal of Religious History* 5, no. 3 (1969): 258–59.

7. See Chapters 1 and 6 of T. Asad, *Genealogies of Religion* (Baltimore: Johns Hopkins Univ. Press, 1993).

8. K. McClure, "Difference, Diversity, and the Limits of Toleration," *Political Theory* 18, no. 3 (1990).

9. I. Hacking, *The Emergence of Probability*, Cambridge, 1975; L. Daston, *Classical Probability in the Enlightenment*, Princeton, 1988; and I. Hacking, *The Taming of Chance*, Cam-

bridge, 1990, together give a superb account of the transformations leading to modern statistical theory—whose domain is precisely the calculation of (social and natural) uncertainties.

10. S. Mendus, *Toleration and the Limits of Liberalism* (Atlantic Highlands, NJ: Humanities Press, 1989).

11. A. Flew and G. Vesey, *Agency and Necessity* (Cambridge, MA: Blackwell, 1987), 17.

12. Cited in O. Chadwick, *The Reformation* (New York: Penguin Books, 1972), 56. As Chadwick remarks, the famous words, "Here I stand: I can do no other" were probably never uttered, although they express very well the sentiment of his actual statement at the Diet of Worms.

13. op. cit., 33

14. Mendus's book as a whole is important for stating a powerful case against the liberal theory of toleration and for recommending a socialist theory in its place. She puts forward the interesting (but by now not unfamiliar) argument that socialism has greater ideological resources for developing a modern politics devoted to constructing a complex solidarity out of disparate loyalties.

15. English literature taught in missionary schools in British India included many Victorian poems in the style of Muscular Christianity. I remember one verse that might be taken as the motto of certain kinds of "agency" theories:

> It matters not how strait the gate,
> How charged with punishments the scroll,
> I am the master of my fate:
> I am the captain of my soul.
> (From *Invictus* by W. H. Henley, 1849–1903)

CONTRIBUTORS

Talal Asad is Professor of Anthropology at Johns Hopkins University. His books include *Anthropology and the Colonial Encounter* (ed), (1973); *The Kababish Arabs* (1971); and *Genealogies of Religion* (1993).

Nicholas B. Dirks is Professor of History and Anthropology and director of the Center for South and Southeast Asian Studies at the University of Michigan. His publications include *The Hollow Crown: Ethnohistory of an Indian Kingdom* (1987); *Colonialism and Culture* (1992); and *Culture/Power/History* (coedited with Geoff Eley and Sherry Ortner, 1993). He is currently working on a variety of projects on colonial transformations of Indian society, as well as on postcolonial politics and the crisis of modernity in contemporary India.

Margaret Jolly is the Convenor of the Gender Relations Project, Research School of Pacific and Asian Studies, the Australian National University, Canberra. She has published extensively on women, colonialism, and Christianity in the Pacific, and Vanuatu in particular. Her major publications include *Family and Gender in the Pacific: Domestic Contradictions and the Colonial Impact* (coedited with Martha Macintyre, 1989); *Women of the Place: Kastom, Colonialism and Gender in Vanuatu* (1994); *Women's Difference: Sexuality and Maternity in Colonial and Postcolonial Discourses* ed., (1994); and *Transformations of Hierarchy* (coedited with Mark Mosko, 1994).

Webb Keane is Assistant Professor in the Department of Anthropology, University of Pennsylvania. He is presently completing a book with the working title *Signs of Recognition: The Power and Hazards of Representations in Eastern Indonesia*, based on his fieldwork in Sumba.

Keith P. Luria is Associate Professor of History at North Carolina State University. He is the author of *Territories of Grace: Cultural Change in the Seventeenth-Century Diocese of Grenoble* (1991). He is presently working on Catholic-Protestant coexistence and conflict as well as the issue of conversation in early-modern France.

Birgit Meyer studied pedagogy and comparative religion at the University of Bremen and cultural anthropology at the University of Amsterdam. She recently finished the manuscript of her dissertation, *Translating the Devil. An African Appropriation of Pietist Protestantism*. Presently she is a Lecturer at the Research Centre Religion and Society at the University of Amsterdam.

Judith Pollmann studied history at the University of Amsterdam and the Warburg Institute in London. Funded by a grant from the *Stichting voor Historische Wetenschappen* in The Hague, she is presently completing her Ph.D. thesis on "Religion in the World View of Arnoldus Buchelius (1565–1641)" at the University of Amsterdam. She has published articles on patronage in the *Ancien Régime*, and on the sixteenth-century origins of the "Black Legend." An article on Arnoldus Buchelius is due to appear in 1995.

Peter van Rooden is Lecturer at the Research Centre Religion and Society in the Faculty of Social Sciences at the University of Amsterdam. He is presently working on the social history of Dutch Christianity. His main publication is *Theology, Biblical Scholarship and Rabbinical Studies in the Seventeenth Century*.

Patricia Spyer is Lecturer at the Research Centre Religion and Society in the Faculty of Social Sciences at the University of Amsterdam. She is presently completing a book with the working title *The Memory of Trade*, based on her fieldwork in the Aru Islands, Eastern Indonesia.

Peter van der Veer is Professor of Comparative Religion and Director of the Research Centre Religion and Society in the Faculty of Social Sciences at the University of Amsterdam. His publications include *Gods on Earth* (1988); *Religious Nationalism* (1994); *Orientalism and the Postcolonial Predicament* (coedited with Carol A. Breckenridge), (1993); and *Nation and Migration* ed., (1995).

Gauri Viswanathan is Associate Professor of English and Comparative Literature at Columbia University, New York. She is the author of *Masks of Conquest: Literary Study and British Rule in India* (1989) and numerous articles on the overlapping cultural histories of England and India. The essay included in this volume is from her forthcoming book, *Outside the Fold: Conversion, Modernity, and Belief.*

Index

Warren, Max, 262
Weber, Max, 9–10, 197–98, 209
Wesleyan Methodist Missionary Society,
8
Whigs, the, 91
White, G., 149
Wielenga, D.K., 147–48, 149–50,
153–54, 160
Williams, John, 6
Williams, Raymond, 18
Wit, Johan Stephenszoon de, 53
witchcraft, 214–16
women: in Buddhism, 103; in caste sys-
tem, 116–17; and private sphere, 71;
roles in traditional religions, 207–208

working class, uplifting of, 8
world religions, 171–72
World War II, 189
written vs. spoken language, 208–209,
232–33

Xavier, Franciscus, 191

yams, 236, 245

Zinzendorf, Count, 77
Zwingli, Ulrich, 48–49